Political Campaigns

Concepts, Context, and Consequences

COSTAS PANAGOPOULOS
Fordham University

New Ycrk   Oxford

OXFORD UNIVERSITY PRESS

FLIP

Oxford University Press is a department of the University of Oxford.
It furthers the University's objective of excellence in research, scholarship,
and education by publishing worldwide. Oxford is a registered trademark
of Oxford University Press in the UK and certain other countries.

Published in the United States of America by Oxford University Press
198 Madison Avenue, New York, NY 10016, United States of America.

For titles covered by Section 112 of the US Higher Education
Opportunity Act, please visit www.oup.com/us/he for the
latest information about pricing and alternate formats.

Library of Congress Cataloging-in-Publication Data
Names: Panagopoulos, Costas, author.
Title: Political Campaigns: Concepts, Context, and Consequences / Costas
    Panagopoulos, Fordham University.
Description: New York, NY: Oxford University Press, 2016. | Series: Oxford
    series on elections, opinion and democracy | Includes bibliographical
    references and index.
Identifiers: LCCN 2016014866 | ISBN 9780199341399 (paperback : acid-free
    paper)
Subjects: LCSH: Political campaigns--United States. | Elections--United
    States. | United States--Politics and government. | BISAC: POLITICAL
    SCIENCE / Government / General. | POLITICAL SCIENCE / Government /
    National. | POLITICAL SCIENCE / Political Process / Elections.
Classification: LCC JK2281 .P36 2016 | DDC 324.70973--dc23
LC record available at https://lccn.loc.gov/2016014866

9 8 7 6 5 4 3 2 1

Printed by R.R. Donnelley, United States of America

TABLE OF CONTENTS

LIST OF TABLES AND FIGURES

Tables

Figures

PREFACE

"Just as water retains no constant shape, so in warfare there
are no constant conditions."

— Sun Tzu, *The Art of War*

Etymologically speaking, the origins of the word campaign can be traced back to
the French word *campagne* ("open country") or to the Latin *campania* ("level
country") or *campus* ("open field"). Originally used in the context of military battles that took place in open fields, the term became associated with political activity
prior to an election early in the 19th century. There are many parallels between
political and military expeditions, as players devise strategies and tactics to win,
but, as we will see throughout this volume, the playing fields in which campaigns
unfold are not always level and in a state of perpetual fluctuation. Paraphrasing the
quote above from the 6th century Chinese general, military strategist and philoso-
pher, Sun Tzu, perhaps the only constant in campaigns, or political warfare, is that
nothing is constant. Just as politicians must remain vigilant, mindful of developments that can affect their prospects, analysts and observers must also remain attentive to the social and political consequences that arise from the ways in which
parties and political campaigns respond to changing circumstances in their relentless quest for power. This is one of the main reasons why I love studying political
campaigns. As the political, legal, regulatory, cultural, social and technological
landscapes change, political candidates, parties, operatives and the campaigns they
wage to pursue electoral victories must evolve and adapt to ever-changing circumstances, challenges and opportunities.

This book reflects on the nature of contemporary political campaigns, highlighting both continuity and change over the past few decades and exploring the
implications of these changes for campaign strategy and execution as well as democratic principles and society at large. A central goal of the book is to provide a detailed and comprehensive glimpse into modern campaigns, but I also aim to provide
a framework with which to think about aspects of the electoral process in practice.

The insights summarized in this volume have accumulated over the course of decades as I have observed, studied, and participated in campaigns as a candidate, consultant, academic, media analyst, voter and citizen. In all of these roles, I have benefitted from countless interactions with colleagues, students, voters and political operatives of all types and from all over the world, and I am indebted to each of these individuals for sparking and sustaining my intellectual curiosity about the world of political campaigns. I am especially indebted to Donald Green, Bob Erikson, Bob Shapiro, Richard Fleisher, David Mayhew, Greg Huber, Jonathan Krasno, Jonathan Nagler, Chris Wlezien, Jamie Druckman, David Nickerson, Todd Rogers, Kevin Arceneaux, David Lublin, Jan Leighley, Marisa Abrajano, Gary Jacobson, Jim Gibson, Leonie Huddy, Stanley Feldman, David Redlawsk, Jim Campbell, Paul Herrnson, Jim Garand, Alan Abramowitz, Michael McDonald, Lynn Vavreck, John Lapinski, Richard Johnston, John Aldrich, Joe Lenski, Kathy Frankovic, Jeff Plaut, Bart Robbett, and many others.

In the course of writing this book, I owe a special debt of gratitude to a number of individuals and organizations. First and foremost, I thank Mike Alvarez, the series editor for Oxford University Press, for encouraging me to take on this project and supporting it throughout by generously providing feedback and suggestions on multiple manuscript drafts. His input, along with suggestions provided by the other reviewers, helped me to strengthen the volume considerably.

I am profoundly grateful to the Institution for Social and Policy Studies and the Center for the Study of American Politics at Yale University which provided a rich and stimulating intellectual environment and an academic home for me as a Visiting Professor of Political Science during a sabbatical year (2015–2016) and enabled me to complete the manuscript. I thank especially Alan Gerber, CSAP Director and my friend, mentor and collaborator—and one of the brightest scholars I've encountered in the academy—as well as my colleague, former Harvard classmate, and ISPS Director, Jacob Hacker, for making this possible.

I am grateful also for the outstanding research assistance provided by Mara Suttmann-Lea. Kyle Endres and Daniel Weiss, one of the best editors I have encountered in my professional career and someone who I was smart (or lucky) enough to hire as my managing editor when I was editor-in-chief of *Campaigns & Elections* magazine, also read the complete manuscript several times and provided thoughtful comments and suggestions.

Finally, I appreciate the support and professionalism of the editorial and production teams at Oxford University Press. Jennifer Carpenter is a consummate professional and a genuine joy to work with, and Matthew Rohal and Roxanne Klaas are top-rate. Of course, as always, any errors of commission or omission, are purely my own.

Costas Panagopoulos
New Haven, CT
May 2016

REVIEWER ACKNOWLEDGMENTS

I owe a debt of gratitude to the following people who reviewed the manuscript in its various forms and have provided invaluable insight in putting together the final book:

Steven Greene
North Carolina State University

Hans Hassell
Cornell College

Thomas R. Marshall
The University of Texas at Arlington

Shad Satterhwaite
University of Oklahoma

Carl L. Palmer
Illinois State University

Travis Ridout
Washington State University

Michael W. Wagner
University of Wisconsin–Madison

The book would not have been the same without the assistance and insight from these outstanding scholars and teachers. Any errors you might find in the book remain my own. I welcome your feedback and thank you for your support.

For Mark

CHAPTER 1

Modern Political Campaigns
Why and How They (May) Matter

O n November 6, 2012, Americans witnessed a memorable display of awe and disbelief from news commentators and political pundits on Fox News' Election Night coverage. Most notably, the well-known Republican strategist Karl Rove publicly challenged, on air, Fox's decision to declare that Barack Obama, the incumbent Democratic president, had bested Mitt Romney, his Republican opponent, in Ohio, effectively capturing reelection. Ultimately, Fox sent the anchor Megyn Kelly to the decision desk to verify the results with the analysts, who confirmed the decision to proclaim Obama the winner in Ohio despite Rove's objection (Sherman 2012).

Although at first glance this might appear to be merely an embarrassing political gaffe for Rove, between the lines of this episode runs a story of contemporary political campaigns in the United States. Propelled to a second term partly by a "data-driven" campaign, the Obama organization relied heavily on a strategy that necessitated the use of a range of experts, data crunchers, and analysts. Indeed, the campaign manager, Jim Messina, promised, "We are going to measure every single thing in this campaign," hiring an analytics department five times bigger than the Obama campaign had used in the 2008 election. There was even an official "chief scientist" named Rayid Ghani who had spent a good chunk of his life analyzing data to boost the effectiveness of supermarket sales promotions (Scherer 2012). Although there was no single reason for Romney's loss, one important explanation is rooted in differences in how the two campaigns analyzed and treated data (Issenberg 2012d). The Romney campaign's vastly different approach to data in comparison with the Obama campaign could be seen in Rove's and other Romney supporters' visible disbelief on Election Night.

Romney's campaign staff often insisted that polls from swing states were wrong, overestimating the number of Democrats who would turn out to support Obama. Any model indicating that the race would be closer than they expected was dismissed as incorrect. Even as late as the morning of the election, Romney's advisors asserted that he was going to win "decisively" (Dickerson 2012). Ignoring components of the Obama campaign that were paramount to its success, including its immensely successful use of data-driven targeting, Romney and his supporters were shell-shocked when the election was called for the incumbent. Indeed, in the aftermath of the 2012 presidential election, many observers concluded that Obama's data-driven campaign strategy had played a central role in his success and in Romney's demise (Issenberg 2012d; Wagner 2015). Romney's campaign was by no means unsophisticated and had other hallmarks of contemporary campaign strategies. For example, his highly sophisticated and persistent early voting campaign played an important role in his success in the 2012 Republican presidential primary elections. Romney also raised enormous amounts of money—and he raised it early—which helped him greatly with his early voting campaign strategy during the Republican primaries (Issenberg 2012c). Romney's fundraising contributed to the record-breaking spending of the 2012 presidential election and was on par with Obama's efforts. In addition, the Republican candidate actually had more money to spend than the incumbent president in the last two and a half weeks of the race (Cilizza and Blake 2012).

These stories highlight some of the key features of contemporary campaigning in the United States. Intensive fundraising efforts to raise vast sums of money are all but essential to a campaign's success. Although mass public appeals remain an important component of contemporary campaigns, they have been supplemented by increasingly sophisticated uses of data to target specific groups of voters, leading to a new era of "mass customization" in which voters are targeted by campaigns based not only on their voting histories, but also on specific attributes, interests, and characteristics (Burton and Shea 2010). Reliance on political consultants and data-driven approaches are an integral part of political campaigns as strategists seek to learn as much as they can about the voters who are solidly in their corner, as well as those who are persuadable, and to develop the best messages to get those voters to turn out and cast a vote for their candidate. These highly sophisticated tactics require an increasing cadre of experts to run effective political campaigns. Enter political consultants, individuals and firms specializing in everything from data analytics, as was the case with Rayid Ghani working for the Obama campaign, to media and digital communications management, fundraising, and volunteer coordination. In 2012, the Obama team recruited and hired over 50 statisticians, mathematicians, quantitative scientists, software developers, and data analysts from leading Internet firms such as Twitter, Google, Facebook, Microsoft, and Craigslist, among others, to design and build a new database infrastructure code named "Project Narwhal." The system was designed to integrate databases and build programming interfaces that allowed the campaign to fuse information about the "multiple identities" of the engaged citizen—the online activist, the offline voter, the donor, the volunteer—into a single, unified political profile (Rubinstein 2014: 878). Political scientists David Nickerson, who was the director of experiments for Obama for America in 2012, and Todd Rogers, who founded the Analyst Institute, point out that "the improved capability to target individual voters offers campaigns an opportunity to concentrate their resources where they will be most effective. This power however, has not radically transformed the nature of campaign work. One could argue that the growing impact of data analytics in campaigns has amplified the importance of traditional campaign work" (Nickerson and Rogers 2014: 71).

Change is constant in American politics. Shifts in partisan attachments, the ebb and flow of presidential administrations, and the turnover of elected officials, whether by defeat or by retirement, are just a few of the transformations that routinely occur in the American political system. Political campaigns are far from immune to changes in the contexts in which they are operating. In recent years, a rise in partisan polarization, changes in election laws, U.S. Supreme Court decisions on campaign finance, and technological advances in communication strategies are just a few of the changes in campaign contexts with which contemporary campaigns grapple.

This volume is designed to describe different dimensions of contemporary political campaigns with respect to the ongoing changes in American politics. I introduce key *concepts* related to modern campaigns and consider how *context* affects campaigns' strategic calculations and decisionmaking. I also explore the potential *consequences* for three primary tenets of democratic theory: *representation, information,* and *engagement.* This "3 C's" approach highlights the influence and significance of each element as it relates to the campaign dimensions discussed in the following chapters. Understanding key concepts is vital. Context refers broadly to the features of the political, institutional, legal, and regulatory landscapes in which contemporary campaigns operate. It can include anything from the competiveness of an election to the compositions of electorates, the type of election (local, state, or national), broader national trends such as the state of the economy, and local nuances, such as voting laws, registration deadlines, and campaign finance regulations. Like much in American politics, these contexts have inevitably changed and will continue to change over time. Campaigns make strategic decisions about their resource allocations based on such contextual factors and the type of resources they are allocating. For example, instrumental resources, such as funds for advertising and appearances by candidates, tend to be allocated to populous, competitive races, whereas other resources, such as state-level funding and campaign personnel, can be more widely dispersed (Bartels 1985; Nagler and Leighley 1992). In presidential elections, for example, the attention given to a state is determined not only by the competiveness of that state, but also by the cost of advertising in its media markets and the effort expended by opponents (Shaw 2006).

Context undoubtedly influences campaigns' strategic decisions as well as citizen choices. Campaigns' choices and decisions, or ways they are conducted, are responsive to context and, in turn, have consequences for election outcomes and democratic principles writ large. The principles of representation, information, and engagement discussed in this volume are deeply embedded in the fabric of American democracy. Political campaigns have the capacity—some argue, the responsibility—to contribute meaningfully to these principles, democratic processes, and governance. Many critics argue that contemporary campaigns fall short of these aspirations.

A central goal of this volume, then, is to reflect on how aspects of contemporary campaigns, the contexts in which they operate, and recent developments in electioneering help (or hinder) these goals of democratic theory. Although there are countless dimensions against which to benchmark campaign performance, I focus on three that are directly related to campaign strategy and execution. Representation refers to how well campaign practices help to produce election outcomes that install accountable representatives who reflect the preferences of their constituencies as "political equals" (Dahl 1971: 1). That is, does the campaign conduct required to win an election encourage elected officials to more or less listen to the preferences of *all* of their constituents or to focus more on one segment of constituents, such as the wealthy and interest groups, than on the average citizen (see Bartels 2008; Gilens 2012; Gilens and Page 2014)?

Accurate and reliable information that guides citizens' vote choices and enables them to make informed decisions is another indispensable component of democratic politics. Under ideal conditions, citizens are expected to make informed political decisions. But candidates arguably play a role in informing the public about their policy positions and the actions they would take as leaders. Although some scholars argue that the mass public does not possess a coherent ideology and that it can be easily misguided by actors like those in political campaigns (Converse 1964; Zaller and Feldman 1992; Althaus 1998), others suggest that when "effectively motivated, the public is awesomely competent" (Fishkin 2006, 158). Political elites campaigning for public office, then, should play a role in motivating the public to be more informed. Furthermore, heuristics and shortcuts, such as partisan identification, ideology, and others perpetuated by campaigns, can serve as good replacements for fully informed decision making by citizens in elections (Downs 1957; Lupia 1994; Druckman and Lupia 2000). I assess the role of contemporary campaigns and the information they provide to the public in enhancing or diminishing citizens' preference formation, their decision-making process, and the extent to which they present meaningful policy alternatives to their constituents (Leighley and Nagler 2013).

Finally, democratic societies also depend on broad citizen participation and engagement, not only in terms of voting but also through other political activities such as expressing interest in the political process, volunteering, donating money to politicians, and contacting elected officials. Unfortunately, many citizens do not participate in politics, and those who do participate tend to be wealthier, better educated, and more engaged citizens (Rosenstone and Hansen 1993; Brady et al. 1995). For better or worse, political campaigns play a central role in influencing voter participation and engagement, especially in the context of competitive, high-stakes elections (Aldrich 1993). I assess the role that contemporary campaigns play in promoting participation, not only in terms of absolute levels but also in terms of who participates in American politics.

The remainder of this chapter discusses when and how campaigns matter, introduces the reader to the structure and organization of contemporary campaigns, and discusses the functions of key campaign staff. It also highlights the transition from party-centered to candidate-centered elections and the growth of political consultants and strategists in contemporary campaigns. The chapter concludes with a brief overview of the remaining chapters.

WHEN (AND HOW) CAMPAIGNS MATTER

For years, scholars focused on determining the extent to which the decisions made by political campaigns actually matter for election outcomes. After all, elections offer citizens an important chance to determine who will govern and represent them (Schumpeter 1942). For better or worse, campaigns have been a part of this process for most of American history. Some of the earliest studies concluded that campaigns did *not* actually matter much for election outcomes. Voters seemed to more often cast ballots in line with socioeconomic status, party affiliation, and retrospective running tallies of candidate evaluations, rather than as a direct result of campaign messages (Lazarsfeld et al. 1944; Berelson et al. 1954; Campbell et al. 1960; Key 1966; Fiorina 1981). Political scientists also uncovered basic fundamentals that carried over from year to year and played a role in determining election outcomes. For example, presidential approval ratings are typically tied to the success of their party members running for other offices (Abramowitz and Segal 1996), and economic performance during a presidential term is also an important indicator of a party's success, especially if its opponents exploit a poorly functioning economy in their campaign messaging (Vavreck 2009; Lewis-Beck and Stegmaier 2000).

All these factors are external to the behavior of political campaigns and their conduct during an election cycle. However, voters do rely on the campaigns to inform them about the status of the economy, about candidates' past successes and failures in office, and about their policy positions and plans (Vavreck 2009; Alvarez 1997). To that end, scholars have also concluded that although campaign effects may be minimal in certain contexts, they are real and can have an effect on election outcomes (Panagopoulos 2009a; Erikson and Wlezien 2012; Campbell 2008). This is an updated version of what was previously known as the minimal effects thesis, which holds that campaigns are only able to persuade voters to their side on the margins and that campaign activities make little difference in election outcomes (Klapper 1960). This generally occurs partly because citizens tend to consume information selectively, in a way that reinforces preexisting beliefs and discounts information and messages that are inconsistent with these views (Zaller 1992), and because they are not constantly tuned to the ebbs and flows of a political campaign. Moreover, voters who are tuned in may be more likely to seek out sources that echo rather than contradict their preferences (Taber and Lodge 2006). If exposed to information that is inconsistent with their firmly held beliefs, citizens are not likely to update their attitudes in response to such new information (Zaller 1992; Zaller and Feldman 1992; Kunda 1990; Gaines et al. 2007). This makes persuasion by campaigns particularly difficult.

Nevertheless, campaigns can and do persuade. Especially in close races, a campaign needs only to succeed in persuading enough of the electorate to tip the election outcome in its favor. The effectiveness of campaigns (in terms of both persuasion and mobilization) must be considered within the broader context of increasingly competitive election cycles. Figure 1.1 highlights this trend for presidential elections. The eventual vote margins between the major-party presidential contenders in general elections have become increasingly narrow over the past three decades. In fact, the four most recent presidential elections have been decided by margins smaller than 10 percentage points. The margins in three of the four cycles (2000, 2004, and 2012) have been less than 5 percentage points. In such scenarios, campaigns can persuade a minimal number of voters and still affect election outcomes. Of course, as we will see in subsequent chapters, not all elections are as competitive as recent presidential elections; ironically, as competition in presidential races and over majority party control of Congress has intensified in recent years, competition in the vast majority of electoral settings across the country, including for individual congressional races as well as state and local contests, is dwindling (Jacobson and Carson 2015), creating both challenges and opportunities for campaigns at these levels.

A simple thought experiment in which one imagines what elections would look like without campaigning should suffice to demonstrate the point that campaigns do matter. After all, given the narrow margin of victory in many recent elections, the electoral outcome could have changed had one or both candidates opted not to campaign. Of course, such a scenario is strictly hypothetical because candidates believe campaigns matter and much of the empirical evidence I

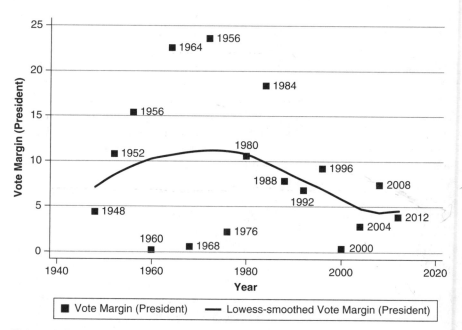

Figure 1.1 Two-Party Vote Margins in Presidential Elections, 1948–2012 (Panagopoulos and Endres 2015)

summarize in this volume confirms it does. Meaningful changes in voter preferences occur over the course of a campaign in response to mobilization efforts, advertisements, and other campaign activities (Gerber et al. 2011; Panagopoulos
2009a). Although broader national trends and economic contexts can color citizen
choices during a given election season, campaigns are also a key component in the
crystallization of these choices. Campaign events such as conventions and debates
can lead to meaningful—and enduring—shifts in candidate preferences over the
course of a campaign season and also encourage citizens to make vote choices that
are in line with their already-held beliefs and partisan identity (Erikson and
Wlezien 2012; Gelman and King 1993; Holbrook 1994; Panagopoulos 2012, 2013a).

To put it another way, basic determinants of vote choice in presidential elections such as socioeconomic status, party identification, or broader economic conditions create a sort of equilibrium, which campaigns have the ability to disturb
when it is strategically advantageous for them to do so. This explains the well-
known patterns of heightened campaign intensity in competitive races, particularly as Election Day approaches (Erikson and Wlezien 2012). These dynamics can
be seen in the different effects of campaign activities in presidential races between
battleground and nonbattleground states; campaign events held in battleground
states have both short- and long-term effects on voter preferences, whereas effects
in nonbattleground states can be fleeting and limited (Panagopoulos 2012). Grassroots mobilization efforts are also concentrated in battleground states; in close
races especially, these activities can be consequential (Bergan et al. 2005).

Rather than trying to answer the question of whether campaign conduct
matters, scholars are now far more interested in answering "where, when, for
what, and for whom they matter" (Jacobson 2015: 1), questions we will revisit
throughout this volume as we explore the different components and consequences
of campaign conduct in contemporary contexts. Contemporary campaigns at all
levels are notably different from their predecessors. Campaigns have grown larger
and more sophisticated, the role of the candidate has evolved, and professional
consultants have emerged to play a more important part in the ever-growing
campaign apparatus. Each of these aspects is discussed in greater detail later in
the chapter and throughout this volume.

CAMPAIGN STRUCTURE AND ORGANIZATION

In some respects, contemporary political campaigns are similar to the operations
of a growing business, increasing in both size and budget with each election cycle
(Dulio 2004). The need for large budgets and operations requires outside help
from a variety of consultants and advisors. Political candidates may have high
aspirations for the policies they want to put into place, for how to govern, and
even for advancing their party's interests, but it is rare to find a candidate or even
a campaign manager who is also an expert in budget planning, marketing and
advertising, targeting and mobilizing voters, and raising money. For many political newcomers, outside expertise is essential. For example, when newcomer

Ken Vaughn of Virginia ran for Congress in 2012, he initially cashed in a substantial portion of his 401(k) and invested $100,000 in his campaign. Vaughn noted, "It's not nearly enough to win, but it's enough to get started . . . it takes a lot of money to run for office, but that's what it takes like any businessman or whatever, you have to do what the job takes" (A. Jones 2012). Vaughn ultimately fell short in his primary race against fellow Republican Chris Perkins, but his experience speaks to the difficulty of breaking into politics in the United States and the importance of having a well-funded, well-organized political campaign and the expertise necessary to execute effective campaign strategies. A similar fate met Christine Jones, a Republican candidate for governor in Arizona in 2014, who put $5.4 million of her own money into the Republican primary that year, only to end up third in the race (Christie et al. 2015).

Not all candidates play it by the books. In the 2014 midterm elections, an independent candidate for the U.S. Senate from South Dakota, Larry Pressler, surprised everyone with his strong showing against the Republican governor Mike Rounds, Democratic congressional aide Rick Weiland, and independent conservative state legislator Gordon Howie. Not only was Pressler an independent, which put him at a disadvantage given the importance of partisan labels for cueing voters about candidate issue positions, but also he had just one paid campaign staffer and acted as his own campaign manager. In addition, he raised substantially less money than his opponents. In the end, his efforts fell short and he lost the election to Rounds. As Pressler noted, "I am like a naked little rabbit with all the guys with shotguns starting up the hill" (Sullivan 2014).

Speaking of throwing out the playbook, we can scarcely proceed in our discussion of modern campaigns without mentioning businessman-and-reality-superstar-turned-GOP-presidential hopeful Donald Trump and the rollercoaster 2016 presidential election cycle. In many ways, the Trump phenomenon inspired analysts to reassess, and quite possibly, eventually, recalibrate, our understanding of the effectiveness of a range of campaign strategies and tactics. It is conceivable that circumstances surrounding the Trump campaign are unique and idiosyncratic, with few, lasting ramifications. But it is also possible that Trump's success speaks directly to ways in which campaigns may be changing and evolving long term. After all, Trump managed to send political scientists and pundits alike scrambling with his meteoric rise in the polls and success in primaries and caucuses across the country in 2016, despite a campaign run on a "shoe string" and an organization considered skeletal and "unsophisticated" (Schreckinger and Vogel 2016). Through the end of February 2016, the Trump campaign had spent a grand total of $33 million but won 19 state contests and racked up 680 delegates to the GOP convention; according to the Federal Election Commission, Trump's inflation-adjusted spending was lower than any other presidential primary front-runner since 1980, but he had managed to secure nearly $2 billion worth of earned (free) media—more than twice what Democratic Party presidential front-runner Hillary Clinton, and more than six times the amount that GOP contender and second-place earner Sen. Ted Cruz, received over the same period (Blumenthal

2016). Clinton's Democratic opponent Sen. Bernie Sander has received only about $28 million in free media coverage. By contrast, former Florida governor and early GOP front-runner Jeb Bush spent over $130 million in his bid for the White House before suspending his campaign in February, 2016, after devastating losses in early-voting states including Iowa, New Hampshire and South Carolina (Confessore and Cohen 2016). These developments suggest change but also reveal continuities in electoral campaign strategy, execution and candidate performance, and the chapters that follow will help to contextualize the contours of successive election cycles and how they fit into broader themes and patterns.

Although campaign strategy may vary from place to place, in contemporary campaigns there are core elements that can be found at most levels of elections. A central necessity is a campaign plan that is detailed and meticulous and prevents members of the campaign team from going off message (Burton and Shea 2010). A comprehensive campaign plan that has explicit descriptions of roles and responsibilities helps campaigns to save time and money and to make better decisions in the face of changing contexts and developments. With so many players and moving parts involved, a thorough plan also helps campaigns stay on message, a factor I will discuss in greater detail in Chapter 5. This is not unlike an ideal organization for a small business, which, to be successful, needs clearly communicated and well-executed plans. Unlike many small businesses, however, campaigns are required to quickly adapt to a variety of electoral contexts, from different media markets and shifting national trends to mid-campaign decisions by their opponents.

In contemporary campaigns, various responsibilities are delegated to different actors. These individuals, in turn, are responsible for supervising and delegating to staff and volunteers within each area of responsibility. As I will discuss throughout the book, in contemporary campaigns the number of roles that must be filled has increased as a result of changes to and advances in campaign strategy that require new kinds of expertise. I describe some of the key roles that must be filled in many political campaigns, especially on high-profile, high-ticket operations, and briefly detail the multitude of other positions that are integral for campaign success.

Campaign managers are at the head of campaign organizations, acting as the primary coordinators of a campaign plan and overseers of day-to-day operations to ensure that the rest of the staff stays on target. Campaign managers must be adept at evaluating the context of a given race to develop a winning strategy and put together the staff and volunteers who will best implement it. For example, Matt Rhoades, who served as the campaign manager for the former Massachusetts governor Mitt Romney's 2012 presidential bid, brought with him a wealth of expertise. He had previously served as the communications director on Romney's presidential campaign in 2008, as well as a deputy director in charge of research for the Republican National Committee during the 2006 midterm elections. Finance directors, in contrast, are primarily responsible for raising money and work closely with the candidate and campaign manager to help meet fundraising goals. In today's high-priced elections, they are in charge of developing far-reaching fundraising operations. Bradley Crate served as Romney's chief financial officer during the 2012 election, but his relationship with Romney began during his work as a fiscal policy analyst and as director of capital planning and policy in Romney's gubernatorial administration between 2003 and 2006 (Sides et al. 2014).

Communications directors manage all candidate interactions with the media, including interviews, speech writing, and campaign website management. Romney's 2012 communications director was Gail Gitcho, who previously served as the national press secretary for the Republican National Committee between 2009 and 2010 and then as the communications director for Massachusetts senator Scott Brown until Romney announced his candidacy for president. Communications directors and their staff are charged with developing and managing the campaign's message and work with a team of media and public relations specialists to do so. Field directors are often in charge of a campaign's on-the-ground operations, coordinating staff and volunteers who contact voters in person or by phone and try to persuade them to vote for the candidate. They typically work closely with a volunteer coordinator to help enlist and manage volunteers. Part of their responsibility may also involve coordinating registration and get-out-the-vote efforts among citizens likely to support their candidate (Sides et al. 2014). President Barack Obama's presidential campaigns, both in 2008 and in 2012, had a highly successful team of field directors and coordinators, which ultimately led to two of the most successful grassroots campaigns in presidential election history (McKenna and Han 2014). Reporting to all of these actors is a range of staffers and volunteers, including multiple deputies and advisors, who help to coordinate and execute responsibilities.

In addition to the campaign manager and his group of senior advisors, the Romney campaign had more than 18 different areas of expertise that needed to be filled by multiple staffers. These included communications, field operations, finance, and policy directors; speechwriters, digital communications experts, and operations and scheduling liaisons; and directors for the publicity and schedule of Ann Romney, the candidate's wife, and congressman Paul Ryan, the vice presidential nominee (Appleman 2012). The sheer number of staffers and volunteers needed, however, also challenges campaign managers to put together a coordinated, efficient, well-functioning team that stays on message.

Campaign operatives are tasked with coordinating to achieve one goal: winning the election. An inherent part of this goal includes three objectives: inform, persuade, and turn out voters. Campaign strategists conduct fundraising, media, and outreach branches of campaigns to help achieve these objectives. Candidates and their staff members put together plans of action organized around four interconnected categories: management, money, message, and mobilization (McKenna and Han 2014). Table 1.1 illustrates these four categories. Management, money, message, and mobilization constitute the strategies campaigns undertake to achieve the goal of winning an election, and each strategy consists of means or tactics needed to successfully implement these strategies.

Not all political campaigns are constructed and organized the same way, however. It is instructive to contrast the actual structures of the Romney and Obama campaigns in 2012 to get a general sense for how different campaigns can be

Table 1.1 Sample Campaign Schema (McKenna and Han 2014, 38)

CATEGORY	MANAGEMENT	MONEY	MESSAGE	MOBILIZATION
GOAL	IMPLEMENTATION	RESOURCES	PERSUASION	VOTER CONTACT
Means	• Operations • Human resources • Advance and scheduling	• Bundling • Online Fundraising • PACs • Public financing • Events • Budgeting	• Traditional media (print, TV, radio) • New media, social media, and digital outreach • Candidate and surrogate events • Issue and opposition research • Data targeting and analytics	• Field operation (door-to-door, calling, registration, literature drops, community meetings, candidate events) • GOTV drives • Data targeting and analytics
Actors	• Campaign managers • Consultants	• Wealthy individuals • Online donors • Fundraising professionals	• Paid staff • Mainstream media • Consultants • "Blogosphere"	• Paid field staff • Out-of-state volunteers • Local volunteers

organized. Figure 1.2 shows Romney's campaign structure and Figure 1.3 displays the organizational structure of the Obama campaign (Sides et al. 2014: 143, 144). Whereas Romney's campaign was structured to emphasize a top-down approach to organization, Obama's campaign was more circular and egalitarian, allowing different individuals to have a say in the decision-making process. Indeed, the Obama campaign introduced an important feature that may become a more permanent feature of future political campaigns: a decentralized campaign structure. Romney's campaign, in contrast, was highly centralized and loaded with political operatives. On Election Day, Obama's campaign had 4,000 employees (including 2,700 field staffers) who managed more than 8,000 neighborhood team leaders and 32,000 well-trained volunteers, also known as core team members. The Ohio field organizer Tony Speare explains what this type of decentralization looked like in action:

> Rather than trying to do all the work ourselves, the idea was to spend the majority of my time building up volunteer teams and then making them self-sufficient so that by the end of the campaign, volunteers were calling other volunteers to recruit them. They were running all of the trainings. They were entering all of the data. They were making all the phone calls, knocking on all the doors. And by the end, the last four days we were able to remove ourselves and just coordinate with all of the teams but let them run their own operation. (McKenna and Han 2014: 8)

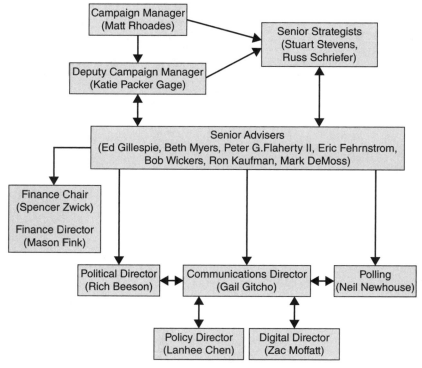

Figure 1.2 Organizational Chart: Romney for President (2012)
SOURCE: Sides et al. 2014, p. 143

The differences in campaign structure were also apparent in the Obama campaign's hiring of technology experts. The Romney campaign featured a small group of "well-connected" political consultants, whereas the Obama campaign thought outside of the box in terms of hiring, reaching beyond established political staffers to recruit data analysts from Silicon Valley, Fortune 500 companies, and academia (Leahy 2013).

The Obama campaigns were groundbreaking in terms of their structures and unprecedented use of data, but most campaigns today understand that a basic component of their strategy must involve sophisticated use of voter information, targeting, and messaging. Contrary to traditional, retail campaigning, which involved a more direct relationship with voters through political machines, as well as to mass marketing as pioneered in the 1960s and 1970s, today's campaigns are much more focused on *mass customization* (see Burton and Shea 2010), a topic I will discuss in depth in Chapter 5 in the context of microtargeting.

Candidate speeches are a good example of how mass customization functions in the context of a political campaigns. It may seem hard to believe, given the number of times we hear talking points repeated over and over in the news media, but candidates do *not* give the same speech every time they speak. Instead,

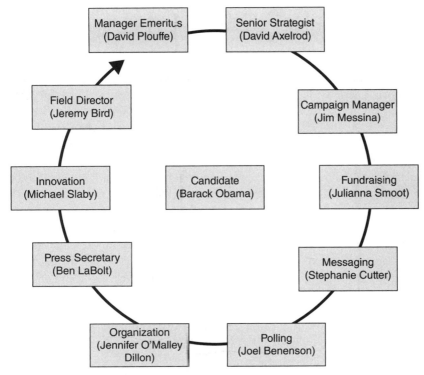

Figure 1.3 Organizational Chart: Obama for President (2012)
SOURCE: Sides et al. 2014, p. 143

they adapt their speech to the specific audience, type of event, and location using speech modules, which are single units of speech. Friedenberg and Trent (2011) write, "Typically, candidates will have a speech unit, or module, on each of the ten to twenty issues on which they speak most frequently . . . the length of each can be varied simply by adding or subtracting examples, statistics, illustrations or other support material" (200–201). Most campaigns have speechwriters on hand to assist with the adaptation of speeches based on where a speech is given, an important example of how context can shape the strategic decisions of candidates and their campaigns.

Overall, the structure of the contemporary political campaign can be described as many parts moving in concert to help the candidates win the election. Different speeches, advertisements, and mobilization efforts are required from place to place, but more often than not, the components of these efforts come from a common, well-tested core of strategic messages. Key campaign staff members help coordinate a wide spectrum of specialized activities that share a common plan and message. As I will discuss throughout this volume, context-contingent strategies have implications for the effectiveness with which political conduct promotes representation and accountability from elected officials, informs citizens, and motivates them to participate in politics.

TRANSITION FROM PARTY-CENTERED
TO CANDIDATE-CENTERED ELECTIONS

Contemporary political campaigns differ from campaigns of previous eras in a number of ways, but one of the most important changes has been in the role played by political parties. Although no one would argue that parties play no role in modern American elections, their position in relation to candidates has decidedly shifted. In 1950, the American Political Science Association (APSA) published a report of the Committee on Political Parties in which political scientists advocated for stronger, better centralized, more clearly defined party organizations, ones that were independent from interest groups and held accountable by their members and responsible to the public (American Political Science Association 1950). The report presents itself as an ideal statement of what makes a "good" party, and its recommendations align with the democratic norms that are the emphasis of this volume. Under these guidelines, parties and their candidates were meant to inform and engage voters with distinct, meaningful policy alternatives, to make firm policy commitments, and to faithfully represent these interests while in office.

Indeed, in the early decades of the 20th century, political parties embodied some form of the APSA committee's report. Candidates for political office stood for election as representatives of their party. Parties were more than a useful identifying label for candidates to use on the campaign trail. They played an integral role in ensuring the organizational and strategic success of their candidates. Elections were largely characterized by direct relationships between parties and the public. Political machines reigned supreme, using their ability to hand out patronage jobs when in power as a powerful political resource. The grip of the party machine was loosened by reforms such as civil service reform, which reduced the number of patronage positions parties could give to their supporters, and the secret ballot, which prevented parties from directly coercing citizens for their votes (Judd and Swanstrom 2007; McCormick 1979).

Following these reforms, candidates were better able to run for office without the aid of parties. However, some debate remains as to whether and how the significance and role of political parties have declined. Political scientists have put forward a nuanced discussion of the shifting roles of parties. For example, one argument in favor of the parties-in-decline thesis focuses on the increasing number of citizens identifying as "independent" when asked about their party identification. This refers specifically to the role that parties play in the electorate, that is, the extent to which the public identifies with one party or the other (Wattenberg 1990). However, political scientists recognize that most independents still actually lean toward one party (Keith et al. 1992). In recent years, party identification has been increasing in importance across a wide range of elections and, as mentioned previously, remains an important shortcut for citizens to assess candidates without expending enormous amounts of time learning detailed information about them. In addition, studies find a close relationship between partisanship and ideology, which generally refers to whether voters see themselves as liberals, conservatives, or moderates, especially for politically sophisticated voters (Box-Steffensmeier and De Boef 2001), and this correspondence seems to be strengthening in the past few decades (Jacobson and Carson 2015). As Box-Steffensmeier and De Boef (2001: 232) note, "the incentives for politicians to link popular ideology with partisanship are strong; the people who pay attention to politics and put them in office (or kick them out) are the same people who connect ideology and partisanship."

Although the identification with parties in the electorate is of obvious importance for political campaigns, party relationships with campaign organizations have gone through a substantial shift as well. In response to the parties-in-decline thesis, Schlesinger (1991) asks a set of compelling questions: "What do we make of political parties that do not control their nominations, yet win elections; whose support among the electorate has declined while their electoral record improves; parties whose organizations have supposedly decomposed, yet whose personnel and payrolls have blossomed; parties that have no control over their members, yet present clear partisan choices to the electorate?" (2–3). Echoes of questions precisely along these lines reverberated in the 2016 race for the Republican presidential nomination as many party leaders, fearful of a general election calamity, sought to thwart Trump's success at the polls and his steady march toward the nomination, as well as in the Democratic presidential contest, in which a serious challenge to front-runner and establishment-favorite Hillary Clinton by Bernie Sanders raised questions about the proper role of party-leaders and unpledged, so-called superdelegates to the party nominating convention.

Answers to these questions come both from the new role of parties in relationship to candidates and from the continued need for candidates to identify with a major party as a virtual prerequisite for running for public office in the United States. Instead of losing their relevance, parties have been forced to energetically respond to the shift in focus of American elections. In response to the rise in candidate-centered campaigns, parties have remained an integral force in political campaigns by offering more services to candidates (Schlesinger 1991; Aldrich 2011). Whereas candidates once followed the lead of parties, parties now aid candidates with a bevy of campaign activities, including fundraising and advertising, as well as by endorsing candidates. Parties provide candidates with a recognizable label to attach to themselves so they appeal to the electorate and draw in further money and support from outside groups aligned with a particular party. As Aldrich (2011) notes, "Nomination by a major party, most fundamentally, remains an all but necessary condition for election to a major office" (285).

Although no one factor can be singled out as the cause of this transforming role of political parties, changes in advertising and marketing technology, particularly the rise of television, have undoubtedly played significant roles. As parties and candidates had to spend more and more time fundraising to meet the costs of advertising on television, greater pressure was placed on candidates to recruit staff to meet these fundraising needs and to manage the growing costs of campaigns. Television also shifted the focus from parties to candidates as the faces of political candidates were projected into the living rooms of millions of Americans. Politicians more or less became "stars" and their relationship with the public became more personal than in the era of party prominence (Sides et al. 2014).

A rise in partisan polarization has also had implications for the strategic behavior of political campaigns. For years, conventional wisdom held that there was little distance between American parties in terms of ideology. In today's political climate, groups such as the APSA's 1950 commission on political parties may in some sense be getting what they asked for, although not without negative consequences. In recent years, observers have contended that parties have grown increasingly polarized; that is, their ideological centers are moving farther apart from one another and becoming more distinct. Empirical evidence also suggests members of Congress that belong to the same party are becoming more similar in their respective policy positions and that there are growing divides between the two major parties with respect to these positions (Layman et al. 2006).

As such, increasing partisan polarization has been one of the main contextual changes within which campaigns must operate. Polarization affects how campaigns unfold, candidate discourse, strategy, and the choices of elected officials once in office. Although partisan polarization has been especially notable among political elites, there has been increased sorting and ideological consistency within the American public as well (Fiorina and Abrams 2014; Fiorina et al. 2010). In 1994, the median Democratic voter was to the left, ideologically speaking, of 64% of Republican voters, whereas the median Republican was to the right of 70% of Democrats. In other words, in 1994, 23% of Republicans were more liberal than the median Democrat, and 17% of Democrats were more conservative than the median Republican. As of 2014, those numbers were 4% and 5%, respectively. Figure 1.4 illustrates these changes over time.

These developments mean it is less feasible for candidates to take positions that compromise their party's issue positions and win elections, given that Americans have become more clearly sorted along ideological lines into their respective parties. As Americans become more firmly entrenched in their party's positions,

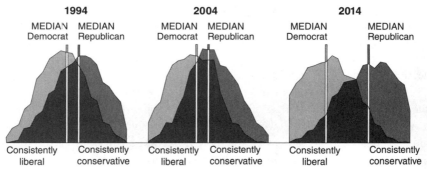

Figure 1.4 Ideological Polarization of the Electorate (Pew Research Center 2014)
SOURCE: 2014 Political Polarization in the American Public, Pew Research Center

with less ideological mixing between parties, and as the parties themselves move farther apart, it becomes far more difficult for elected officials to work across the aisle and develop bipartisan compromises on important policy issues. Instead, candidates feel increasing pressure to stick to the party line. One prominent example of this dynamic comes from Grover Norquist's taxation protection pledge, which asks candidates and elected officials to commit in writing to oppose any and all tax increases. Since the pledge was rolled out in 1986, it has become increasingly necessary for Republicans—and Democrats elected in traditionally Republican districts—to sign the pledge to win election, although in recent years some Republicans have begun to back away from the pledge (Robinson 2012).

Nevertheless, growing partisan polarization does not mean that parties have reverted to the same role they played in eras past. Campaigns in the United States are still largely candidate centered, with parties serving as important and necessary attachments for candidates to be seen as electorally viable, a relationship I will discuss more in depth in Chapter 3.

GROWTH AND PROFESSIONALIZATION OF THE POLITICAL CONSULTING PROFESSION

Shifting means of communication with the public, increased costs of campaigning, and continued candidate prominence at the center of American elections have also led to another drastic change in the American electoral landscape: the rise of political consulting.

The growth of political consulting in contemporary campaigns can partially be attributed to the shift from party-centered to candidate-centered campaigns that began during the 1960s. However, political consulting has its origins in the 1930s. In 1933, Clem Whitaker and Leone Baxter, a husband-and-wife team, formed Campaigns, Inc., and served as consultants in the 1934 race for California governor in which Upton Sinclair, author of *The Jungle* and well-known socialist, uprooted the California political establishment as the Democratic Party's nominee for governor. Whitaker and Baxter were hired by Sinclair's opponents and countered him through smear campaigns and negative advertising tactics (Dinkin 1989). By the 1960s, in large part thanks to the rise in television advertising, professional campaign management became more regularized. The rise of consultants as we know them today, however, as providers of area-specific expertise to candidates, did not arrive until the 1980s and 1990s in the form of media and polling firms (Johnson 2000).

Whereas political consultants at first worked only on campaigns for federal offices such as the U.S. Senate, the U.S. House of Representatives, and the presidency, this is no longer the case. Political consultants are a common element of many political campaigns, from federal to local elections, and also work on ballot initiatives and issue advocacy campaigns (Johnson 2000). Along with the rise in the role of television in politics, the growing importance of political advertisements, and the increasing costs of running successful political campaigns, political consulting has grown into a bona fide profession. Political consultants help to formulate strategies for different candidates based on preexisting (and previously tested) slogans, policy stands, and media strategies to suit their clients. Consultants tend to offer specialized services: some help candidates gauge public opinion, whereas others help craft a candidate's image and increase his or her appeal. Some consultants develop strategies to implement targeted voter contact programs based on demographics and known voting history, and others help the campaign raise money (Burton and Shea 2010; Dulio 2004).

The decisions consultants make depend on who they are working with and in what context they are working (Burton and Shea 2010). For example, Burton and Shea write, "the strategy and tactics of *mass customization*, where consultants narrowly target their message, hoping to optimize their efforts at the level of the individual voter, is a one-to-many approach that functions on a one-to-one basis" (18). Consultants thus have several previously tested strategies for political campaigns that they can choose from depending on the race they are working on, the opponent their candidate is facing, the candidate's constituency, and a host of other dynamic elements. Candidates, especially those in high-profile races, do not typically rely on just one or two consultants. In a U.S. Senate race, for example, candidates will hire a range of consultants with different areas of expertise, from strategists who manage campaigns, conduct polls, and manage media efforts to specialists with expertise in specific areas such as campaign finance law, speech writing, and microtargeting. One of the most important developments in consulting of the past few decades has been the specialization in managing a candidate's online image, including everything from website management, e-mail blasts, blogs, and social media presence, a change I will discuss in Chapter 9 (Kazin et al. 2011).

Many decry the rise of political consultants, claiming that they have led to the demise of the party system, putting candidate interests ahead of party interests and leading to manufactured messages and "unholy alliances" among money, television, and consultants (Stuart 2006). In his critique of modern political consultancy, the journalist Joe Klein (2007) bemoans the loss of the impassioned and authentic politician. Referring to the presidential candidate Robert Kennedy's speech from a flatbed truck in Indianapolis, Indiana, in 1968 following the assassination of Martin Luther King Jr., Klein writes, "Kennedy's words stand as a sublime example of politics in its grandest form, for its highest purpose, to heal, to educate, to lead—but also sadly they represent the end of an era: the last moments before American political life was overwhelmed by marketing professionals, consultants, and pollsters who, with the flaccid acquiescence of the politicians, have robbed public life of much of its romance and vigor" (quoted in Stuart 2006).

Many argue that the rise in political consulting is at least partly responsible for the ever-increasing cost of running for elected office. After all, political consultancy is a profit-driven enterprise. By the middle of 2012, months before the actual presidential election, the top 150 political consulting companies, including those that specialize in media, fundraising, and direct mail, had already grossed $465.76 million. Some critics express concerns about the motivations and effects of these developments. Fred Wertheimer, the founder of Democracy 21, a nonprofit, nonpartisan organization dedicated to promoting government integrity and accountability, contends that "the whole industry is not only bigger and more lucrative, but more negative. . . . The consultants go where the money is; the money is in outside spending; the outside spending is almost uniformly negative" (Fineman and Blumenthal 2012). As I will discuss in Chapter 6, there are a number of implications of negative advertising for democratic principles; some scholars argue negative campaigning has a detrimental impact on voter turnout in certain contexts, whereas others suggest it has the potential to actually increase both engagement and the amount of political information received by voters.

Others see the rise in political consulting as necessary in a fast-paced and technologically advanced world rife with an increasing number of media outlets and a diverse array of professional expertise needed to run for public office. In fact, some view political consultants as essential to the infrastructure of the modern political party and to the success of candidates. In other words, "modern consultants aren't in competition with the parties; they *are* [emphasis mine] the parties" (J. W. Doherty 2006, 39). In fact, evidence exists that the political consulting industry has developed into two rival networks of Republicans and Democrats. That is, consultants have learned it is better to collaborate and share information with their ideological allies than to be in competition with one another within their own party networks (J. W. Doherty 2006).

Some further suggest that political consultants can play a role in promoting some of the democratic ideals emphasized in this volume. No longer are candidates simply competing against one another; outside actors, such as labor unions and special interest groups, spend a great deal of money to influence the outcome of important races. Contests once perceived as local, for all intents and purposes, have become nationalized through the influence of these actors. Political consultants serve to help candidates to navigate increasingly complex fields of communication and to develop clear, coherent messages. As such, they are in a position to help inform voters by clarifying the debate between candidates and by sifting through complex webs of information (Dulio 2004).

The increasing role of political consultants in campaigns raises a host of concerns regarding campaign conduct and the democratic norms of representation, information, and engagement, especially given the changing electoral contexts to which campaigns must respond and adapt. Parties are weaker and their relationships with campaigns have changed; they no longer run the show when it comes to American elections. Changes in campaign finance law allow candidates to raise funds more directly, and advances in technology and media enable candidates to plan, produce, and implement their own media campaigns. Campaigns operating in these contexts will naturally require additional expertise to help guide them through these changes. But consultants are an unelected class of political actors who may not necessarily feel accountable to the public. Consultants are tasked with developing and implementing strategies that help candidates win elections, and these strategies do not always align with democratic ideals.

Regardless of where one stands on the consultant debate, one thing is clear: political consultants are here to stay. They have become pervasive in contemporary campaigns. As early as 1992, almost 66% of candidates running for the U.S. House of Representatives hired at least one professional consultant (Medvic 2001). By 1998, this number averaged approximately five, with incumbents averaging almost seven hires (Herrnson 2000). By 2008, there were at least 3,000 firms that specialized in political consulting (Kazin et al. 2011). In contemporary campaigns, the relationship among candidates, consultants, and parties is complex and intertwined, making the implications of their activities less than clear for democratic principles in American politics. Making the equation even more complicated is the contingent nature of their decisions. Although the basic pieces of the campaign puzzle may remain the same in many cases, they are pieced together in different ways depending on the setting in which campaigns operate and shifting contexts over time. As we will see in subsequent chapters, these decisions have implications for the extent to which contemporary campaigns help or hinder progress toward democratic representation and an informed and engaged citizenry.

ORGANIZATION OF THE BOOK

Each of the chapters in this volume is designed to help scholars of American politics understand how different components of contemporary campaigns help advance or hinder the three democratic norms outlined above. Each chapter discusses these components, emphasizing how the context in which campaigns operate influences their strategic calculations and decisions, which, in turn, produce consequences with implications for democratic processes and governance.

Chapter 2 considers how campaigns adapt to the contexts and circumstances of races at different levels of elections, as well as the growth of ballot measures, initiatives, and the campaigns designed to promote these causes. Chapter 3 discusses the other players campaigns often interact with, including political parties, interest groups, and the media. It also highlights the challenges and opportunities presented by these interactions as they have changed over time.

Chapters 4 through 8 walk the reader through a discussion of the different steps and strategies necessary for political campaigns to persuade and mobilize voters and how well these steps align with the democratic ideals described above. Chapter 4 tackles a major source of controversy in modern campaigns: money and campaign finance. It includes a discussion of the changing context of campaign financing regulations and fundraising, as well as of the effects of campaign spending in elections and the growing role of super PACs and other independent spending groups. Chapter 5 discusses what campaigns actually do with the money they raise, outlining the strategic choices they make and their implications for representation, information, and engagement.

Chapter 6 focuses on how the messages crafted by campaigns are actually delivered and includes an overview of the media options available to campaigns and the effectiveness of political advertising. Chapter 7 brings the discussion of campaign strategies and messaging together to highlight how campaigns actually get out the vote, presenting an overview of a wide array of mobilization tactics, including a discussion of recent advances in our understanding of which tactics are effective. Chapter 8 provides a more nuanced focus on campaign strategy and voting, presenting the factors that influence vote choice, including partisanship and issue positions, candidate traits and characteristics, emotions, and some of the emerging findings about how personality traits, genetic predispositions, and other dimensions of voter psychology challenge campaigns to devise ways to influence voters.

Shifting gears, Chapters 9 and 10 examine the changes taking place in the broader sociopolitical landscape. Chapter 9 discusses how developments in technology and social media have forced campaigns to adapt, focusing on campaign software, the availability of data, and the need to manage the campaign's online presence, including social media platforms such as Facebook and Twitter. Chapter 10 presents an overview of how changing electoral processes and election law, such as convenience voting, same-day registration, and the possible implementation of Internet-based voting, challenges campaigns to use these developments to their advantage.

Chapter 11 brings attention to political campaigns in international contexts, offering insights into how political campaigns operate in democracies abroad and the extent to which changes in American campaign strategies have been applied to international contexts. Finally, Chapter 12 concludes with an assessment of the current state of political campaigns, summarizing how well contemporary campaigns advance the democratic norms of representation, information, and engagement. Looking forward, I discuss some of the popular reforms proposed to improve the conduct of American campaigns and democracy writ large, concluding with reflections on the "permanent campaign" and speculating about the prospects for the future of political campaigns.

KEY TERMS

Campaign plan

Candidate-centered
    elections

Data analytics

Data-driven campaign

Ideology

Minimal effects thesis

Mobilization

Parties-in-decline thesis

Partisan polarization

Persuasion

Political consultants

Political engagement

Political machines

Professionalization

Representation

SUGGESTED READINGS

Alvarez, R. M. 1997. *Information and Elections*. Ann Arbor: University of Michigan Press.

Dulio, D. A. 2004. *For Better or Worse?: How Political Consultants Are Changing Elections in the United States*. New York: State University of New York Press.

Erikson. R. S., and C. Wlezien. 2012. *The Timeline of Presidential Elections: How Campaigns Do (and Do Not) Matter*. Chicago: University of Chicago Press.

Sides, J., and L. Vavreck. 2013. *The Gamble: Choice and Chance in the 2012 Presidential Election*. Princeton, NJ: Princeton University Press.

Zaller, J. 1992. *The Nature and Origins of Mass Opinion*. New York: Cambridge University Press.

CHAPTER 2

Layers of Democracy: Federal, State, and Local Campaigns

In 2009, the New York mayor, Michael R. Bloomberg, set electoral records: he spent more of his own money than any other single person in the history of the United States to win elected office. Ultimately, he exhausted more than $140 million by the time he was reelected to a third term. His spending left political consultants flabbergasted; they had presumed his popularity in New York and advantage as an incumbent should have been enough to win him reelection without excessive spending. In contrast, his Democratic competitor, Bill Thompson, only had $3 million dollars available for the final week and a half of the race and spent a total of $8.3 million over the entire campaign (Barbaro and Chen 2009; Katz 2009).

Despite having outspent his challenger 12 to 1, Bloomberg ultimately eked out a victory with a mere 50.7% of the vote. The Bloomberg–Thompson race broke records for personal contributions to a campaign and illustrates the expansion of record-breaking campaign spending beyond the domain of high-stakes, high-purview elections for federal office. For example, in New Jersey, the 2013 Jersey City mayoral race between councilman Steve Fulop and the incumbent, Jerramiah Healy, $5.2 million was spent between the two campaigns. In the 2014 Newark, New Jersey, mayoral race, a near record $12.6 million was spent as Ras Baraka defeated Shavar Jeffries, an amount second only to the 2006 mayoral election (Villanova 2015). As of 2014, the average cost of a winning city council race in Ann Arbor, Michigan, had more than doubled since 2009 (Leonard 2014).

Although higher-profile presidential, congressional, or gubernatorial campaigns have long been known for their high price tags and professionalization, these features have only recently become associated with state and local elections. Once run on a tight budget with the help of dedicated friends, family, and volunteers, these elections are now characterized by increased costs, professionalization, and use of political consultants.

Bloomberg's election spending and prominent place in the United States' largest city garnered national media attention. But this is unusual for local or even

Table 2.1 Governments in the United States (Elective Offices)

	NUMBER OF ELECTIVE BODIES	NUMBER OF ELECTED OFFICIALS
Federal Government	1	
Executive branch		2
U.S. Senate		100
U.S. House of Representatives		435
State Government	50	
State legislatures		7,382
Statewide elected offices		1,036
State boards		1,331
Local Government		
Municipal governments	19,429	135,531
Town or township governments	16,504	126,958
County governments	3,034	58,818
School districts	13,506	95,000
Special Districts	35,052	84,089
Total	87,576	510,682

NOTE: Data on the breakdown of local governments are from the National League of Cities (2010), except school district data, which were provided by the National Association of School Boards. State government elected officials data come from the National Conference of State Legislatures (2010) and the Bureau of the Census (1992).

SOURCE: Adapted from Lawless (2012); modified to correct a transposition error in original after confirmation with author.

state-level elections. Federal elections are generally higher-salience affairs in terms of public and media attention, but, as Table 2.1 illustrates, the United States boasts more than a half-million elective offices, most of which are found at the state and local levels.

In this chapter, I discuss state and local elections with respect to the changing context of national elections, considering the differences and similarities in factors that influence campaign conduct at each level, the ways strategies used in each have converged over time, and how they have remained distinct. I first describe the different types of elections held in the United States, providing an overview of the differences and similarities in rules and regulations among national, state, and local elections and their impact on campaign strategy. Incumbency bias is an important factor in elections at all levels and is increasing in prominence. Competiveness plays a strategic role in determining campaign strategy, spending, and voter interest. As I highlighted at the beginning of the chapter, more state and local elections are beginning to look like federal elections in terms of their professionalization, use of political consultants, and total expense. Differences in campaign finance law from state to state undoubtedly affect the decisions made by campaigns. Partisanship also factors into the strategic calculus of campaigns at different levels of elections, although as we will see, there are some distinct differences in the role that partisanship plays between local and federal elections. Finally, decisions made by voters in state and local elections are often made within the context of national trends and forces. For each of these factors, I discuss whether and how campaign conduct will differ between the context of federal and subnational elections, concluding each section with an assessment of these interactions for the democratic norms of the representation, information received by, and engagement of American citizens.

LEVELS OF AMERICAN ELECTIONS: VARIATION ACROSS STATES

The U.S. Constitution stipulates the basic parameters for federal elections, but states, counties, and municipalities hold elections for thousands of executive and representative positions in cycles that often can (but do not need to) coincide with presidential or congressional elections. These include elections for statewide positions (for example, governor, lieutenant governor, attorney general, treasurer) or state legislative offices, local offices (mayor, city council, school board), or county posts (county executive). Local governmental structures can have important implications for campaigns and democracy. For example, some cities have mayors and city councils, while others have city councils that work with professional city managers. Oliver and Ha (2007) argue that council-manager structures tend to create low information political environments that enable incumbents seeking reelection to fare better. Councilors in these cities have fewer opportunities to influence policy, so they are less likely to seek reelection (Oliver and Ha 2007).

In the United States, many judicial offices are also elected. At the state level, 22 states use elections to fill state supreme court seats, whereas 24 use bipartisan commissions to appoint court justices. As Figure 2.1 shows, 26 states also allow ballot initiatives or referenda that enable citizens to vote directly on state laws and legislative proposals. An initiative allows citizens to propose a statute or constitutional amendment, whereas a referendum allows citizens to transfer a statute passed by the state legislature to the ballot, on which voters can choose to affirm or repeal it.

As I note above, some of these elections take place concurrently with federal elections, but others occur during off-year cycles, that is, those that do not feature a federal midterm or presidential election. In advance of general elections, primary elections are generally held to select party nominees for positions, and the timing of these elections varies considerably across jurisdictions. Timing is an important consideration for campaign operatives because it could have important implications for campaign strategy. For example, turnout in presidential years tends to be higher than in other cycles, which will affect how many (and possibly which) voters show up to vote on Election Day. As I will discuss

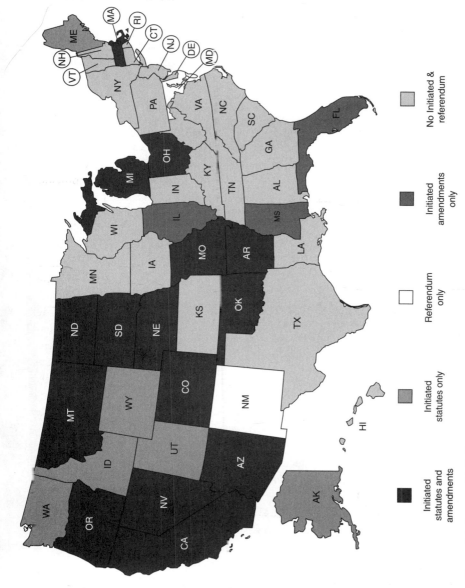

Figure 2.1 States with Ballot Initiatives or Referenda (Ballotpedia 2015)

No Initiated & referendum

Initiated amendments only

Referendum only

Initiated statutes only

Initiated statutes and amendments

below, it could also have implications for the overall electoral context in which state and local campaigns unfold given the outcomes in these races often (but not always) reflect national forces or broader conditions.

In many ways, state and local campaigns are distinct from their counterparts at the federal level. State and local races are often fought over the policies or issues relevant to their respective constituencies, for example. The rules can also be quite different across jurisdictions and offices as well. For instance, signature requirements for candidates to get on the ballot, filing fees, deadlines, and campaign finance laws vary greatly (Panagopoulos and Weinschenk 2016). But state and local elections do not operate in a vacuum and are not immune from developments that are characteristic of American elections more generally. Many of these patterns apply to state and local elections and affect the overall context in which these campaigns unfold. I will summarize some of the key features commonly found across the landscape of American elections and discuss how these can affect considerations for campaign strategy and implementation at various levels.

One commonality across the majority of American elections is the advantage enjoyed by incumbents (Cox and Katz 1996; Krebs 1998; Berry et al. 2000; Gelman and King 1990). At the federal level, incumbent reelection rates for members of Congress have typically exceeded 90% over the past few decades (Panagopoulos and Weinschenk 2016). One explanation for this phenomenon is that incumbents exploit the resources of their offices, and constituency service in particular, to cultivate a "personal vote" that ingratiates voters to support them in subsequent races (Cain, Ferejohn, and Fiorina 1987). Incumbents also typically enjoy greater name recognition among their constituents, essential for garnering votes as well as financial support from parties, interest groups, and individual donors. Incumbency bias presents a sort of catch-22 for the recruitment of potential challengers. Challengers need name recognition to garner support from the public and to be seen as viable candidates by important donors, but are less likely to have this name recognition in the first place. Incumbency bias can make it difficult to recruit quality challengers to strong incumbents or even to incumbents who have not been effective, but who remain in office because they are well known to and established with voters, interest groups, and parties. After all, politicians tend to be strategic in deciding when to run, and they will often wait for incumbent vulnerability or an open seat before tossing their hat into the rink (Jacobson and Kernell 1981).

Incumbency bias influences would-be challengers' decisions to run for office in the first place and affects campaign strategy throughout an election. Whether challengers think they can run a strong campaign depends on the vulnerability of the incumbent and resources that can be mustered to give them momentum. Throughout an election, challengers typically must work far harder than incumbents to convince donors and supporters that they deserve to win. Challengers do, however, enjoy at least one advantage: spending by challengers is typically more effective in garnering support than is spending by incumbents (Panagopoulos and Green 2008; Jacobson 1978). This is because challengers have more room to grow in terms of voter approval and electoral support; incumbents almost always begin an election season with higher levels of awareness and approval than their opponents.

Despite some clear advantages, incumbency does not always assure victory. In the 2015 Chicago mayoral election, for example, the incumbent, Rahm Emanuel, was forced into a runoff in the election, the first in Chicago mayoral history. Despite having vastly outspent his challengers in the first round, Emanuel failed to win a majority and faced Jesus "Chuy" Garcia in a runoff election. Emanuel ultimately won, but the runoff forced the incumbent mayor to change his tone and show his constituents he was serious about representing them and admitting to his shortcomings.

The 2015 Chicago mayoral runoff was an unusual and highly publicized race, both because Chicago is one of the largest cities in the country and because it was so unprecedented. Challengers in less high-profile local elections often face an even greater uphill battle because they must deal with not only an incumbent's advantage, but also a public that is likely to be far less engaged and interested in the dynamics of local elections. One reason for this—and a key difference between local and state/federal elections—is that the vast majority of local elections are nonpartisan. At the turn of the 20th century, progressive reformers, targeting the perceived corruption of the party machines, adopted a number of reforms, one of which was the nonpartisan ballot. Without partisan affiliation, party machines lost an important cue by which they could mobilize supporters to their cause (Bridges 1997; Erie 1988). Today, nonpartisan elections pose unique challenges for campaigns operating in these contexts, especially challengers looking to upset the status quo, because they can no longer rely on partisan cues to stimulate voters' interest and attract support.

At the national level, both chambers of Congress are highly professionalized legislatures, with sizable salaries, staff, and benefits (Polsby 1968), this is not the case in all state legislatures. Some state legislatures have unlimited legislative sessions, provide ample budgets for staff, and pay salaries high enough that elected officials do not need a second career to make ends meet. Others only meet for a few months every year, offer little to no staff support, and pay such low salaries that elected officials are effectively required to hold a regular job to support themselves while in office (Squire 1992, 2007). These differences have implications for the reelection campaigns of current legislators and incentives for viable challengers to run for elected office. Elected officials in professionalized legislatures have more time, money, and staff resources to actively engage their constituents and meet their needs, accomplishments they can tout when running for reelection. Incumbents in professionalized legislatures are typically more likely to attract challengers interested in pursuing a career in state politics, but they are not as likely to lose reelection because of the extensive resources at their disposal (Carey et al. 2000; Hogan 2004).

Federal elections in the United States each feature different election cycles, which have implications for incumbency advantage and campaign strategy. The president is elected every four years and can only be elected for two terms. Senators are elected every six years and face no term limits, nor do members of the House of Representatives, who face reelection every two years. Term limits on the presidency have consequences for policy initiatives. In their first term, presidents face the challenge of running for reelection and thus must carefully consider how their decisions affect their likelihood of success in the next election. If elected for a second term, presidents theoretically have less constraint on the decisions they make, but they can be checked by other members of the legislative branch who do face reelection and must tread more carefully in terms of the decisions they make and the laws they support. Presidents have no formal lawmaking power (although they can issue executive orders), but often draft legislation and can play a substantial role in proposing and supporting initiatives that are then taken up by Congress. After he was first elected to office in 2008, Barack Obama drafted and proposed comprehensive health care reform in conjunction with several of his Democratic allies in Congress. The legislation ultimately passed, but did not receive a single Republican vote in the U.S. House of Representatives. Republicans then used the public's ambivalent feelings about the legislation to lambast the president during his reelection bid and unseat several Democratic supporters of the legislation (Fuller 2014).

Presidential candidates must contend with a unique rule that greatly impacts how they conduct their campaigns. Most elections in the United States feature a winner-take-all system, in which seats are awarded to the highest vote getters. Because of the Electoral College, presidential candidates develop their campaign strategy with the goal of winning multiple "winner-take-all" elections in specific states rather than winning the majority of votes nationwide in a popular vote. Each state is allocated a certain number of electors based on the number of members of Congress that each state sends to Washington, meaning there are a total of 538 electors, 435 for members of the House of Representatives and 100 for Senators (3 additional electors come from the District of Columbia). To win the presidency, a candidate must receive a majority of the Electoral College, or at least 270 electoral votes. With the exception of Maine and Nebraska, electoral votes are awarded on a winner-take-all basis. The candidate who wins the plurality of the vote in a given state is awarded all of that state's electors.

What this means for presidential campaigns is that they must be highly strategic with regard to where they allocate their resources, both in terms of the number of electors a state has and in terms of the competiveness of elections across states. California, for example, has the most electors available to any candidate, with 55 electoral votes, but it has been a reliably Democratic state for the past several elections. Ohio and Florida, in contrast, are perennial battlegrounds given their partisan makeup and number of potential swing voters, although they had only 18 and 29 electoral votes respectively in the 2016 election. As a result, presidential candidates typically spend more resources and time campaigning in battleground states than in places where their efforts are unlikely to affect the outcome. For example, presidential campaigns focus their television advertisements on media markets that overlap with battleground states. As a result, in the 2012 election, the campaigns heavily advertised in only 71 of the 210 U.S. media markets (Fowler and Ridout 2010).

Other elected members of the federal government do not face the same kinds of constraints that presidential candidates do. Members of the U.S. Senate have more leeway because they only face reelection every six years and are elected in statewide, winner-take-all elections. Senators can thus spend more time crafting policy and are theoretically more immune to the whims of their constituents. Members of the U.S. House of Representatives, however, are said to be almost "constantly campaigning," given the short period they have between election and reelection. After the 2012 elections, Tracy Jan, a reporter for the *Boston Globe*, wrote that "newly elected congressional Democrats had just a week to savor their victories before coming face to face with a harsh reality of Washington. . . . Raise money. Raise more. Win." As I will cover in greater depth in Chapter 4, members of the House are often expected to devote at least four hours of every workday to raising money to build a war chest and defend their seats (Jan 2013). To be sure, senators are not immune from fundraising necessities, but the amount of time between elections allows them more breathing room than their counterparts in the House of Representatives.

Nonfederal elections, too, feature varied election cycles and term-limit rules. Some state governments have election cycles that line up with federal elections, whereas others feature off-cycle elections. Virginia and New Jersey, for example, hold "postpresidential," off-cycle elections. That is, their governors are up for re-election in the year following a presidential election. Kentucky, Louisiana, and Mississippi, in contrast, have "prepresidential" off-cycle elections. Governors, for the most part, are elected every four years, with the exception of New Hampshire and Vermont, whose governors serve two-year terms. State senators in 31 states have four-year terms, whereas senators in 12 states have two-year terms. In Arkansas, Delaware, Florida, Illinois, Minnesota, New Jersey, and Texas, senators have terms that are sometimes two years and sometimes four depending on whether their election is held close to the redistricting that occurs every 10 years after a federal census. Within states, municipalities have a fair amount of autonomy in determining when to hold elections for mayor, city council, school board, and other locally elected positions. Many local elections are also held, that is, at different times than the traditional midterm and presidential elections. This has implications for campaign strategy because off-cycle elections, especially if they only feature local races, tend to garner far less interest and turnout, which affects the calculations campaigns must make when developing mobilization strategies.

In federal elections, term limits only exist for the president. In nonfederal elections, however, term limits vary from state to state and can affect the recruitment of viable challengers because they can increase the number of open-seat races in a state. Currently, governors in 36 states and state legislators in 15 states are subject to term limits (Panagopoulos and Weinschenk 2016). Advocates for term limits initially thought that this institutional change would make state leg-islative campaigns more competitive and less expensive, but some empirical evi-dence suggests this is not the case. In a study of California state legislative elections, Masket and Lewis (2007) found that elections in California in the early 2000s were just as expensive as they were in the late 1980s, that incumbents were in no greater danger of losing their seats, and that open seat races were no more competitive than they were prior to the adoption of term limits. In a comparison of state legislatures with and without term limits, Schaffner et al. (2004) argue that term limits strengthen the overall electoral prospects of the majority party because they are more inclined to move supporters from the safe districts of term-limited legislators into competitive districts.

Voting and registration laws also vary from state to state. These variations affect not only state and local candidates, but also candidates for federal office, including the presidency. A given state's deadlines for registering to vote can in-fluence when campaigns conduct voter registration drives. Even in terms of get-ting on the ballot, there is considerable variation across states and municipalities in terms of the number of signatures and filing fees required for ballot access. For example, candidates seeking to run in a major-party congressional primary in Florida in 2014 were required either to pay a filing fee of $10,440 or to submit petitions with at least 2,298 signatures. By contrast, the filing fee in Maryland for the same office was $100; candidates in Rhode Island are only required to submit 500 signatures and nominating petitions in Tennessee require just 25 signatures from the candidate's district. Collecting signatures or sufficient funds to pay filing fees is often the first hurdle new candidates must face in entering a race. Other developments, such as early or convenience voting, also have implications for how contemporary campaigns are run. In Colorado, Oregon, and Washington, citizens vote by mail. Instead of going to a polling station on Election Day, citizens receive their ballot in the mail weeks before the deadline of "Election Day" and make their decisions from the comfort of their own home. As one can imagine, this type of election can be a source of frustration for political cam-paigns because they no longer target their mobilizing efforts toward Election Day, but must spread out their resources over a span of several weeks. I will talk more about changing election realities such as convenience voting in Chapter 10 in my discussion of the evolving electoral process.

THE IMPLICATIONS OF STRUCTURAL AND LEGAL VARIATIONS FOR DEMOCRATIC NORMS

Naturally, the institutional variation across levels of democracy in America has implications for campaign conduct and democratic norms. The two-term limit on presidents seems to have some influence on representation, although not nec-essarily in the way one would expect. Presidents at times make public appeals for policy positions that might otherwise not be considered or passed by Congress but are popular with the public. However, they are only likely to do so when they face a contest for reelection and have approval ratings that are average, not high or low. Presidents who no longer face the threat of reelection or are very popular or unpopular do not have the same incentives to pander to public opinion (Canes-Wrone 2006).

Election cycles for the U.S. House and Senate also have normative implications, especially with regard to incumbency bias in these institutions. The short period of time between elections for members of the U.S. House of Representatives is supposed to hold them more accountable to their constituencies. However, the incumbency rate in the U.S. House has steadily increased and can be even more pronounced at the level of state and local elections where voter interest and engagement are lower (Abramowitz et al. 2006; Trounstine 2011, 2013). Incumbent senators, too, have won reelection almost 80% of the time since 1914, in large part because of a lack of quality challengers (Gowrisankaran et al. 2004). In many respects, incumbency bias has similar *types* of implications across local, state, and federal elections for the extent to which campaigns can help uphold democratic norms of representing, informing, and engaging citizens. However, because incumbency bias is more prominent in state and local elections, it is these elections that can often be the most problematic for the extent to which campaign conduct in these contexts promotes democratic norms. Can we realistically expect elected officials who are virtually assured reelection to remain responsive to citizens' preferences and needs? Higher voter turnout can put more pressure on incumbents and has the potential to attenuate structural advantages, so it is no surprise that state and local elections, which generally feature lower turnout, have more advantaged incumbents (Hansford and Gomez 2010; Trounstine 2013).

The implications of incumbency bias for democratic norms initially come into play at the stage when potential challengers are deciding whether to run for office. Incumbency advantage might scare off otherwise strong and viable opponents, preventing the public from even having the opportunity to consider and vote for candidates better suited to represent them. Some argue that the routine reelection of incumbents serves citizens because it allows elected officials to spend more time worrying about citizen concerns and less time campaigning for reelection. Empirical evidence suggests otherwise: on average, entrenched incumbents do not seem to do a better job of representing their constituents. In the context of the U.S. House of Representatives, for example, as incumbency advantage has increased, incumbents have become significantly less responsive to their constituents (King and Gelman 1991). Because they tend to be more electorally secure, incumbents likely feel less need to be responsive to their constituents' preferences to win reelection.

Other realities of state and local elections have consequences for democratic norms in ways that differ from federal elections. As I mentioned above, many local elections feature nonpartisan races. In such elections, one of the main issues campaigns must deal with is how to efficiently inform citizens of their policy positions without partisan cues. As I will discuss further in Chapter 8, voters frequently rely on partisan labels for signals about candidates' likely positions on issues. Although one of the original intents of the nonpartisan ballot was to encourage citizens to seek more detailed information about candidates, some suggest that party labels provide important and perfectly acceptable cues that help citizens learn about candidates for office while saving them the time of having to learn specifics about each candidate running for office (Downs 1957; Druckman and Lupia 2000). As a result, a lack of party labels can actually reduce citizen engagement in local races.

Local elections already tend to draw low turnout. In addition, the *bias* in who votes across race and class can lead to biased outcomes in local elections because nonwhites and individuals of low socioeconomic status turn out at even lower rates in local elections. Low turnout hurts the extent to which minorities are actually represented on city councils and in mayoral offices across the United States (Hajnal 2011). Nonpartisan elections seem to exacerbate these trends and further depress turnout (Schaffner et al. 2001). In the absence of partisanship, voters tend to search out other cues from which to make their decisions, mainly incumbency (Shaffner et al. 2001; Iyengar 2002). This makes it difficult for campaigns operating in these contexts to uphold a normative commitment to citizen engagement and discourages viable, potentially more representative challengers from running for office.

Even if voters show up at the polls and cast ballots, they will not always make their way completely through the ballot. This is somewhat understandable considering the average state ballot in 2010 consisted of 17 elections for office and five ballot questions; many were much longer. In Cook County, Illinois, for example, there were 93 candidate races and four ballot measures on the 2010 ballot (Hedlin 2015). Often voters will simply skip making decisions or else make hasty selections based on shortcuts like voting for incumbents or for the first candidate listed in a race as the position of a contest on the ballot drops (Augenblick and Nicholson 2016). Scholars attribute this phenomenon, known as "roll-off," to voter fatigue, lower contest salience, or simply confusion (Bowler and Donovan 2000). Sometimes, the degree of roll-off can be sufficient to alter the outcome of elections or ballot measures (Augenblick an Nicholson 2016). Strategists for lower-salience state and local campaigns are wise to be mindful of roll-off when devising campaign strategy, even when races are concurrent with higher-stimulus elections, like presidential races.

One component of state and local elections that is not present at the federal level, with the exception of the presidency, is term limits. Although term limits may not make elections less expensive and more competitive, they do have some normatively redeeming qualities. In particular, evidence suggests they can improve the quality of representation among state legislators; term-limited representatives spend less time securing pork for their districts and place a higher priority on the needs of their entire state. Although some may contend that state legislators have a strict responsibility to respond directly to their constituents, advocates of term limits tend to see these effects as positive since they cause state legislators to spend less time working to pass policies that increase their electability at the expense of the collective good of their state and more time engaging in meaningful governance (Carey et al. 1998). At the same time, critics of term limits contend they artificially constrain choice and potentially disqualify effective and responsive elected officials from retaining their positions. This is an enduring controversy that pits a variety of democratic ideals against each other.

THE ROLE OF COMPETITIVE ELECTIONS

A highly competitive election changes the strategic decisions made by campaigns and drives the need for more money, a greater role for political consultants, and expanded professional advertising and mobilizing campaigns. Competitive elections generally attract more resources from parties and outside groups and more interest from voters and inspire greater efforts on the part of campaigns to mobilize supporters to their cause. The closer an election, the less certainty for candidates and the more likely they are to make any effort possible to tip the deciding votes in their favor (Lipsitz 2011). Nonetheless, competiveness varies between federal and nonfederal elections. It is one of the primary influences on campaign strategy and, because it varies so greatly depending on the level of election, the extent to which campaigns are actually motivated to engage and inform citizens is not constant across American elections.

Although elections for federal offices such as the U.S. House of Representatives and U.S. Senate garner a fair amount of attention during an election cycle, they are not markedly more competitive as a result. In U.S. Senate elections, because the constituency consists of an entire state, competition is often more widespread, variable, and dependent on factors such as the partisan and ideological makeup of a given state and the extent to which each candidate's national legislative delegation is more ideologically diverse (Winer et al. 2014). The competiveness of U.S. House elections, in contrast, has been steadily decreasing over the years. U.S. House incumbents seeking reelection are generally able to retain their seats, and the costs to entry for newcomers have steadily escalated in recent years (Jacobson and Carson 2015). This is in part because incumbents in the U.S. House of Representatives rarely face challengers strong enough to pose a serious threat (Cox and Katz 1996). Instead, strong challengers often wait until conditions, including the partisan distributions resulting from the ways district lines are drawn following decennial redistricting, are more favorable to them (Jacobson and Carson 2015; Cox and Katz 2002; Jacobson and Kernell 1981). Although it generally (but not always) occurs only once per decade after the national census is conducted and seats in the U.S. House are reapportioned to states based on their relative populations, redistricting can exert enormous influence on elections, in part because district boundaries delineated by lawmakers or commissions are often gerrymandered to achieve partisan or racial compositions that advantage one party, group, or individual incumbent in ways that can create structural barriers to entry (Cox and Katz 2002). The rise of political consultants, however, appears to be changing the fortunes of individuals wishing to challenge incumbents. S. A. Cain (2011) finds that challengers, especially general election challengers, are able to increase the competiveness of a race if they are able to hire top consultants. He suggests that hiring these consultants serves as a signal to interest groups and party leaders that a challenger is serious about winning an election, from which endorsement and donations follow.

Of course, the ability to hire top consultants depends on the amount of money a challenger can bring to the table in the first place. In her successful campaign against the Democratic incumbent Ron Barber in the 2014 midterm elections, Arizona representative Martha McSally had to spend nearly $4.5 million, narrowly winning the race by only 167 votes after a recount (AZPM Staff 2014). Other challengers were not so lucky. In a high-profile Kentucky Senate race, the challenger, Alison Lundergan Grimes, spent more than $18.8 million, only to be defeated by the incumbent senator Mitch McConnell, who spent more than $21.1 million to retain his seat (Federal Election Commission Data 2014). Although the race was relatively close in comparison to the defeats often suffered by challengers to incumbents (Lundergan Grimes lost by about 7 percentage points), it is nonetheless an illustration of the exorbitant amounts of money challengers must raise and spend to even stand a chance against incumbents.

Presidential elections are where the wealth of resources and attention go during a presidential election cycle. The relationship between competition and campaign strategy has been well documented for these elections, especially because of the role that key battleground states play. Advertisements (Goldstein and Freedman 2002), spending (B. J. Doherty 2007; Shaw 2006), and mobilization efforts (Bergan et al. 2005; Cann and Cole 2011) are almost always more intense in battleground states. In many safe states, campaign activity is all but nonexistent (Panagopoulos 2009a).

Compared to federal campaigns and even campaigns for the U.S. House of Representatives, most state and local elections are fairly uncompetitive (Masket and Lewis 2007; Ballotpedia 2014). Incumbents often face no challengers, and districts are sometimes deliberately drawn so that one party is consistently favored. In addition, the national media typically pay little attention to these types of elections. Although statewide races, such as those for governor, may attract greater attention and be more competitive, this is not the case for state legislative and local races. As a result, spending levels are lower for state and local elections, and strategists rely far less on help from professional consultants and more on friends and family volunteering their time (Sides et al. 2014). Nonetheless, campaigns for state and local elections have become more professionalized and expensive in recent years. In many respects, local races are beginning to look more and more like expensive federal campaigns for U.S. House and Senate elections. The increase in the cost of running an election does not always coincide with the level of competiveness, however, especially in the context of lower-interest elections at the state and local level (Bonneau 2004).

IMPLICATIONS OF COMPETITIVE ELECTIONS ACROSS THE UNITED STATES FOR DEMOCRATIC NORMS

Electoral competiveness is one of the most widely cited motivators of campaign strategy. Thus, it has substantial implications for democratic norms, especially voter engagement and information. The closeness of an election is correlated with higher turnout across a wide array of electoral contests (Cox and Munger 1989; Lipsitz 2011, 2009). Aldrich (1993) further suggests that turnout in the context of an election hinges on the decisions made by strategic politicians to invest more of their resources, time, and energy in these elections. In the context of campaigns fighting vigorously to sway a close vote in their favor, citizens are likely to receive more information and have more incentive to volunteer, donate, and ultimately vote in that election.

At the level of presidential elections, the variation in competition between battleground and safe states has implications for campaign conduct and for democratic norms. Preferences for presidential candidates tend to be less stable in less competitive states (Panagopoulos 2009a). This means candidates must work harder to sway votes in the states that matter most to their election chances. Battleground states also tend to have higher turnout among lower-income citizens who are otherwise less likely to turn out in response to campaign activities in these states (Gimpel et al. 2007), an outcome that aligns well with the normative goals of an electorate that is representative of the general population (Dahl 1971).

The intensity of campaigning in terms of spending, advertising, and mobilizing efforts will almost always be greater in elections that are competitive across the spectrum of races in American politics. I will explore in more detail the role that advertising and spending play in advancing and hindering democratic norms in Chapters 4 and 6, but competitive elections, because they are likely to attract more media attention and campaign effort, can have profound effects on the amount of information received by citizens and their motivation to participate in politics.

Competitive elections also have consequences for representation and may do something to dampen the incumbency bias discussed previously in this chapter. Using a dataset of more than 40,000 closely contested races, Eggers et al. (2015) found that, in the context of very close elections, incumbents do not systematically win over their challengers. It seems that reforms enhancing competitive elections might alleviate some concerns about the implications of incumbency bias for representation in American politics.

Given what is known about the relationship among electoral competition, campaign strategy, and citizen representation, information, and engagement, it appears that there are starkly different implications for these norms across the different levels of elections in the United States. Because state and local elections stimulate less interest, are less competitive, and ultimately tend to attract lower turnout, other organized groups such as parties and interest groups stand a greater chance of influencing campaign behavior and election outcomes that do not necessarily coincide with the preferences of a district or state's constituency. As Sides et al. (2014) point out, "state and local races—the ones that most affect schools, homes, roads, and many other aspects of citizen's daily lives—are often the ones that live up to the ideals of political campaigns the least" (283).

CAMPAIGN FINANCE AND CONSEQUENCES

Although state and local elections used to be famous for being run on "shoestring budgets," this is no longer the case (Sides et al. 2014, 282; Girzynski and Breaux 1991). The amount of money spent on state and local races has steadily increased alongside spending in federal contests. In addition, outside interest groups, super PACs, and other wealthy donors appear to be increasing their focus on state and local elections. In 2014, for example, the Committee for Economic Growth and Social Justice sent mailers to voters in Elizabeth, New Jersey, pressing them to vote against several incumbent members of the school board. The group spent more than $150,000 and largely succeeded in its efforts (Schouten 2014). The increasing amount of money flowing to local campaigns means it is now more common to see professionals come in to run campaigns (Strachan 2003).

Consultants and outside groups alike are starting to weigh in more often on ballot initiatives and referenda that occur in state elections. Also known as "direct democracy," these initiatives allow citizens to have a direct say in the passage of laws in their states and municipalities (Matsusaka 2005, 2006). Initiatives and referenda theoretically give voters the opportunity to address mistakes made by their elected officials in their representation of constituency preferences (Besley and Coate 2008), although some evidence suggests that individual legislators may not be responsive to their constituents' efforts to change public policy in this way (Smith 2001). In contemporary elections, however, expensive campaigns are now being run in efforts to influence citizen choice on these initiatives. In 2005, a proposed amendment to the state constitution in Ohio was put on the ballot that would have changed how state and congressional districts were drawn, created a state board of elections, allowed for no-excuse absentee voting, and lowered campaign contribution limits. Two independent groups—Ohio Now and Ohio First—battled for and against the amendments, respectively (Niquette 2005). Even national figures, such as John Kerry, who narrowly lost the state of Ohio in the 2004 presidential election, came in to campaign in favor of the proposed constitutional amendment. In 1997, the billionaire Paul Allen used more than $3.2 million of his own money to fund television advertising in a campaign to try to convince voters in the state of Washington to approve a ballot initiative that would finance the construction of a new stadium for the Seattle Seahawks, ultimately succeeding in his efforts (Penhale 1997). The irony of these anecdotes is that the expansion of direct democracy through ballot initiatives and referenda was introduced by the populist and progressive movements of the early 20th century to make state legislatures more responsive to their constituents and to prevent them from being beholden to powerful special interests (Beard and Schultz 1912).

The U.S. Supreme Court has made several well-known decisions on campaign finance in recent years that have affected the conduct of campaigns at all levels. I will discuss these decisions in detail in Chapter 4. In *Citizens United v. Federal Election Commission*, the Court ruled that the First Amendment prohibits the government from restricting independent political spending by corporations, nonprofits, labor unions, and other organized entities, a move that many suggest has played a significant role in the explosive spending in recent American elections. However, in the context of elections held within specific states and localities, the extent to which money can (and does) matter depends on regulations in place within given states. As we have seen, the regulatory landscapes can vary significantly across jurisdictions and offices.

There are a few key differences in campaign finance laws across states. A state may impose limits on the amount of money individual citizens can donate directly to a candidate or party organization. This, of course, means that campaigns operating in these states must adjust their fundraising strategies accordingly. Currently, 12 states have no limits on individual contributions, whereas in states that impose caps on individual contributions, limits can range from a few hundred dollars to more than $10,000 in state legislative races and to more than $40,000 (in New York) for gubernatorial elections. Thirty-seven states limit political action committee contributions, and all but 4 states limit direct, corporate giving to campaigns. Twenty-two states outright prohibit direct, corporate contributions (see Medvic 2014 for details). This variation implies the campaign finance environments in which campaigns operate differ widely across states, and one can reasonably question whether candidates' degrees of reliance on individuals, corporations, or other entities shift focus toward (or away from) ordinary voters or constituents as the landscape changes. We will return to this debate in the discussion about campaign finance laws more generally.

Another difference across several states is the extent to which they require the *disclosure* of political contributions (Cruikshank 2015). In 2008, the states receiving the worst rating from the Campaign Disclosure Project on disclosure laws included New Mexico, Nebraska, Vermont, Mississippi, Nevada, Delaware, North Dakota, South Dakota, Alabama, and Wyoming (Grading State Disclosure Laws 2008). Disclosure allows citizens to observe, often in real time, the sources of campaigns' financial resources. Variation in campaign finance disclosure effectively means voters in some states and localities can operate (and vote) with greater detail and information about candidates financing than in other contexts. Although such information inequalities are often neglected in debates about the consequences of the institutional variation in campaign contexts, they raise important questions about the availability of accurate and accessible campaign information that can be used to evaluate candidacies and to reach informed voting decisions.

Half of the states (25) provide some form of public funding of state and local campaigns. Often called "clean elections," these programs can take many forms, with subsidies to eligible campaigns financed through voluntary check-offs on state tax returns or budget allocations. Some jurisdictions offer eligible candidates lump-sum payments, whereas others provide candidates who opt in to the system with matching funds (up to a certain limit) (see Panagopoulos 2011). In New York City, for example, where a public funding system for local elections has been in place since 1988, eligible candidates can receive as much as $6 for each dollar raised up to a maximum that depends on the office sought. Accepting public funds typically requires campaigns to agree to certain restrictions, such as spending caps or fundraising restrictions, which affect campaigns' strategic decisions, but the programs are designed to level the playing field between candidates and encourage candidates to spend more time and effort on interacting with voters rather than fundraising. Critics contend there are drawbacks, however. One main disadvantage is that candidates cannot be forced to opt in to the program, so publicly funded candidates often face spending restrictions, whereas their privately funded opponents do not. Some states relax spending restrictions in such circumstances, although the Supreme Court has struck down private spending thresholds that trigger infusions of additional public funding to participating candidates as unconstitutional on the basis that the thresholds curtail privately funded candidates' free speech. It is also unclear how public funding programs should respond to independent expenditures that support (or oppose) participating candidates. Public funding programs often fail to take independent spending into account, but these could alter the strategic environment considerably for candidates. Variation in programs can also affect the extent to which candidates rely on small versus larger campaign donors. Several states have adopted what is known as a multiple matching systems, where public money is used to match small contributions up to a certain amount. This approach has been designed to mitigate the influence of larger donors in these jurisdictions.

In states without public financing laws, campaigns are incentivized to seek out large amounts of money from a few wealthy donors, potentially alienating the rest of their constituents and opening the door to disproportionate influence from smaller, less representative groups of citizens and interest groups. For example, races featuring candidates who were publicly financed in Arizona and Maine were far more competitive than before the public financing option was adopted in these states (Mayer et al. 2006; Malhotra 2008). However, a much larger dataset using gubernatorial races between 1978 and 2004 suggests otherwise (Primo et al. 2006). A study of New York City elections found the introduction of the public financing program encouraged more candidates to run for city council positions, but that most of these candidacies were hopeless, concluding the program did not ultimately render city council contests more competitive (Kraus 2011). There is also debate about how effectively public finance programs promote citizen participation and engagement; although some studies find evidence of positive effects (Migally and Liss 2010), others find no such effects (Milyo et al. 2011). Public financing can provide candidates with more time to focus their efforts on discussing issues with their constituents, encourage quality candidates who would otherwise be unable to run for public office because of a lack of personal wealth or connections with wealthy donors, and improve the representation of minorities and women in public office (Center for Governmental Studies 2003). Levin (2006: 46, 47) notes that although minorities represent only 16% of all candidates in general elections, they account for 30% of publicly financed candidates. Women account for only 31% of all candidates, but 39% under public funded systems. In Arizona alone, the number of Native American and Latino candidates tripled in the two election cycles after public financing was put in place.

As the need for campaign resources and the sources of campaign messages have proliferated, and in the aftermath of rulings like *Citizens United*, disclosure has taken center stage. In many electoral contexts, detailed disclosure of donors or ad sponsors is required. Ad sponsors and the identities of individual donors who contribute more than $200 to candidates in federal races must be disclosed, for instance, but disclosure regimes vary greatly, or simply do not exist, across states and municipalities and even across the types of groups operating in federal elections. Inaccurate or incomplete disclosure, or poor enforcement, is commonplace, however, diminishing the credibility, efficacy and informative capacity of disclosure data and depriving citizens of useful informational cues (Heerwig and Shaw 2014). One goal of such transparency is to provide a safeguard against misleading (and anonymous) attack advertising. In October 2014, for example, campaign finance regulators in Texas decided to broaden transparency for spending in state elections. The Texas Ethics Committee unanimously adopted a new regulation that requires politically active nonprofits to disclose donors if they spend more than 25% of their annual budgets on "politicking." The change was designed to address "dark money" groups that are not required to disclose their donors under federal laws (Rauf 2014).

In the absence of disclosure laws, campaigns by independent groups have more leeway to advertise misleading or even patently false information about candidates and initiatives they oppose. This can pose challenges for the campaigns being attacked and have a negative impact on the quality of information citizens receive about candidates. Ads sponsored by unknown independent groups can be more effective at influencing citizens than those sponsored by candidates (Brooks and Muroy 2012). In the 2014 Kansas governor's race, outside groups spent millions in efforts to influence the election outcome in a flood of "mostly untraceable cash" (Helling 2014). In 2010, the Republican State Leadership Committee spent $30 million dollars to flip 22 state legislatures to the control of the Republican Party (Kardish 2014). Even judicial candidates are not immune to this trend. In 2013, Ed Sheehy, a candidate for the Montana supreme court, fell victim to a misleading set of advertisements accusing him of being soft on crime after he represented a man accused of murder in court (Beckel 2013).

THE NATIONALIZATION OF STATE
AND LOCAL CAMPAIGNS

The increasing prominence of professionalization and money in state and local campaigns is in line with another trend occurring in these contexts: nationalization. Studies reveal evidence that election outcomes at various levels of office are electorally interconnected or responsive to similar short and long-term, national factors, like presidential approval, whose effects can be detected in congressional but also in gubernatorial and state legislative elections (Simon, Ostrom, and Marra 1991), and that these nation forces have become increasingly potent in recent election cycles (Jacobson and Carson 2015). In other words, campaigns for mayor or state senator in Peoria, Illinois must be mindful of what happens in Washington or the national as a whole because election outcomes in Peoria will likely reflect the influence of national developments as well as local or district-specific forces like incumbency or potholes in the streets. Some studies find evidence of coattail effects, that is, candidates at the top of a party's ticket (like presidential candidates in presidential years or gubernatorial candidates in off-year or midterm cycles) can influence how voters vote in down-ballot races for lower-level offices (Broockman 2009; Campbell and Sumners 1990), for example, found that presidential coattails exerted a modest but statistically significant effect on voting in U.S. Senate races between 1972–1988. Mondak (1990) also found evidence of presidential coattail voting, but argued that the magnitude of the effect is affected by the strength of voters' evaluations of the presidential candidates, sensitivities to the local political scene, and the political climate in voters' local neighborhoods. More recently, Broockman (2009) has considered the possibility of reverse coattails, positing that views about lower-level (congressional) candidates may be able to influence voting in higher-level races (presidential), but finds little supporting evidence for such an effect. More and more then, state and local campaigns are becoming "echoes" of broader national partisan issues and debates (Jacobson 2009, 2012; Jacobson and Carson 2015; Aguiar-Conraria et al. 2013). Since Barack Obama was elected, opinions of him have had a more substantial effect on attitudes toward his party than has been the case with previous presidents (Jacobson 2012). Increasingly, voters appear to view candidates in elections based on partisan identification first and based on their performance as individual policy makers in their respective states and localities second. This can occur in the context of nonpresidential elections as well, as in the 2010 midterm elections in which Republican congressional candidates benefitted from voters' dissatisfaction with President Obama and the Democratic Party. Other voters held both Republicans and Democrats responsible for national problems, but ultimately chose to push Democrats out of office (Aldrich et al. 2014). According to the American National Election Study, the 2012 election had the highest levels of party-line voting of any survey in the studies' history. Figure 2.2 illustrates this trend and shows that 90% of partisans reported voting for their party's candidate for president. Further, 90% of partisans

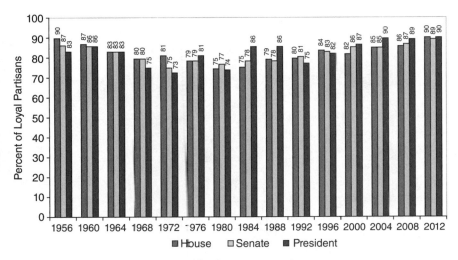

Figure 2.2 Party-Line Voting in U.S. Elections, 1956–2012

reported voting for their party's candidate for the U.S. House of Representatives and 89% for its Senate candidate

Nationalization is clearly evident in congressional elections (see Jacobson 2014; Jacobson and Carson 2015). Incumbents seeking reelection are keenly aware of this trend, especially in midterm elections in which it is common for members of the incumbent president's party to lose seats both in Congress and in state legislative chambers across the nation (Campbell 1986). Before the 2014 midterm elections, for example, Democrats controlled 41 state legislative chambers and Republicans controlled 57; after the election, Democrats controlled 30 and Republicans 68 (Storey 2014). Between 1946–2010, the president's party has lost on average 27 seats in the U.S. House, and 7 seats in the U.S. Senate, in "midterm slumps," a phenomenon apparently driven by voters' quest for ideological balancing rather than a negative referendum on presidential performance (Bafumi, Erikson and Wlezien 2010). In the 2006 midterm elections, Republicans up for reelection were all but running from George W. Bush, fearing that any connection with his unpopular policies—the Iraq war in particular—would tarnish their election chances. Representative Mark Kennedy of Minnesota and Senator James M. Talent of Missouri, both "loyal Republican soldiers," made no mention of Bush in their advertisements and distanced themselves from their party affiliation, saying things such as, "Most people don't care if you're red or blue, Republican or Democrat" (Abramowitz 2006).

As I argue above, the influence of national forces on state and even local election appears to be on the rise. Empirical evidence links gubernatorial election outcomes, for example, to perceptions about the performance of the president's party (Simon 1989; Carsey and Wright 1998). In fact, presidential vote choice has become, over the past few decades, an increasingly strong predictor of who will ultimately prevail in gubernatorial races. Figure 2.3 displays conditional correlations between county-level votes for president and governor in presidential

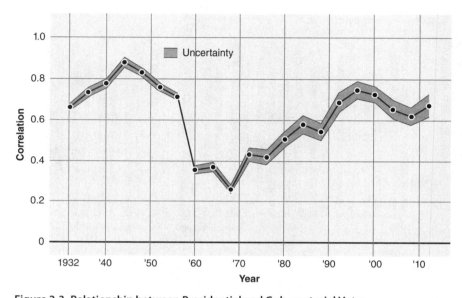

Figure 2.3 Relationship between Presidential and Gubernatorial Votes
NOTE: Conditional correlation between party votes in presidential election years in 29 states outside the South
SOURCE: Hopkins 2014.

election years to demonstrate this trend (Hopkins 2014). A similar pattern emerges when midterm elections are considered, implying nationalization in gubernatorial elections has been rising steadily since the 1970s (Hopkins 2014).

CONCLUSION

Because of the federalist nature of American governance, the electoral realities of local, state, and federal campaigns can seem like different worlds. Although federal elections still receive the majority of attention from major media outlets, interest groups, and citizens, state and local elections have begun to resemble these elections. In many ways the contextual changes occurring at the national level of politics have also occurred at nonfederal levels of governance and elections. State and local elections have become increasingly expensive and professionalized and outside groups are starting to expend more efforts to influence their outcomes. Furthermore, state and local elections are more often being judged on the context of national politics; the president's popularity is often a strong predictor of the support lower-level elected officials will receive depending on which party they represent.

Campaign strategy and implementation will vary markedly depending on the features of the states or localities in which they unfold. Some of these features, like the structural, institutional, or legal constraints (nonpartisan ballots, term limits, legislative professionalization, or registration, voting or ballot access requirements) will be unique to the specific jurisdiction, but other trends are more pervasive. If recent patterns persist, state and local elections will continue to become increasingly expensive, professionalized and nationalized, challenging campaigns to navigate the intersections between local constraints and broader forces to devise effective strategies.

There are a number of implications of these trends for how well campaigns at all levels of American elections represent, inform, and engage citizens. More expensive state and local campaigns may not be indicative of increasing participation and donations from broad swaths of constituents. More professionalized campaigns at state and local levels might provide incumbent candidates with the resources to more effectively inform and engage voters, but low turnout will likely continue to be an issue for off-year elections that do not feature a presidential contest, in particular for local elections that are held apart from the two-year midterm and presidential cycle. Because state and local elections often attract less interest and turnout, elected officials are often less accountable for representing the preferences of their constituents. Challengers to incumbents face steep challenges, although I touched on some reforms and trends that may improve their prospects. Overall, the thousands of elections that occur across the United States during every election cycle present a distinct challenge for campaigns and for clearly determining the extent to which campaign conduct helps or hinders the advancement of democratic norms.

KEY TERMS

Ballot initiative
Ballot referendum
Battleground states
Citizens United v.
    Federal Election
    Commission
Dark money
Direct democracy

Disclosure
Electoral College
Gerrymander
Ideological balancing
Incumbency advantage
Interest groups
Matching funds
"Midterm slump"

Nationalization
Off-year elections
Party-line voting
Public financing
Redistricting
Super PAC
Term limits
Winner-take-all

SUGGESTED READINGS

Gelman, A., and G. King, 1990. "Estimating Incumbency Advantage without Bias." *American Journal of Political Science* 34, no. 4: 1143–1164.

Jacobson, G. and J. Carson. 2015. *The Politics of Congressional Elections*, 9th ed. Lanham, MD: Rowman & Littlefield.

Mayhew, D. R. 1974. *Congress: The Electoral Connection*. New Haven, CT: Yale University Press.

CHAPTER 3

External Actors: Parties, Interest Groups, and the Media

In early 2015, news media organizations, political parties, and interest groups were looking forward to the 2016 presidential campaign. Although few candidacies had been formally announced, parties and interest groups were already beginning to consider which candidates they would ultimately support and endorse. Recognizing that it is never too early to start laying the groundwork for a campaign, potential candidates were hard at work crafting their messages for potential supporters. Although the 2014 midterm elections had just ended, the early months of 2015 saw a flurry of 2016 presidential campaign activity.

In early speeches, potential Republican candidates made a point of emphasizing their humble upbringings as a means of connecting with voters, suggesting an early theme in the GOP discourse for 2016 (Rappeport 2015). Jeb Bush, the first Republican to form an exploratory committee to run for president, launched two new political action committees to get a head start on fundraising and organizing (Costa 2015). In late 2014, the all-but-certain Democratic nominee Hillary Clinton increased her efforts to forge ties with Democratic interest groups that would be integral to fundraising success (Gearan and Gold 2014). In early March 2015, potential 2016 GOP presidential contenders attended an agriculture summit in Iowa to vie for the favor of agriculture-based interest groups (Reinhard 2015).

The news media, for its part, was already beefing up its own staff in preparation for the elections, bringing on more political journalists even as they were cutting back on staff in other areas. In the first few months of 2015, Bloomberg Media brought on an additional two dozen people to a new unit on national politics. CNN made 20 new hires, with plans to add an additional 20. As Sam Feist, CNN Washington's bureau chief noted, "This is the biggest story I know of that we'll be covering in the next two years. . . . We'll spend more money on the 2016 campaign than on any campaign in history" (Fahri 2015).

As these examples demonstrate, contemporary campaigns do not operate in a vacuum. They make decisions and act within the context of a complex relationship between parties and interest groups, whose endorsements and support

are integral for electoral success. The news media ultimately shapes much of the public perception surrounding candidates and their campaigns and has grown increasingly complex and instantaneous in its coverage in recent years with the advent of the 24-hour news cycle. Together, these key actors exert considerable influence on the conduct of campaigns during an election season. This chapter discusses the role of parties, interest groups, and the media in contemporary campaigns, how their roles in American elections have changed over time to shape the context in which campaigns operate, and how they interact with internal campaign organizations to create both challenges and opportunities. For each class of actors, I will consider how these developments can affect campaign decisions before turning to the consequences of these interactions for representation, information, and engagement.

Parties and interest groups have the most direct interaction with one another *and* with campaigns. In fact, some argue that "parties in the United States are best understood as coalitions of interest groups and activists seeking to capture and use government" (Bawn et al. 2012: 571). Given this, there is some degree of overlap in the relationship between these actors and campaigns, and I will consider their relationships with campaigns before turning my attention to the news media. On the one hand, parties and interest groups can support candidates by running advertisements, mobilizing voters and volunteers, and playing a part in recruiting viable candidates. On the other hand, they can and often do run campaigns *separate* from candidates in their own attempts to influence the way citizens vote and bring awareness to issues that are of importance to them (Sides et al. 2014). As we will see, the goals and interests of these actors may not always coincide with those of a candidate running for office, posing potential challenges to campaigns.

POLITICAL PARTIES: CHANGING CONTEXTS

As I discussed in Chapter 1, what constitutes a "party" is not always clear. In my view, parties are not necessarily in decline relative to campaigns, but I acknowledge their role has shifted within the context of U.S. electoral politics (Aldrich 2011). Parties may no longer run the show in American elections and be the centralized, powerful machines they once were, but it would be imprudent to discount their relevance or to render them to obscurity.

Political scientists typically identify three different aspects of parties in American politics (Key 1942). Parties-in-the-electorate refers to citizen identification with political parties. In the United States, this usually means citizens identifying with one of the two major parties (Democratic or Republican), although some citizens identify as "independents" or with less prominent, minor parties. Parties-in-government refers to the influence of parties in actual governance, that is, when they are proposing, debating, and passing legislation. Although U.S. legislators are elected to represent the interests of their districts or their states, they can also be held accountable to their parties. For example, they may be asked to toe the party line on certain policy issues or face repercussions. Finally, parties-as-organizations refers to local, state, and national party organizations dedicated to promoting their agenda by nominating and helping to elect candidates aligned with their goals.

Parties-in-the-electorate certainly play a role in the conduct of campaigns because the partisan makeup of a candidate's constituency will inevitably influence who runs for office, the issues they choose to emphasize, and their positions on those issues. Candidates cannot ignore the partisan makeup of their constituencies in terms of both garnering support at the polls and maintaining a base of supporters, donors, and volunteers to help run their campaigns. Parties-in-government, too, influence campaign conduct because certain legislative stances, co-sponsorships, or accomplishments, such as bills that are proposed or passed that advance a party agenda, can become records on which incumbent candidates can run (Harbridge 2015; Mayhew 1974). Even if a candidate did not have a direct hand in writing and cosponsoring a bill, his or her yay or nay vote can be an important signal to partisan constituents and their supporters within party organizations, as well as something he or she can boast of on the campaign trail (Harbridge 2015). Instances when an incumbent representative does not vote with the party line on certain issues may be held against them—by party organizations and supporters—when they run for reelection.

After the passage of the Affordable Care Act (ACA), for instance, which the GOP unanimously opposed in both chambers of Congress, many Republicans used their nay votes as a signal to their bases and as a rallying point for voters with misgivings about the new law. Indeed, in the years after its passage, U.S. House Republicans have voted to repeal the ACA (or Obamacare) in every session of Congress since the law passed. These votes have been largely symbolic as the 60 votes necessary to invoke cloture and overcome filibusters by opponents in the U.S. Senate were never really available (Moe 2015). Such symbolic votes have become a key element of what has been termed the "permanent campaign," the notion that the line between governance and campaigning has become blurrier over time as politicians' actions are increasingly publicized and analyzed by a variety of different outlets for electoral purposes (S. Blumenthal 1980). Policy positions, issue framing, and even votes become a part of a politician's "campaign," which can help or hurt them depending on how they are covered and whether the politician is able to use them to his or her advantage.

When House Republicans voted to repeal the ACA for the 56th time in early February 2015, the Republican House speaker John Boehner openly acknowledged that the vote was, practically speaking, futile. Instead, he said the vote was for the sake of the 47 House Republicans who had taken office after the 2014 midterm elections and had thus never had the "privilege" of voting to repeal Obamacare. With the vote under their belts, these freshmen lawmakers could go back to their constituents and say they had done everything within their power to repeal the law (Berman 2015).

Although actions by parties-in-government are important signaling points for incumbents to bring back to their constituencies during a campaign, it is the parties-as-organizations that play the most direct role in contemporary campaigns. Although certainly not as influential as they were in previous eras, when candidates more or less "stood" for election, parties can still influence candidate issue positions and the types of campaigns they run because support from and endorsement by one's party are all but essential for electoral success.

For better or worse, parties-as-organizations provide money, endorsements, and publicity to contemporary campaigns. Federal law permits party organizations to raise and spend money on behalf of their candidates. Some of this support can be contributed directly to candidate committees or coordinated with their campaigns, but parties can also engage in unlimited independent spending (see Chapter 4). Table 3.1 shows that national party committees actively raise millions of dollars to support presidential and congressional campaigns. The figures distinguish between hard and soft money. Hard money represents regulated funds raised by parties—in other words, sums that were raised subject to federal contribution limits. Soft money refers to unlimited, unregulated funds the parties were allowed to raise and spend on "party-building" activities in the past. Party building was never clearly defined, but was generally interpreted as anything short of directly advocating for or against a particular candidate. The Bipartisan Campaign Reform Act of 2002 eliminated soft money.

In 2014, the Democratic and Republican party committees raised more than $1 billion. Table 3.2 displays expenditures in congressional elections between 2000 and 2014 broken down by chamber and party as well as by whether the spending was coordinated with campaigns or independent. Although Republicans held an advantage in overall spending levels early in this period, Democrats have managed to turn the tables in recent cycles, especially in U.S. House elections. Parties provide important labels to which candidates can attach themselves, providing voters with cues about their policy positions or ideology, a role I will discuss in Chapter 8. Parties also help with the actual running of campaigns by providing expertise, helping to mobilize voters, and running advertisements on behalf of candidates. Parties can also engage in coordinated expenditures with campaigns, working with them to help develop clear messages for voters and providing them with extra financial resources. But limited party resources often lead to a sort of zero-sum game in which candidates who are more electable or engaged in particularly competitive races are given preferential treatment. Parties also make independent expenditures that are not coordinated with campaigns and put forth advertisements that may or may not align with a candidate's vision for his or her campaign.

As I note above, the role of parties in campaigns has changed dramatically since the 1960s in response to the changing sociopolitics and technology of the times but also because of reforms undertaken by the party organizations themselves. One class of reforms, designed to give the parties' rank-and-file voters greater control over candidate selection, involved the increased use of direct, primary elections to choose nominees. Previously, this was generally done by

Table 3.1 Hard and Soft Money Raised by National Party Committees, 1996–2014 (in millions of nominal dollars)

	1996			1998			2000			2002			2004	2006	2008	2010	2012	2014
	HARD	SOFT	TOTAL	HARD	SOFT	TOTAL	HARD	SOFT	TOTAL	HARD	SOFT	TOTAL	HARD	HARD	HARD	HARD	HARD	HARD
Democratic																		
National Committee	108.4	101.9	210.3	64.8	57.0	121.7	124.0	136.6	260.6	67.5	94.6	162.1	394.4	130.8	260.1	224.8	301.4	163.3
Senatorial	30.8	14.2	45.0	35.7	25.9	61.5	40.5	63.7	104.2	48.4	95.0	143.4	88.7	121.4	162.8	129.5	145.9	167.6
Congressional	26.6	12.3	39.0	25.2	16.9	42.0	48.4	56.7	105.1	46.4	56.4	102.9	93.2	139.9	176.2	163.9	183.8	206.8
Total	165.8	128.4	294.2	125.6	99.7	225.3	212.9	257.0	469.9	162.3	246.1	408.4	576.2	392.1	599.1	518.3	631.1	537.7
Republican																		
National Committee	193.0	113.1	306.2	104.1	74.8	178.9	212.8	166.2	379.0	170.1	113.9	284.0	392.4	243.0	427.6	196.4	425.0	194.9
Senatorial	64.5	29.4	93.9	53.4	37.9	91.3	51.5	44.7	96.1	59.2	66.4	125.6	79.0	88.8	94.4	114.6	117.0	129.9
Congressional	74.2	18.5	92.8	72.7	26.9	99.6	97.3	47.3	144.6	141.0	69.7	210.7	185.7	179.5	118.3	133.8	155.7	153.5
Total	331.8	138.2	470.0	230.2	131.6	361.8	361.6	249.9	611.5	370.3	250.0	620.3	657.1	511.3	640.3	444.7	697.7	478.3

NOTES: 2012 RNC and DNC receipts reflect contributions from presidential joint fundraising committees that are attributed to the RNC and DNC, but not included in reported total receipts. The national party committees were prohibited from raising soft money by the Bipartisan Campaign Reform Act of 2002. Soft money referred to unlimited amounts of money the parties could raise for "party-building" activities. What constitutes party building was never clearly defined, but was generally interpreted as anything short of directly advocating for/against the election of a particular candidate.

SOURCE: Campaign Finance Institute Analysis of Federal Election Commission data.

Table 3.2 Political Party Contributions, Coordinated and Independent Expenditures for Congressional Candidates, 2000–2014 (nominal dollars)

	SENATE			HOUSE			TOTAL
	CONTRIBUTIONS	EXPENDITURES		CONTRIBUTIONS	EXPENDITURES		
		COORDINATED	INDEPENDENT		COORDINATED	INDEPENDENT	
2014							
Democrats	270,188	7,584,598	59,853,924	651,159	4,204,232	68,985,088	141,549,189
Republicans	587,772	7,390,184	34,286,962	368,576	4,297,692	65,537,939	112,469,125
2012							
Democrats	646,500	5,318,835	52,034,293	585,363	5,348,835	62,685,918	127,449,744
Republicans	790,800	7,600,476	32,114,674	749,025	4,718,800	61,881,122	107,854,897
2010							
Democrats	782,710	17,509,201	41,496,478	293,045	6,746,051	65,745,376	132,572,861
Republicans	1,597,170	18,196,872	34,351,039	1,022,314	8,295,592	48,785,092	112,248,079
2008							
Democrats	558,600	3,822,922	73,028,432	1,027,132	1,654,208	81,641,424	161,732,718
Republicans	135,000	1,530,624	40,650,902	3,109,174	3,420,315	30,971,545	79,817,560
2006							
Democrats	596,800	5,796,005	42,627,472	2,429,919	2,409,914	64,141,253	118,001,363
Republicans	386,782	8,784,685	32,156,053	785,435	4,519,856	83,085,694	129,718,505
2004							
Democrats	1,082,388	10,154,423	21,710,954	806,115	2,880,867	32,036,890	68,671,637
Republicans	1,875,740	9,277,459	11,500,079	1,156,771	3,220,419	43,440,699	70,471,167
2002							
Democrats	493,852	2,085,319	413	891,626	2,730,563	250,262	6,452,035
Republicans	2,027,001	10,378,872	501,208	2,131,531	5,388,717	1,362,431	21,789,760

(Continued)

Table 3.2 (Continued)

| | SENATE | | | HOUSE | | | |
| | EXPENDITURES | | | EXPENDITURES | | | |
	CONTRIBUTIONS	COORDINATED	INDEPENDENT	CONTRIBUTIONS	COORDINATED	INDEPENDENT	TOTAL
2000							
Democrats	356,618	5,149,704	257,920	977,690	3,325,207	2,031,421	12,098,560
Republicans	519,110	10,823,862	395,190	1,747,012	4,394,759	1,161,612	19,041,545

NOTES: The table includes three different kinds of party support for candidates: direct contributions, coordinated expenditures, and independent spending. Direct contributions: House candidates may receive a maximum of $20,000 in primary and general election combined from national and state party committees. In 2012, Senate candidates could receive $43,100 from national party committees and another $10,000 from state parties. The National Party to Senate candidate amount is indexed for inflation.

Coordinated expenditures: For most House candidates, party committees may spend an inflation-adjusted amount that in 2012 came to $45,600. The limit is doubled (to $91,200 in 2012) for states with only one congressional district. For Senate candidates, the limit goes up with a state's population as well as inflation. In the smallest states, this was $91,200 in 2012. In the largest states (California) it was $2.6 million. The median states (Kentucky and Louisiana) had party-coordinated spending limits of $305,000 and $315,400, respectively.

Independent spending by the parties cannot be limited since the Supreme Court's decision in *Colorado Republican Federal Campaign Committee v. Federal Election Commission* 518 U.S. 604 (1996). Despite this ruling, the parties did not do a great deal of independent spending between 1996 and 2002 because such spending must be funded entirely with money raised under federal contribution limits.

The parties preferred to use "soft" money (no contribution limits) to help pay for communications that were designed to get around these restraints. After the Bipartisan Campaign Reform Act of 2002 prohibited national party soft money, the parties shifted more money into independent expenditures. Unfortunately, it is not possible to know how much soft money was spent to help congressional candidates in the elections through 2002. In 2012, party-independent spending in House contests spread out to more than 74 districts, with a maximum of $5.0 million spent in one district. Senate independent spending focused on 17 races, with $14.4 million spent in Virginia.

SOURCE: Campaign Finance Institute analysis of Federal Election Commission data.

nominating conventions or caucuses, which included mainly party insiders. The importance of control over nominations is summarized best perhaps by the corrupt and notorious leader of New York's Tammany Hall political machine in the 1860s and 1870s, Boss Tweed, who famously said, "I don't care who does the electing, so long as I get to do the nominating." The reforms had important consequences for the parties. As Jacobson (2004: 15–16) puts it, "primary elections have largely deprived parties of their most important source of influence over elected officials. Parties no longer control access to the ballot and, therefore, to political office. They cannot determine who runs under their label and so cannot control what the label represents . . . parties typically have few sanctions and little influence [over nominations]." Some scholars, however, argue that an "invisible primary" exists in which party leaders narrow the field of candidates and ultimately build support for a single candidate (Cohen et al. 2008). Nevertheless, parties did retain some control in determining key aspects of candidate selection, such as the format of nominating procedures and who is allowed to vote. These decisions vary from state to state and help determine the types of candidates who are selected to run on a party's ticket in the general election (Gerber and Morton 1998).

Primary elections are a sort of partisan litmus test. Primary candidates must often demonstrate a commitment to their party's base, which has implications for the policy positions they adopt and how they communicate these to the electorate. Primaries tend to attract fewer voters than general elections, and those voters who do turn out generally favor more ideologically extreme policy positions, compared to general election voters (Panagopoulos 2010b). Accordingly, the type of primary held in a particular state affects the composition of the electorate, and candidates must take the form of the primary system into account when making strategic decisions. There are three main types of primaries: open primaries, closed primaries, and semiclosed primaries. Figure 3.1 depicts the primary type currently used in each state. The states and parties determine the rules for their primaries. In some states, the Republican and Democratic parties may adopt different rules. Open primaries allow voters to participate in the party primary of their choosing regardless of their party affiliation, although they may only vote in one party's primary in each election cycle. In closed primaries, only those officially registered with the party may participate in its primary. In a semiclosed primary, those registered with a party can only vote in the primary of the party with which they are registered, whereas those who are unaffiliated with a party may participate in the primary of their choosing. Since its voters are most tightly restricted to the party faithful, closed primaries may influence a candidate to adopt more ideologically extreme positions than open or semiclosed primaries.

Some states use a more tailored process to nominate candidates for the general election. California, Nebraska, and Washington use a process commonly referred to as "top two" for the nomination of all candidates except those for president. Under the top-two system, all candidates are listed on the same

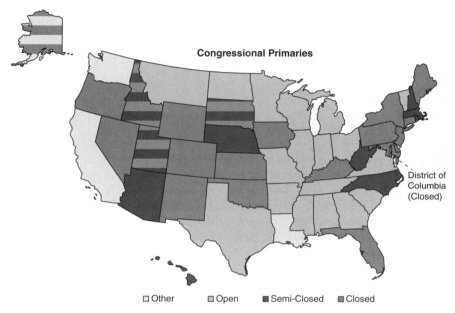

Figure 3.1 Primary Election Type by State

primary ballot, and the two candidates who receive the most votes in the primary appear on the general election ballot. This means that two candidates from the same party may face off in the general election. In Louisiana, instead of a primary, all candidates appear on the general election ballot and a runoff is held between the top two candidates if no one wins a majority.

The type of primary directly affects the composition of primary electorates, which in turn affects candidates' strategic decisions. For example, candidates must adjust their strategy in open-primary states to account for an electorate that includes independents and members of other parties. In the 2012 presidential primary in Michigan, an open-primary state, the Michigan Democratic Party sent e-mails encouraging its supporters to vote against Romney in the state's Republican presidential primary in an attempt to draw out the Republican nominating contest (Blake 2012). This is an example of what political scientists have termed strategic voting, or voting for a candidate who does not reflect one's true preference for strategic reasons. (The alternative is called sincere voting.) In sum, depending on where they are located, candidates may face primary electorates that range from strongly partisan to diluted with independents or even members of the opposing party. These contextual variations are especially difficult for presidential candidates to navigate because they must compete in a number of different primary contexts.

In presidential campaigns, candidates also must deal with states that hold caucuses instead of primaries. A caucus is an organization of local gatherings where voters decide which candidate to support and then select delegates to their party's nominating conventions. Attendees at each caucus elect a county delegate, who then casts a vote for another delegate at a higher level, and so on until the delegates to the national convention are determined. Caucuses are unusual because they allow participants to openly express support for a candidate, which is prohibited in primaries that take place in traditional polling places.

Presidential candidates often allocate more money to primaries than to caucuses because there are more delegates available in primaries and media coverage is usually greater in these races (Gurian 1993). One major exception to this rule is the Iowa caucuses, which constitute the first contest in the presidential primary season and are subject to intense media attention. Therefore, candidates typically make great efforts to win in Iowa to demonstrate their viability to supporters, donors, and interest groups. Victories in early presidential nominating contests such as the Iowa caucuses or the first-in-the-nation New Hampshire primary can be especially consequential because they create momentum and accrue advantages for candidates as they head into subsequent nominating contests (Bartels 1988). The news media brings attention to the Iowa caucuses well before they take place. Nearly two and a half years before the 2016 presidential nomination season, Public Policy Polling was already releasing polls predicting who would win the Iowa caucuses, and media outlets were already speculating over the meaning of these polls and the likelihood of candidate success. All of this was occurring before any of the "candidates" included in the polls had formally announced a run for president (Weigel 2013).

There are other exceptions to the rule that presidential campaigns generally devote greater attention to states that hold primaries, especially when locked in a contentious primary battle. In 2008, Barack Obama's campaign focused on caucus states whereas other candidates, notably Hillary Clinton, neglected them. In response to speculation that Obama's caucus strategy might not be effective, one of his press team members said, "it may not be California, but smaller states like Idaho and Delaware add up" (Sizemore 2008). And indeed, they did. In the Democratic Party's system of delegate allocation in 2008, delegates were awarded based on the portion of the vote received by each candidate, provided they met the minimum viability threshold of 15 percent of the vote in the state contest. In a closely contested race, such as the 2008 Democratic nomination race, it is difficult for any candidate to establish a commanding lead in the delegates. One way to build up a lead, however, is to rack up lopsided victories in states where one's opponent fails to compete aggressively. By the end of the long-contested 2008 Democratic primary campaign, Obama led Clinton by 117 pledged delegates; without Obama's landslide victories in caucus states, Hillary Clinton may well have won the nomination. In a winner-take-all system, Clinton would have gotten 700 delegates from the states where she claimed victory. But, as illustrated in Figure 3.2, because of the proportional allocation of votes, Obama came out only slightly behind in delegates awarded in primaries because his wins were more lopsided than Clinton's. Obama ultimately won the nomination in part because of the attention his campaign paid to caucuses (Sizemore 2008).

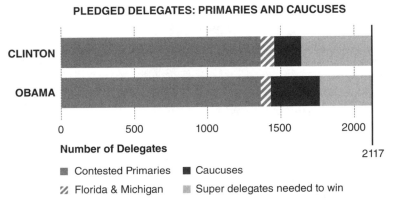

PLEDGED DELEGATES: PRIMARIES AND CAUCUSES

Figure 3.2 The Race for Delegates (2008 Democratic Presidential Nominating Convention)
SOURCE: Sizemore (2C08)

In the 2016 presidential election cycle, a similar pattern emerged on the Democratic side, with Bernie Sanders besting Clinton in several caucus states (as well as in some primary states). Caucuses tend to be time-intensive (deliberations can last for hours) and to attract fewer voters; it is not uncommon for turnout in caucuses to be in the single digits. In 2008, participation rates in states with caucuses lagged behind states that held primaries by more than 20 percentage points on average (Panagopoulos 2010b). Lower turnout has implications for campaigns, as such contests will attract voters who are more enthusiastic and ideologically extreme in their political views (Panagopoulos 2010b). In 2008 and 2016, these voters, including younger Democrats, disproportionately favored Obama and Sanders respectively. In an odd twist, Texas adopted a unique, hybrid procedure in 2008 that allowed Democrats to vote *both* in caucuses as well as in a primary on March 4. Clinton won the primary, but Obama won the caucuses—in the same state, on the same day! (The "Texas Two-Step," as it was dubbed, was abandoned in 2016.) National and state party leaders are instrumental in devising the rules that govern key aspects of presidential contests, including contest type, voting eligibility and delegate allocation, and these can vary considerably across the states. The implications for persuasion and mobilization strategies can be consequential, challenging campaigns to take such variation in electoral features and structures into account to be successful.

Whether through a caucus or primary election, it is imperative for candidates to demonstrate their alignment with their party during the primary season to consolidate the support of the party base and encourage the broader party organization to support their efforts. If state and national party committees think a candidate will do more harm than good for a party's interests, they may be less inclined to support the candidate's efforts. In addition, the positions adopted by candidates early on can influence the support and endorsements their campaigns receive from these groups because many are informally aligned with different parties (Steger 2000). In some cases, it can be difficult to disentangle the influence of parties and interest groups because both can have an effect on the positions candidates take during campaigns. The National Rifle Association, for example, is notably aligned with the Republican Party and may serve as a king-maker when two Republicans face off. In March 2014, for example, the association endorsed U.S. Representative Mike Simpson (R-Idaho) in a highly competitive primary against Tea Party challenger Bryan Smith (Lachman 2014). Simpson went on to defeat Smith in their primary election race.

Often the race for party endorsements begins well before citizens take to the voting booth in what has become known as the "invisible primary," the period of time between when a candidate expresses an interest in running and when the actual caucus or primary contests formally begin. Although elected officials and other party notables may not officially endorse before or during the primary phase, behind-the-scenes potential candidates are hustling to raise money and support to attest to their viability In presidential nominations, in particular, can-didates typically conduct these preprimary "campaigns" to win the support of their party and relevant interest groups since a candidate's level of funding and national political support at the beginning of a primary season has a strong rela-tionship with his or her chances of winning the nomination, presumably because it sends clear viability signals to the electorates that vote subsequently in prima-ries and caucuses (Steger 2000, 2007; Cohen et al. 2008). Thus, although party organizations may have less influence in the nominating process than in decades past, they can still influence primary outcomes with financial support and endorsements. Voters generally capitulate, ratifying choices when party activists and leaders are in lockstep behind one of the candidates, but not always; for ex-ample, Democrats in 2008, and Republicans in 2016, failed to nominate Hillary Clinton or Jeb Bush, respectively, despite their early support within the party es-tablishments. Furthermore, depending on the party, there may be more or less variation in the selection of delegates by state parties for presidential nominating conventions. For Republicans, the national party lays out general guidelines for the nominating process but leaves many details up to state parties. Delegates to the GOP convention were allocated by a winner-take-all method in most states, for example, but many switched to proportional allocation after 2008, in part be-cause some party operatives considered the extended Democratic nomination battle to have helped Obama in 2008. Both the 2012 and 2016 Republican nomina-tion races were likely protracted as a result of these changes. Democrats, in con-trast, rely on a national set of election rules. State Democratic parties must submit their delegate selection plans to the Democratic National Committee Rules and Bylaws Committee to ensure compliance with the party's national rules (Coleman 2012). In short, this discussion makes clear that the rules matter, and it is often the parties that create and revise the rules, altering the terrains in which presidential, but also potentially other, campaigns must unfold.

After winning their party's primary, candidates must pivot to compete in general election in which they must typically appeal to much broader and more diverse constituencies. Parties care not only about a candidate's position on the issues, but also about their electability. Thus, candidates must pull off a fairly tight balancing act in maintaining the support of their party as well as the broader electorate through the primary and general elections.

This balancing act has come into focus in contemporary campaigns in recent years with the growth of the Tea Party. Although it is not an official party organization in the United States, the Tea Party is a potent movement within the broader Republican Party known for taking more conservative and antiestablishment positions. This wing of the Republican Party has become a major force in recent primary elections, making active efforts to target and unseat more moderate Republican candidates. One example, with an unusual twist, was the defeat of Senator Lisa Murkowski by Joe Miller in the 2010 U.S. Senate primary in Alaska, although Murkowski ultimately won the general election because of a successful write-in campaign (Yardley 2010). Murkowski was somewhat moderate as Republicans go, but even staunch conservatives are not immune. In 2014, the U.S. House majority leader Eric Cantor lost his primary bid to the little-known college professor David Brat, who was backed by the Tea Party. Although Cantor spent millions of dollars more than Brat and was one of the more conservative members of the party, his position as a Washington establishment insider made him vulnerable enough to lose his primary election (Enten 2014).

Party organizations generally pour their resources into races that are closely contested and more likely to help win or maintain control of the state or federal legislature for their party. This type of resource allocation by parties can affect a potential candidate's decision to run for office in the first place, presenting a sort of catch-22 to those interested in running. To be taken seriously by parties and their affiliates, a candidate must have resources and name recognition and must be electable. However, as I highlighted in Chapter 2, political newcomers typically need party support in the first place to be considered serious contenders. Candidates who make it through the primary process and emerge as their parties' nominees but are nonetheless considered to be futile by the party organizations, face an uphill battle to secure campaign resources or endorsements.

Party organizations retain central roles in candidate emergence, campaign staffing, and volunteer recruitment. Despite the fact that prospective candidates can increasingly toss their proverbial hats into the ring directly, organizing and financing their campaigns independently, party leaders at all levels continue to engage actively in identifying promising candidates. Candidate recruitment by party leaders and political elites remains extensive (Fowler 1993; Kazee and Thornberry 1990). Given candidate quality exerts considerable influence on election outcomes (Jacobson and Carson 2015), recruitment is critical. Candidates with prior elective experience tend to fare significantly better in elections, for example (Jacobson and Carson 2015). Furthermore, campaigns rely routinely on party loyalists and the local party infrastructures for volunteer recruitment (McKenna and Han 2014). Volunteer-led grassroots voter contact activities, including canvassing and phone-bank outreach, were central to Obama's presidential victories; the Obama campaign empowered over 2 million volunteers in 2012 to conduct extensive mobilization efforts, using technology and data analytics to monitor and refine these activities on an ongoing and dynamic basis (McKenna and Han 2014). Extended party networks also include operatives, consultants and professionals on whom candidates rely for expertise (Herrnson 2000).

Consequences for Democracy

Scholarly debates about whether parties help or hinder the realization of democratic ideals are not settled within political science. Schattschneider (1960) contends that a competitive party system gives the American public the greatest opportunity to have a clear voice in the decision-making process. He suggests that citizens will only vote if they can discern clear differences between parties. In other words, citizens are more motivated to engage in politics if they perceive they have distinct choices. In fact, he asserts "people are powerless if the political enterprise is not competitive" (Schattschneider 1960: 137).

The arguments against political parties as arbiters and upholders of democratic norms in the context of political campaigns are not advanced over whether political parties should exist in the context of American elections, but over whether incentives to engage in partisan battles designed to elect their favored candidates can be reconciled with more general democratic ideals. In contemporary campaigns, parties provide candidates with vital resources, but also exert pressure on the decisions they make in ways that affect how their campaigns are conducted. In this way, candidates and their campaigns often become the standard-bearers of a party's message although campaigns are far more candidate centered than they were in previous eras.

If parties encourage campaigns to distinguish themselves and provide clear alternatives to voters, this can help campaigns both inform and engage voters, as Schattschneider (1960) contended. Partisan labels make it easier for candidates to inform citizens of their positions. Partisan identification also serves as a strong motivator for getting citizens engaged in politics and out to the polls in the interest of supporting "their" party. In recent years, increasing partisan polarization has pushed parties and, in turn, campaigns, farther apart on the ideological spectrum (Layman and Carsey 2002). But there is some debate among political scientists over whether increased partisan polarization has increased turnout and participation or has turned off and disengaged voters. Whereas Fiorina et al. (2010) suggest that polarization depresses turnout, others have demonstrated that it actually energizes voters and motivates participation (Downs 1957; Abramowitz and Stone 2006).

The changing relationship between parties and candidates in an era of polarization has implications for representation. Party influence in primary elections may prevent the candidate whose views are most representative of his or her constituency from running for office. Evidence further suggests that the type of primary system used in a state affects the types of candidates who are elected to office. Closed primary systems tend to lead to more ideologically extreme candidates winning office. States with semi-closed primaries tend to produce the most moderate candidates (Gerber and Morton 1998).

Finally, in the race for endorsements and financial and organizational support, both incumbents and challengers can be motivated to move away from the average preferences of their constituents to gain the favor of their party's base and organizations. It is becoming more difficult for candidates to be fully representative of their constituents in their policy positions *and* to garner the support of the institutional actors needed to win office (Layman et al. 2006). This is true not only for their conduct on the campaign trail, but also for their conduct in office (Binder 2003; Jones 2001). Oftentimes, the candidates who face the greatest difficulties are those with highly mixed constituencies, that is, constituencies with roughly balanced shares of Democrats and Republicans, who tend to agree with Republican positions on some issues and Democrats on others. In 2010, Bart Stupak (D-Michigan), a pro-life Democrat, provided integral support and a key vote in the passage of the ACA, a bill that many Republicans and pro-life groups viewed as promoting government-subsidized abortions. In the wake of this vote, Stupak ultimately decided not to run for reelection because he would have likely lost support from voters in his district who may have supported him but for his vote on the ACA which included provisions related to abortion that pro-life supporters opposed (Davey 2010).

INTEREST GROUPS: CHANGING CONTEXTS

Interest group activity has become more pronounced in American politics, largely in response to the expansion of government that occurred in the late 19th and early 20th centuries (Lowi 1979). With the increase in government regulation, interest groups were formed with the goal of getting more favorable regulations and resources from government. Contemporary interest groups draw on the large-scale social movements of previous decades and centuries as models for organizing around their own policy goals. The women's suffrage movement of the late 19th and early 20th century and the civil rights movement of the 1960s are prominent past examples of successful interest group organization.

Interest groups, like parties, seek to influence public policy. They do so not by running candidates for office, but by campaigning for candidates and initiatives that align with their policy interests. Many prominent interest groups, such as the National Rifle Association or National Right to Life, tend to be associated strongly with one party or the other. Nevertheless, although interest groups certainly have incentives to join partisan coalitions, they also build bipartisan coalitions to pursue legislative goals (Grossman and Dominguez 2009; Grossman 2012).

In the context of contemporary campaigns, interest groups provide far more active support for candidates and issues than they did in decades past. They recognize that election outcomes exert great influence on the policies that are ultimately adopted and seek to support candidates who are supportive of their

Figure 3.3 Example of Interest Group Voter Contact

agenda. Interest group involvement in campaigns can come in many forms. Although interest groups may not always adopt partisan strategies, evidence suggests they allocate resources in ways that are similar to the strategies used by candidates and political parties, at least in the context of presidential elections. This occurs although there are numerous, disconnected, and diverse interest groups in the United States (Panagopoulos 2006). Interest groups focus their efforts not only on candidates, but also on campaigns for ballot initiatives. In the 2014 midterm elections, a group known as Save Birth Control Illinois sent out mailers like the one pictured in Figure 3.3 urging voters to vote yes on a birth control initiative the group had helped draft.

Some interest groups, like political action committees, can also contribute regulated sums of money directly to and endorse candidates. Member organizations communicate with and attempt to mobilize their members to volunteer and help turn out the vote on behalf of a candidate or an initiative. In the context of contemporary campaigns, interest groups not only use extensive databases of citizen e-mails to get their messages out, but also exploit new forms of media such as Twitter and Facebook to help mobilize supporters. This type of activity can provide campaigns with distinct advantages. Coordinated interest groups can do some of the heavy lifting for political campaigns. Their donations can bring in much-needed infusions of cash, and they often come with an army of volunteers dedicated to their cause who will line up behind a group to support a candidate. Because interest group advertisements are far more likely to be focused on policy issues rather than candidate information, candidates may have more leeway to focus on their biographies and background information, which can be more engaging and appealing to voters.

The majority of interest group resources are dedicated to communicating with voters through advertisements designed to influence their vote choice (Panagopoulos 2006). In recent years, interest groups not only have engaged in more advertising, but also have done so independently from candidates. According to the Wesleyan Media Project, in presidential primaries alone since 2000 less than 15% of all ads were aired by outside groups. But by 2012, their share of advertisements ballooned to nearly 60% (Franz 2013). Between December 2011 and Election Day 2012, independent groups spent more than $360 million on advertising in the presidential race alone. Some estimates hold that in the 2012 election cycle, outside groups spent more than $1 billion dollars, almost three times the amount they spent in the 2010 midterm elections (Jamieson 2013). Table 3.3 displays total, non–party independent expenditures in congressional elections alone between 2000 and 2014. The data confirm the explosive growth in outside spending in elections, especially in cycles following the *Citizens United* decision. In the 2014 cycle, more than $500 million was spent independently by outside groups to influence election outcomes. Table 3.4 presents a list of independent expenditure groups including super PACs and 501(c) organizations (see Chapter 4 for a discussion of differences between these groups) that were active in the 2012 election cycle and spent at least $10 million, along with their ideological viewpoint and total amounts spent. On both sides of the political aisle, independent spending amounts were considerable.

As I noted previously, the remarkable growth in outside spending by interest groups in elections is in large part a result of recent Supreme Court decisions on campaign finance, which I will discuss in greater detail in Chapter 4. In the aftermath of *Citizens United v. Federal Election Commission* and *McCutcheon v. Federal Election Commission*, which freed them from previous restrictions on aggregate contribution limits, wealthy donors can now give up to about $3.5 million in total contributions to federal candidates, political action committees, and party committees given current limits to individual campaign committees that remain intact (Lioz and Bowie 2013). The latter outcome is particularly pertinent in the discussion of interest groups because wealthy donors can more or less contribute to these groups without fear of having their identities disclosed. Super PACs affiliated with interest groups are effectively allowed to spend unlimited amounts of money during a given election, as long as they do not directly coordinate with a candidate's election committee.

These developments in interest group campaigning mean these groups play a significant role in shaping the messages citizens receive about candidates and initiatives during a campaign season. This has direct consequences for the conduct

Table 3.3 U.S. House and Senate

	FOR DEMOCRATS	AGAINST DEMOCRATS	FOR REPUBLICANS	AGAINST REPUBLICANS	TOTAL
2014					
House	15,263,587	40,597,011	39,445,914	48,052,065	143,358,577
Senate	36,596,536	120,655,341	82,767,574	147,253,985	387,273,436
2012					
House	23,413,464	77,171,121	34,082,403	63,247,389	197,914,377
Senate	18,265,873	101,547,974	42,596,491	96,890,762	259,301,100
2010					
House	20,586,631	37,047,762	14,609,781	25,624,537	97,868,711
Senate	13,510,171	43,396,775	22,532,780	17,803,878	97,243,604
2008					
House	8,474,409	2,037,373	8,387,039	7,062,990	25,955,811
Senate	5,417,350	1,846,788	5,506,228	5,004,986	17,775,352
2006					
House	6,441,484	771,557	6,382,708	12,084,897	25,680,646
Senate	2,924,466	305,268	5,700,633	1,474,496	10,404,863
2004					
House	1,346,007	66,693	3,898,440	545,190	5,856,330
Senate	415,371	311,123	7,740,022	364,568	8,831,084
2002					
House	2,664,722	261,922	2,522,441	538,808	5,987,893
Senate	5,275,291	181,233	3,547,488	1,173,796	10,177,808
2000					
House	4,112,071	234,237	2,893,836	1,665,755	8,905,899
Senate	1,481,901	607,809	4,378,023	2,729,069	9,196,802

NOTE: An independent expenditure is defined by the Federal Election Commission as an expenditure for a communication "expressly advocating the election or defeat of a clearly identified candidate that is not made in cooperation, consultation, or concert with, or at the request or suggestion of, a candidate, a candidate's authorized committee, or their agents, or a political party or its agents." 11 CFR 100.16(a).
SOURCE: Campaign Finance Institute analysis of Federal Election Commission data.

of campaigns during election season. Previously, campaigns retained greater control over the content of their campaign communications. Now, parties and interest groups often put out advertisements and communications without the approval of the candidates they are supporting. This can be challenging for candidates, especially because these advertisements are far more likely to be negative (Fowler and Ridout 2012). Insulated from concerns about electability, interest groups are generally less concerned about backlash or repercussions from negative advertising, compared to candidates and parties which must protect their images at all costs. Table 3.5 presents an analysis conducted by the Wesleyan Media Project of the tone in television advertisements, broadcasted between September 1 and

Table 3.4 Outside Spending (more than $10 million) by 2012 Super PACs and 501(c) Organizations

GROUP	VIEW	TOTAL SPENDING
American Crossroads/Crossroads GPS	C	$176,215,829
Restore Our Future	C	$142,097,336
Priorities USA/Priorities USA Action	L	$65,166,859
Majority PAC	L	$37,498,257
Americans for Prosperity	C	$33,542,051
U.S. Chamber of Commerce	C	$32,255,439
House Majority PAC	L	$30,470,122
American Future Fund	C	$24,499,533
Service Employees International Union	L	$19,645,293
National Rifle Association	C	$18,607,356
FreedomWorks	C	$19,638,968
American Federation of State/County/Municipal Employees	L	$17,027,319
Club for Growth	C	$17,960,737
Winning Our Future	C	$17,007,762
Americans for Job Security	C	$15,872,864
Americans for Tax Reform	C	$15,794,552
Ending Spending	C	$13,250,766
League of Conservation Voters	L	$13,867,752
Planned Parenthood	L	$11,855,885
American Action Network	C	$11,689,399

SOURCE: Center for Responsive Politics.

Election Day in 2012 in federal races, by ad sponsor. The results show that while candidates' campaigns broadcasted roughly even numbers of positive, contrast and negative (or attack) ads, parties and especially interest groups ran largely negative ads (Fowler, Franz and Ridout 2016). In addition, negativity is most pronounced in competitive races; fewer than two in ten television advertisements aired in the 2012 U.S. Senate elections were positive, for example, while 61 percent were negative; by contrast, 80 percent of the ads in uncompetitive Senate races were positive in tone (Fowler et al. 2016: 54).

Table 3.5 Tone in 2012 Federal Races by Ad Sponsor, September 1-Election Day

SPONSOR	POSITIVE	CONTRAST	NEGATIVE
Candidate	32.5%	28.5%	39.0%
Party/coordinated	4.5%	17.2%	78.3%
Interest group	5.9%	11.0%	83.1%

SOURCE: Wesleyan Media Project (Fowler et al. 2016: 55)

This does not mean campaigns must stand idly by. Although candidates are barred from directly coordinating with super PACs, enforcement of this provision is rare given the uncertainty about what constitutes coordination. Candidates can theoretically speak out "as citizens" and ask super PACs to change their campaign strategies, as Newt Gingrich did during the early months of the 2012 Republican presidential primaries. In a speech to his campaign supporters in which he noted that he was "speaking as a citizen," Gingrich called on the super PAC supporting his election bid, Winning Our Future, to withdraw commercials criticizing Mitt Romney (Powers 2012). Such signals are routinely used in contemporary elections, and there is evidence that the resource allocation strategies of campaigns, parties, and interest groups are often highly correlated in elections (Panagopoulos 2006).

More broadly, campaigns often face difficult decisions about whether—and how—to respond to interest group attacks. The strategic calculus can be complicated. Campaigns can choose to respond with their own negative ads in response to interest group ads that target them, but in doing so they run the risk of being seen as too negative and alienating potential supporters. The influence of negative advertising on citizen preferences and behavior is a point of intense debate among political scientists (to be discussed in greater depth in Chapter 6), but the source of the lion's share of negative campaign messages can often be traced back to interest groups.

Consequences for Democracy

Overall, as with parties, it is unclear whether interest groups have incentives to promote democratic ideals. After all, their efforts are typically focused on advancing their interests, which do not necessarily coincide with those of the public. Pundits and political scientists question the role that interest groups play in enhancing representation, transmission of information, and public engagement in American politics. On the one hand, interest groups can theoretically both inform the public and help them engage with issues they care about but feel are not being adequately represented by elected officials. On the other hand, however, false and misleading campaign claims can misinform citizens; in fact, some studies show that ads sponsored by groups that adopt nonpartisan, nonideological, or noncontroversial-sounding names (such as "Citizens for a Working America") tend to be more effective in influencing the preferences of citizens than those sponsored by candidates (Brooks and Muroy 2012).

For decades, political scientists have debated whether the proliferation of interest groups is beneficial for upholding democratic norms in the United States, especially in terms of voter representation. David Truman put forward one of the seminal arguments in favor of interest groups (1951 [1981]). Truman argued that latent groups, that is, interest groups that have not yet organized, will always rise up to protect interests and preferences that are being ignored or violated. Groups will inevitably clash and disagree with one another, thus preventing a tyranny of the majority, which was a primary concern expressed by James Madison in the *Federalist Papers* (Madison 1961 [1787–1788]). Representative democracy is thus maintained as a result of the organization and interaction of interest groups. The structure of U.S. governance allows latent groups to play a role in representing public interests.

Of course, Truman did not have the final word on the role of interest groups. As more interest groups organized in the United States, other scholars weighed in on the positives and negatives of interest group expansion. In the presence of an increasingly complex and large bureaucracy, Theodore Lowi (1979) contended that the U.S. government expanded in response to the demands of organized interests, assuming responsibility for the administrative agencies that were created to respond to their concerns. As the number of government agencies increased, they were confined by the influence of major interest groups. Another normative concern is the role that interest groups and parties play in influencing political agendas, known as the second face of power (Bachrach and Baratz 1962). Whereas pluralist scholars such as Dahl (1961) focused on who in government is making decisions and what those decisions are, others recognized that influencing what gets on the decision-making agenda in the first place is a form of representation and power as well. With the increase in the number of interest groups and their ability to campaign for and donate to political campaigns, there are greater concerns over the extent to which contemporary interest groups have an inordinate amount of influence on the policy positions taken by candidates for public office.

MEDIA: CHANGING CONTEXTS

The news media play an integral role in the electoral and campaign processes. In an ideal world, the media would be objective and focused on substantive policy, but news coverage of campaigns has evolved as news organizations grapple with tectonic economic and technological shifts. Audience sizes have shrunk, and media proliferation has caused fragmentation. As a result, the partisan press has been revitalized and campaign coverage has become increasingly sensationalized, less substantive, and focused more on negativity and controversy (Wayne 2014). In the 2012 general election, for instance, there were twice as many horse race stories as there were policy stories (Wayne 2014). Coverage also tends to be superficial, as evidenced by the fact that the length of the average presidential candidate sound bite dwindled from 43 seconds in 1968 (Hallin 1992) to 7.7 seconds in 2004 (Bucy and Grabe 2007). Consequently, public confidence in the media and about news accuracy have eroded (Mattes and Redlawsk 2014), while perceptions of political bias in news reporting has climbed, especially among Republicans (Wayne 2014). In addition, Marcus Prior has linked the vast array of media choices now available to citizens to inequality in political involvement and polarization and argued these developments also affect political learning and incumbency advantage (Prior 2007).

Despite these changes, most Americans still get their campaign news from the media, especially from television, which remains the dominant source of campaign news, and, increasingly, from the Internet (Wayne 2014). However, because citizens consume media messages selectively and tend to discount information that is inconsistent with their preexisting beliefs, attitudes and opinions about candidates and campaigns are not easily influenced by media messages (Zaller 1992). That is not to say that citizens' preferences are completely immune from media influence. For example, the media possesses considerable power over which issues the public thinks *about*, an effect known as agenda setting. For instance, if news media outlets focus predominantly on the state of the economy in an election cycle, the average citizen will be more likely to draw on economic considerations when choosing who to vote for. The more often the media reports on a topic or an event, the more likely the public is to think about it and see it as something important to consider when making decisions (Iyengar and Kinder 1987).

This can be especially problematic for "in-power" parties, particularly presidents, because they are often blamed if the state of the economy is poor (Nadeau and Lewis-Beck 2001). Because there was a Republican president in office at the time of the financial crisis of 2008, a topic of intense media scrutiny, some scholars argue the election of Barack Obama and a wave of congressional Democrats in 2008 was a referendum on George W. Bush's handling of the economy (Jacobson 2009).

By drawing attention to some issues at the expense of others, the media can also prime audiences, or shape the considerations they take into account when making political judgments about issues or candidates (Iyengar and Kinder 1987). In evaluating Obama's ACA, for example, a voter might focus on the reform's economic implications (How will the ACA affect the economy or the budget overall?) or on its moral, social, or ethical implications (Is it fair for so many Americans to be uninsured?). The evaluative emphasis citizens adopt is often a function of how media coverage has framed the issue.

Of course, campaigns compete for media attention in the first place, and most campaigns operating at subnational levels find it difficult to attract this attention. The races that get the most attention from prominent media outlets are almost always those higher up on the ballot, with presidential elections garnering the majority of the coverage. The news media are also more likely to cover competitive races and those that are more consequential for broad-scale outcomes, such as races that could potentially shift the balance of power in the U.S. House of Representatives or the U.S. Senate. Notably, given their prominent role in contemporary campaigns, the media have also begun to pay more attention to political consultants (Panagopoulos 2006). The extent to which this helps or hurts candidates and campaigns is not clear, although in the past the public has appeared skeptical toward political consultants (Panagopoulos and Thurber 2003).

The primary way the media influences the conduct of political campaigns depends on the extent to which campaigns are advantaged or hurt by the content of news coverage. Although positive coverage is ideal, coverage of a scandal or dubious claims made by a candidate can be more damaging than no coverage at all. A prime example of the latter was the leaked video of a speech by Mitt Romney to a group of donors during the 2012 presidential election. The speech, originally leaked by the left-leaning news outlet *Mother Jones*, was picked up by national networks, with one quote in particular repeated over and over again: "There are 47 percent of the people who will vote for the president no matter what," Romney said. "All right, there are 47 percent who are with him, who are dependent upon government, who believe that they are victims, who believe the government has a responsibility to care for them, who believe that they are entitled to health care, to food, to housing, to you-name-it. That's an entitlement" (Bingham 2012). Although some argue the "47 percent" video was not fundamentally devastating to Romney (Sides and Vavreck 2014: 155), it did change the campaign narrative and force Romney to deviate from his message to address the video.

Nonetheless, contemporary campaigns recognize that the news is an important channel through which to communicate with voters. This can include direct interaction with the media through interviews, meetings with editorial boards, and press conferences, as well as inviting reporters to attend public events and issuing press releases. Indeed, candidates are eager to attract the free publicity that comes from news coverage. As Sides et al. (2014) note, "nearly everything a candidate does is designed to be picked up in the next day's newspaper, the night's television broadcast, the next hour's update to a Web site, or the next minute's tweet" (203). During the 2016 presidential campaign, GOP contender Donald Trump leveraged this approach masterfully, often with bombastic rhetoric and controversial statements, to fuel support for his campaign. But such "earned media," as I will discuss in Chapter 6, is not always advantageous to candidates. For example, a politician's image can suffer if interviewers appear to be more hostile than friendly to the candidate in an interview (Babad 1999, 2005).

In fact, there is often considerable tension between the news media and political candidates, who generally aim to stick to talking points in the hope of avoiding gaffes that might lead to negative coverage (Sides et al. 2014). Furthermore, news reporters are generally uninterested in simply reporting a candidate's platform. In fact, reporters are typically far more interested in focusing on the competiveness of a given race and the latest polling numbers than they are to report on substantive policy content (Hayes 2010). Leading media outlets, sometime in partnership with other polling organizations, devote considerable resources to fielding their own polls over the course of political campaigns, often in the interest of producing "news" (Panagopoulos and Farrer 2014). Poll aggregators, such as realclearpolitics.com, pollster.com, and others, now provide comprehensive compilations of all available poll results online, making it easier for ordinary citizens to monitor campaign dynamics virtually in real time. Final, preelection poll estimates tend to be accurate, projecting actual presidential vote shares to within 2–3 percentage points on average since 1956 (Panagopoulos and Farrer 2014). However, publicizing poll results is not necessarily a neutral act, which is one reason why countries such as France do not permit publication of poll results in the media in the final weeks of an election. Studies have revealed that viewers can be significantly influenced by poll reports, adjusting their preferences in favor of the leading candidate (Ansolabehere and Iyengar 1994).

In national general elections as well as high-profile primary elections, a consortium of media outlets (NBC, CBS, Fox News, CNN, and the Associated Press) known as the National Election Pool conducts exit polls of voters in most states across the country. These surveys probe respondents about their vote choices, demographic characteristics, and issue preferences to help explain election outcomes by deciphering patterns in voting behavior. These data are also used to develop projections that enable the networks to declare election winners well before all (or sometimes any) votes are counted. Relying partly on exit poll results, several television networks initially—and erroneously—declared the Democratic presidential candidate Al Gore the winner of the 2000 election, although George W. Bush ultimately became president after a protracted struggle over Florida's electoral votes. Exit polls can be useful in elucidating underlying patterns that help us understand why voters voted the way they did in elections. However, methodological shortcomings, including growing numbers of voters who refuse to participate, challenges in accounting for early voters, and the fact that some types of voters (for instance, Democrats) appear to participate at rates different from Republicans (Panagopoulos 2013c), can severely hamper the accuracy of election projections based on these data.

From a normative perspective, media coverage of exit poll projections can distort election outcomes. In 1980, for example, NBC projected Ronald Reagan would win the presidency at 8:15 pm Eastern Standard Time based on analysis of exit poll data. This decision raised speculation about the impact on voting in states where the polls were still open (on the West Coast, for example), and one study found the early call had a small but measurable impact on both presidential and congressional turnout and a somewhat larger impact on depressing the vote for Democratic candidates at both levels. The author found the overall impact was too small to have affected the outcome of the presidential race, but that as many as 14 congressional races were won by margins smaller than the estimated impact of the early call in those districts (Delli Carpini 1984). In recent cycles, the National Election Pool networks have voluntarily agreed not to declare winners or to make projections until polls in respective states (or, in the case of presidential elections, nearly all states) have closed, but the pressure to capture ratings and prestige by declaring winners as quickly as possible persists and has the potential to result in hasty decisions. Moreover, the networks continue to make other projections—about majority control in the U.S. House or the U.S. Senate, for example—long before polls close across the country, raising concerns about whether (and how) these declarations may affect, distort, or bias election results.

It is also important to note the trend toward increasing fragmentation of the news media. There are now multiple 24-hour news networks, a seemingly infinite number of online newspaper sources, and a variety of social media sites from which citizens can get information and updates about politics. For campaigns, this means citizens are no longer getting information from a few centralized resources, such as their main local newspaper, national newspapers, and nightly news programs. Instead, citizens can choose from different sources, some of which tend to lean one way or the other in their ideological framing of news stories. Cable news outlets such as MSNBC and Fox News are the best-known examples of this type of coverage. Campaigns that are more closely aligned with the ideological leanings of a given news organization might be more likely to interact with it to obtain favorable coverage and garner the interest of their base party members (Morris 2005, 2007).

Consequences for Democracy

News media coverage of campaigns alone has implications for democratic norms. The news can help to inform citizens about candidates, their issue positions, and the experience they would bring to office. The more coverage a campaign gets, the more likely citizens are to recall the candidate's name and to identify issues associated with him or her. Empirical evidence suggests that news media coverage of campaigns does not always live up to the ideal of fully informing the public about their voting options during an election season. Most campaigns attract little or no attention in the news, and those that do often do so for reasons other than their policy and issue stances. Although competitive campaigns might receive greater media attention, this attention likewise does not necessarily focus on substantive policy issues. Instead, the media often focus greater attention on candidates' personal characteristics or on the race for money and voter support. In other words, voters are least likely to get detailed, accurate information about candidates and their policy differences when they need it most (Hayes 2009). When the media does provide campaign coverage, reports often distill candidates' statements into sound bites lasting just a few seconds. One can reasonably question whether complicated policy views or positions can be effectively summarized in 7-second sound bites.

In the context of highly competitive races, campaigns may exacerbate the effects of the news media on the quality of the information citizens receive. In a bid for greater coverage, campaigns might attack their opponents over issues unrelated to policy or do whatever they can to amp up the perception of a close race to garner more free coverage. Such scenarios can deprive voters of news coverage of substantive issues on which they can rely to reach informed decisions.

Other developments in the media landscape have also had implications for campaign conduct and democratic norms, as we will discuss in greater depth in Chapter 9. New and social media, for example, enable near-instantaneous dissemination of news stories, making it easier, among other things, to spread candidate attacks. But it also facilitates rapid response, allowing campaigns to set the record straight before irreparable damage is done. As we have seen in the 2016 presidential election cycle, Twitter in particular has played a central role in influencing news coverage of campaigns and enables both supporters and opponents to spread views and information about candidates rapidly (L. Mair 2012).

One type of new news media that has become particularly prominent is online blogs. Blogs have become a mainstay of major news organizations, from the *Huffington Post* to *Politico* to the *Washington Post*. Many of these outlets carry well-known blogs as a part of their brands, such as Nate Silver's *Five Thirty Eight* blog, which was carried by the *New York Times*. All of this means that the difference between who is a "blogger" and who is a "reporter" has, in certain instances, become far murkier. Many blogs have ideological leanings, which has implications not only for how citizens are informed, but also for campaigns. Campaigns now often hire individuals to coordinate with the traditional news media as well as influential, high-profile bloggers within and outside of news organizations.

CONCLUSION

Over the course of a campaign, candidates and their staff must both navigate their relationships with their opponents and deal with a host of outside influences, some with a direct stake in the outcome of an election, such as parties and interest groups. Although the news media may not have a direct stake in the outcome of an election, they do have a stake in covering races that will increase their viewership and improve profits. The goals of these groups do not always align with the goals of contemporary campaigns. Although attention, resources, and organizational support from parties and interest groups certainly help campaigns, they can also hamper candidates' ability to represent their constituencies and also *win* elected office. News media coverage, when favorable, can be a great asset to campaigns, but there is always room for gaffes, slip-ups, and otherwise negative press to make its way into the news. When running for office, candidates and their campaigns must interact with, manage, and in some cases appeal to all of these actors in their bid for limited attention, resources, and electoral support.

KEY TERMS

24-hour news cycle	Hard money	Parties-as-organizations
Agenda setting	Independent	Parties-in-government
Campaign coordination	expenditure	Parties-in-the-electorate
Caucus	Issue framing	Pledged delegates
Closed primary	Nominating	Priming
Earned media	conventions	Semiclosed primary
Exit polls	Open primary	Soft money

SUGGESTED READINGS

Aldrich, J. H. 2011. *Why Parties? A Second Look*. Chicago: University of Chicago Press.

Bartels, L. 1988. *Presidential Primaries and the Dynamics of Public Choice*. Princeton, NJ: Princeton University Press.

Cohen, M., D. Karol, H. Noel, and J. Zaller. 2008. *The Party Decides: Presidential Nominations before and after Reform*. Chicago, IL: University of Chicago Press.

Iyengar, S., and D. R. Kinder. 1987. *News That Matters*. Chicago, IL: University of Chicago Press.

CHAPTER 4

Money and the Modern Campaign

Prior to the Watergate scandal of 1972, there were few federal campaign finance laws on the books. One of the more notable provisions related to campaign finance law at the time was the Pendleton Civil Service Reform Act, passed in 1883, which made it illegal for government officials to ask for or receive contributions from civil service workers or to hire individuals for these positions in exchange for political favors. Prior to the act, government workers were expected to donate money to politicians to keep their jobs in quid pro quo arrangements. Other notable efforts at campaign finance reform came from President Theodore Roosevelt, who lobbied for the passage of the Tillman Act in 1907. This act made corporate contributions to federal candidates illegal, but provided no effective means of enforcement. Other attempts to reign in campaign finance were made throughout the first half of the 20th century, but it was not until the 1970s when Congress actually decided to collect campaign finance reports, adopted the Federal Election Campaign Act (FECA), and responded to the Watergate scandal of 1972, that meaningful changes with the possibility of real enforcement were enacted (Fuller 2014).

On June 17, 1972, several burglars were arrested at the Democratic National Committee headquarters located in the Watergate building in Washington, D.C., while attempting to wiretap phones and steal documents. It remains unclear whether then–Republican president Nixon knew about the operations beforehand, but it was eventually revealed that he was involved in extensive efforts to cover it up by raising hush money to be paid to the burglars, attempting to stop the Federal Bureau of Investigation from investigating the crime, firing uncooperative staff, and destroying documents. The scandal ultimately led to Nixon's resignation and changed the course of American campaign finance regulation. In 1974, motivated by public reactions to the Watergate scandal, Congress passed amendments to the 1971 FECA, which had initially required broad disclosure of campaign spending. Amendments included public financing options for presidential campaigns and the creation of the Federal Election Commission

(FEC), alongside limits on contributions to campaigns and on candidate expenditures.

In 1976, the U.S. Supreme Court reached a landmark decision in *Buckley v. Valeo*,[1] a case that featured Senator James L. Buckley as the primary plaintiff, along with numerous others from both sides of the aisle. The defendant was Francis R. Valeo, then secretary of state and a former member of the FEC, who represented the U.S. federal government. In the decision, the Supreme Court struck down several provisions of the 1974 FECA amendments, the most significant of which limited spending by candidates in campaigns, on the grounds that they violated free speech rights guaranteed by the First Amendment. *Buckley v. Valeo* also struck down caps on candidate contributions to their own campaigns and paved the way for corporations and unions to do their own electioneering in the form of issue advocacy, as long as they did not explicitly call for the election of one candidate or another.

In the years that followed, several bills were considered but ultimately defeated in the U.S. Senate that would have imposed stricter regulations on campaign spending. In 1996, in response to an alleged effort by the People's Republic of China to funnel money into American presidential races, the U.S. Justice Department formed a task force to investigate these efforts. The Justice Department found evidence that the Chinese government had provided contributions to the Democratic National Committee before the 1996 presidential campaigns, a direct violation of U.S. campaign finance law prohibiting non–American citizens and nonpermanent residents from providing donations to U.S. politicians or political parties. Eventually, both the president, Bill Clinton, and the vice president, Al Gore, came under intense scrutiny as a result of these allegations and investigations.

Following these events, U.S. senators John McCain (R-Arizona) and Russell Feingold (D-Wisconsin) pushed forward a campaign finance reform bill to limit special interest funding of campaigns, including a ban on unregulated soft money donations to party organizations. Over the next few years, multiple campaign finance reform bills were proposed in Congress, but no comprehensive campaign finance reform was passed until the Bipartisan Campaign Reform Act (BCRA) in 2002. Among other things, BCRA eliminated all soft-money donations to national party committees, but doubled individual hard-money contribution limits in federal races from $1,000 to $2,000 per election (primary and general) and pegged these limits to inflation. Under FECA, political parties had been allowed to use soft-money donations to raise and spend unlimited sums as long as the money was directed to "party-building" activities, such as get-out-the-vote efforts and non–candidate specific advertising such as issue ads promoting a party's platform.

Since 2002, campaign finance regulation in the United States has undergone further changes. In 2010, the Supreme Court ruled on *Citizens United v. Federal Election Commission*. Citizens United is a nonprofit organization that produced a

---

[1]*Buckley v. Valeo*, No. 75-546 424 U.S. (1976).

documentary film called *Hillary: The Movie* using corporate finances. The group wanted to run commercials promoting the movie during the 2008 presidential primaries. Because the film was technically electioneering in that it argued that Clinton should not be elected, a lower court ruled that it could not be aired in a state during the 30 days before its presidential primary. When the Supreme Court took up the matter, conservative justices went beyond the limited question of whether the documentary should be allowed to air and addressed whether corporations and unions could be banned from spending money on electioneering altogether. In a highly contentious decision, the court ultimately ruled that the limitations on Citizens United were unconstitutional, arguing that "associations of persons," such as corporations and unions, also have the right to free speech.[2]

In 2013, the Supreme Court again loosened the restrictions on campaign finance in American elections with its ruling in *McCutcheon v. Federal Election Commission*. This decision struck down the aggregate limits on how much individuals can contribute during a two-year election cycle.[3] Although limits remain on the amount one can contribute to *individual* candidates, parties, and political action committees (PACs), the total limit for the amount one can contribute to *all* of these groups across the board is no longer in place.

During this period, the amount of money spent in American elections has increased dramatically, although it has been on the rise since the 1970s. In 1996, the average election winner in the U.S. House of Representatives spent $673,739, and the average election winner in the U.S. Senate spent $4,692,110. By 2012, the corresponding numbers were $1,567,379 and $11,474,362, respectively (OpenSecrets .org 2015a). Figures 4.1 and 4.2 illustrate these trends.

In contemporary campaigns, money is an all-but-necessary ingredient. It allows campaigns to hire political campaign consultants and to air television

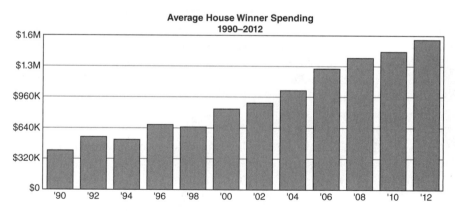

Figure 4.1 Average House Winner Spending, 1990–2012
SOURCE: OpenSecrets.org and the Center for Responsive Politics

---

[2]*Citizens United v. Federal Election Commission*, No. 08-205, 558 U.S. 310 (2010).
[3]*McCutcheon v. Federal Election Commission*, No.12-536 572 U.S. (2014).

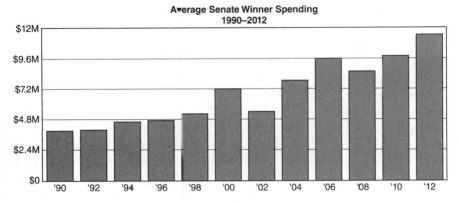

Figure 4.2 Average Senate Winner Spending, 1990–2012
SOURCE: OpenSecrets.org and the Center for Responsive Politics

advertisements. Campaigns have become more expensive over time as the result of technological advancements as well as rising communications, media, and staffing costs. In previous eras, campaigns relied heavily on endorsements and volunteers, as well as infrastructure provided by political party organizations, but in contemporary political campaigns, money has become necessary for candidates to be perceived as viable in the first place by parties, interest groups, and individual donors.

This chapter discusses campaign finance in contemporary campaigns. I first discuss current campaign finance regulations and how they affect campaign fundraising, budgeting, and the actual spending of financial resources. Then, I consider the effects that campaign spending can actually have, focusing primarily on election outcomes. Finally, I direct attention to the regulation of new actors that have begun to significantly impact the role of money in American elections: super PACs and other independent groups. I discuss each of these components in the context of the contemporary campaign finance environment, giving historical context where necessary to provide background for how changing campaign finance regulations have shifted the behavior of political campaigns. Not surprisingly, the changing role of money in politics since the 1970s has had important implications for campaign conduct along with corresponding consequences for democratic norms, but it has also raised penetrating normative and ethical concerns with which the nation continues to wrestle.

CONTEMPORARY CAMPAIGN FINANCE REGULATIONS AND FUNDRAISING

Individuals and organized interest groups are the primary contributors during any given political campaign. Although interest groups that are tax exempt cannot provide contributions (because this would mean the government was partially subsidizing campaigns), almost all organizations that are not tax exempt, corporations and unions included, can donate during election cycles. Although some groups, such as corporations and unions, are prohibited from donating directly to candidates, they can create their own political action committees (PACs) whose purpose is to work toward the election of favored candidates and advance political agendas. For the most part, PACs must raise money on their own, although a small amount of money from an organization's revenue can be used to set up the PAC. Like unions, other membership organizations (groups in which members pay dues) may also create PACs. Finally, political parties are also free to establish their own PACs.

In federal elections, there are limits on who can donate, the amounts they can contribute, and the disclosure of such political giving. There are different regulations and limitations on contributions depending on who is doing the contributing and to whom they are contributing. Table 4.1 shows the contribution limits set in place for the 2015–2016 election cycle. After the passage of the BCRA in 2002, the limits for individuals giving to federal candidates and parties were increased. Prior to April 2, 2014, there were also limits on how much individuals could give to candidates, parties, and PACs in the aggregate for an election cycle. In the wake of *McCutcheon v. Federal Election Commission*, individual donors are no longer bound by aggregate limits and can give to as many candidates and committees as they want, although they must still comply with per-candidate, PAC, and party committee limits.

Limits on the amount of money individuals, parties, and interest groups can contribute to candidates have implications for campaign fundraising strategies. These limits are in place for a reason. If individuals could donate unlimited amounts of money to one campaign, candidates would run the risk of being beholden to a small, unrepresentative portion of the population. The existence of donation limits makes it more challenging for candidates to raise money because they must reach out to a larger number of donors. Members of Congress often spend large chunks of their day calling potential donors or meeting with them at fundraisers in Washington and back home in their districts. In Figure 4.3, a slide from a PowerPoint presentation provided to incoming freshmen congressmen by the Democratic Congressional Campaign Committee shows how much of an incumbent's time is dedicated to fundraising (Grim and Siddiqui 2013). Based on the committee's schedule, members of Congress should expect to spend up to four hours per day calling potential donors and another two hours per day meeting face to face with constituents, donors, and other interests.

Fundraising and contributions are important for two basic reasons: They provide resources with which to run viable campaigns and serve as signals of viability to future donors, interest groups, and parties, as I touched on in previous chapters. Although money is only one marker that can provide signals about a candidate's viability (alongside support in polls, media coverage, web presence and other indicators), it can be an important one (Mutz 1995; Christenson et al. 2014). As we will see in Chapter 9, advances in online fundraising have significantly improved candidates' ability to pursue financial support, helping them generate more small-donor contributions and amplifying their fundraising after

Table 4.1 Contribution Limits for 2015–2016 Federal Elections

DONORS	CANDIDATE COMMITTEE	PAC[1] (SSF AND NONCONNECTED)	STATE/DISTRICT/LOCAL PARTY COMMITTEE	NATIONAL PARTY COMMITTEE	ADDITIONAL NATIONAL PARTY COMMITTEE ACCOUNTS[2]
			RECIPIENTS		
Individual	$2,700* per election	$5,000 per year	$10,000 per year (combined)	$33,400* per year	$100,200* per account, per year
Candidate committee	$2,000 per election	$5,000 per year	Unlimited transfers	Unlimited transfers	
PAC—multicandidate	$5,000 per election	$5,000 per year	$5,000 per year (combined)	$15,000 per year	$45,000 per account, per year
PAC—nonmulticandidate	$2,700* per election	$5,000 per year	$10,000 per year (combined)	$33,400* per year	$100,200* per account, per year
State, district, and local party committee	$5,000 per election	$5,000 per year	Unlimited transfers	Unlimited transfers	
National party committee	$5,000 per election[3]	$5,000 per year			

* Indexed for inflation in odd-numbered years.

[1] "PAC" here refers to a committee that makes contributions to other federal political committees. Independent-expenditure-only political committees (sometimes called "super PACs") may accept unlimited contributions, including from corporations and labor organizations.

[2] The limits in this column apply to a national party committee's accounts for: (i) the presidential nominating convention; (ii) election recounts and contests and other legal proceedings; and (iii) national party headquarters buildings. A party's national committee, Senate campaign committee, and House campaign committee are each considered separate national party committees with separate limits. Only a national party committee, not the parties' national congressional campaign committees, may have an account for the presidential nominating convention.

[3] Additionally, a national party committee and its senatorial campaign committee may contribute up to $46,800 combined per campaign to each Senate candidate.

SOURCE: Federal Election Commission

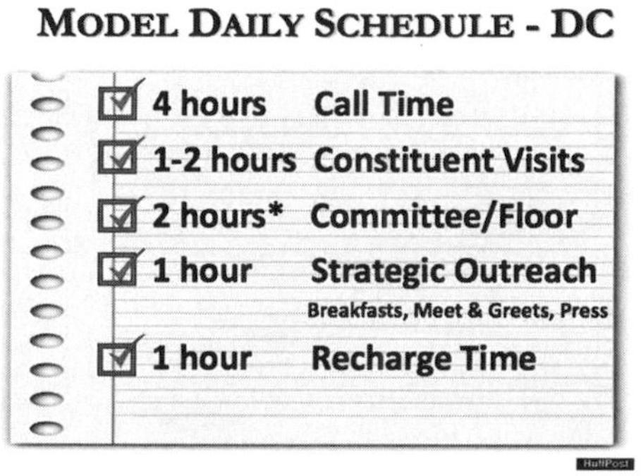

MODEL DAILY SCHEDULE - DC

- ☑ **4 hours** **Call Time**
- ☑ **1-2 hours** **Constituent Visits**
- ☑ **2 hours*** **Committee/Floor**
- ☑ **1 hour** **Strategic Outreach**
  Breakfasts, Meet & Greets, Press
- ☑ **1 hour** **Recharge Time**

Figure 4.3 Model Daily Congressional Schedule
SOURCE: *Huffington Post*

early primary victories (Christenson et al. 2014). Most strategists suggest that campaigns should not make their plans given a calculation of the amount of money that *can* be raised, but figure out how much money is needed to implement an effective campaign strategy in the first place (Winston 2013). Although wealthy candidates can have an edge . . . jump start their campaigns, their organizations generally adopt elaborate fundraising strategies to solicit support from donors large and small. The 2008 Obama campaign exemplified such a strategy, touting its efforts to gather small-donor contributions from a broad number of citizens. For the 2012 election, Obama doubled down on these efforts. In 2011 alone, nearly half of the donors to his reelection were individuals who gave $200 or less. This was more than double the amount he had received from small donors during the same time period for his 2008 election bid (Malbin 2012).

Before we discuss the various ways in which campaigns can approach fundraising, either directly or by retaining professional political fundraisers, it is worth thinking about what motivates individuals to contribute in the first place. Although this result is likely somewhat inflated, survey evidence from the past few election cycles suggests that only about one in six Americans generally reports contributing money to a political campaign and that these donors tend to be more affluent, educated, partisan, and ideologically extreme in their policy views than individuals who do not report contributing to a political campaign (Lipsitz and Panagopoulos 2009; Panagopoulos and Bergan 2004). Francia et al. (2003) analyzed survey data from the 1996 congressional elections to group donors into four general categories. About one-fourth of all donors are considered "investors," who are primarily motivated by material incentives. These include considerations about whether a candidate is (or has been) helpful or receptive to the donor's business or industry interests. "Ideologues," who comprise about one-third of the donor pool, give mainly for purposive reasons, or to advance a certain ideological agenda or specific policy positions. Another fourth of donors, called "intimates," give primarily for social reasons, for example, to attend a fundraising dinner, reception, or event or to receive some sort of recognition for giving. The remaining 15%, called "incidentals," do not have strong or consistent motivations for giving.

Candidates appeal to donors using a number of strategies. They can undertake direct-mail fundraising by soliciting donations from databases of citizens who are likely to support a given candidate based on their previous contributing behavior (Sabato 1989). Given the technological advancements in the past decade, more and more candidates are turning to online fundraising and developing databases of donor e-mails from which to solicit donations (Morris 2008). In 2008, the Obama campaign gave citizens the option of locking in recurring monthly donations. This decreased the number of times the campaign had to ask for money and gave the campaign a greater degree of certainty for future budgeting and fundraising estimates. Whether solicitations are made via direct mail or online, well-developed and diversified donor lists are a must for contemporary political campaigns (Christenson 2009).

Another way candidates can fundraise is by hosting events. These include fancy dinners and black-tie galas as well as small, informal events such as ice cream socials, gatherings at diners, and barbecues. These events provide supporters a chance to connect with candidates on a more intimate level and are often successful at raising large amounts of donations. Recently, campaigns have developed strategies that combine the benefits of online fundraising and candidate events. E-mails are sent to potential donors notifying them that if they donate certain amounts, they will have the chance of being selected to be flown in to meet candidates and engage in some sort of social activity, often a dinner, sporting event, or the like. In Hillary Clinton's bid for the 2016 Democratic presidential nomination, her election committee sent out e-mails and posted announcements on social media such as the one pictured in Figure 4.4 from Clinton's official Facebook page that offered her supporters a chance to meet her nearly a year out from the beginning of the 2016 primary season.

One prominent and controversial means by which campaigns raise money is by relying on what are known as campaign bundlers. Individual donors may hit personal limits, but if they are well connected, they can help raise more money for the campaign from others, which is then "bundled" and given to candidates. This method of fundraising is controversial because there are limited laws in place requiring the disclosure of bundlers. The FEC only requires money that is bundled by registered lobbyists to be disclosed, although some candidates agree to disclose other bundlers who raise more than a set amount of money. Barack Obama and John McCain did this during the 2008 presidential election for bundlers who raised more than $50,000. Figure 4.5, put together by the campaign finance watchdog group Center for Responsive Politics (OpenSecrets.org), illustrates the role that bundlers can play in presidential elections. Although bundlers themselves cannot contribute beyond individual contribution limits, they serve to channel a large amount of money to campaigns through a narrow subset of individuals.

Important to note is that federal campaign finance laws only apply to federal elections. As discussed briefly in Chapter 2, states and localities have widely

Figure 4.4 Hillary for America Social Media Example

different campaign finance laws for nonfederal elections held within their jurisdictions, including gubernatorial, state legislative, and other local elections.
Some states have limits that are more permissive than at the federal level, whereas
others have more restrictive limits. Certain states have virtually no restrictions
on individuals or direct corporate giving. Alabama, Missouri, Nebraska, Oregon,
Utah, and Virginia are among the states that place no limits on contributions at all.
Indiana, Iowa, Mississippi, North Dakota, Pennsylvania, and Texas have minimal
limits on contributions. They may limit contributions by corporations and unions
to candidates, but have no limits on contributions from other sources. In the remaining states, there are limits on the amount of contributions to candidates by individuals, parties, PACs, corporations, and unions. In certain states, such as Alaska,
Arizona, Colorado, and Connecticut, donations by corporations and unions are
completely prohibited. Other states, such as Massachusetts, Minnesota, and Iowa,
do not allow contributions by corporations, but do allow contributions by unions.
New Hampshire, in contrast, prohibits contributions by unions but allows contributions by corporations up to a certain amount. Other states have even more
complex regulations on campaign finance. New York, for example, has different
limits on who may contribute and how much in primary and general elections.
There, state parties are prohibited from contributing to a candidate during a primary election, but may do so during a general election (National Conference of
State Legislatures 2011).

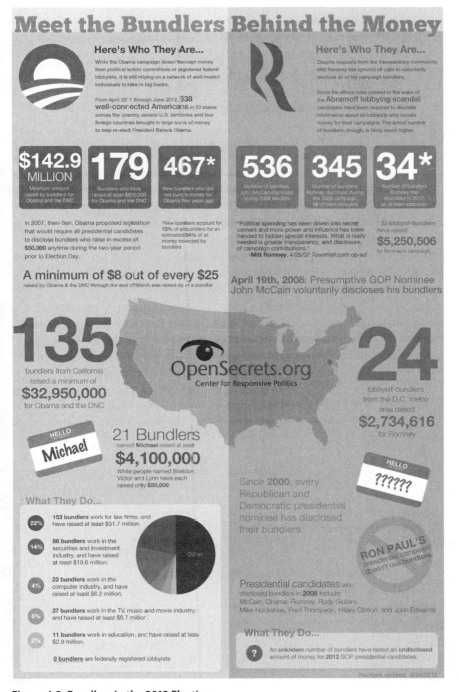

Figure 4.5 Bundlers in the 2012 Election

SOURCE: Center for Responsive Politics

These complexities mean that the implications of campaign finance regulations for campaign fundraising conduct will vary widely depending on the context in which a campaign is operating. For example, candidates running for office in a state where there are greater restrictions on contributions may have to expend more effort raising money from a broader base of small-dollar donors. Depending on the extent to which corporations and unions can contribute to campaigns, this will also affect the different interests campaigns in a given state choose to court. None of the state limitations on contributions to candidates, however, prevents individuals, parties, corporations, and unions from donating to or setting up their own PACs in support of particular candidates within a given state.

CAMPAIGN FINANCE REGULATIONS, BUDGETING, AND SPENDING RESOURCES

Despite regulating contributions to political campaigns, federal campaign finance law places virtually no restrictions on candidate spending in elections. Presidential races are the only level of elections where total campaign spending can potentially be limited. Even at this level, this limitation can only occur with the consent of the candidates. The FECA set up a system of public financing for presidential elections that is still in place today. Financing for this funding comes from a check-off system wherein taxpayers allocate money to the funding pool on their federal tax returns. The allocation limit per taxpayer was previously $1, but was changed to $3 in 1994. For primaries, candidates are eligible to receive primary matching funds, in which the federal government will match up to $250 of an individual's total contributions to an eligible candidate. Only candidates who are seeking nomination by a political party for the presidency are eligible to receive these funds. Furthermore, primary candidates must demonstrate that they have broad-based support by raising more than $5,000 in at least 20 different states.

For the general election, the nominee of each major party is eligible to receive a public grant ($91.2 million in 2012). If candidates accept public funds in either the primary or the general election, they must agree to limit their spending. In 2012, the limit on spending in the general election was $91.2 million, and the overall primary spending limit was $45.6 million. Accepting public funding in the primary elections also requires abiding by spending limits that vary depending on a state's voting-age population. California, for example, had an expenditure limit of $20,744,600 during the 2012 presidential elections, whereas Hawaii had a limit of $912,400.

These systems are entirely voluntary, and candidates can choose to opt out. In 1996, the Republican Steve Forbes became the first presidential candidate to opt out of the public financing system in the primary elections, and he did the same in 2000, along with Republican George W. Bush, who feared that accepting public funding in a race against Forbes could have put him at a disadvantage. Rejecting public funding meant the candidates could bypass spending limits and, in 2000, Bush raised more than $100 million (Weber 2011). Candidates opt out in the primaries because they want to raise and spend more money than is allowed by national public financing limits and state-by-state limits in primary races. The ability to spend is particularly important in early presidential primary states such as Iowa and New Hampshire. These states have small populations and, thus, fairly low spending limits in primaries for candidates who accept matching funds. Candidates tend to opt out of public financing in primary elections because victory in these early voting states sends a signal to groups and donors of a candidate's viability at the beginning of the primary season.

In 2008, Barack Obama became the first presidential candidate to opt out of the public financing system in both the primary and general elections. The Obama campaign argued the system was no longer sustainable and that participation would put Obama at a significant disadvantage. Obama stated,

> The public financing of presidential elections as it exists today is broken, and I face opponents who've become masters at gaming this broken system. . . . John McCain's campaign and the Republican National Committee are fueled by contributions from Washington lobbyists and special interest PACs. And we've already seen that he's not going to stop the smears and attacks from his allies running so-called 527 groups, who will spend millions and millions of dollars in unlimited donations. (Nagourney and Zeleny 2008)

Obama's decision to forego public financing foreshadowed a lasting shift in the use of public funding for presidential general elections. In 2012, both major-party nominees rejected public funding. Spending caps in both the primary and general elections can potentially prevent a candidate from responding effectively to attacks or spending by opponents or outside groups. In 2004, when both candidates opted in to the system of public financing in the general election, the Democratic candidate John Kerry was the victim of a smear campaign from a PAC known as the Swift Boat Veterans for Truth, which ran a series of advertisements claiming Kerry was not fit to serve as president because he had supposedly exaggerated his service in the Vietnam War. Kerry maintained he was not able to adequately respond to the smear campaign given the money he had available to spend, conjecturing that presidential elections were ultimately headed toward a system where it would become politically unfeasible for future candidates to opt in to the public financing system (Parti 2011).

Given that candidates have been trending toward opting out of both general and primary election public funding in recent years and that 2012 saw the first presidential election in which both nominees refused public funding, many argue the system is more or less defunct. There are questions about whether the system should be dismantled or reformed. If reformed, aggregate spending limits might be changed in places such as Iowa and New Hampshire for primary elections to account for their importance in the primary system as early voting states or the match or check-off amounts that citizens are allowed to contribute could be raised. As it stands, the check-off system is withering because the amount that taxpayers can allocate has been kept constant, whereas the costs of running a campaign have skyrocketed (Parti 2011).

For state and local-level elections, there is a wider array of public financing laws on the books. As I noted in Chapter 3, 25 states offered some form of public financing for campaigns, although where this money comes from and how it is dispersed varies from state to state (National Conference of State Legislatures 2013; Panagopoulos 2011). In recent years, public financing in some states has been under attack. Wisconsin's public financing system was controversially shut down by its state legislature in 2011 (Lueders 2011), an ironic turn of events, given that Russell Feingold (D-Wisconsin) was one of the primary co-sponsors and architects of the 2002 BCRA. In 2006, Vermont's strict limits on contributions to campaign and campaign spending were struck down by the U.S. Supreme Court, a decision that likely increased the difficulty states have had and will continue to have in placing limitations on money in politics down the road (Lane 2006).

CAMPAIGN SPENDING AND BUDGETS

Let us now turn our attention to how campaigns spend their money is recent election cycles. Many campaign decisions on how to allocate funds are contingent on contextual factors. Primary elections have fewer voters who must be contacted. Challengers must spend more money raising awareness and name recognition than incumbents. In some states, candidates may be able to rely more heavily on support from state or local party organizations, freeing up some of their own funds for expenditures they may have not otherwise been able to afford. In most races, however, a large chunk of the money that candidates raise is allocated to television advertisements (Fowler and Ridout 2010; West 2010). By June 2012, Mitt Romney had spent 39% of his funds on media buys, whereas Barack Obama had spent a whopping 63% of his campaign's money on media advertising, the lion's share of which was directed to television (Sullivan 2012). Figure 4.6 summarizes how expenditures were allocated across spending categories by the two major-party candidates and their allies in the 2012 campaign.

Figure 4.7 presents an overview of how money was allocated to various categories of spending by federal campaigns during the 2014 midterm election cycle.

	Advertising	Mail	Fundraising	Payroll	Admin.	Travel	Polling	Events	Consult.	Lists
OBAMA	$580.1m	$97.3	$106.4	$102.3	$52.0	$35.7	$34.9	$25.3	$13.2	$16.8
ROMNEY	$470.3	$133.4	$96.2	$50.8	$21.3	$39.6	$14.2	$7.0	$24.7	$9.6

Figure 4.6   2012 Presidential Campaign Expenditures
SOURCE: *Washington Post* (www.washingtonpost.com/wp-srv/special/politics/campaign-finance/)

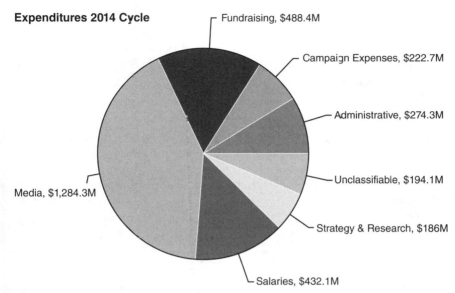

Expenditures 2014 Cycle

Fundraising, $488.4M

Campaign Expenses, $222.7M

Administrative, $274.3M

Unclassifiable, $194.1M

Strategy & Research, $186M

Salaries, $432.1M

Media, $1,284.3M

Figure 4.7 Overall Spending by Category (Federal Elections, 2014)
SOURCE: OpenSecrets.org (2015b)

An example of a general election campaign budget for a competitive U.S. House race, or a statewide U.S. Senate or gubernatorial contest, in a moderately expensive media market (see also Chapters 6 and 7) is displayed in Figure 4.8. Overall spending in this hypothetical race approaches $6 million and could reasonably reflect a relatively expensive U.S. House race or an average U.S. Senate or gubernatorial race. The budget estimates provide a sense of how expenditures are disbursed over the course of a yearlong campaign and serve as a guidepost for fundraising goals.

EFFECTS OF CAMPAIGN SPENDING IN ELECTIONS

Scholars have debated the effects of campaign spending on election outcomes for decades. While some argue campaign spending can influence vote shares for both incumbents and challengers (Green and Krasno 1998), especially in close races (Erikson and Palfrey 2000), other researchers find campaign spending only affects challenger performance at the polls (Jacobson 1978, 1990; Jacobson and Carson 2015). Quantifying the impact of spending is methodologically challenging in part because its effects may be endogenous: that is to say, incumbents spend most heavily when they are in danger of defeat. While the question of whether spending affects incumbent performance remains open, there is broader consensus that challenger spending is effective. The political scientist Gary Jacobson argues there are good theoretical reasons to expect challenger

	JAN	FEB	MAR	APR	MAY	JUNE	JULY	AUG	SEPT	OCT	NOV	TOTAL
ADMINISTRATION												
Manager	$10,000	$10,000	$10,000	$10,000	$10,000	$10,000	$10,000	$10,000	$10,000	$10,000	$5,000	$105,000
Deputy	$4,000	$4,000	$4,000	$4,000	$4,000	$4,000	$4,000	$4,000	$4,000	$4,000	$2,000	$42,000
Scheduler	$4,000	$4,000	$4,000	$4,000	$4,000	$4,000	$4,000	$4,000	$4,000	$4,000	$2,000	$42,000
Rent	$5,000	$5,000	$5,000	$5,000	$5,000	$5,000	$5,000	$5,000	$5,000	$5,000	$2,500	$52,500
Copy Machine	$600	$600	$600	$600	$600	$600	$600	$600	$600	$600	$600	$6,600
Computer Equip	$2,000	$2,000	$2,000	$2,000	$2,000	$2,000	$2,000	$2,000	$2,000	$2,000	$2,000	$22,000
Phone/Fax	$750	$750	$750	$750	$750	$750	$750	$750	$750	$750	$750	$8,250
Postage/Courier	$300	$300	$300	$300	$300	$300	$300	$300	$300	$300	$0	$3,000
Office Mgmt/Volunt	$3,500	$3,500	$3,500	$3,500	$3,500	$3,500	$3,500	$3,500	$3,500	$3,500	$1,750	$36,750
Misc Staffing	$0	$0	$0	$2,000	$4,000	$6,000	$6,000	$8,000	$10,000	$20,000	$0	$56,000
Office Supplies	$200	$200	$200	$200	$400	$200	$200	$200	$300	$300	$100	$2,500
Contingency	$2,500	$2,500	$2,500	$2,500	$2,500	$2,500	$2,500	$2,500	$2,500	$20,000	$0	$42,500
SUBTOTAL	*$32,850*	*$32,850*	*$32,850*	*$34,850*	*$37,050*	*$38,850*	*$38,850*	*$40,850*	*$42,950*	*$70,450*	*$16,700*	*$419,100*
												7%
FUNDRAISING												
Finance Director	$7,500	$7,500	$7,500	$7,500	$7,500	$7,500	$7,500	$7,500	$7,500	$7,500	$7,500	$82,500
Compliance	$3,500	$3,500	$3,500	$3,500	$3,500	$3,500	$3,500	$3,500	$3,500	$3,500	$3,500	$38,500
Deputy FD	$3,500	$3,500	$3,500	$3,500	$3,500	$3,500	$3,500	$3,500	$3,500	$3,500	$3,500	$38,500
Event Exp.	$0	$0	$0	$0	$30,000	$30,000	$30,000	$30,000	$30,000	$30,000	$30,000	$210,000
Misc Exp	$1,000	$1,000	$1,000	$1,000	$1,000	$1,000	$1,000	$1,000	$1,000	$1,000	$1,000	$11,000
SUBTOTAL	*$15,500*	*$15,500*	*$15,500*	*$15,500*	*$45,500*	*$45,500*	*$45,500*	*$45,500*	*$45,500*	*$45,500*	*$45,500*	*$380,500*
												7%
MEDIA												
TV/Radio Prod	$0	$0	$0	$0	$0	$50,000	$25,000	$25,000	$40,000	$25,000	$25,000	$190,000
TV/Radio Time	$0	$0	$0	$0	$0	$0	$0	$2,000,000	$500,000	$500,000	$50,000	$3,050,000

												Total
Media Consultant Fe	$5,000	$5,000	$5,000	$5,000	$5,000	$5,000	$5,000	$5,000	$5,000	$5,000	$5,000	$55,000
Press Secretary	$6,000	$6,000	$6,000	$6,000	$6,000	$6,000	$6,000	$6,000	$6,000	$6,000	$6,000	$66,000
Web/Online/Social	$10,000	$10,000	$1,000	$1,000	$1,000	$1,000	$1,000	$100,000	$100,000	$100,000	$20,000	$246,000
SUBTOTAL	*$21,000*	*$21,000*	*$12,000*	*$12,000*	*$11,000*	*$62,000*	*$37,000*	*$651,000*	*$2,037,000*	*$636,000*	*$106,000*	*$3,607,000*
												62%
MAIL												
Mail Consultant	$1,000	$1,000	$1,000	$1,000	$1,000	$1,000	$1,000	$1,000	$1,000	$1,000	$1,000	$11,000
Printing/Postage	$5,000	$5,000	$5,000	$5,000	$5,000	$5,000	$5,000	$5,000	$5,000	$250,000	$25,000	$320,000
Mail Expenses	$5,000	$5,000	$5,000	$5,000	$5,000	$5,000	$5,000	$5,000	$5,000	$25,000	$10,000	$80,000
SUBTOTAL	*$11,000*	*$11,000*	*$11,000*	*$11,000*	*$11,000*	*$11,000*	*$11,000*	*$11,000*	*$11,000*	*$276,000*	*$36,000*	*$411,000*
												7%
FIELD												
Field Director	$6,000	$6,000	$6,000	$6,000	$6,000	$6,000	$6,000	$6,000	$6,000	$6,000	$6,000	$66,000
Voter Lists	$0	$0	$0	$0	$0	$0	$0	$0	$0	$5,000	$0	$5,000
Field Operation	$5,000	$5,000	$5,000	$7,500	$7,500	$7,500	$10,000	$15,000	$5,000	$30,000	$200,000	$297,500
GOTV Call	$0	$0	$0	$0	$0	$0	$0	$0	$0	$200,000	$0	$200,000
ID Call	$0	$0	$0	$0	$0	$0	$0	$0	$0	$75,000	$0	$75,000
SUBTOTAL	*$11,000*	*$11,000*	*$11,000*	*$13,500*	*$13,500*	*$13,500*	*$16,000*	*$21,000*	*$11,000*	*$316,000*	*$206,000*	*$643,500*
												11%
RESEARCH												
Polling/Focus Grp	$0	$36,000	$40,000	$0	$15,000	$15,000	$50,000	$15,000	$0	$80,000	$0	$251,000
Pollster Fee	$5,000	$5,000	$5,000	$5,000	$5,000	$5,000	$5,000	$5,000	$5,000	$5,000	$5,000	$55,000
Opposition Research	$0	$20,000	$0	$0	$0	$5,000	$0	$0	$0	$0	$0	$25,000
SUBTOTAL	*$5,000*	*$61,000*	*$45,000*	*$5,000*	*$20,000*	*$25,000*	*$55,000*	*$20,000*	*$5,000*	*$85,000*	*$5,000*	*$331,000*
												6%
TOTAL	**$96,350**	**$152,350**	**$127,350**	**$89,350**	**$124,050**	**$190,850**	**$170,850**	**$791,450**	**$2,205,350**	**$1,428,950**	**$415,200**	**$5,792,100**

Figure 4.8 Sample Campaign Budget

spending to exert a greater effect on outcomes than incumbent expenditures (Jacobson 2006). He notes,

> Incumbents usually begin the campaign seasons with a large advantage in familiarity which, if retained, guarantees comfortable re-election . . . voters are very unlikely to turn them out without a good reason and an acceptable replacement, and it is usually up to the challenger's campaign to inform them of both the reason and the alternative. Diminishing returns apply to campaigning, so marginal returns on campaign activities are smaller for incumbents (coming on top of past campaigns and extensive efforts to cultivate constituents) than for challengers who have not previously engaged voters at this level. (Jacobson 2015: 6)

In other words, increased campaign spending should favor challengers simply since they have more room to increase their support among voters than incumbents do. The type of election and electoral context may also determine the extent to which campaign spending matters for election outcomes. Spending may matter more in local elections that are nonpartisan and feature new candidates because these environments lack party cues and prior information about candidates that can help stimulate voter engagement. Candidates in these contexts may need to spend more money to inform citizens of their positions, engage them, and turn them out on Election Day. Conversely, spending may matter less in contexts where such information is more readily available and candidates are well known to voters, although it no doubt remains important, especially in highly competitive races (Jacobson 2015). As I noted in Chapter 1, Donald Trump managed to do quite well in the 2016 GOP presidential nomination race despite being outspent by most of his leading rivals (Confessore and Cohen 2016).

Many advocates for campaign finance reform have suggested that limits on campaign spending may spur electoral competition. However, it is difficult to determine whether campaign spending causes or is the result of electoral competition. Some political scientists have provided evidence that limitations on donations might make elections more competitive, but these changes do not necessarily produce more losses for incumbents. Nevertheless, lower contribution limits do seem to lead to smaller margins of victory (Stratmann and Aparicio-Castillo 2006). Public financing programs do not seem to improve competition either, although they help limit the amount of time candidates must devote to fundraising (Francia and Herrnson 2003; Mayer et al. 2006). In 2012, the Campaign Finance Institute reported that the average Senate incumbent who won election with less than 60% of the vote spent almost $13 million, whereas their challengers spent just over $10 million. For incumbents who won with more than 60% of the vote, incumbent senators outspent their challengers to a much greater degree, with incumbents spending just over $7 million and challengers spending just under $1.5 million (Campaign Finance Institute 2014). Logically, it makes sense that more competitive races might spur greater spending by incumbents and challengers and that incumbents have less motivation to raise more money the more assured they are of victory. At this point, however, it remains questionable whether increased spending limitations would strengthen electoral competition, especially given the rise of new sets of independent expenditure groups in the political arena.

OUTSIDE ACTORS: ISSUE ADVOCACY, INDEPENDENT EXPENDITURE GROUPS, AND SUPER PACs

Issue advocacy organizations are political groups formed to engage in advancing (or opposing) specific issues, rather than in "express advocacy" for specific candidates. Issue advocacy organizations can serve as a conduit for candidate support as long as the "magic words" of direct support or opposition (e.g., "vote for," "elect," "support," and "defeat") are not used in their appeals to voters. There are several types of advocacy groups in the United States. Some of the more common types include 501(c) groups, 527 groups, and PACs. Each group is organized under a different section of the U.S. Internal Revenue Code. 501(c) groups are nonprofit, tax-exempt organizations. There are several subtypes under this heading including 501(c)(3), 501(c)(4), 501(c)(5), and 501(c)(6), each of which has different requirements and can engage in different degrees and types of political activity based on those requirements. 501(c)(3) groups operate for religious, charitable, scientific, or educational purposes. A 501(c)(3) is not technically permitted to engage in political activities, although in some cases they may be allowed to participate in voter registration activities. 501(c)(4) groups are commonly called "social welfare" organizations and may engage in political activities as long as these activities are not their primary purpose. Similar rules apply to 501(c)(5) organizations (labor and agricultural groups) and 501(c)(6) organizations (business leagues, chambers of commerce, real estate boards and boards of trade).

527 groups are tax-exempt organizations and are allowed under Section 527 of the Internal Revenue Code. These groups' main purpose is to organize voters, raise money for political causes, and advocate for specific political issues. Many 527s "are advocacy groups trying to influence federal elections through voter mobilization efforts and so-called issue ads that tout or criticize a candidate's record. 527s must report their contributors and expenditures to the IRS, unless they already file identical information at the state or local level."[4] Currently, the FEC only requires a 527 group to file regular disclosure reports if it is a political party or PAC that engages in either activities expressly advocating the election or defeat of a federal candidate or in electioneering communications. Unless the 527 organization meets this specific definition, it is required only to register with the Internal Revenue Service or with the state in which it is based. Despite the restrictions on directly advocating for a specific candidate, the ability of 527s to raise and spend unlimited amounts of soft money makes them potent political

---

[4]OpenSecrets.org, "Expenditure Breakdown—Federally Focused Organizations," OpenSecrets.org. Available at http://www.opensecrets.org/527s/527cmtes.php?level=E&cycle=2008.

forces. During the 2014 midterms, the top-spending 527 groups included Next-Gen Climate Action, dedicated to addressing climate change, which spent just over $23 million. Another group topping the list was ActBlue, a pro-Democratic organization dedicated to helping small-dollar donors allocate their money in effective ways, which spent about $14.5 million in the 2014 cycle. The College Republican National Committee is a youth organization committed to helping elect Republican candidates and promoting the Republican agenda; it spent nearly $13 million during the 2014 midterm cycle (OpenSecrets.org 2015e). In recent elections, as I will discuss, the greatest expenditures by 527s have come from groups focused on state and local politics. In 2014, 527 groups spent just over $520 million in total on these elections, compared with around $200 million on federal elections (OpenSecrets.org 2015e).

PACs are often the political arm of organized commercial interests. In the United States, most PACs represent business, labor, or ideological interest groups. Unlike 527 and 501(c) groups, PACs are unable to raise soft money. Instead, PACs operate under a system in which they can spend limited hard-money contributions for the express purpose of electing or defeating candidates. PACs contribute money directly to parties and candidates, although contribution limits apply. In the 2013–2014 cycle, PACs were permitted to give up to $5,000 to a candidate for each election (primary or general) and up to $15,000 to a party each calendar year. Similarly, PACs are limited in the amount of money they can accept because individuals, other PACs, and party committees may only contribute $5,000 per year to a given PAC.[5]

In the 2008 election cycle, outside soft-money groups raised and spent an estimated $400 million (Campaign Finance Institute 2008). Federal 527 groups spent an estimated $202 million in 2008 (down from $426 million in 2004). However, 501(c) organizations, which, as I discussed previously, are subject to far less scrutiny and regulation, were far more active in the cycle, and helped to close the partisan divide in spending by outside groups that had disproportionately favored Democrats in 2004. Spending by 501(c) groups tripled in 2008, reaching nearly $200 million (Campaign Finance Institute 2008). Interestingly, Democratic-oriented 527s outspent their GOP-oriented counterparts by a margin of nearly 3 to 1 in 2008 ($143 million to $56 million, respectively), much like in 2004, but spending by 501(c) groups favored Republicans by a similar margin in 2008 ($142 million to $54 million, respectively) (Campaign Finance Institute 2008). Figure 4.9 shows that overall spending by outside groups has generally been on the rise in recent years, especially after the 2010 *Citizens United* decision.

In contemporary American politics, issue advocacy groups are also active in nonfederal and noncandidate elections across the country. As an example, consider the role of issue advocacy in a statewide issue—same-sex marriage—that was up for a vote in California in 2008. In 2000, California voters passed, by

---

[5]*Ibid.*

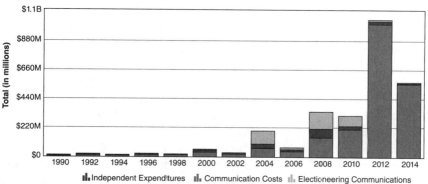

Figure 4.9 Outside Spending by Cycle, Excluding Party Committees
SOURCE: OpenSecrets.org (2015g)

referendum, a ban on same-sex marriage, but the state supreme court overturned that statute, making same-sex marriage legal in California as of June 16, 2008. California voters were asked to reconsider the issue of same-sex marriage as a ballot measure (Proposition 8) in November 2008. In what became a hotly contested campaign, issue advocacy groups took center stage. The main organization supporting the ban was Protect Marriage, whereas Equality California was the main opposition group. These and allied groups conducted large-scale mass media advertising campaigns and canvassed, called, and contacted voters, drove them to the polls, held rallies and protests, and distributed campaign literature in support of their respective views. According to campaign filings, groups on both sides of the issue spent a total of more than $83 million on the Proposition 8 initiative. The final tally showed that opponents of Proposition 8 raised $43.3 million, whereas the measure's sponsors raised $39.9 million (Leff 2008, 2009). These totals dwarfed those of previous same-sex marriage initiatives. Between 2004 and 2006, 22 such measures were on ballots around the country, and donations to all of them combined totaled $31.4 million, according to the nonpartisan National Institute on Money in State Politics (Morain and Garrison 2008).

Religious communities were some of the strongest advocates for Proposition 8. As Election Day approached, Protect Marriage issued an urgent appeal and managed to raise more than $5 million in a matter of days, including a $1 million donation from Alan C. Ashton, the grandson of a former president of the Mormon Church. The funds were used primarily to finance an advertising campaign that many analysts believe succeeded in boosting support for the measure (McKinley and Johnson 2008). For many Mormons, Proposition 8 was "a kind of firewall to be held at all costs" (McKinley and Johnson 2008). Describing the support of the Mormon community for the ballot measure, Michael R. Otterson, the managing director of public affairs for the Mormon Church said, "we've spoken out on other issues, we've spoken out on abortion, we've spoken out on those other kinds of things. . . . But we don't get involved to the degree we did on this" (McKinley and Johnson 2008).

Mormons were not the only religious group involved; the Roman Catholic Archbishop of San Francisco suggested that many Catholics, evangelical Christians, conservative black and Latino pastors, and a variety of other ethnic groups with strong religious ties were involved in the "struggle to protect traditional marriage against what they saw as an encroachment" (McKinley and Johnson 2008). Other grassroots groups also supported the measure, holding rallies and engaging in other forms of outreach to voters.

Opposition to Proposition 8 came from a variety of traditional Democratic contributors, including party leaders, Hollywood elites, and labor unions, as well as California-based businesses. The California Teachers' Association, the teacher's union organization of California, donated more than $1.25 million to help defeat Proposition 8. Similarly, a group of San Diego–based biotechnology executives banded together to oppose Proposition 8, saying the proposed constitutional ban on gay marriage would be bad for business. These executives, along with other technology companies such as Google and Apple, publicly voiced opposition to Proposition 8, claiming that the ballot measure would make California less appealing to gay workers and put their industry at a competitive disadvantage (Somers 2008). Commercial enterprises including Google, Apple, Pacific Gas & Electric, Levi Strauss, and AT&T also provided funds to oppose Proposition 8 (Leff 2008). In the end, voters passed the measure with 52% support.

This example clearly demonstrates how critical issue advocacy organizations can be in advancing or thwarting issue-based campaigns in the United States. Support for or against social change in American can be galvanized, often quickly, and interest groups can amass vast resources to conduct large-scale, highly advanced campaigns to mobilize and persuade voters. Even as the regulations that govern issue advocacy in statewide settings vary across jurisdictions, interest groups are highly capable of getting involved and exerting a significant impact on election and referendum outcomes.

Since 2010, and spurred in part by *Citizens United*, a different type of independent expenditure group—commonly known as super PACs—has exploded onto the scene. These organizations can collect money in unlimited sums from individuals as well as labor unions and corporations, provided they do not donate money directly to candidates or coordinate with them in any way. As of March 2015, there were 1,340 groups designated as super PACs, reporting total expenditures of about $350 million during the 2014 election cycle alone. These included groups such as the Senate and House Majority PAC, liberal-leaning groups dedicated to electing ideologically similar candidates, and the Freedom Partners Action Fund, a conservative-leaning group that supports candidates who promote free markets and economic liberty (OpenSecrets.org 2015c).

Overall, campaign finance in American elections has shifted drastically over the past few decades, in large part because of the rise of these independent expenditure groups. In the wake of the *Citizens United* decision in particular, candidates have likely been spurred to raise even more money because the growth in independent spending increases the likelihood that candidates will be attacked by outside groups. These changes have also had implications for the extent to which campaigns help to uphold democratic principles.

CONSEQUENCES FOR DEMOCRACY

Since the 1970s, changes in the regulatory landscape of campaign finance in American elections have altered the context in which campaigns operate and required them to adapt, which in turn have had consequences for the extent to which campaign conduct helps uphold democratic norms. After landmark Supreme Court decisions such as *Buckley v. Valeo, Citizens United v. Federal Election Commission*, and *McCutcheon v. Federal Election Commission*, all of which eased restrictions on election contributions, not only have campaigns had an incentive to chase after more money, but also it has become all but necessary for them to increase their fundraising goals to keep up in the race for political resources.

Over time, campaign finance in the United States has been on a path toward increasing deregulation, despite the persistent efforts of reformers in the 1970s, the late 1990s, and the early 2000s. The BCRA is an excellent example of the unintended consequences that reforms can have on American elections. Many observers believed the act would weaken the prevalence of unlimited soft-money contributions to political parties, which were typically directly solicited by candidates for federal office, and encourage them to rely instead on a larger number of small donors. In a defense of the reform published as a letter to the editor in the *Washington Post* in October 2004, the reform's authors contended, "Ending the practice of the president, party leaders, and members of Congress soliciting huge donations from corporations, unions and wealthy individuals improved the system. And, despite predictions to the contrary, the parties have thrived in the new hard-money world" (McCain and Feingold 2004: A22). Ultimately, however, the BCRA shifted the flow of money from political parties to outside groups such as 527 organizations, groups that are subject to less regulation from the FEC than are parties themselves. McCain and Feingold saw this as a problem with the FEC, not with the reform itself. They argued that the Federal Election Commission's failure to properly regulate 527s under existing federal election law has allowed wealthy individuals to pour millions into this election. But that failure does not change the fact that McCain–Feingold succeeded in ending the corrupting practice of politicians asking for $100,000 or $500,000 checks (McCain and Feingold 2004).

The BCRA is illustrative of the debate over the extent to which campaign finance reforms help to improve American democracy and promote the representation and engagement of American citizens. After all, campaigns, donors, and other political actors themselves do not sit idly by after reforms are adopted; instead, they use whatever options they have to adapt to the reforms in ways that may or may not promote democratic norms. The shift in the funneling of money from parties to 527 groups after the passage of the BCRA is illustrative of this type of adaptation. Donors found another way to exercise influence in politics and created a new set of actors that campaigns had to consider in the race for political resources. In the October 31, 2004, edition of the *Denver Post*, a week before the first presidential election following the reform, David Harwood argued, "The McCain–Feingold campaign finance reform law—much debated and ballyhooed—has been an ineffectual speed bump in the chase of money after politicians. The so-called reforms have done nothing at all to alleviate the influence of big money in politics and very well may have exacerbated it" (Harwood 2004: E 04; as cited in Malbin 2006: 1).

Campaigns are capitalizing on the opportunities ushered in by recent reforms. Because candidates still face limitations on the amount of money they can accept directly from any one individual, they are required to court a broader, more representative swath of the public in their search for financial resources. Through various fundraising events and with the efforts of dedicated volunteers reaching out for donations, candidates can engage directly and indirectly with citizens, informing them of their policy positions and encouraging them to donate and participate. Indeed, the number of citizens donating to campaigns has increased in recent decades, as has the proportion of small contributions. In the 2008 election, 21% of total individual contributions to John McCain (in the pre-nomination phase) and 24% of contributions to Barack Obama (in the primaries and general election combined) came from donors whose contributions aggregated to $200 or less, demonstrating small donors play an central role in financing contemporary campaigns (Campaign Finance Institute 2010). Obama made a point of explicitly courting small donors in addition to wealthy ones during his 2008 and 2012 presidential bids, demonstrating that campaigns can be won with the aid of small donations as well as large ones. An analysis by the Campaign Finance Institute revealed that small donors played a significant role in funding Obama's 2012 reelection campaign. Fully $216 million, or 28% of the $782 million in individual contributions raised by the Obama campaign in 2012, came from donors who contributed $200 or less. By comparison, $59 million, or 12% of the $494 million in total individual contributions raised by Romney's 2012 campaign (Campaign Finance Institute 2013), came from these small donors. The Obama campaign reportedly had 4.4 million unique donors in 2012, and the Campaign Finance Institute estimates that this figure includes more than 3.6 million small donors (Campaign Finance Institute 2013). From a normative perspective, this type of campaign strategy leads to engagement among a broader swath of Americans and, if employed more widely by other candidates for office in the future, may make elected officials less beholden to big-money interests and more likely to represent their constituents' preferences. From the perspective of campaign strategy, small-dollar donations, now typically collected electronically, also provide campaigns with something perhaps just as valuable: supporters' contact information. E-mail addresses, phone numbers, and mailing addresses can be used to call donors, knock on their doors, encourage them to volunteer, and target them with personalized online ads (Levinthal 2012).

Of course, there are limits to the argument that the drive to raise more and more money helps promote democratic norms. Although opponents of more stringent campaign finance regulations often suggest that they would violate the First Amendment—indeed, this was the argument made by the Supreme Court in the *Citizens United* ruling—there is evidence suggesting that limiting political spending does not actually limit political speech (Dowling et al. 2012). In this case, the controversy seems to focus on one's interpretation of the breadth of the First Amendment right to free speech.

Even if candidates increasingly solicit donations from large swaths of small-dollar donors, these donors may still not be representative of the electorate as a whole. Individuals who donate to political campaigns tend to be wealthier and more educated than other citizens on average (Brady et al. 1995). Nevertheless, although donors are not necessarily representative of the electorate in terms of their socioeconomic characteristics, they may not be entirely different across the ideological spectrum. Evidence from Panagopoulos and Bergan (2004) suggests that between 2000 and 2004 the number of individual and first-time contributors grew, noting that enhanced participation likely caused a more ideologically representative donor pool.

Nevertheless, candidates, once elected to office, may be beholden to the preferences of their wealthier donors. In the 2016 Democratic presidential nomination race, Bernie Sanders made criticisms along these lines a central line of attack against his rival, Hillary Clinton. In 2012, the top 100 individual donors to super PACs represented only 1.0% of all individual donors to super PACs in that election cycle, but delivered 67% of all the money that went to the groups. In the 2014 midterm elections, the top 1% of donors contributed even more—69%—of all money that went to super PACs (OpenSecrets.org 2015g). Oftentimes, individuals donate to specific groups and candidates in an effort to influence policy on issues important to them. This kind of concentrated spending cannot be ignored. Although groups supporting the Republican Party initially dominated outside spending following the *Citizens United* decision, excessive spending by outside groups has become a feature of both parties and their individual supporters. In 2014, Democrats topped the list of super PAC mega donors. In this cycle, Thomas Steyer was the top donor to super PACs, contributing $74.2 million of his money to his own super PAC, NextGen Climate Action, as well as other super PACs that supported Democratic candidates for the U.S. Senate. On the Republican side, the brothers Charles and David Koch are two prominent and extremely wealthy businessmen who have helped create a network of nonprofit groups that control hundreds of millions of dollars that support campaigns to advance their libertarian ideas and support free-market Republican candidates. The Koch brothers have grown controversial in part because they channel much of their money into 527 nonprofit groups, which do not have to identify their donors. Some super PACs benefit candidates from both parties. For example, the former New York mayor, Michael Bloomberg, has donated more than $20 million dollars to his super PAC, Independence USA PAC, which supports Democrats and Republicans at the federal and state levels (Blumenthal and Bycoffe 2014).

Evidence that political contributions directly influence legislators' votes is scarce (Ansolabehere, de Figueiredo and Synder 2003), but recent scholarship reveals elected officials are more responsive to the preferences of more affluent Americans. Although some scholars find few policy differences across income levels (Enns and Wlezien 2011), other studies find lawmakers support policies that align with wealthier citizens' views when their preferences diverge from those held by the average citizen (Gilens and Page 2014; Bartels 2008; Gilens 2012). This is not to say elected officials routinely ignore average citizens' preferences, but that they appear to represent those views primarily when they happen to align with those of more affluent citizens. Studies also suggest legislators may be more accessible to donors (Kalla and Broockman 2015) and exert more effort on behalf of their policy positions in committees (Hall and Wayman 1990). It is difficult to parse out which comes first, donor preferences or candidate preferences (Hall and Wayman 1990), but it seems likely that the donors candidates must solicit for donations to get elected and stay in office do exert some influence on the decisions they make as legislators.

In contemporary American elections, the most troubling phenomenon in terms of its influence on democratic norms seems to be the rise of independent expenditure groups discussed earlier in this chapter. Even regular interest groups and PACs appear to potentially hinder the representation of the citizens. Gilens and Page (2014) show that, as was the case with the preferences of wealthy citizens, when the preferences of interest groups diverge from the preferences of the average citizen, elected officials are more likely to follow the preferences of interest groups. Although certain states have stricter limitations on the amount of money that can be donated to candidates, even there, these groups manage to be effective. Interest groups seem to inevitably find new ways to influence elections beyond directly contributing to candidates, such as engaging in direct contact with voters, endorsing candidates, and donating money to political parties (Hogan 2005).

The regulations surrounding some of the newer independent expenditure groups also have direct implications for democratic norms. For example, because 501(c)4's are not required to disclose their donors, citizens are not fully informed about the funding sources behind the political ads they are seeing during an election cycle. Although candidates cannot directly coordinate with super PACs, if they hold policy positions that are not favorable to wealthy donors interested in contributing to a super PAC, it is plausible that candidates may shift their policy positions to earn the indirect support of such donors. The proliferation of such groups may also further affect the actual policy information citizens receive from candidates. In an increasingly cluttered field of political advertisements, often supported by organizations with generic and positive-sounding names such as Americans for Responsible Solutions or American Crossroads, citizens may be less likely to be able to discern the relevant information they need to make informed decisions about candidates.

CONCLUSION

The Supreme Court decision in the *Citizens United* case extended free speech rights to corporations, allowing them for the first time to spend money as they wished in elections at all levels under the protection of the First Amendment. This decision, alongside the court's decision in *McCutcheon vs. Federal Election Commission*, has raised questions over the purview of the amendment. The First Amendment is meant to protect free speech, but opponents of these rulings question whether spending money should be considered a form of speech. It is also unclear how far to extend this line of argumentation, and many observers anticipate free speech considerations could eventually end up dismantling individual contribution limits altogether.

Opponents of campaign finance regulation are in favor of the precedent set by Supreme Court rulings like *Buckley v. Valeo*, *Citizens United v. Federal Election Commission*, and *McCutcheon v. Federal Election Commission*. Bradley Smith, a policy analyst at the libertarian-leaning Cato Institute and a professor at Capital University Law School in Ohio, contends that campaign finance regulation that limits contributions is actually undemocratic, arguing that it creates disincentives for challengers and political outsiders to get involved in politics, dampens grassroots political participation, and distorts the political process in favor of the more wealthy and powerful (Smith 1995). On the other side of the argument, advocates and researchers at the Brennan Center for Justice at the New York University School of Law argue that unfettered campaign spending is the true threat to American democracy, giving power to "a handful of special interests" that "threaten to dominate political funding, often through super PACs and shadowy nonprofits" (Brennan Center for Justice 2015). The consequence, they contend, is that public trust in government has dropped precipitously, which has implications for the extent to which the average citizen is interested in and engaged in the political process.

Meaningful attempts at reform that directly try to curb the amount of money in politics will likely not be accomplished without a major reversal of the Supreme Court's recent campaign finance decisions. Any laws passed by Congress attempting to limit spending would be ruled unconstitutional based on the precedents set by these decisions. For now, the Supreme Court has determined that free speech is an integral component of democracy and that limiting campaign spending violates essential First Amendment rights. As I will discuss more in depth in Chapter 12, reformers have set their sights on more attainable goals aimed at requiring the disclosure of all contributors to elections. Another problem with current disclosure laws is that they make it hard for the average citizen to track who is spending money; even the data that are available from the FEC are difficult to interpret. Advocates at the Brennan Center for Justice have proposed making the tracking of campaign donations more "consumer friendly" by developing websites and apps where donations are easy to find and readily available (Basseti 2015). For example, Open Secrets' app, Dollarocracy, pictured in Figure 4.10, provides easily accessible data on contribution profiles for every member of Congress and every major industry and interest group. It also features spending and contribution profiles for every congressional race.

But some reformers feel that transparency through disclosure is not enough and, in fact, may be contributing to the problem because candidates are all but guaranteed to have a clear picture of where the money is coming from and still be motivated to focus more on the preferences of wealthy donors than on the public at large. Instead, it has been suggested that all campaign contributions be made anonymous, that is, to let wealthy and nonwealthy donors alike spend money on politics but not take credit for their donations. If it were difficult or impossible for candidates to confirm the sources and amounts of contributions to their campaigns, they would have less incentive to follow the contributions with policy favors or obtain contributions through threats or intimidation (Levine and Johnston 2014).

The landscape of campaign finance in American politics has changed dramatically over the past two decades. Candidates and donors on all sides of the political spectrum have adapted their strategies in the wake of the major changes in campaign finance we have discussed in this chapter. The cost of running a campaign goes up with every election cycle, and there has been a proliferation of outside expenditures by a diverse array of groups. It has become extremely difficult to implement effective campaigns without extensive amounts of money and even support from outside groups. Observers have become increasingly concerned

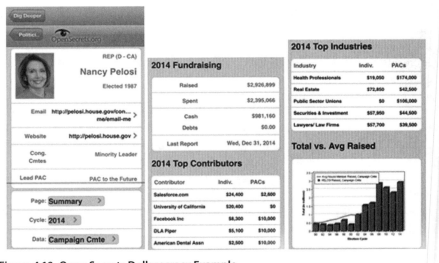

Figure 4.10 Open Secrets Dollarocracy Example
SOURCE: Open Secrets Dollarocracy App

about the implications of these developments for candidate behavior and key principles of democratic representation. Given the recent decisions by the U.S. Supreme Court in the *Citizens United and McCutcheon* cases, and absent new restrictions on campaign contributions and expenditures and regulations on independent groups, these concerns are likely to become exacerbated.

KEY TERMS

501(c) groups

527 groups

Bipartisan Campaign
   Reform Act (BCRA)

Buckley v. Valeo

Bundlers

Citizens United v.
   Federal Election
   Commission

Express advocacy

Federal Election
   Commission

Federal Election
   Campaign Act
   (FECA)

Ideologues

Incidentals

Intimates

Investors

Issue advocacy

Matching funds

McCutcheon v. Federal
   Election
   Commission

Political action
   committee

Public financing

Super PAC

SUGGESTED READINGS

Gilens, M. 2012. *Affluence and Influence: Economic Inequality and Political Power in America*. Princeton, NJ: Princeton University Press.

La Raja, R. 2008. *Small Change: Money, Political Parties and Campaign Finance Reform*. Ann Arbor, MI: University of Michigan Press.

Magleby, D. B. 2014. *Financing the 2012 Election*. Washington, D.C.: Brookings Institution Press.

CHAPTER 5

Campaign Strategy

In late 2011, President Obama faced a harsh political landscape as he approached his 2012 reelection bid. Unemployment nationally remained fairly high, at 8.5%. Most polls showed his approval rating was below 50% and a majority of voters thought the country was going in the wrong direction. In addition, polls suggested that Republicans were far more excited about the upcoming elections than Democrats and that support for Obama among likely voters in most swing states was eroding.

In developing the campaign strategy for his reelection bid, Obama and his team had to shift the campaign's message away from the lackluster economic recovery and the president's dismal approval ratings. To do so, they developed a campaign strategy designed to paint the Republican presidential nomination race as increasingly ideological, suggesting that the GOP had pushed its platform too far to the ideological extreme to be taken seriously in the general election. At the same time, the Obama campaign did not try to move attention entirely from the faltering economy; instead, echoing a message honed in Obama's 2008 campaign during the economic meltdown, the Obama team shifted the frame of the debate to focus on the notion that all citizens deserve a "fair shot" at the American dream (Dickerson 2011). The message encapsulated a sharp and effective contrast against Mitt Romney, the GOP nominee, who was viewed by many as a wealthy businessman indifferent to the problems facing average citizens, and especially poor and middle-class voters across the country.

The Obama campaign did what any well-run campaign should do when developing its strategy: it paid attention to the broader context of the campaign and election cycle, understood where President Obama stood in relationship to this context and to his opponent, and crafted a message that played to his strengths and Romney's weaknesses. It understood it was necessary to shift perceptions of Obama from a president who was unable to turn the country around to one who was committed to fighting against the perceived source of the economic crisis in the first place: economic greed. Obama may not have been able to bring about economic recovery or to significantly reduce unemployment in his first four years in office, but he understood the value of communicating a message of fair access to the American dream to voters, a message that he could then effectively leverage against Romney and the Republican Party.

Developing an effective campaign strategy is akin to creating a road map that candidates can follow to victory. The map outlines what campaigns ultimately must accomplish, detailing the strategies and tactics that will help achieve victory. A goal is a broad outcome, such as improving the public's perception of a candidate or raising a certain amount of money. Strategies are the approaches campaigns will take to achieve their goals on the road toward winning an election. In other words, a campaign strategy describes, "*what* is to be done, *when* it should be done, and *how* the work will be implemented" (Burton and Shea 2010: 25; see also Beaudry and Scheaffer 1986: 44). In this chapter, we will focus mainly on four aspects of campaign strategy: resource allocation, voter targeting, message development, and timing and sequence. Tactics are the tools campaigns use to achieve campaign goals and implement strategy.

Candidates and their campaign staffers must have a firm understanding of roadblocks they might face on the way to achieving their goals and the political landscape in which they are running. Campaign strategies are almost always driven by two essential questions: Who will vote for me, and why will he or she do so? (Sides et al. 2014). The political scientist David Winston (2013) defines strategy as "achieving a desired outcome using a structured approach based on understanding existing and potential environment elements and your opponent's potential strategies . . . crafting a successful strategy takes good instincts, an understanding of politics, historical context, and detailed quantifiable and qualitative research" (24–25). In other words, developing a campaign strategy is all about taking into account the context in which a campaign is operating.

There is no one-size-fits-all strategy for contemporary campaigns. Although there are certain broad-stroke principles one can adhere to when developing strategy, the actual implementation of these principles will vary greatly depending on where the campaign is taking place and at what level of election it is running. The decisions a campaign makes change based on the opponent, the office he or she is running for, and the voting history, partisan makeup, and demographic makeup of the electorate, in addition to factors like the rules and regulations that apply to the particular race. In light of the virtually unlimited array of possible electoral contexts, the development of a successful campaign strategy depends greatly on the research conducted about that environment. Candidates and their staffers must answer several important questions: What is the partisan, ideological, and demographic makeup of the district? What types of messages might be most effective for this group of voters? What is the evidence for this? How does my opponent stack up? Are there things about his or her past, track record, or character that might be useful in developing my own campaign strategy? What are some of the rules and regulations I must account for when developing a campaign strategy (Burton and Shea 2010)?

The goal of this chapter is to outline how campaigns typically develop campaign strategy and set in motion plans to implement it using a wide range of tactics. I examine how campaigns determine what they are trying to accomplish and how they are going to achieve those goals. I first discuss the major factors that almost all campaigns must consider when formulating strategy. I then turn to the nuts and bolts of strategy development and use the example of strategy development in presidential elections to illustrate how context affects campaign strategy. Next, I discuss the types of research campaigns must conduct, highlighting the roles of voter targeting and polling as means of developing effective strategy. Specifically, I focus on the use of demographic and electoral targeting based on partisan identification and previous voting behavior, as well as the rise of microtargeting. I also discuss the use of opposition research and the context in which this strategy is most likely to be effective, as well as how all of these factors play into the successful development of a campaign message. Finally, I bring our discussion back to the consequences these strategic decisions have for democratic norms of representation, information, and engagement.

CAMPAIGN RESEARCH: WHAT IS IMPORTANT?

Constituency research is an essential first step in formulating campaign strategy. Survey research and prior election results can be marshaled to provide campaigns with information about the relevant electorates in their districts. Because campaigns do not necessarily need to win every vote, and because resources are scarce, campaign efforts must be prioritized. A well-crafted campaign strategy will rely on turning out a candidate's base and winning over enough undecided or persuadable voters to swing the election in the candidate's favor.

Winston (2014) outlines five steps that candidates and their campaign managers must take to have a strong change of success. Although it may seem like it should go without saying, campaigns must first develop a desired outcome. For many campaigns, this is as simple as setting a winning percentage, that is, a percentage of the vote more than 50%. However, some candidates seek more than a simple victory. They may instead have the goal of winning with a mandate, that is, by a significant margin. A politician with a mandate has greater legitimacy to govern because he or she can claim the support of a broader swath of constituents.

But goals go beyond merely setting a winning vote percentage. Campaigns must ask the right questions and conduct the right research to define what it will take to achieve the goal. To do this, they must develop situational awareness. This involves keeping track of party registration and the identification of a candidate's base, the previous turnout and vote choices, demographic makeup, and which issues are most important to voters. This situational awareness can be subject to changes in issue salience, the national brand of one's party during a given election year, and unexpected shifts in the broader political environment. In the lead-up to the 2012 elections, for example, the death of the U.S. ambassador J. Christopher Stevens in an attack on an American diplomatic compound in Libya, resulted in political upheaval for the Obama campaign, forcing Obama to go on the defensive after Mitt Romney and other Republicans placed heavy blame on his administration for the attacks (Rubin 2012).

Campaigns must also pay close attention to their opponents. Opposition research can help bring to the fore both an opponent's strengths but also vulnerabilities that can be marshaled for effective attacks or rebuttals. But it is also necessary to remain attentive to the opposition's strategies, which are not generally disclosed. Instead, campaigns must look for hints or indications about the opposition's strategy from statements and issues emphasized on the campaign trail or by tracking and analyzing advertising or mobilization activities.

Situational awareness, knowledge of an opponent's strategy, and defining a winning coalition all help candidates to develop a strategic communications plan and are part and parcel of a successful campaign strategy. An effective communications plan includes details about both strategy and tactics. Strategic components integrate an understanding of the political environment, insights about the opponent's strengths and weaknesses, details about effective message development, and voter targets. Tactics are the means by which a strategy is pursued, for example, how a campaign's message gets delivered. This typically involves how messages reach voters, through tools such as direct mail, phone banks, and advertising, some of which I will discuss in further detail in Chapter 6. As Winston notes, "tactics are the tools to build the house. Strategy creates the context [reason] for tactical decisions. Don't buy an ad because you think you should buy an ad. Do it for a reason" (2014: 35).

CONTEXT MATTERS: CAMPAIGN STRATEGY IN PRESIDENTIAL ELECTIONS

In presidential elections, the U.S. Constitution stipulates that general election victors must secure a majority (currently 270) votes in the Electoral College. Electoral votes in all states but Maine and Nebraska are allocated using a winner-take-all method, which means that the candidate who wins the popular vote is rewarded with all of the state's electoral votes. Given the consistency in voting patterns over successive elections in states across the country, candidates can be strategic in allocating resources mainly to those states in which the outcome is not a foregone conclusion. Emphasis is placed almost entirely on battleground states, with virtually no campaigning done in states that are deemed to be safe wins for one candidate or another. This means that presidential candidates and their campaign teams must not only make decisions on how to best allocate their resources, but also develop messages that will resonate with voters in a particular state. Thus, issues important to voters in a battleground state may become part of the campaign's message, whereas issues important to voters in nonbattleground states may receive little or no mention from the candidates and their campaigns. Figure 5.1 shows the allocation of ad spending for presidential candidates in the 2012 elections, which was largely concentrated in a few key swing states like Colorado, Florida, North Carolina, Ohio, and Virginia. In the media markets shaded dark brown—Cleveland, Denver, Las Vegas, Orlando, and Tampa—there were more than 40,000 presidential ads aired (Wesleyan Media Project, 2012).

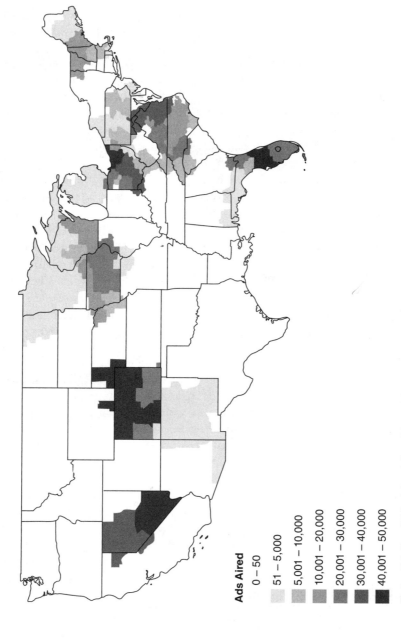

Ads Aired

- 0 – 50
- 51 – 5,000
- 5,001 – 10,000
- 10,001 – 20,000
- 20,001 – 30,000
- 30,001 – 40,000
- 40,001 – 50,000

Figure 5.1 Total Television Advertising Airings in the Presidential Race by Media Market (April 11–October 29, 2012)

SOURCE: Wesleyan Advertising Project

State differences matter for presidential campaign strategies in primary elections as well. States that hold early primaries matter most. During the nomination process, victories in early-contest states like Iowa and New Hampshire can provide candidates with the momentum, donations, and support needed to propel them forward and increase their likelihood of success in later primaries (Bartels 1988). With the exception of Iowa, campaigns typically devote more attention to states that hold primary elections as opposed to caucuses. The type of primary, too, makes a difference. Presidential campaigns operating in states with open primaries must account for the fact that it is not just loyal partisans who will be casting their ballots, and states that have closed primaries may require targeted messages aimed at their more partisan constituencies.

As I highlighted in Chapters 2 and 3, primary elections are somewhat of a conundrum for campaign strategists. Because primary electorates tend to be more ideologically extreme, campaigns must try to strike a balance between appeals to which their bases are receptive and those that will not alienate general election voters who tend to be more moderate overall. The logic of this strategy is illustrated by what political scientists have termed the "median voter theorem," which suggests an optimal strategy for candidates is to appeal to the ideological ideal points of the median voter in a distribution of voters (Downs 1957); this is the point at which a candidate's chances of victory are maximized, and, incidentally, it is the same point for both candidates in a two-person contest. The challenge for campaigns, however, is that the ideological distribution of voters in a primary can (and generally is) entirely different from a general election. Given the two-stage electoral process in place in U.S. elections, candidates must navigate two different sets of electorates, a more partisan one in primaries and a more moderate one in general elections.

The assumption of the median voter theorem is that the farther away a candidate is from a voter's most preferred outcome, the less likely the voter is to select that candidate. Figure 5.2 presents a stylized view of what this theorem looks like: candidates

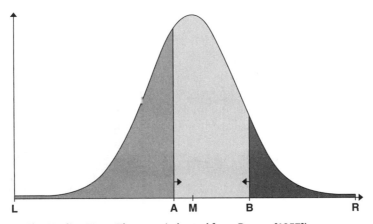

Figure 5.2 The Median Voter Theorem (adapted from Downs [1957])

A and B are placed along an ideological continuum that goes from left/liberal positions to right/conservative positions. In this model, candidates A and B should theoretically move their policy stances toward the preferences of the median voter, M. At this point, the candidates maximize their chances of capturing the voter's support.

Such stylized assumptions naturally have problems when applied to persuading citizens in the real world. Candidates cannot always be placed cleanly along a left–right ideological continuum. (For example, where would one place a pro-life Democrat who supports social welfare?) And adopting more ideologically extreme views to appeal to primary voters can cause problems for candidates if they advance to the general election in which the median voter in the electorate is likely to espouse more moderate views. This delicate balancing act can create incentives for candidates to provide voters with ambiguous information about themselves, their records, and their issue positions (Alvarez 1999). Growing partisan polarization also has implications for campaign strategy as voters become increasingly sorted and move toward the ideological extremes. In such a scenario, campaigns may have fewer incentives to engage in persuasion or conversion in general elections because it may suffice to rely primarily on mobilizing their base voters (Panagopoulos 2015). Evidence suggests that this is indeed the case because campaigns have increasingly sought to maximize turnout among more consistent supporters in recent elections rather than risk courting swing and independent voters whose support is less reliable (Panagopoulos 2015).

Of course, the causal direction in the relationship between campaign strategy and polarization is unclear. It is conceivable that campaign decisions may drive partisan polarization and be affected by it. In particular, technological advancements and a growth in the ability of campaigns to microtarget ever precisely selected segments of the electorate alongside new insights from social and behavioral science about the effectiveness of different voter mobilization tactics seem to have led to a renewed emphasis on mobilizing reliable partisan bases, instead of making the riskier move of reaching out and trying to persuade new supporters (Panagopoulos 2015).

TARGETING VOTERS

Scarce resources require campaigns to be strategic in their outreach and communications efforts. As Nielsen (2012: 169) has put it, "no partisan political organization engages in undifferentiated or blanket personalized political communication." All strategies developed and tactics employed by campaigns serve the purpose of developing a winning coalition and turning out enough supporters to help give a candidate the edge on Election Day. Thus, candidates must develop specific vote targets or goals for different groups of voters and understand the messages that will be most effective in reaching these groups. Campaigns must determine not only the number of votes needed to win, but also how many votes they can reliably count on from their base and what percentage of the electorate is persuadable. Before getting to targeting individual or specific groups of voters, campaigns will begin with electoral, or aggregate-level, targeting to get a sense of the lay of the land in terms of how many votes are needed and where they can be found.

Electoral targeting takes advantage of regularities or patterns in voting behavior across geographic units (like precincts, towns, or counties) over time. A well-known adage, applicable to politics, as will be discussed further in subsequent chapters, is that the best predictor of future behavior is past behavior. Because voters tend to vote similarly across election cycles, presumably for their preferred party's candidates, past election results can provide excellent guidance to campaigns about baseline levels of likely support (or opposition) in areas across a district or state. Campaign strategists can then adjust this information to take into account differences in the specific electoral context (for example, variation in voter turnout by election cycle type [i.e., presidential vs. midterm vs. off cycle] or other features, such as the introduction of same-day registration or other changes to the voting process) to come up with reasonable projections that enable them to prioritize how much effort or attention the campaign should direct to particular locales. This approach can help campaigns to be strategic in allocating resources, guiding campaign activities, and providing a roadmap to victory.

More refined approaches that zoom in on individual-level attributes can facilitate greater precision in strategic targeting. As I have noted throughout this volume, this is one of the cornerstones of the modern campaign. An excellent example of how campaigns can target voters comes from the 2014 governor's race in Texas. In the election, the state attorney general, Greg Abbott, soundly defeated the popular Democratic challenger, Wendy Davis. Part of the Abbott campaign's winning strategy was to capture the votes of groups that might normally vote reliably Democratic, but were vulnerable to persuasion in this particular election. To implement this strategy, the Abbot campaign targeted voters whose attributes were comparable to those of its known supporters and continually refined this subset of voters using data gathered from multiple sources. Using this information, the campaign was able to continually update a model of which voters were supporters, which were persuadable, and which were firmly in the opposition's camp, while keeping track of every contact the campaign made. The campaign focused all of its communication efforts on a subset of about 5 million voters based on their likelihood of support and propensity to turn out and vote. Abbott's campaign identified a substantial group of women and Hispanic voters, groups that traditionally vote with the Democratic Party but were determined by Abbott's campaign to be receptive to the campaign's efforts (Carney 2015).

This example represents a shift in contemporary campaigns from mass-marketing appeals to a broad range of audiences to the mass customization of appeals aimed at the specific subsets of voters most needed for a candidate to win, as discussed in Chapter 1. Although candidates running in reliably safe races may have to engage in fewer of these targeted appeals, in close races, candidates must craft messages that rally not only their base supporters to turn out but also enough independent and undecided voters to tip the scales in their favor. In an era of mass customization, mobilizing these undecided voters requires advanced and specific forms of communication to help candidates reach out to voters in a more personally tailored way. As Burton and Shea (2010) note, "Broad-based understanding of entire districts is being refined into narrowly focused analytics that traffic in neighborhoods and individuals" (116).

These targeting approaches make sense given that campaigns have access to limited resources; time and money should be spent judiciously and focused on engaging the segments of voters that are most needed to secure victory. In recent presidential elections, for example, residents living in battleground states were more likely to be contacted by *both* parties (Panagopoulos and Wielhouwer 2008). However, candidates must be careful to not focus too heavily on middle-of-the-road voters, lest they alienate their base voters and motivate them to stay away from the polls.

Of course, voters' policy preferences and ideological positions can be inconsistent and do not always fit nicely into clear boxes. Politics is far more complicated than simply fitting every voter on a one-dimensional ideological spectrum. Campaigns must also consider citizens who might be cross-pressured, that is, who support one party on certain issues but the opposing party on others. A voter might be highly supportive of traditionally Democratic programs, such as welfare and Medicaid, but more conservative on social issues like abortion. As Hillygus and Shields (2008) argue, "the most persuadable voters in the electorate are those individuals with a foot in each candidate's camp" (5). I will discuss in greater detail the factors that play a role in vote choice in Chapter 8.

Another factor that complicates targeting is the mode of message delivery, something we will discuss more in depth in Chapter 6 in the discussion of how campaigns get the word out about their candidate's message. Tactics such as direct mail, e-mail, and even online advertisements can be individually or narrowly targeted, but broadcast outlets like television and radio cover broader geographic areas known as designated market areas. Designated market areas are regions where residents receive largely the same television and radio options. Candidates can determine whether to air an ad in a specific designated market area based on the partisan and demographic makeup of that area, but they cannot target messages to reach specific individuals viewing television or listening to a radio program. It may be risky for a Democratic presidential candidate campaigning in a swing state, for example, to air a pro–gun control television ad in Republican-dominated designated market area. Using more targetable tactics like direct mail or e-mail may mitigate the risk.

Targeting involves three specific goals: *reinforcement*, *persuasion*, and *conversion*. Reinforcement makes sure partisan voters will actually turn out to vote for a candidate. Persuasion helps convince undecided voters. Conversion tries to convince voters from the opposition to switch their support (Burton and Shea 2010). It is easier to reinforce one's own voters than to persuade undecided voters, and it can be especially difficult to convert opposition voters. In a reliably partisan district, campaigns should focus on making sure their supporters get out to vote. If a race is a toss-up, persuasion might be as important, but there are races in which even the best persuasion strategy cannot hold up against an electoral landscape where the odds are stacked against a candidate. In 2014, in Louisiana's Senate runoff race, the incumbent Democrat, Mary Landrieu, faced the immense challenge of running as one of the last remaining white Democrats in the Deep South during a midterm election that did not bode well for Democratic fortunes across the country. Landrieu lost to the Republican challenger Bill Cassidy in a runoff election, in part because she failed to get the support she needed among white voters that she had in previous elections. Landrieu won 30% of the white vote in the general election in 2008, but only 18% in 2014. Although Landrieu received more than 90% of the black vote in 2014, its overall turnout was not high enough to save her seat (Easley 2014).

A recent development in voter targeting tactics is the use of microtargeting, which first came into play during the 2000 presidential and 2002 midterm elections. Microtargeting leverages information from surveys and other research to develop sophisticated statistical models that can be used to predict voters' preferences and behaviors. This information is then combined with state voter files supplemented with demographic, political, and consumer data to produce voter-specific likelihood scores about everything from how likely a voter is to vote, volunteer, contribute to a campaign, or support specific policy positions. The voter files are maintained and updated by the states and made available to campaigns. The content of the voter files varies from state to state. In terms of identifying supporters, the key information in voter files is party registration and/or past participation in primary elections. Table 5.1 breaks down what party

Table 5.1 Party Registration and Primary Participation by State

PARTY PRIMARY DATA ONLY	PARTY REGISTRATION DATA ONLY	PARTY REGISTRATION AND PARTY PRIMARY DATA	NO PARTY REGISTRATION AND NO PRIMARY DATA
Arkansas	Alaska	Arizona	Alabama
Georgia	Connecticut	California	Hawaii
Ohio	Washington, D.C.	Colorado	Minnesota
Illinois	Delaware	Iowa	Missouri
Indiana	Florida	Massachusetts	Montana
Michigan	Idaho	Maryland	North Dakota
Mississippi	Kansas	Maine	Vermont
South Carolina	Kentucky	North Carolina	Wisconsin
Tennessee	Louisiana	New Hampshire	
Texas	Nebraska	New Jersey	
Virginia	Oklahoma	New Mexico	
Washington	South Dakota	Nevada	
	Utah	New York	
	Wyoming	Oregon	
		Pennsylvania	
		Rhode Island	
		West Virginia	

SOURCE: Hersh (2015)

registration and party primary participation information is collected by each state. States with closed primaries require registration with a party to participate in their primary election. States with open primaries do not require party registration, but often list past primary participation in the voter file, which signals partisan affiliation. The more information that states collect on individuals' party affiliations, the easier it is for campaigns to identify their supporters (Hersh 2015). John Phillips of Aristotle, a nonpartisan company that provides information to candidates of both parties, describes registered voter files as being "the DNA of the electorate." Information is added to voter files from commercial marketing firms and includes e-mail addresses, telephone numbers, demographic information, and even what magazines a given voter subscribes to. All of this allows campaigns to take that data and target voters with more precision than ever before (Sreenivasan 2012). This kind of information is not infallible, but it arms political campaigns with powerful targeting tools that can be used to persuade, mobilize, and communicate effectively with voters. The practice of microtargeting has been turbocharged by the wealth of information provided by people's Internet browsing records, a topic I will discuss further in Chapter 9. Surfing the Internet leaves a trail of data that allows companies to develop an understanding of an individual's personal interests, which political strategy firms, in turn, use for their own purposes. They match it to publicly available voter rolls and can then take detailed information about a potential voter's consumer behavior, interests, and voting history to determine the most effective message to target them with.

Alexander Lundry (2012: 162) defines microtargeting as follows: "Employing the same marketing methods corporate America uses to sell credit cards and coffee machines, political micro-targeting collects and studies the enormous amount of data that is available about individual voters in order to answer a campaign's most fundamental questions: Who supports my candidate? Where do I find them? How do I persuade others to support my candidate?" Answering these questions allows candidates to build an efficient and effective direct voter-contact program. One of the pioneers of microtargeting is Alex Gage. In 2002, Gage sold his share of a high-profile polling firm and made a pitch to Karl Rove, George. W. Bush's chief campaign strategist, about how to ensure the president's reelection. His argument was not complex: he wanted to take the business world's tactic of learning everything about its customers, "carving up the country into smaller and smaller clusters of like-minded consumers," and apply this to political campaigns (Cilizza 2007). The Bush coalition would be made up of groups of like-minded voters whom the campaign could target with messages about the issues they considered the most important. Gage says that microtargeting is like "trying to unravel your political DNA . . . the more information I have about you, the better." The more information, the easier it is to group people into target clusters, such as "Flag and Family Republicans" or "Tax and Terrorism Moderates" (Cilizza 2007). This strategy differs from the more common precinct-by-precinct electoral targeting of likely supporters; with microtargeting, individual voters are targeted using interests, demographics, and other characteristics, not just aggregated units of voters living in precincts, towns, or states.

As I discuss throughout this volume, microtargeting is becoming ubiquitous in campaigns, even in elections for lower-level offices. There are many advantages to microtargeting because it leverages predictive modeling techniques and statistical predictions to extrapolate what specific individuals care about or believe or how they may behave; similar techniques have been used to create credit scores since the mid-1970s and adopted for direct marketing purposes since the early 1980s (Nielsen 2012). The approach is useful and attractive for political campaigns, which would otherwise need to depend on less reliable techniques, but it is not foolproof. In the first place, the estimates it produces are just that: educated guesses based on input data; these scores are often as good as the quality of the data that is used to create them, and they can be wrong. A predictive model can estimate the likelihood that a voter opposes gun control, for example, based on a series of other known attributes; often, the projections will be right, but they will occasionally be off the mark. One study finds accuracy rates range from 36% to 82% depending on the issue and state (Endres 2016). Moreover, it is conceivable that voters are not as receptive to micro-targeted appeals as campaign operatives believe they are. A recent study by Hersh and Schaffner (2013) cautions users about the potential limits of microtareting. Using a series of survey experiments, the authors found that voters rarely prefer targeted pandering to general messages and that "mistargeted" voters penalize candidates enough to erase the positive returns to targeting. They concluded targeting may allow candidates to quietly promise particularistic benefits to narrow audiences, but voters seem to prefer being solicited based on broad principles and collective benefits (Hersh and Schaffner 2013).

POLLING TO DEVELOP CAMPAIGN STRATEGY

Candidates often believe they know a great deal about a district or that they have a clear sense of what voters want. Sometimes they are right, but often their expectations are inaccurate or incomplete. Since they will spend anywhere from thousands to millions of dollars, campaigns need reliable information on which to base their spending decisions. In contemporary elections, campaigns use polling (or survey research) to determine levels of support among voters, to develop targeting strategies, and to identify segments of the electorate where improvements in campaigning might be made. Polls are also used to measure levels of name recognition and candidate support, as well as to identify the issues that are most important to voters to help develop campaign messages. Campaigns will often hire firms to conduct polling; although media outlets often commission their own polls for reporting purposes, the findings are typically general and do not go into the level of detail needed by political campaigns. Thus, it has almost become a necessity for candidates to hire political survey research firms to conduct their polling (Burton and Shea 2010).

Polls are ideally conducted using probability samples, which give each citizen in a candidate's race an equal probability of being selected, so that inferences can reliably be made to the entire population of interest (voters in a state or congressional district, for example). Often the results reported are restricted to likely voters who are most likely to comprise the actual electorate, but this involves guessing games that vary across polling organizations (Erikson et al. 2004). Other times, polls are conducted among all registered voters who may potentially participate in a given race to put together a general picture of who is likely to turn out and what might be done to motivate less likely voters to come out in support of a given candidate. Sometimes, campaigns test specific messages to determine what types of appeals resonate (or not) with voters using focus groups, which are guided conversations with small groups of voters, although these approaches are unscientific. They can also use split ballot testing, in which a traditional sample of survey respondents is divided randomly into two or more subsamples. Each subsample is then given a survey that is embedded with one or more different questions between the surveys. Often, the goal of this method is to see whether any differences exist in responses to the framing of specific questions. For example, a Republican campaign may wish to determine whether Democratic voters in a sample who are parents would be more likely to support its candidate's position to increase national security spending if their identity as a parent is primed. Empirical evidence suggests that citizens who experience a threat to their identity (for example, national security threats on the well-being of a parent's child) that also competes with their party identification may express preferences that contradict their partisanship (Klar 2013).

Campaigns will typically start with a benchmark poll, ideally conducted during the early stage of a campaign, to gauge some basic details about familiarity and preferences in a state or district in a systematic, rigorous, and scientific way. Benchmark polls take an initial, political temperature reading of the district and can be used later to assess changes or progress toward a desired goal. These surveys generally probe voters about their issue preferences and priorities, their recognition of candidates' names, their favorability toward and approval of key political figures, and, crucially, their evaluation of the target candidate and his or her opponent, their vote intentions, their receptiveness to campaign messages, and their basic demographic information. Benchmark polls tend to include a few hundred voters (400–800) and ask about 25–35 questions. Most polling firms conduct these surveys by telephone using computer-assisted technology coupled with live interviewers, and a campaign can expect to pay about $10,000–$25,000 (depending on the length and the number of completed responses) to complete the survey and obtain a report with an analysis of the results. Increasingly, campaigns have the option to use alternative methods to field polls, for example, Internet-based polls or automated, interactive voice response technology that does not require a live interviewer. This technology uses automated software to call respondents and prerecorded voice prompts to ask questions, and respondents key in answers using their telephone keypads. These alternatives tend to be much more affordable, but some analysts have raised concerns about the quality and reliability of the responses. Ongoing polling, or tracking polls, conducted at various intervals over the course of a campaign tend to be shorter and include fewer respondents.

These tracking polls are generally less expensive and are designed mainly to keep a finger on key elements related to the political pulse of the districts.

To bring to life how survey responses can aid in the development of campaign message strategy, Figure 5.3 provides an excerpt from a benchmark poll conducted

---

(Framing the Campaign Message)
This September, there will be a Democratic primary election for [DISTRICT]. If this election were held today, and the candidates were (READ LIST AND ROTATE), for whom would you vote?

Positives on [CANDIDATE]
Now I am going to read you a few statements about [CANDIDATE] that have been made by his supporters. After I read each one, please tell me whether it is a very convincing, somewhat convincing, not very convincing or not at all convincing reason to vote for [CANDIDATE] in the Democratic primary this September.

(Randomize statement order)
1. Unlike the other candidates in the race, who are mostly former political aides and political operatives, [CANDIDATE] has real world experience solving problems and working for the people in our community.
2. [CANDIDATE] has spent five years as a federal prosecutor in the Eastern District of the United States Attorney's office. He has participated in dozens of operations to break up violent gangs and prosecute criminals to keep our streets safe.

(SPLIT-SAMPLE A/B; ½ sample each)
3.A   [CANDIDATE] understands that the only way we can keep our streets and schools safe is to have a mix of smart policies that include drug treatment and rehabilitation and specific programs aimed at non-violent, younger offenders.
3.B   [CANDIDATE] understands that the only way we can keep our streets and schools safe is to have a zero tolerance policy toward drugs and violence, and has been on the front lines with police putting criminals behind bars and protecting victim's rights.
4. [CANDIDATE] is committed to fighting for more increased affordable and accessible housing, so that teachers, doctors, firemen, policemen and regular families can do a little better trying to make ends meet in our community.
5. [CANDIDATE] knows we must do more to expand educational opportunity, and knows that the first step in creating opportunity is having safe, secure schools that focus on preventing violence and weapons in their schools.

Thinking about what you just heard: This September, there will be a Democratic primary election for the [DISTRICT]. If this election were held today, and the candidates were (READ LIST AND ROTATE), for whom would you vote?

Negatives on [CANDIDATE]
Now I am going to read you a few statements about [CANDIDATE] that have been made by his opponents. After I read each one, please tell me whether it is a very convincing, somewhat convincing, not very convincing or not at all convincing reason to vote against [CANDIDATE] in the Democratic primary this September.

6. [CANDIDATE] is too inexperienced with the workings of the City Council to deliver for our area. With the budget, schools, stadium and all of these issues on the table, need someone who can make sure our voice in the Council is not ignored.

Figure 5.3 Benchmark Poll Sample (Excerpt)

by telephone I commissioned on behalf of a recent campaign. Note that respondents are initially asked a question about their voter intentions in the Democratic primary and then asked to determine whether each of a series of messages pertaining to the candidate's profile or experience is convincing. The respondents are then probed again about their vote intentions so that the researchers can observe any change in preferences that may follow exposure to the biographical statements. Look closely at items 3A and 3B: only half of the sample selected at random will be asked each version of the question. This allows the pollster to compare whether one version—or message—is superior to the other in terms of attracting support. Respondents are also asked to evaluate negative messages that could potentially emerge in the campaign. Note that responses to these and other items can be broken down (generally using cross-tabulation) by demographics (age, race, gender) or other factors (residential location) to compare responses across different groups of voters. More sophisticated statistical techniques (like regression) can also be used to model responses to poll items as a function of demographics or other attributes. Such a model can then be applied to a larger database of voters who were not necessarily surveyed but about whom campaigns possess basic demographic information to predict issue preferences or vote intentions based on their shared demographics. The scores produced by modeling risk being inaccurate, but oftentimes this information is better than nothing. This is the essence of microtargeting discussed previously and throughout this volume.

Surveys and focus groups do not always extract accurate responses from participants because people have a tendency to report socially desirable responses or filter them in other ways that can affect the analysis of these responses. One of the most common survey responses for which citizens give incorrect answers is on likelihood of voting (or, after an election, whether they have actually voted). Social desirability bias causes voters to overreport participation in elections on surveys (Holbrook and Krosnick 2010). If someone is speaking to a pollster on the phone or in person, they may also feel pressure to support one candidate or another depending on which campaign the pollster is working for or whether a candidate in question is a minority or female. The logic behind this latter type of bias is that individuals do not wish to appear to be racist or sexist, even if in reality they prefer another candidate for different reasons (Streb et al. 2008). These effects seem to be attenuated by levels of education; that is, socially desirable responses decrease as education increases, and attitudes toward minority candidates grow more tolerant (Heerwig and McCabe 2009).

Increasingly, campaigns have access to other kinds of technologies to test reactions to messages. Some firms offer campaigns services that take advantage of biometric technologies to track peoples' heart rates, pupilometrics (which examines the dilation of pupils in response to different stimuli), and the measurement of body temperatures. These techniques can determine how people react to specific messages or other features used in campaign appeals, such as music, images, and the framing of a message. Brain imaging is also available, but is usually cost-prohibitive except for the best-funded campaigns (Randall 2015).

As I discussed previously, conducting polling at the beginning of campaigns is integral to developing campaign strategy. Having a clear picture of how well recognized a candidate is, his or her initial levels of support among voters, and what issues are important to him or her will help campaigns develop their strategy and determine what their goals are for the remainder of the campaign. Some believe that in this day and age, campaigns should *never* stop polling. Candidates need regular information to make effective decisions. Although large swaths of voters are fairly predictable in their behavior, in close races, undecided or persuadable voters can change their minds multiple times over the course of an election cycle as they receive new information. Without regular polling data, campaigns face becoming "lost" over the course of the campaign in terms of where their candidate stands in relationship to the voters. A shift in voter opinion and support might necessitate a shift in message and strategy (Brown 2015).

In the 2012 Republican presidential primaries, Rick Santorum served as a prime example of how important polling has become when he opted *not* to use it for his campaign. Santorum's top strategist, John Brabender, argued, "There's a way that polling makes people crazy with data and they want to build a whole campaign around that," recalling that Santorum had noted, "I don't want someone telling us what to believe." The strategy was not without its drawbacks. The Michigan primary is an example of an instance where his campaign would have benefitted from polling. In Michigan, Santorum's campaign decided to send robocalls containing the message "join Democrats who are going to send a loud message to Massachusetts Mitt Romney by voting for Rick Santorum for president." Without proper polling, the calls were targeted at voters who looked like Democrats who had participated in previous Republican primaries, but included socially conservative Reagan Democrats and moderate Republicans. Although Santorum's strategy seemed to work in some of his other primary races (he was the frontrunner for a good portion of the Republican primary season), he ultimately lost the Michigan primary and the Republican presidential nomination. In Michigan, Santorum had almost the same levels of support among men, but lost by 5 percentage points to women, ultimately losing the state by 3 percentage points. Although it is difficult to say for certain, more detailed and reliable information may have helped Santorum stay away from issues that potentially alienated women, such as his conservative position on contraception, which he continued to push during the Michigan primary (Elving 2012).

OPPOSITION RESEARCH

Opposition research has become a key feature of contemporary campaigns, although it has been a part of American elections from the beginning. Famously, during the presidential election of 1800, the Federalists contended that Thomas Jefferson had slave mistresses, one of whom gave birth to his child (Burton and Shea 2010). In what is widely considered to be America's first political sex scandal, an incident made infamous by the 2015 hit Broadway musical "Hamilton,"

Democratic-Republicans in the 1790s dug up details about Alexander Hamilton's affair with Maria Reynolds and the fact that her husband was paid to keep silent about the affair. In an effort to get ahead of the scandal, Hamilton wrote openly about the affair after being confronted by the Democratic-Republicans to dispel rumors that he had engaged in speculation with federal funds, nevertheless failing to rescue his political career (Bonanos 2016). Opposition research involves in-depth investigations of an opponent, looking to uncover anything about his or her past experiences, political or otherwise, that might give one's campaign an advantage. Another, perhaps more crass, way of thinking about opposition research is that it is essentially digging up dirt on one's opponent, although there are limits on what qualifies as politically advantageous dirt and inappropriate attacks on a candidate's past, character, or family.

The Internet has greatly affected how opposition research is conducted and the role that it plays in political campaigns. For much of the 20th century, paying political consultants to conduct opposition research was a luxury not afforded to most campaigns. Now, it is almost unimaginable, at least for higher-level campaigns, not to hire a consultant to do opposition research. Indeed, many consulting firms specialize in this research. Before the rise of the Internet, examining an opponent's record could take a significant amount of time, requiring multiple months and extensive manpower to do the job. In contemporary campaigns, much, if not most of the information needed on an opponent can be found online (Bovee 1998). Although political consultants make up the bulk of those conducting opposition research directly for campaigns, the increasing prominence of social media and a wider variety of news outlets and online bloggers means that more and more individuals and groups outside of campaigns can conduct and widely publicize their own form of opposition research. With more and more information becoming publicly available and an expanding array of channels for disseminating it, it can be difficult for candidates to keep anything unsavory from their past in the dark.

Conducting effective opposition research is not simply a matter of digging up the most dirt on a candidate. Effective use of opposition research considers both the positives of exploiting it and the potential blowback of engaging in what the public might perceive as dirty politics. During the 2008 presidential campaigns, many Republicans felt that the McCain campaign did a poor job of vetting his vice presidential candidate, Sarah Palin, after a number of public gaffes exposed what appeared to be her lack of competence and experience. However, the Obama campaign made clear that it would not exploit potentially unsavory aspects of Palin's family, especially the out-of-wedlock pregnancy of her teenage daughter, presumably to avoid any backlash doing so might inspire (Marquardt 2008).

With so much information floating around and publicly available, it is important for opposition researchers to wrap their heads around what is relevant to a campaign and what is more likely to be a distraction or backfire. Most often, highly personal attacks, such as claims leveraged against an opponent's family or past personal relationships, are not effective in rallying voters. Misrepresented information can be equally damaging. As information becomes more checkable and verifiable, consultants and campaigns must be clear on whether the claim they are making is represented accurately or even true in the first place. Candidates, too, should ensure that they themselves have not engaged in the behavior they are accusing their opponents of. Just as important as conducting opposition research is conducting counteropposition research. Candidates must take an in-depth look into their own background before going on the attack. After all, one's opponents are also conducting opposition research.

It is important for candidates to know what their opponents might potentially find and use against them and to not leverage attacks for actions that are similar to mistakes they have also made. As Burton and Shea (2010) note, "campaigns should not throw stones unless they know what sins their own candidate has committed" (61). For example, in the 1998 race for U.S. Senator in New York, Senator Alphonse M. D'Amato accused his opponent, Chuck Schumer, of missing more than 100 votes, including critical ones, while in Congress. But D'Amato had missed a similar number of votes when running for Senate in 1980. Accused of being a hypocrite, his argument against Schumer backfired (Nagourney 1998).

Although some of the better remembered instances of damning opposition research (as well as opposition research gone awry) seem to come from the surfacing of personally embarrassing stories and questionable behavior of candidates, most opposition research focuses on an opponent's political record. In this sense, opposition research is inherently retrospective: it encourages voters to think about a candidate's past voting behavior, bills he or she has supported, and his or her general record in elected office, if one exists. In other words, past actions are considered by voters to make a determination about what a candidate's future behavior might be. If an opponent is a newcomer to politics or has previously held lower-level offices, a candidate might focus on his or her opponent's lack of experience. Conversely, challengers to incumbent candidates might focus on the extent to which the opponent's record reflects one of an entrenched politician, out of touch with his or her constituents (Fiorina 1981). I will talk more about the role that retrospective evaluations play in voter decision making in Chapter 8 when I discuss vote choice.

MESSAGE DEVELOPMENT

Properly done, voter targeting, opposition research, and candidate positioning aid the development of an effective campaign message. A campaign message constitutes the central idea that a campaign is trying to get across to voters and should be coherently articulated throughout the course of a campaign, a topic I will touch on more in Chapter 6. Campaign messages help candidates connect with voter concerns and help voters identify the major differences between a candidate and his or her opponent. A well-crafted message, repeated over and over again throughout an election cycle, reminds voters why a given candidate should be elected instead of another. The development of such a message depends greatly on the electoral context a candidate encounters. Partisan appeals will work in heavily partisan areas, whereas toss-up races may require more carefully crafted messages.

A key part of message development is gaining control over the agenda. Candidates want *their* message to be the one that resonates with voters, about both their own record and their framing of their opponent's record. Citizen attention is at a premium during a campaign, and candidates only have a few opportunities to tell voters what an election is about in a way that is advantageous to their campaign. During the 2008 presidential election, Barack Obama's campaign did an excellent job of developing a message that resonated with voters: that Obama, not John McCain, would be best to handle the economic crisis gripping the country. Obama's campaign did this in large part by successfully linking John McCain to the outgoing president, George W. Bush, for whom many Americans blamed for the country's economic woes and the increasingly troublesome situation in Iraq (Kenski et al. 2010).

In message development, campaigns carefully choose which issues they will emphasize and which ones they will ignore and work hard to ensure the issues they are tackling are discussed on the terms that are most advantageous to them. To gain the support of persuadable voters, candidates often focus on issues which the voters align with their policy positions and which they are advantaged and their opponent is disadvantaged (Petrocik 1996; Petrocik et al. 2003). In addition, candidates are not afraid to infringe on issue territory that typically belongs to the opposing party, as long as they are the ones who get to control the message and frame the opposing party's issues in a way that is beneficial to them (Sides 2006).

Although campaigns have some control over the substantive content of their messages and how they are presented, oftentimes the focus of campaign messages is driven by realities outside the candidates' control. One of the best documented contexts that affect candidate message development is the state of the economy, which comes into play largely at the level of presidential elections. Evidence suggests that the candidate advantaged by the state of the economy—for example, an incumbent if the economy is strong or the challenger if the economy is poor— would do well to exploit this positioning to his or her advantage in the development of the campaign message. In 11 of the past 15 presidential elections, the candidate favored by economic conditions won by conducting what the political scientist Lynn Vavreck calls "clarifying" campaigns. She argues that "the economy matters because the candidate who benefits from it talks about it a lot during the campaign and this makes voters more aware of the condition and this candidate's relationship to it" (Vavreck 2009: 158). In three of the four presidential elections in Vavreck's study where the candidate favored by economic conditions did not take full advantage of his or her position, the candidate lost the election.

Timing and Sequence

Implementation of campaign communications and outreach strategies require important decisions about the timing and sequence along which activities will unfold. On this score, campaign strategists have a plethora of basic options, with no one-size-fits-all solutions (Faucheux 2002). A traditional formulation for persuasion and mobilization suggests campaigns start by creating and reinforcing their base supporters, then proceed with identifying and persuading undecided voters or converts, and close with turning out supporters. A base strategy advises focusing on reinforcing the base and then turning it out; one study finds this strategy is becoming more common in recent presidential elections (Panagopoulos 2015); a corollary strategy sometimes called the "Marion Barry," after the Washington, D.C. mayor who used it to make a spectacular comeback in 1994 after scandalous legal troubles nearly ended his career (Faucheux 2002), advises campaigns to start with reinforcing their base, then enlarge the base and then turn it out. Faucheux (2002) also discusses diverse intensity strategies including: The "tortoise" (start slowly, steadily build), the "bookend" (open big and loud, then build steadily, close big and loud), "Pearl Harbor" (open very quietly, causing the opposition to underestimate strength then close big and loud) and "hold your fire" (slow, steady build, big and loud close) (Faucheux 2002). Message tone strategies include: "Ignoring the opposition" (open on a positive note and remain positive); "aggressive" (open positive but go negative before the opposition; then respond to attacks and close either positive or on dual positive/negative or comparative tracks); "frontal assault" (open negative, then go positive and respond to attacks on a dual track, close either positively or on a dual track); "relentless attack" (start and stay negative, with some positive messages in between; a classic strategy is to start positive and not provoke but respond to attacks and to end positively (Faucheux 2002: 52–58).

Strategists often adopt different approaches depending on a wide-range of factors. For example, Clinton and Clinton (1999) assert the prototypical telephone/direct mail campaign has four phases: sensitizing (establishes contact and elicits a small but affirmative commitment), identification (4–6 weeks before an election, another call identifies a voter's attitude about the candidate and the issue of greatest importance), persuasion (7–10 days before Election Day, targets persuadable voters and attempts to convince voter to support), and GOTV (a minimum of two phone calls to voters identified as favorable; the first a few days before the election, and the second call on the eve or day of the election). In the 2012 election, the Obama for America field operation unfolded in four, interrelated phases: capacity building (January–October), persuasion (January–October), expansion of the electorate (January–registration deadline), and mobilization and GOTV (October–November 6) (McKenna and Han 2014). The campaign placed an emphasis on metrics in each phase, quantifying, measuring and tracking the activities of its massive and decentralized infrastructure comprised on over 2.2 million volunteers daily by each state's in-house analytics team (McKenna and Han 2014). Reports also calculated each organizer's progress toward weekly goals and used this information to take stock of the overall effort, assign responsibilities and hold teams accountable (McKenna and Han 2014). This program highlights the significance of the role volunteers play in contemporary campaigns; effective and efficient volunteer recruitment, and management are integral to successful campaign execution.

We will discuss timing strategies further in the chapters that follow, but I introduce the discussion here to emphasize the fact that this is a critical dimension of campaign planning. Insights about how and when voters make decisions in campaigns can shed further light on timing considerations. As we will see, large shifts in voter preferences over the course of a presidential campaign are uncommon and mainly in place by the end of the summer preceding the fall campaign (Erikson and Wlezien 2012). This early solidification suggests the opportunity for candidates to get crossover support from opposing partisans may already have passed by the time the general election begins (Erikson and Wlezien 2012: Erikson et al. 2010). Persuasion strategies that hold off until closer to Election Day, which are common in recent campaigns (Ridout 2009; Fowler et al. 2016), may fall on deaf ears by then, implying such an approach may be overly simplistic and potentially ineffectual. Then again, delivering late-breaking appeals may be optimal if persuasion effects decay rapidly (Gerber et al. 2011). Timing considerations are complicated, and strategists must weigh these carefully when designing outreach, communications and activity timelines. In Chapter 10, we will discuss how changing electoral laws in states across the country may also affect timing considerations in campaign strategy.

CONSEQUENCES FOR DEMOCRACY

By design, campaigns cannot speak to *all* citizens in their electorate; to do so would be a waste of time and money and would likely lead to a fairly unsuccessful campaign. As such, the need for efficiency in political campaigns does not necessarily line up with the needs of a well-functioning and representative democracy.

Because campaigns focus on targeting specific subsets of likely supporters, they must leave portions of the electorate out of their persuasion and mobilization efforts by default. This includes not only voters who are more likely to support their opponent, but also citizens who are less likely to vote in the first place. Unfortunately, this can affect the participation of lower-income, less educated, and minority voters who, on average, have a lower propensity of being mobilized by campaigns (Rosenstone and Hansen 1993). Generally, individuals who have a spotty voting history will be less likely to be targeted by most campaigns for mobilization (Panagopoulos and Weilhouwer 2008). Campaigns are not interested in turning out the most voters; they are interested in turning out the *right* voters.

One of the strategies candidates use to persuade and mobilize the right voters, microtargeting, has also brought with it concerns about the extent to which it can be used to misinform citizens. Representative government necessitates that voters be able to learn accurate information about the candidates who seek to represent them in elected office. With the increased use of microtargeting, however, some suggest this tactic could be used to misinform citizens and suppress votes in ways that are not likely to be identified by election officials or reporters. As the political scientist Kathleen Hall Jamieson (2013) notes, "In a world of micro-targeted messages, it is difficult for reporters and scholars to know who is saying what to whom, where, and with what effect . . . and without knowing what is being whispered to whom, scholars have no good way to determine what effects, if any, this new form of campaigning is having on the candidates, the voters, and the process writ large." (430, 434).

Some critics contend microtargeting can give voters a false sense of representation. Carefully crafted messages can successfully secure voters' support, but failure to deliver on key claims and promises may ultimately disillusion voters resulting in lower levels of engagement and participation in the long term. Such disenchanting realizations have the potential to turn citizens away from politics (Ridder 2014).

Tactics like microtargeting also raise concerns over the extent to which they constitute an invasion of citizen privacy. During the 2012 elections, the Obama and Romney campaigns had the technological ability to know more about the voters they were courting than had any other election campaign in history. In fact, contemporary campaigns can procure affordable, comprehensive databases of registered voters from commercial vendors that have been enhanced to include not only demographics but also information about political habits (for example, contributing behavior) and consumer behavior. For example, Aristotle, one of the nation's leading providers of voter lists, offers campaigns more than 500 data fields. Aristotle partners with consumer marketers to provide data that goes far beyond basic demographic and political information, including details about whether voters have children, pets, pools, air conditioning, or gold cards, for example, as well as whether voters own or rent their homes, invest in the stock market, contribute to a wide range of charities, garden, have fireplaces, play sports, travel, subscribe to magazines, speak a second language, and attend church. The debate over microtargeting reflects the competition between two intractable American values: individuality and privacy. As Terrence McCoy (2012), a writer for *The Atlantic* magazine notes, "We're social animals, tweeting every trenchant and insipid thought, but, somehow, we still prize anonymity. We're more open than ever, but less trusting. We want things to be easy—Amazon, tell us which book to buy, Pandora, which song to play—but we don't want it done behind our backs. Because that makes us feel stupid and tricked."

Indeed, evidence suggests that voters' privacy concerns regarding microtargeting can potentially backfire on candidates. What if a campaign were to wrongly target a Republican who prefers hybrid cars with a Democrat-oriented advertisement or were to target a gun-owning Democrat with an ad about government deregulation when the voter in fact prefers more government control over policies relating to gun ownership? If people are targeted inappropriately, it can become confusing to individuals or even downright offensive. Echoing the findings reported by Hersh and Shaffner (2013) and discussed above, survey data reinforce the notion that the public does not necessarily embrace microtargeting tactics. In a survey done by the University of Pennsylvania's Annenberg School of Communication in 2012, 86% of those surveyed said they did not want political advertising to be tailored to their interests, and 64% said that their support for a candidate would decrease if they found out that a candidate targeted him or her differently than their neighbors (Turow et al. 2012). These statistics also have implications for the extent to which campaign uses of microtargeting directly contradict the ideal that campaigns should help promote representation. As the Annenberg study highlights, Americans roundly reject tailored political advertising at a time when political campaigns are embracing it.

Of course, there are some positive normative upsides to contemporary campaign tactics like microtargeting, especially for engagement and the information received by voters. Individual messaging can be used to make sure a voter receives an absentee ballot, knows where the polling place is, or knows where and how to register to vote. Greater personalization has the capacity to increase the likelihood that voters will notice and respond to campaign appeals (Green and Gerber 2008, 2012; Nielsen 2012). The Obama campaigns successfully mobilized blacks and Latinos in 2008 and 2012 using these strategies (Sinclair 2012; Jamieson 2013). Tailored messages perceived by voters to be more pertinent or relevant to them can also potentially overcome exposure barriers, heightening voter information levels overall. However, it is not difficult to imagine situations where campaigns use targeting, especially microtargeting, to their advantage, misinforming voters in the process. In the next chapter, I go into detail on the different ways campaigns can get their message out, as well as the factors that influence its delivery and effectiveness, and delve deeper into the implications of this important component of campaign strategy for democratic norms.

KEY TERMS

Base voters	Microtargeting	Reinforcement
Benchmark poll	Name recognition	Split-ballot test
Conversion	Opposition research	Tracking poll
Issue ownership	Persuasion	
Median voter theorem	Probability sample	

SUGGESTED READINGS

Burton, M. J., and D. M. Shea. 2010. *Campaign Craft: The Strategies, Tactics, and Art of Political Campaign Management*. Santa Barbara, CA: Praeger, from the Collections of ABC–CLIO.

Downs. A. 1957. *An Economic Theory of Democracy*. Boston, MA: Addison–Wesley.

Vavreck, L. 2009. *The Message Matters: The Economy and Presidential Campaigns*. Princeton, NJ: Princeton University Press.

CHAPTER 6

Get Out the Word

Effective communication, including advertising and other tactics designed to get out the central message or theme, is a critical component of the modern campaign. Strategists working for the reelection campaign of the senator Harry Reid in 2010 echoed this sentiment in their discussion of the Reid campaign's advertising strategy against his Republican opponent, Sharron Angle.

> "Our first ads hit just days after she [Sharron Angle] became the Republican nominee," noted one strategist, "taking her to task for advocating the elimination of Social Security. Over the next four months, our efforts to fill in the picture on Angle were unrelenting. We ran spots about her belief that it wasn't a senator's job to fight for jobs, for wanting to abolish the Department of Education, for voting to protect the privacy of sex offenders and for letting insurance companies deny coverage for cancer screening. The spots were anchored with her own words; we let the voters see her for themselves. And the spots all led to the same conclusion—that Sharron Angle was too extreme. The ads proved devastating. Angle's unfavorables increased more than 30 points in just two months" (Sides 2011).

On the surface, the Reid campaign's strategy seemed to work because Reid eked out a narrow victory over Angle during the midterms that year. But what is not clear from the strategist's statement is how much of an effect the campaign's advertising blitz actually had itself or, indeed, whether it exerted a meaningful effect at all. Post hoc assertions about the effectiveness of an advertising campaign prove little about the extent to which that campaign actually mattered for the election outcome.

That said, no political consultant would argue that a candidate should forego advertising campaigns simply because they do not have hard evidence of the extent to which a campaign will be effective. As it stands, one of the most important and equally challenging aspects of executing campaign strategy is the delivery of campaign messaging. In contemporary campaigns, political consultants are savvy to the fact that campaign success is not a matter of whether campaign advertising matters, but when and for whom it matters.

Message delivery in contemporary campaigns is complex and requires increasingly specialized and diversified knowledge to be executed effectively. Although the candidate and the campaign manager play a role in helping to develop a campaign's message, the primary person in charge of getting out the word and interacting with the media is the communications director, often in tandem with media consultants. They need detailed knowledge about the ins and outs of multiple different paid media sources, including broadcast and cable television, radio, print, and new media technologies like blogging, Twitter, Facebook, and Instagram—with more cropping up all the time. In addition, they must orchestrate their paid media presence in concert with the need to attract earned media, that is, news coverage of campaign happenings and events, in an electoral environment where attention is at a premium.

In this chapter I address the intricacies and challenges of effectively delivering campaign messaging. We begin with an introduction to the delivery of campaign messaging, that is, the basic components that communications directors must take into account when executing a campaign communication strategy. Next, I discuss the various paid media strategies that campaigns have at their disposal, the process of media buying, and how campaigns can manage the multitude of media options available to them. I then juxtapose the use of paid media with a discussion of earned media and the tactics campaigns can use to effectively leverage news coverage of their activities. Earned media is "free" in the technical sense, but it takes carefully crafted planning to earn the right kind of media coverage—indeed, to earn any coverage at all. Finally, I discuss the effectiveness of campaign advertising in shifting election outcomes as well as the implications of campaign advertising for citizen opinion and behavior. The effects of campaign advertising is one of the more hotly debated aspects of campaigns by political scientists, in terms of both whether advertising can actually influence election outcomes and the implications it has for democratic norms, specifically the engagement of citizens in politics and the information they receive during the course of an election season.

REVISITING THE BASICS OF CAMPAIGN MESSAGING

At the core of the complex range of media strategies that must be navigated by campaigns, communications directors should keep two basic questions in mind: what does the candidate want to say about him- or herself and how does he or she want to be differentiated from the opposition? Campaign messages must draw clear contrasts between the candidate and the opponent in a way that is easily disseminated and understood by voters. This includes accounting for what the opposition might say about a candidate. In the development of message delivery strategies, it can be helpful for campaign strategists to begin by organizing the basics of message delivery into a message box that clarifies what a candidate wants to say, helps to defend against what the opposition is saying, and frames the debate in a way that is advantageous. Burton and Shea (2010) further develop this idea to incorporate positive and negative messages from both a candidate and his/her opponent, as illustrated in Figure 6.1.

Our positive message	Their positive message
Our negative message	Their negative message

Figure 6.1 Message Box (Adapted from Burton and Shea [2010: 161])

There are three basic categories of campaign advertising and message delivery that communications directors must choose from when developing their messaging strategy. Positive messaging, as the name implies, focuses on candidates' own attributes and strengths and tries to establish their policy positions and explain why they are the right person for elected office. Comparative messaging highlights the differences between candidates, often drawing comparisons with an opponent's track record or policy goals to attract support. Finally, negative messaging focuses solely on an opponent's vulnerabilities.

The quintessential attack ad that changed the tone of modern political advertisements aired during the 1964 presidential race. In his presidential bid, with national tensions about the Cold War and the danger of a nuclear holocaust running high, Democratic President Lyndon Johnson aired the "Daisy" ad, a commercial that opened with a little girl counting down the number of daisy petals in a meadow that slowly morphed into a countdown for an enormous nuclear blast filling the screen. President Johnson's voiceover stated, "These are the stakes: to make a world in which all of God's children can live, or to go into the darkness. We must either love each other, or we must die." This was followed by an announcer's voice saying "Vote for President Johnson on November 3rd. The stakes are too high for you to stay home." The ad clearly suggested that Johnson's opponent, Barry Goldwater, was trigger-happy and would likely lead the United States into a nuclear war. Prior to this advertisement, which was only aired once, political commercials tended to be upbeat and positive. But, as Drew Babb, a teacher of political advertising at American University, notes, the Daisy ad was a "full-throated, gloves-off, take-no-prisoners negative message. Arguably, and for better or worse, it's the mother of all attack ads" (Babb 2014).

Another famous example of negative campaign messaging comes from the 1988 presidential campaign. In 1986, Willie Horton, a convicted felon serving a life sentence for murder, was released from a prison in Massachusetts as a part of a furlough program. During his furlough, he escaped and raped a woman. The governor of Massachusetts at the time, Michael Dukakis, had supported the furlough program. In his 1988 presidential bid, his opponent, George H. W. Bush, used Dukakis's support of the furlough program against him to portray the Massachusetts governor as soft on crime. From the beginning of his campaign, then–vice president Bush had declared that Dukakis was soft on crime, and it became a repeated theme in his campaign messaging. The controversy eventually came to a head when an outside political action committee aired a now infamous advertisement against Dukakis, accusing Dukakis of allowing "first degree murderers to have weekend passes from prison" and then giving details of the crimes Horton committed when on furlough, concluding the ad with the statement, "Weekend Prison Passes. Dukakis on Crime." The political action committee responsible for the ad had notified James Baker, the Bush campaign chairman, about the ad and told him they would not air it if the campaign disapproved. It took 25 days for Baker to voice his candidate's disapproval (*New York Times* 1988).

Although the most controversial element of Bush's 1988 presidential campaign came from an outside group, the Bush team made Dukakis's alleged softness on crime a centerpiece of its campaign messaging agenda. Instead of picking apart each component of an opponent's record, candidates will often focus on one or two salient issues with which to target their opponent. In 1988, crime was a primary concern for many Americans. In the 2008 presidential election, Obama was able to pin his Republican opponent John McCain to the failed economic policies of the George W. Bush administration as well as the Iraq War, two issues that were of top concern to Americans that year.

PAID MEDIA

PQ Media, a leading provider of media research, reported that $4.55 billion was spent by campaigns on political media in 2010, up 8% compared to 2008, a presidential election cycle, and up 44.9% compared to 2006 (PQ Media 2010). Spending was projected to exceed $5.6 billion in 2012 (PQ Media 2010). The organization tracked advertising spending on broadcast and cable television, radio, newspapers, out-of-home (media designed to reach consumers outside of the home, such as billboards), Internet, mobile, and magazines as well as marketing media including direct mail, telemarketing, public relations, event marketing, promotions, and marketing research. PQ Media's 2010 report on political media spending noted that broadcast television remained the primary medium that political campaigns used to reach voters in 2010, accounting for $2.29 billion in advertising, or just over half of all campaign media spending, and commanding nearly three-quarters of total ad spending. The report noted that although broadcast television's share of overall political media spending declined each election year from 2000 (55.8%) to 2010 (50.2%), the amount spent on this medium increased 237% during the period. Although radio's share of ad spending also declined every campaign cycle of the decade, newspapers were the only medium in which overall spending actually declined in any year from 2000 to 2010. Newspaper ad spending decreased for the second consecutive election cycle in 2010, as its share of total campaign media spending (2%) and advertising (3.1%) continued to slide for the third straight election. Meanwhile, advertising media that consistently grew and gained share of ad spending over the 2000–2010 period included cable television (7.9% share in 2010), Internet (4.3%) and mobile, which tripled in spending from 2006 to 2010, but still accounted for well under 1% of total political advertising in 2010. Direct-mail spending accounted for almost three-quarters of all marketing expenditures in 2010, increasing 2.9% (to $1.03 billion), compared with 2008, and 46.2% compared to 2006. Among the other five marketing media, which combined accounted for only $356 million in 2010, public relations was the fastest growing segment, climbing 13% to $52 million compared to 2008 (PQ Media 2010).

Despite the expense associated with political advertising, paid media presents an array of communications outreach tactics that are attractive to political campaigns because they allow them to control the messages put out for public consumption as well as the timing and targeting of those messages. In contemporary campaigns, there are an increasing number of ways in which campaigns can use paid media, some more expensive than others. As I noted, broadcast television accounts for the largest share of political campaign advertising. Although television ads are highly engaging, they can also be expensive to produce and air, especially during peak periods closer to Election Day when ad space is at a premium (Burton and Shea 2010). Production costs are diminishing, however, because video technology and editing software has become less expensive and more widely available, enabling rapid production.

Even lower-level state and local campaigns are increasingly attracted to television advertising to deliver their messages, and the medium typically takes up the largest chunk of a campaign's budget (West 2010; Fowler and Ridout 2011). When advertising on television, the effectiveness of an ad campaign depends on both reach (how many viewers will see the ad) and frequency (how many times viewers will see the ad). In the wake of *Citizens United*, campaigns must now contend with media environments in which they are competing for air time not only with their opponents and other candidates running for office, but also with outside groups trying to get on the airways with their own messages, especially those that buy up the bulk of air space months before an election.

Contemporary campaigns have a vast array of outlets to consider for ad placement. In previous decades, campaigns used to be able to focus their television advertising efforts on broadcast television alone; the growth of cable news allows campaigns to target narrower audiences on niche channels. With broadcast television, a campaign's message can be widely dispersed to the electorate, which can be especially useful for candidates looking to mobilize potential supporters with lower incomes who may not be able to afford a cable television subscription. Candidates do not have to worry that they are only reaching paid subscribers because broadcast television is widely available.

The caveat, however, is less precision in targeting voters. Cable affords candidates more confidence that their ads are targeting groups of voters likely to be responsive to them. This is because of the structure of cable companies and the variety of programming options available to cable subscribers. Local cable companies have zones of broadcasting that are more or less fixed and easily identified by candidates and can be somewhat close to the boundaries of a candidate's district (Federal Communications Commission 2012). Another advantage is that more specialized programming on cable networks allows candidates to target voters in ways similar to advertisements designed to sell products. In 1992, Matt Stanton, a sales manager for National Cable Advertising, noted that the "microtargeting" techniques that sell products to consumers are also a factor in elections. Media buyers for candidates can focus their efforts on specific networks and programs to reach the right voters (Nordheimer 1992). Well-known, partisan-leaning cable news networks include Fox News, which tends to lean conservative, and MSNBC, which has a more liberal bent. But campaigns can also use other demographic information to reach the voters they want; different channels and programs are designed to reach different sets of viewers. A candidate interested in mobilizing younger voters might take out advertisements on MTV, whereas a candidate interested in mobilizing women voters might focus on the cable channel Oxygen (Burton and Shea 2010).

Campaigns have many media outlets available to them beyond television. Other mediums offer comparable advantages even if they are not as widely utilized and can often be less expensive. Although radio advertising does not have the visual advantages that television does, it allows campaigns to reach beyond paid subscribers *and* potentially target narrower audiences because radio programs are often segmented to reach different types of audiences. For example, Hispanic voters tend to listen to radio at higher rates than do non-Hispanics. Thus, Spanish-language radio is a potentially useful means of targeting Hispanic voters and of improving turnout among this demographic group (Panagopoulos and Green 2011).

Ads in print newspapers have for the most part dwindled in recent years with the rise of online newspapers and new media. However, there are certain advantages to putting a candidate's message in newspapers. First, a campaign is far more likely to find ad space available in newspapers (no space or air-time limitations!) and newspaper advertising can be relatively less expensive and highly-targetable. We can look at Minnesota for an example of newspaper ad pricing. Rates for an ad in a regional newspaper like the *Duluth News Tribune* (circulation: 39,500 [Sundays], 27,500 [weekdays]) differ for state and local and federal candidates. The rate for a full-page, black-and-white ad for a local candidate would cost about $8,138 (Sunday) or $6,958 (weekday), whereas federal candidates would pay $10,800 for a Sunday ad and $9,276 for a weekday ad. Second, newspaper readers appear to be more likely to vote, and newspaper ads can slightly boost voter turnout (Helliker 2007; A. S. Gerber et al. 2009; Panagopoulos and Bowers 2012). Finally, people consider newspapers more trustworthy than other media outlets, so they may be more likely to find a candidate's message in a newspaper ad believable and convincing than if it were in ads placed elsewhere (Hendricks 2012).

Finally, the Internet has made "new media" an attractive option for campaigns. Although candidate websites are important for providing voters with a central location through which to learn about candidate positions, their biography, and upcoming campaign events, voters must have a reason to visit pages in the first place. To accomplish this, campaigns can buy ads that are linked to specific web searches that will show an Internet user an advertisement for a candidate's website. This way, campaigns can have some assurance that their message is reaching individuals who at least have some interest in supporting them. New media encompasses a host of messaging options; today, candidates not only have websites, but also Facebook pages, Twitter accounts, and Instagram accounts (Williams and Gulati 2012). A recent study of political campaigning during the 2012 elections suggests that campaigns use social networking sites to enhance the effectiveness of their messages, to engage citizens online and promote activism on behalf of candidates, and to help candidates better understand the opinions of the electorate (Bor 2014).

Although in some respects campaigns stick to traditional modes of message delivery, the actual placement of messaging has become much more complicated. The number of paid media outlets has increased drastically since the advent of television changed political campaigns; candidates now must decide among traditional network, cable, satellite channels, radio messages, and Internet advertisements. In addition, video on demand, streaming video, and DVRs allow voters to watch content wherever and whenever they like and allow them to rely less on traditional forms of entertainment and news. How do candidates reach college students who canceled their cable plan to save money but pay for Netflix, which is free of advertisements? What about families who use their DVRs to fast-forward through commercials?

Because of this fragmented media environment, campaign strategists need an understanding of how different types of media are bought and the different audiences each can target. "Broadcast" targeting reaches a large subset of people, for example, television viewers or radio listeners for specific channels and stations within a metropolitan area. This differs from "narrowcasting," which allows campaigns to be more direct in their message targeting. Campaigns can narrowcast using more traditional tactics, like direct mail, but the Internet is also allowing candidates to become more targeted using e-mails and by purchasing ads that are shown to specific subsets of users based on their Internet browsing history.

Nevertheless, the most established type of media buying remains television advertising. Gross ratings points (GRPs) are the standard unit of consideration for television ad buys. GRPs represent "the sum total of the ratings achieved for a media schedule" (Berkovitz 1996). They are a calculation of ratings for a given program multiplied by the number of times a campaign advertisement is aired in each program time slot. The cost per point is the cost of purchasing a single rating point. To estimate media costs, the person in charge of ad buys for a campaign will multiply the total GRPs by the cost per point to get an estimate of the media cost for an advertising schedule. Generally, 100 GRPs means the average television viewer will see a commercial once (or that 50% of viewers will be exposed twice, and so on). A general rule of thumb in the industry is that a voter should be exposed to an ad at least five times weekly (so 500 GRPs) for it to impact his or her vote choice (Berkowitz 1996).

Advertising costs for television vary depending on the format and programming. The cost for a national 30-second spot on channels like ABC, NBC, CBS, or FOX can range from $35,000 to nearly $2 million. Cable television rates are generally lower; as of 2011, the average cost of a 30-second spot on one of the top 15 networks was around $13,000, with ESPN charging the highest rate ($31,551 on average) (Crupi 2011). Local spots cost less money, but prices can vary. Ad buys in big media markets, like Chicago or New York, can be as expensive as national advertising. The costs of airing ads on television can also depend on the desirability of the audiences as well as the time of day (known as "daypart") because this can affect audience sizes; the largest audience sizes can usually be found during primetime (8–11 PM EST), so ads aired during these times can be more expensive (Fowler et al. 2016).

Campaigns can leverage information about programs and channels, and the characteristics of their viewing audiences, to design television ad buys that reach target voters. Tracking firms like Nielsen or Mediamark Research and Intelligence (MRI), for instance, can provide useful information like: In 1999, CNN viewers aged 50 and older were 29% more likely to vote; the median age of Weather Cannel viewers was 43 and audiences skewed female; 69% of History Channel viewers skewed male during prime time; and Lifetime was the top network for women 18 and older and women 25-44 in total day, prime and weekend viewing (Shaw 2004).

An illustration provided by Kolodny and Hagen (2009) is instructive. The authors analyze television ad buys in competitive races in the Philadelphia media market in 2006 to show that campaigns actually spent more on advertising between 5:00PM and 8:00PM (compared to between 8:00PM and 11:00PM) in part because the percentage of the desired, older (55+) demographic grows from 22% to 39% during the late afternoon. Overall, the median price for a 30-second spot grew from $700 at 6AM to $1,200 at 9AM, dropped in the early afternoon, spiked to $3,000 at 7:30PM, peaked at $9,000 at 9PM and dropped to $3,750 during the late local news. The specific shows on which ads air also affect pricing. A 30-second spot aired by the National Republican Congressional Committee (NRCC) at 9:15PM on Wednesday, November 1, 2006 on ABC's *Lost* cost $35,000, more than twice as much as a spot that aired at the same time on CBS's *Jericho* ($14,000). To ensure ads will be aired as scheduled, campaigns must also consider paying a premium to buy nonpreemptible airtime; Kolodny and Hagen (2009: 200) report that the premium for a nonpreemptible spot during *The Biggest Loser* on October 25, 2006 was 63% higher ($6,500) than a preemptible spot on the same program ($4,000). Prices were also considerably lower for candidate campaigns than for parties or interest groups and for ads purchased far in advance, but campaigns often find it difficult to make such early resource commitments (Kolodny and Hagen 2009).

Campaign strategists also must develop buying strategies for radio advertisements. In general, radio advertisements are far less expensive in terms of production and ad cost. For example, a 30-second spot on WBBM-FM, a popular radio station in Chicago owned by CBS, costs about $362.00 (Gaebler 2015a). Conversely, a 30-second advertisement on WAAG in Galesburg, a rural town on the western side of Illinois owned by Galesburg Broadcasting Company, is only about $26.00 (Gaebler 2015b).

Consider an example. Imagine you are the media director or campaign manager for a statewide, general election campaign to promote a Democratic candidate in Minnesota. The map presented in Figure 6.2 shows that Minnesota is comprised of seven designated market areas (DMAs): Minneapolis–St. Paul, Sioux Falls, Fargo–Valley City, La Crosse–Eau Claire, Duluth–Superior, Rochester–Mason City–Austin, and Mankato. Although the maps only show Minnesota, keep in mind that DMAs do not generally overlap perfectly with state or district lines. To enhance the effectiveness of ad buying, this map could be overlaid with maps delineating

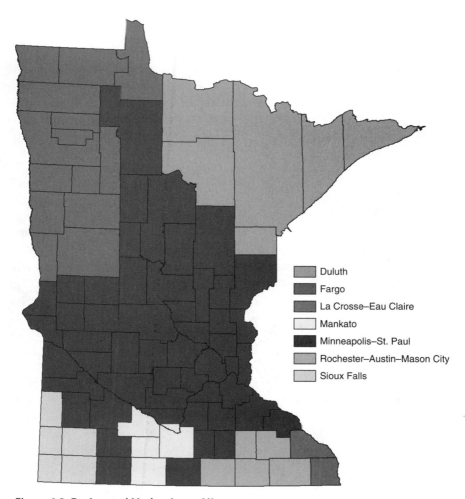

Figure 6.2 Designated Market Areas: Minnesota

SOURCE: http://www.northpine.com/broadcast/mn/tvmarkets.html/.

congressional or other district boundaries, the partisan composition of the state, voting patterns in prior elections (for example, Figure 6.3 displays vote share distributions by county for the November 2012 presidential election), and any other geographically dispersed information that could be useful for targeting purposes. Table 6.1 presents some basic information about each DMA, including television and radio costs per point to advertise in these markets, and Table 6.2 lists the television stations for the Minnesota–St. Paul DMA. A reasonable television and radio advertising media plan (excluding production costs) for a general election campaign expected to last about nine weeks may look something like what is

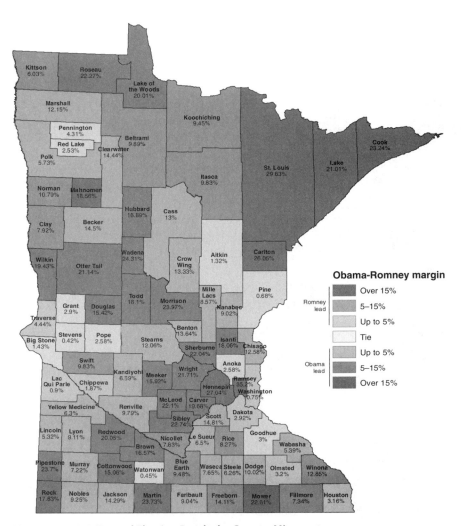

Figure 6.3 2012 General Election Results by County, Minnesota
SOURCE: Minnesota Office of the Secretary of State

Table 6.1 Minnesota Media Profile (Designated Market Areas)

DESIGNATED MARKET AREAS	COUNTIES (NO.)	POPULATION	HOUSEHOLDS	COST PER POINT (TV)	COST PER POINT (RADIO)	TV STATIONS (NO.)
Minneapolis–St. Paul	51	3,820,600	1,753,780	289	69	18
Sioux Falls	5	565,900	263,790	44	10	17
Fargo–Valley City	14	506,900	241,990	40	10	11
La Crosse–Eau Claire	2	473,500	216,510	36	9	8
Duluth–Superior	6	365,400	174,570	29	7	7
Rochester–Mason City–Austin	5	304,700	144,590	24	6	6
Mankato	4	101,100	52,640	9	2	1

SOURCE: http://www.tvnewscheck.com/.

Table 6.2 Television Stations: Minnesota–St. Paul Designated Market Area

TV STATION	AFFILIATION	GROUP AFFILIATION/LICENSEE
KARE	NBC	Gannett Co.
KAWB	PBS	Northern Minnesota Public Television
KAWE	PBS	Northern Minnesota Public Television
KCCO-TV	CBS	CBS Television Stations
KCCW-TV	CBS	CBS Television Stations
KFTC	FOX	Fox TV Stations
KMSP-TV	FOX	Fox TV Stations
KPXM	ION	Ion Media Networks Inc.
KRWF	ABC	Hubbard Broadcasting Inc.
KSAX	ABC	Hubbard Broadcasting Inc.
KSTC-TV	IND	Hubbard Broadcasting Inc.
KSTP-TV	ABC	Hubbard Broadcasting Inc.
KTCA-TV	PBS	Twin Cities Public Television
KTCI-TV	PBS	Twin Cities Public Television
KWCM-TV	PBS	West Central Minnesota Educational Television
WCCO-TV	CBS	CBS Television Stations
WFTC	MNT	Fox TV Stations
WUCW	CW	Sinclair Broadcast Group

presented in Table 6.3. This example is rather crude because we possess few details about the (imaginary) campaign's targeting strategy, overall budget, and opponent advertising, but it provides a launching pad for thinking about structuring a media advertising plan.

Table 6.3 Hypothetical Campaign Media Schedule (Television and Radio)

TELEVISION

WEEKS	MINNEAPOLIS – SAINT PAUL (51 COUNTIES)	DULUTH – SUPERIOR (6 COUNTIES)	FARGO – VALLEY CITY (14 COUNTIES)	ROCHESTER – MASON CITY – AUSTIN (5 COUNTIES)	MANKATO (4 COUNTIES)	LA CROSSE – EAU CLAIRE (2 COUNTIES)	SIOUX FALLS (MITCHELL) (5 COUNTIES)	COST PER WEEK
Week 9	800	500	500	500	500	300	300	$306,200
Week 8	800	600	500	600	600	400	400	$320,400
Week 7	500	200	500	200	200	100	200	$189,300
Week 6	500	200	200	200	200	100	200	$177,300
Week 5	500	600	400	200	200	100	200	$196,900
Week 4	500	200	200	200	200	100	200	$177,300
Week 3	500	200	200	200	200	100	200	$177,300
Week 2	1,500	1,000	800	1,000	1,300	300	400	$558,600
Week 1	1,800	1,800	1,000	1,800	1,800	1,000	1,000	$751,800
Week 0	200	200	200	200	200	200	200	$94,200
TOTAL GRP	7,600	5,500	4,500	5,100	5,400	2,700	3,300	

RADIO

WEEKS	MINNEAPOLIS – SAINT PAUL	DULUTH – SUPERIOR	FARGO – VALLEY CITY	ROCHESTER – MASON CITY	MANKATO	LA CAROSSE – EAU CLAIRE	SIOUX FALLS (MITCHELL)	COST PER WEEK
Week 9	250	250	250	250	250	250	250	$28,250
Week 8	500	500	500	500	500	500	500	$56,500
Week 7	200	200	200	200	200	200	100	$21,600
Week 6	350	200	200	200	200	200	200	$32,950
Week 5	200	350	350	200	200	200	200	$25,150
Week 4	500	200	200	500	500	500	500	$51,400
Week 3	500	200	200	500	500	500	500	$51,400
Week 2	700	500	700	700	700	700	700	$77,700
Week 1	500	500	750	500	750	500	500	$59,500
Week 0	200	100	100	100	100	100	100	$18,200
TOTAL GRP	3900	3000	3450	3650	3900	3650	3550	

Other examples of mass media tactics that campaigns have at their disposal include outdoor advertising, such as billboards. The research and consulting firm PQ Media projected that $63 million would be spent on political advertising on billboards nationwide in the 2008 election cycle (Lieberman 2007), reflecting nearly a fivefold increase since the 2000 elections, when a total of $13 million was spent by campaigns on outdoor media (PQ Media 2004). Relative to other media, outdoor advertising offers campaigns several advantages. Outdoor advertising is relatively inexpensive to produce and has the ability to reach wide audiences and to create awareness quickly. Studies also find that outdoor media reaches Americans who are not (or are only lightly) exposed to other media, including newspaper and local television news (Arbitron 2001), and that unaided recall of messages advertised using outdoor media exceeds recall of messages encountered on network or cable television (Cunningham and Coleman 2003). "Showings" are the units of measurement used to place billboard advertising; for example, 25 showings denotes billboards adequate to reach one-quarter of the population at least once (or 5% of the population five times, and so on). The estimated cost to purchase 25 showings (3 billboards) in Norwalk, Connecticut, for one month, for example, would likely be in the ballpark of $5,000 (including printing), but digital billboards can be even more economical. Experimental tests have also shown lawn signs can effectively boost candidate voteshares (Green, Krasno, Coppock, Farrer, Lenoir and Zingher 2016) and that street signs can raise turnout (Panagopoulos 2009c).

Campaigns often complement their mass media advertising with outreach delivered by direct mail. We also discuss direct mail in the context of voter mobilization in the following chapter, but an introduction here may be helpful. Although many consider direct mail a nuisance and often dispose of direct-mail appeals instantaneously, studies reveal they have the potential to attract voters' attention (Green and Gerber 2012). They are also highly targetable and are an ideal way to deliver specialized messages (for instance, about wedge issues) that candidates may not wish to publicize broadly (Hillygus and Shields 2008). Direct mail can also be cost-effective, especially in some areas (like New York City or Los Angeles) where television and even radio advertising can be prohibitively expensive for local campaigns. By contrast, an 11 × 17 inch color mailer printed on 100-pound paper stock may cost between $.18 and $.25 to produce (depending on the number of units), and an 8.5 × 11 inch color mailer on postcard stock could cost between $.25 and $.40 to print. Postage to mail the letter would range from $.26 to $.43 depending on the size of the mailing, whether it is presorted, and other details.

Campaigns now also have a plethora of options for placing ads within websites and social media platforms. These ads often appear in the sidebars of websites and search services. There are many options to consider when buying digital advertising, so it is a complicated enterprise. Campaign goals should guide the key decisions. There are three main cost models for ad buying: cost-per-click, cost-per-thousand-impressions, and cost-per-acquisition. Cost-per-click is optimal for campaigns trying to drive as much traffic as possible to a website. Cost-per-thousand-impressions is best when trying to raise awareness by exposing as many viewers as possible to a candidate's message. Cost-per-acquisition is preferable when trying to track acquisitions (or conversions), which are actions completed by viewers (e.g., making a donation or signing up for an e-mail list). There is also a cost-per-lead cost model, which is used when collecting e-mail addresses for a list.

Next, campaigns must consider multiple targeting options. Remarketing involves placing a pixel on a website to capture visitors in a remarketing list. Ads can then be served to that list of website visitors, who have already shown interest in the campaign. One can also target contextually, an approach which selects sites to display the ad based on keywords found on the site. For example, a campaign can run ads for a candidate on pages featuring articles about that candidate. One can also target ads based on user interests. There are also ways to match mailing lists to online users. For example, a campaign can match a list of mailing addresses to Facebook and/or Twitter users and serve them specific ads. Campaigns can also perform cookie matches, which find users online who have visited sites that suggest the user may be receptive to the candidate and his or her message. More and more types of data are being made available to campaign advertisers. Targeting can be refined using voter files, consumer habits, household income, geotargeting (down to a zip code or congressional district level), and the many other data segments that are available from data providers like BlueKai or eXelate.

Digital ad buy options include programmatic, direct buys, and ad networks. Programmatic buying is done through a demand side platform, which gives campaign media buyers access to inventory from ad exchanges and ad networks. Demand side platform users typically use real-time bidding, and the best bid wins the impressions. Direct buying is done directly between the campaign and publisher, and the ads are directly placed on the website. Advertising networks buy large amounts of inventory from multiple publishers and sell the inventory to buyers, including campaigns. Buying from an ad network is a good option if a campaign does not wish to bid directly on ads but intends to show ads on many websites.

As far as ad units are concerned, there are also many options, but some are more common than others. For example, the most popular display banner sizes are 300 × 250 (window), 160 × 600 (skyscraper), 728 × 90 (banner), 320 × 50 (mobile), and 300 × 600 (large skyscraper). There are also multiple forms of video ads. First are preroll video ads, which appear before an online video begins and are typically 15 or 30 seconds long. In-banner video ads appear in the banner unit on a website. A campaign can also buy a homepage takeover, which is particularly useful for get-out-the-vote efforts. This features multiple sizes of the same ad creative that appear together on the homepage of a website for a certain amount of time, usually a day or two. Takeovers can be a good way to catch visitors' attention and make it more likely that they will click through to the landing page (like a campaign website). To take over Yahoo's homepage, for example, the

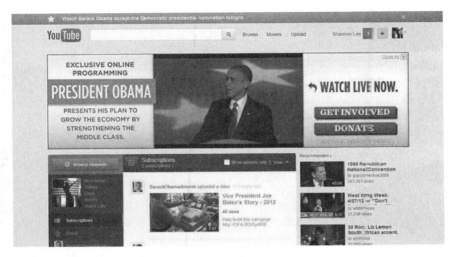

Figure 6.4 Obama Campaign YouTube Example

average cost is between $450,000 and $600,000 per day. YouTube, a video stream-ing service, asks for about $400,000 for a takeover and includes multiple features such as in-stream video advertisements, static display ads, and l stings of adver-tisements on featured video listings. Figure 6.4 shows an example of what an online advertising takeover might look like on YouTube. Hulu, the popular online television-viewing platform, also incorporates advertisements into shows at a cost of $25 to $30 per thousand viewers, and promoted trending topics on Twitter typically sell for about $120,000. Stand-alone log-out screen ads on Facebook can be purchased for around $100,000 (Marshall 2013). Of course, many of these options are inappropriate (and extravagant) for campaigns that operate in geographically circumscribed jurisdictions; as I noted previously, even presidential campaigns strategically concentrate spending and rarely deploy na-tional ad buys, but these details provide a sense of the resources that such a strat-egy would require. In general, online advertising rates vary depending on a complex mix of ad dimensions, location on the site, ad performance, and market demand. Nevertheless, many digital and social media outlets offer more afford-able options, and campaigns can generally expect to be able to expose targeted voters to their online advertisements at a rate of $10–$40 per thousand (cost-per-thousand-impressions) for established, reputable sites. Another example may be useful for illustrative purposes. According to Vincent Harris, the founder of Harris Media, a leading GOP digital public affairs firm based in Austin, Texas, whose clients include the U.S. Senate majority leader Mitch McConnell and 2016 presidential candidate and Texas senator Ted Cruz, a standard month-long digi-tal advertising plan that features video and display for a hypothetical statewide political campaign might look something like what is presented in Table 6.4.[1]

---

[1]Personal e-mail communication with author via Alix Carlin on June 12, 2015.

Table 6.4 Monthly Digital Advertising Plan for Hypothetical Statewide Campaign

AD CHANNEL	AD TYPE	BUDGET	REACH
Facebook	Newsfeed post	$35,000	3.8 million impressions
Twitter	Engagement tweets	$30,000	3.3 million impressions; 50,000 engagements
Google	Sear	$10,000	5,700 clicks
Google	Display ad	$15,000	5 million impressions
Google	TrueView (video)	$10,000	65,000 views
Total		*$100,000*	

Candidates are often strategic in when they launch online advertisements and takeovers and may do so to preempt positive earned media coverage of their opponent that is predictable, such as during presidential nominating conventions. During the 2012 Republican Nominating Convention, the Obama campaign bought a takeover of CNN, pictured in Figure 6.5, where viewers saw the ad placed next to a headline of "earned" media claiming, "It's Mitt Romney's Night." Obama's campaign also took over the websites of newspapers in Tampa Bay, the site of the Republican convention in 2012 (Fitzpatrick 2012).

As I will discuss further in Chapter 9, social media also offers an array of free and priced advertising options. In theory, a campaign could launch a Facebook page and use its initial flow of followers (for smaller campaigns, these might be friends and family members) to attract a wider audience. Each additional "like" on a Facebook page or on a post within a page leads to the page being shared with other connected users in their newsfeed. But campaigns also can and do pay for

Figure 6.5 Obama Campaign CNN Takeover

targeted Facebook ads based on specific interests. For example, a Democratic candidate running for Congress with a pro–health care reform platform might target individuals who identify as Democrats, have health care concerns, express an interest in health care reform, and live near that candidate's district. These potential targets are kept track of using Facebook's user data, which includes information on clicks, likes, posts, and expressed interests that are then matched with an ad's targeted audience. Facebook allows candidates to choose the amount of money they want to spend on an ad, which is then translated into an estimated number of "likes per day." For example, an ad for Hillary Clinton's 2016 presidential campaign running in the state of New York aimed at targeting women might select the interests listed in Figure 6.6 as a part of the ad's target audience. Facebook allows campaigns to set daily budgets and run an ad as long as they see fit. Note that campaigns also have the option of specifying genders in ad targets (in this case, women) and the ability to set limits on the age groups targeted. Here, the ad campaign is set to target individuals 18 years or older, which makes sense given the voting age in the United States. If the campaign wanted to be even more specific in its targeting, say, aiming an ad at young women, it could adjust the age limits set by the advertisement.

In today's campaign environment, campaign organizations spend a lot of time talking about the importance of launching effective digital campaigns, but still seem to spend the bulk of their funds on television and radio advertising. This is both because television advertising is more costly and because online advertising is in some senses more risky and less tested as an effective means of targeting voters. As I

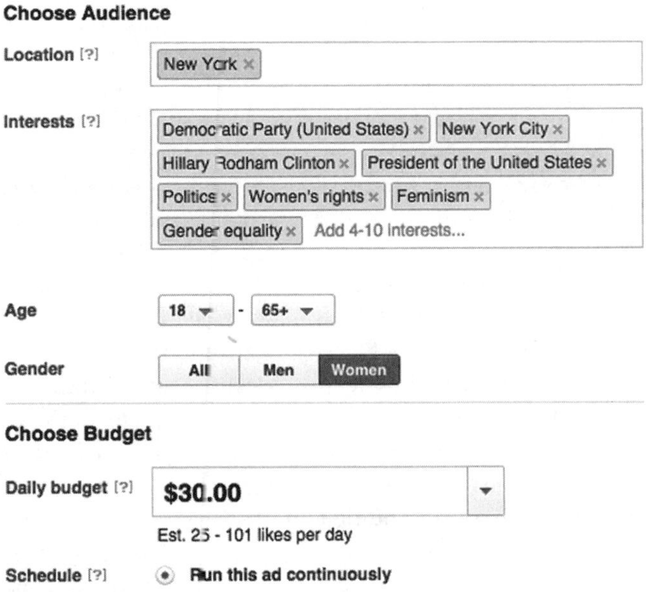

Choose Audience

Location [?]   New York ×

Interests [?]   Democratic Party (United States) ×   New York City ×
                Hillary Rodham Clinton ×   President of the United States ×
                Politics ×   Women's rights ×   Feminism ×
                Gender equality ×   Add 4-10 interests...

Age   18 ▼ - 65+ ▼

Gender   All   Men   **Women**

Choose Budget

Daily budget [?]   **$30.00**   ▼
                   Est. 25 - 101 likes per day

Schedule [?]   ◉ Run this ad continuously

Figure 6.6 Online Advertising Targeting

discussed previously, campaigns may be moving to take advantage of digital advertising, but it is by no means replacing television and radio advertisements. In the 10
most strongly contested House races in the 2014 midterm elections, candidates spent
some money on digital advertising, but it still accounted for a small amount of overall
spending. Confirming the national patterns reported by PQ Media as described
above, these campaigns spent more than $34 million on television and radio adver-
tisements, but only about $1.1 million on their digital outreach (Willis 2015).

The landscape of media use has grown increasingly fragmented and seems to
be constantly changing, making it more difficult than ever to reach voters with
paid political advertising. To deal with the challenges of a more fragmented
media environment, campaigns, vendors, and media outlets have begun to share
information in unprecedented ways. Campaigns have databases that have substantial information about voters, fundraising, field operations, get-out-the-vote
operations, and polling information. Media operations often have information
on individuals' online activity, their social media activity, and their television
viewing. In the 2012 election cycle, both Republican and Democratic campaigns
worked to put this type of information together, merging multiple datasets from
a number of different sources to allow them to make smarter decisions with
regard to the placement of their messaging (Jester and Roberts 2013).

EARNED MEDIA

Although the use of paid media gives candidates a fair amount of discretion over
the timing, audience, and content of their campaign messaging, earned media is
especially valuable given that campaigns have limited resources from which to
draw for paid media advertising. Earned media is coverage of campaigns by news
organizations. As the name implies, although this type of coverage is technically
"free," it does not often come easy for campaigns. Burton and Shea (2010) define
earned media as "news coverage on television, on radio, in the papers, or on Web-
based outlets where others must be persuaded about the value of one's message.
Consultants call it earned media rather than free media in order to emphasize the
hard work that goes into the quest for coverage" (170). Although campaigns
cannot actually manage the news, they do their best to (a) get news coverage of
their candidate's activities and positions and (b) ensure that such coverage is
positive. When campaigns can get it, the advantage of positive earned media is
that candidates get exposure for a low cost relative to the price of paid advertising, exposure that is presented by a theoretically neutral, and therefore more
trustworthy, outlet. Furthermore, as I touched on in Chapter 3, the news reaches
people when they are more likely to be actively seeking political information and
may be more receptive to a candidate's message.

To "earn" media, there are a number of different strategies communications
directors can use. One of the most widely regarded means of earning media coverage is the news release. News releases help news outlets make sense of what is
going on in the context of a race in a way that hopefully paints information about

candidates, new statements, and upcoming events in a favorable light. News outlets receive innumerable news releases during a campaign season, making it difficult for campaigns to be heard amid the din of all of the other races. Another oft-used way of garnering media attention is to hold news conferences, which brings reporters into an organized and coordinated environment to ask questions about campaign developments.

Outside these more traditional methods of earned media, candidates will also "create" media events, doing anything from helping to clean up neighborhoods, to shaking hands with workers, to sitting in on popular television talk shows like *Oprah* and late-night television programming. Cory Booker, the former mayor of Newark, New Jersey, and a current U.S. senator from New Jersey, became famous for living in the one of the most troubled housing projects in Newark alongside impoverished and embattled tenants, which brought him significant media attention during his bids for the mayor's office in Newark in 2002 and 2006. He has since become well known for living in less than desirable neighborhoods to raise awareness of the blight of urban poverty (Jacobs 2006). High-profile candidates can also leverage celebrity endorsements as a means to garner attention and create media events. In 2008, Oprah Winfrey endorsed Barack Obama prior to the start of the Democratic primary. According to a study by economists from the University of Maryland and Northwestern University, this endorsement increased Obama's financial contributions, improved overall voter turnout, and brought in more than 1 million additional votes for Obama (Garthwaite and Moore 2012). Finally, for local candidates or those who are poorly funded, debates can also be a good way to garner earned media coverage. Front runners are often hesitant to debate, whereas candidates who are lagging in the polls and fundraising can benefit from the balanced setting of a debate environment because both candidates get the same amount of attention.

As I discussed in Chapter 3, not all earned media is good media. The news media can be both advantageous and disastrous, an opportunity and a hazard. Candidates naturally need media attention, but they need the right kind of media attention. And withholding access to the candidate from the press can be just as damaging as a gaffe or a misstep. The McCain/Palin campaign found this out the hard way during the 2008 presidential elections. Their campaign had been heavily criticized for not allowing the media to have access to Palin, accusations that led to Palin's infamous interview with CBS reporter Katie Couric. During the interview, Palin did herself and her running mate no favors with her uncertain and vague responses to Couric's questions on her foreign policy experience (Stanley 2008).

Especially in the era of new media, campaigns will do whatever they can to use moments and sound bites from debate events to their advantage to develop content that "goes viral." Viral news is similar to the process of increasing returns; as it is redistributed over and over again on various media outlets and social networking sites, each redistribution creates more buzz and dissemination than the last. During one of the 2012 presidential debates, Mitt Romney suggested that President Obama was not spending enough money on the military, pointing out that the U.S. Navy had fewer ships at present than it did in 1916. The president responded by saying, "Well, Governor, we also have fewer horses and bayonets because the nature of our military has changed." The horses and bayonets comment went viral and was an "Internet hit" even before the debate was over, an earned media win for Obama's campaign and a troublesome gaffe for Romney (Orr 2012).

This example highlights how developments in online outlets and social media create a context in which campaigns can find it difficult to control messaging, a topic to be discussed further in Chapter 9. In previous decades, monitoring a media environment might have involved checking in with daily newspapers and monitoring nightly newscasts. With the advent of 24-hour cable news channels and the Internet, campaigns have had to become more vigilant in their monitoring to keep an eye out for potential opportunistic or challenging breaking news. Now, campaigns must contend not only with these traditional sources, but also with other more grassroots forms of "breaking news," such as Obama's horses and bayonets comment, that can go viral in a matter of minutes with the right amount of public interest. These developments require constant vigilance. In recent elections, campaigns have developed "rapid response teams" or "war rooms" to manage the multitude of ways in which candidates can earn media, both good and bad. In an effort to shape coverage of the 2012 vice presidential debate, both the Romney and the Obama campaigns sent e-mails to supporters urging them to follow their campaign Twitter accounts for fact checks and "real-time" rebuttals of their opponents, giving new meaning to the term rapid response. For the debate, the Obama campaign launched a rapid response twitter handle, @OFAdebates (pictured in Figure 6.7),

Figure 6.7 OFA Debate Response Twitter Account
SOURCE: Nyczepir (2012)

which was then used during the remaining presidential debates. Ultimately, these efforts fell short in terms of taking advantage of some of the more flashy, memorable moments of the debate, focusing instead on carefully crafted policy tweets, but they still paint a picture of what contemporary campaigns must do to try to control the message in an era of fragmented earned media (Nyczepir 2012).

MESSAGE CONTENT, MANAGEMENT
AND DELIVERY

In the previous chapter, we discussed the importance of message development. Effectively communicating and managing messages that have been carefully and strategically developed is just as critical and typically requires orchestration by the campaign communications director, the campaign manager, media consultants, and the candidates themselves. Some mediums may be more effective than others in communicating certain types of messages. Hillygus and Shields (2008), for example, find that campaigns are more likely to deliver attacks via direct mail and other targetable media than broadcast options like television; similarly, Fowler et al. (2016) find online ads to be more negative in tone on average compared to ads aired on television. Adopting an integrated approach that leverages a layered mix of media outlets often results in maximum impact. As Obama's campaign manager David Plouffe has put it, "[b]alanced communications across *all mediums* is critical in any messaging effort today" (quoted in Nielsen 2012: 17).

Beyond balancing media options, strategists must also consider other dimensions of message content. As I note above, the tone of an ad—whether it is positive or negative—is a key decision, but choices have to be made about other elements. Whether the ad or message will emphasize substantive policy positions or personal characteristics, or both, is an equally important decision. Analyses of ads aired on television in the 2014 congressional contests find that most ads (60%) focused mainly on policy matters, while only 13% emphasized personal characteristics; 25% included both personal and policy elements (Fowler et al. 2016). It may be surprising to some that the vast majority of campaign ads on television in 2014—85% in fact—included at least some policy content, and this was generally true regardless of ad tone (Fowler 2016). In policy-focused appeals, there was also considerable variation in the specific issues that were emphasized, likely selected based on research about the district's preferences and priorities.

Peripheral aspects of media messages can also play an important role. Audiovisual elements like music and visual imagery can convey specific points of view. Ominous music and darker, grainy, or black-and-white imagery in television ads are often used to portray candidates in a negative light, while positive communications tend to feature bright colors and upbeat music (West 2010). Even decisions about who does voiceovers in ads are important. Fowler et al. (2016) found most ads (60%) that used voiceovers in the 2014 cycle used male announcers, while 32% used women and 8% used both male and female announcers. Female announcers are more common in negative ads and in ads about so-called women's issues like education or abortion (Fowler 2016: 73). Studies reveal voters are responsive to these types of elements (Brader 2006), perhaps even subconsciously (Graber 2000; Lodge and Taber 2013). In fact, neuroscientific research posits voters' brains may actually be wired to process political stimuli that incorporate audiovisual elements more effectively than purely verbal or written messages (Graber 2000).

The timing of advertisements is another important component of message management. This comes into play most prominently for television advertising. Prime advertising slots are closer to Election Day, and if a campaign waits until the last minute to buy ad time, it may be stuck with an advertising spot at a time with low viewership or no advertising slot at all. The increasing use of early voting and vote by mail may also be changing the calculus of political advertising, topics I will discuss in greater detail in Chapter 10. With more and more citizens voting before Election Day, it may be less viable for candidates to target their advertising efforts near Election Day (Dunaway and Stein 2013).

With an increasing number of media options and the growth of new media, it is likely consultants with more specified areas of expertise will be needed for message management in future campaigns. In today's elections, it seems almost unimaginable that one or two people could effectively manage and execute a campaign's social media campaign, television advertisements, and radio spots, especially for high-profile candidacies. This poses further challenges for campaigns as they seek to maintain a coherent and consistent message in an increasingly diversified and complex messaging environment.

THE EFFECTIVENESS OF POLITICAL ADVERTISING AND CONSEQUENCES FOR DEMOCRACY

Although campaigns now spend billions of dollars every election cycle on getting their messages out, there is no guarantee these efforts will shift election outcomes in their favor. In response to the question of whether political advertising matters, a large body of research in political science says, "it depends." It depends on the type of message (is it positive or negative?), the timing, and the format of the message. It can also depend on who the advertising is reaching in the first place; political advertisements can have differential effects depending on the level of education and political interest of the individuals they are reaching. In many respects, political scientists still have a long way to go in accurately measuring the effectiveness of advertising in political campaigns, in large part because of the wide variety of methods used to capture exposure to advertising (Goldstein and Ridout 2004).

What matters most for campaigns is determining whether ads are effective in shifting the vote share away from an opponent and toward his or her candidate, as well as determining which mode of message delivery is most effective. A study done by the political scientist Daron Shaw, who also advised the Bush campaign during the 2000 and 2004 presidential elections, estimates that 1,000

GRPs for five weeks would produce about a one-point shift in a candidate's relative favorability and a 0.5% increase in his or her vote share (2006: 136). Seemingly small, the vote margin between George W. Bush and Al Gore in the decisive battleground state of Florida in the 2000 presidential election was less than 0.5%.

Some studies provide evidence that advertising can persuade voters. One over-time study suggests that candidate appearances and television advertisements within a given state can affect statewide preferences for that candidate and the Electoral College vote (Shaw 1999). During the 2004 presidential elections, exposure to advertising in favor of John Kerry increased one's likelihood of voting for him, whereas exposure to advertising in favor of George W. Bush decreased one's likelihood of voting for Kerry. During that same election year, voters exposed to ads supportive of Democratic candidates were more likely to support Democratic Senate candidates, and voters exposed to ads in favor of Republican ads showed greater support for Republican candidates (Franz and Ridout 2007).

In reality, political scientists agree that the effect of advertising depends on the context of an election and the timing and content of advertising. Campaign ads seem to matter more when candidates are unfamiliar, for example, in open seat races or for relatively unknown challengers. This echoes the logic of the effects of challenger spending. Simply put, there is more room for movement in favor of unknown candidates than for those for whom citizens already have well-informed opinions (Jacobson and Carson 2015). Furthermore, the volume of ads may have a greater impact than the content of an advertisement, although people tend to become preoccupied with the content of one or two memorable advertisements over the course of an election season. In research comparing presidential ad buys in two presidential elections, one in which both candidates took public financing (2004) and one in which one candidate did not (2008), evidence suggests that the increased capability of the Obama campaign to outspend and outadvertise the McCain campaign in 2008 gave Obama's campaign 1 percentage point more of the vote in counties than John Kerry earned in those same counties in the 2004 elections (Franz and Ridout 2010).

Although recent studies find advertising can be effective, they also raise questions about the longevity of these effects. During the 2006 gubernatorial campaign in Texas, Rick Perry worked with four political scientists to study the effects of political advertising. They found that ads do "matter," but not necessarily for long. The political scientists noted that their advertising treatment raised Perry's vote share by almost 5 percentage points per 1,000 GRPs in the weeks when his ads aired. However, merely a week after the ads aired, although Perry was far more popular than he had been in at the beginning of the experiment in early January 2006, the effects of the ads themselves were virtually gone, amounting to a rapid decay in their effects (Gerber et al. 2011; Issenberg 2012d). Similar decay effects were found for advertising during the 2000 presidential campaign (Hill et al. 2013).

NEGATIVE ADVERTISING

Negative advertising is ubiquitous in modern campaigns, and its effects have attracted considerable scholarly scrutiny. Many question whether it actually helps candidates win elections. Again, the answer might be, "it depends." During the 2000 election, for example, ads attacking Al Gore were more effective at moving support toward his opponent than were ads attacking George W. Bush (Johnston et al. 2004). In the 2012 presidential election cycle, not only was there an unprecedented amount of advertising, but also nearly two-thirds of the ads broadcasted were negative attacks (Fowler and Ridout 2012). Consistent with findings reported in other studies (Geer 2006; Kahn and Kenney 2004), Figure 6.8 shows negativity in political advertisements broadcasted on television has been climbing steadily over the past two decades in both presidential and congressional races. Although campaign consultants appear to think that negative messages are far more effective than positive ads supporting their own candidate or contrasting ads that point out differences between the two candidates, empirical evidence is more ambivalent. Early studies suggested that negative advertising demobilizes citizens and reduces their sense of political efficacy (Ansolabehere et al. 1994), but recent evidence suggests otherwise. The topic has received so

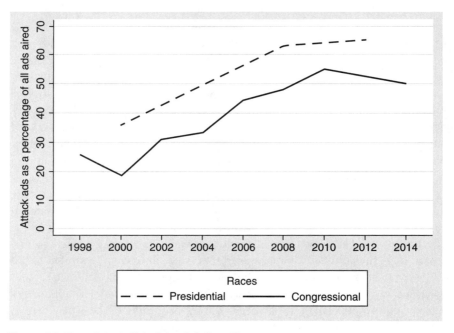

Figure 6.8 Negativity in Television Ads Over Time
NOTE: Percentage of Negative Advertising over Time in the Top 75 markets, September 1–Election Day of Each Year.
SOURCE: Wesleyan Media Project (Fowler et al. 2016: 53)

much attention that the political scientists Richard Lau, Lee Sigelman, and Ivy Brown Rovner (2007) were able to conduct a meta-analysis of these studies. They found that although negative ads left a greater impression and were more informative than other ads, they did little to improve political interest. Most important for the purposes of campaigns, negative advertisements do little to move votes toward candidates who wage negative ad campaigns; although they lower support for the candidate being attacked, they also decrease support for the attacker, canceling out any significant shift toward one candidate or the other.

Given that they are spending so much money on television advertising in particular, it makes sense that political consultants want to know how much bang for their buck they are getting. But other, less expensive forms of message delivery can affect attitudes toward candidates as well. Although their study uses nonpartisan advertisements, findings from Panagopoulos and Green (2012) suggest that radio advertisements can improve electoral competition, particularly benefiting challengers who gain greater returns in response to their efforts. In contrast, although online advertising is undoubtedly on the rise, there is no clear evidence that these ads encourage voters to more positively evaluate candidates (Broockman and Green 2013). In general, it seems candidates should be wary of investing an overwhelming amount of their efforts in new media; they are not likely to reach many undecided or persuadable voters because individuals who are seeking out candidate information or visiting their websites are already likely supporters committed to one side or the other (Sides et al. 2014).

Political advertising and the delivery of campaign messaging have generated some of the most substantial and controversial debates about the role that campaign strategies play in upholding democratic representation, information, and citizen engagement. Most debates seem to focus primarily on the extent to which political advertisements enhance or detract from the quality of information received by citizens and their levels of engagement. Presidential advertisements, for example, do not appear to mobilize citizens or make them any more informed, but they can be persuasive. Huber and Arceneaux (2007) highlight this normative dilemma, arguing that "by manipulating voters' expressed candidate preferences, the partisan balance of the advertising stream has a direct, important, and undocumented effect on election outcomes" (976). Such advertising would not be a problem if it helped voters align their vote choices with their policy preferences and in turn encouraged them to turn out, but at least for advertisements aired during presidential elections, this does not appear to be the case.

With the rise of cable news and partisan-leaning media outlets like Fox News and MSNBC, normative concerns have also arisen over the extent to which these outlets simply "preach to the converted" and become echo chambers where like-minded citizens tune in to hear viewpoints they already agree with mirrored back to them when they watch the news. The development of these outlets has implications both for how well informed these viewers are and for the extent to which they are critical of politicians who share their viewpoints. Evidence suggests that Fox News viewers, for example, were less likely to pay attention to stories that were critical of the Bush administration and were more likely to underestimate the number of American casualties in Iraq, a war that was generally popular with Republicans and unpopular with Democrats (Morris 2005). Such evidence raises concerns over the extent to which avid viewers of partisan-tinted news stations are receptive to information from campaigns that contradict their beliefs and policy preferences.

Not surprisingly, a major point of contention among political scientists is whether there are normatively adverse effects of negative advertising in particular. On the one hand, some contend that negative advertising is detrimental to citizen engagement, arguing that it corrodes citizens' trust in politics, reduces their likelihood of voting, and lowers overall voter turnout and polarizes the electorate (Ansolabehere and Iyengar 1995). On the other hand, some maintain that negative advertising leads to a more informed electorate. In their meta-analysis, Lau et al. (2007) found that negative campaign advertising does not seem to depress voter turnout, although it does lower feelings of political efficacy and trust in government. Two randomized field experiments uncovered no systematic differences of message tone on voter turnout (Arceneaux and Nickerson 2010). Other evidence suggests that negative advertising may have more positive effects than its detractors give it credit for. Mattes and Redlawsk (2014) argue voters are not really as bothered by negativity as conventional wisdom suggests. In some cases, voters, especially those who are less engaged, may actually welcome negativity because counterfactuals help them to sort out the truth about candidates in a race; backlash is limited (Mattes and Redlawsk 2014). Similarly, Kahn and Kenney (2004) show that citizens' familiarity with candidates and campaigns increases as campaign rhetoric becomes more unpleasant and malicious. Moreover, Geer (2006) finds negative ads generally contain more substantive information compared to positive ads, and this may be one explanation for why negative ads can boost citizens' knowledge about the candidate, especially among low-information voters (Franz et al. 2007). Moreover, negative advertising can increase the likelihood that individuals will actually choose one candidate over the other, an often overlooked but highly important step in the process of political engagement (Krupnikov 2012). On the farther end of the spectrum, the political scientists Michael Franz, Paul Freedman, Kenneth Goldstein, and Travis Ridout (2007) contend that negative advertising can actually be healthy for democracy. Goldstein contends, "With negative ads in particular, campaigns have to be very careful about the claims they make because the press puts much more scrutiny on negative ads. . . . If you get an outrageous one, that tends to boomerang on a campaign" (as cited in Chaptman 2008). The authors' evidence suggests that negative advertising can actually lead to a more informed and engaged electorate (Franz et al. 2007). All in all, the jury is still out on whether the use of negative advertising is helpful or harmful in advancing democratic norms.

This type of contingency adds another layer of nuance when considering the normative implications of political advertising. In particular, evidence suggesting that advertising is moderated through political knowledge is potentially troubling; those with less political information tend to be more influenced by television advertising messages, whereas media that is more intellectually cumbersome to process, like news reports and print media, influence the more politically knowledgeable (Franz and Ridout 2007). This is troublesome because it leaves the citizens most in need of more accurate information most susceptible to misinformation and exaggeration in campaign advertisements and less likely to seek out new information after seeing advertisements (see also Valentino et al. 2004).

KEY TERMS

Comparative messaging
Cost-per-acquisition
Cost-per-click
Cost-per-thousand-
    impressions
Decay effects

Designated market areas
Earned media
Gross ratings points
Negative messaging
News conference
News release

Paid media
Positive messaging
Showings
Viral news

SUGGESTED READINGS

Ansolabehere, A., and S. Iyengar. 1995. *Going Negative: How Political Advertisements Shrink and Demobilize the Electorate.* New York, NY: Free Press.

Fowler, E. F., Michael M. Franz and T. N. Ridout. 2016. *Political Advertising in the United States.* Boulder, CO: Westview Press.

Geer, J. 2006. *In Defense of Negativity: Attack Ads in Presidential Campaigns.* Chicago, IL: University of Chicago Press.

Mattes, K. and D. Redlawsk. 2014. *The Positive Case for Negative Campaigning.* Chicago, IL: University of Chicago Press.

Patterson, T. E. 1994. *Out of Order.* New York, NY: Vintage Books.

Shaw, D. R. 2006. *The Race to 270: The Electoral College and the Campaign Strategies of 2000 and 2004.* Chicago, IL: University of Chicago Press.

CHAPTER 7

Get Out the Vote

During the 2014 midterm elections, the Democratic Illinois governor Pat Quinn and the Republican challenger Bruce Rauner were engaged in a fierce election battle that shattered records for spending. Three days before the election, having already spent a combined $96 million, both candidates turned to what would be the most critical phase of their election strategy: getting out the vote, or GOTV. The efforts by these candidates and their campaigns are especially interesting to consider given the nature of politics in Chicago, the state's most populous city by a stretch. The core components of last-minute GOTV efforts such as canvassing door to door and bringing voters to the polls on Election Day typically tend to favor Democrats, whose strengths lie in the voter mobilization traditions of Chicago and their allies in organized labor. In response to this context that favored his opponent, Rauner launched a GOTV effort unparalleled by previous Republican campaigns in Illinois. Rauner's campaign depended on ground-game "foot soldiers" from local Republican organizations and opening several campaign offices where volunteers coordinated with the campaigns of other GOP candidates in the area (Pearson et al. 2014).

The competitiveness of the Quinn/Rauner race spurred classic GOTV efforts put into action with new technological advances. Despite campaigning in an age in which new media developments have made it easier for candidates to reach constituents without actually having to see them in person (via text message, e-mail, and social media, for example), both candidates also had armies of volunteers knocking on doors in the days leading up to the election. In this election, however, they were able to do so in a far more targeted manner thanks to the increasing availability of sophisticated data about individual voters, an advancement I will discuss further in Chapter 9.

Political campaigns make every conceivable effort to persuade citizens to support them and to turn out likely supporters, but there are naturally factors beyond their control. Quinn, for example, had to address the fact that he was running as a Democrat in an election year in which lower turnout meant he faced an uphill battle;

midterm election voters tend to be more conservative than voters in presidential elections, in part because minorities and younger voters, who tend to lean Democratic, generally vote at disproportionately lower rates in midterm cycles (Bevan 2014).

Generally speaking, candidates running for office during midterm elections encounter a decidedly different GOTV challenge than candidates running during presidential election years. Following high turnout during the 2008 election, many presumed that the record-breaking levels of political participation during this cycle would carry over into the 2010 midterm elections. Reality fell short of expectations, however. The rate of overall turnout in 2010 was about average for recent midterm election cycles, 40.8% of the eligible electorate voted, only slightly higher than the turnout in 2006, which was estimated to be about 40.4%. Some suggested that Democrats were not especially motivated by the election given the controversial health care bill and struggling economy, for which many citizens placed blame on President Obama. This apathy was in part overcome, and indeed taken advantage of, by Republicans who were hopeful about their prospects of taking control of both chambers in Congress.

Political scientists have grappled with explaining voter turnout rates for decades (Downs 1957; Leighley and Nagler 2013). This vast literature has produced numerous explanations for why voters vote (or not). Scholars have linked turnout patterns to institutional structures like registration laws (Rosenstone and Wolfinger 1978), party competition (Key 1949) or political culture (Almond and Verba 1963), while others find associations with individual-level factors including: socio-demographics (Leighley and Nagler 2013; Rosenstone and Hansen 1993), partisan attachment (Campbell et al. 1960), interest in politics (Brady et al. 1995), internal and external efficacy (Rosenstone and Hansen 1993) or a sense of civic duty (Blais 2000). Scholars who come at the question from a rational choice perspective argue abstention may be rational because voting represents a classic collective action problem (Downs 1957). Since a single vote is unlikely to be pivotal, voters have incentives to free-ride on the efforts of others. Citizens shirk their civic duties because they receive little tangible benefit from voting. With few measurable benefits from voting, the costs, in terms of both the time and the resources it takes to vote and make an informed decision, exceed the benefits for most people (Downs 1957). But, as is evidenced by the Quinn/Rauner race and competitive elections across the country, campaigns can play a role in influencing voter turnout rates by reducing the costs associated with voting and increasing the perception in voters that their vote matters and is important. Many attribute the decline in turnout after the 1960s to increasingly impersonal forms of electioneering and declining voter mobilization efforts (Green and Smith 2003; Rosenstone and Hansen 1993). Following the 2000 elections, however, campaigns made renewed efforts to develop more sophisticated, targeted, and grassroots GOTV efforts, a move that seems to have spurred a renewed interest in political participation (Bergan et al. 2005).

In Chapters 5 and 6, I focused on campaign strategies and tactics used to get the word out about candidates. In this chapter, I discuss what campaigns do to get out the vote once they have engaged in persuasion efforts and have identified which citizens they can count on for support. I focus particularly on grassroots mobilization tactics and new behavioral insights that enable campaigns to stimulate turnout amongst targeted voters. In recent elections, grassroots mobilization has taken on a primary role in successful campaign GOTV strategies and, in close contests, can be large enough to be politically consequential (Bergan et al. 2005). Advances in grassroots mobilization strategies have come largely as the product of recent field experiments, which have helped to shed light on the impact of different mobilization tactics.

I first provide an overview of basic campaign mobilization strategies before discussing which are the most effective. I then focus in particular on recent advances in field experiments. Finally, as with previous chapters, I turn my attention to how campaign GOTV strategies can both advance and hinder democratic norms, paying particular attention to differences between the perspectives of political scientists studying voter turnout and the goals of campaigns themselves, as well as how increasing polarization has affected campaign mobilization and the consequences for democratic norms. GOTV efforts are the component of campaign strategy that arguably have the most direct relationship to democratic norms, alongside the campaign message and advertising efforts discussed in Chapter 6. In Chapter 10, I discuss how changing legal contexts further influence when and how campaigns mobilize supporters.

GRASSROOTS MOBILIZATION: AN OVERVIEW

In the aftermath of the razor-thin vote margin in Florida that ultimately decided the 2000 presidential election, parties began to pay closer attention to voter turnout and mobilization. Grassroots mobilization was a vestige of campaigns past, as the focus had been on mass media and television advertising in particular for decades. In 2002, Republicans orchestrated STOMP (Strategic Task Force to Organize and Mobilize People) and the so-called 72-hour program to focus on the ground war; the investment continued into the 2004 presidential election, in which the Bush-Cheney campaign reportedly spent five times more on the field operations than they had in 2000 (Nielsen 2012). GOP victories in both cycles (in a departure from established patterns, Republicans gained seats in both chambers of Congress in the 2002 midterm elections) attested to the power of the renewed emphasis on mobilization, and Democrats quickly followed suit (Nielsen 2012). Many GOTV strategies incorporate tactics discussed in previous chapters, such as demographic and survey research, polling, studying the electoral history in a candidate's district, and voter identification calls to ensure voters receive the most effective mobilization messages. Although democratic ideals call for as many people as possible (ideally, everyone who is eligible) to turn out and vote on Election Day, this strategy does not necessarily align with the goals of political campaigns. A campaign's GOTV drive serves one purpose: making sure the people who are likely to support you actually cast their ballots.

A colorful anecdote from Matt Reese, a Democratic consultant who was integral in helping run John F. Kennedy's West Virginia presidential primary campaign, explains the ideal toward which campaigns are constantly pushing: "I wish God gave green noses to undecided voters, because between now and election eve, I'd work only the green noses," notes Reese. "I wish God gave purple ears to nonvoters for my candidate on election eve, because on Election Day, I'd work only the purple voters" (Issenberg 2012d). This is fantasy, of course. Instead, contemporary campaigns try to gather as much data about the electorate as possible to increase the likelihood of identifying the *right* voters to target with GOTV efforts, sorting undecided from decided voters and nonvoters from voters to reduce risk and uncertainty in GOTV efforts.

Despite the campaign's use of individual-level data to increase the probability of targeting voters with the right mobilization messages, there are no guaranteed, surefire campaign mobilization tactics. Different electoral contexts, external events, and campaign shakeups can and often do lead to altered campaign strategies. However, there are general timelines and principles most campaigns adhere to. Campaigns first must identify the number of votes needed to win and how many citizens they can rely on to support them on Election Day. Then, they typically focus all of their efforts on getting those identified supporters out to vote. A good rule to go by when assessing how many people campaigns should try to push to the polls is to aim for 10% of the votes needed to win. "For example," note Burton and Shea (2010), "if you are running a state legislative race and need 14,000 votes to win, you must have at least 1,500 identified supporters whom you will push to the polls" (200; see also Allen 1990).

GOTV efforts are typically planned far in advance. As we will see in Chapter 10, campaigns must identify likely supporters and begin efforts earlier and earlier as more Americans take advantage of early voting and vote-by-mail options. In the Quinn/Rauner race, Democrats began planning their GOTV operation months before they actually put their plan into action. A GOTV plan lays out different deadlines, tasks, and assignments. Campaigns also take account of the resources needed to implement their GOTV, paying careful attention to the resources they will need for their final push as Election Day approaches. The week before an election, mailers might be sent to swing voters and volunteer canvassers dispatched to knock on the doors of known supporters. In recent elections, campaigns have been able take advantage of technological advances to use text messages, e-mail, and social media blasts to remind likely supporters to turn out on Election Day, a topic of discussion in Chapter 9.

In some locales, campaigns are allowed to send poll watchers to record the names of each person who votes and deliver these results to campaign headquarters, where those who have already voted are checked off on a master list. In this way, campaigns can continue to send reminders to identified supporters who have not yet voted. Prospective voters whom the campaign has identified as supporters are called right up until the polls close. Burton and Shea (2010: 200) highlight how important such last-minute campaigning can be, especially for races that are close. In the Oneonta, New York, school board election of Rosemary Shea, her campaign pored over their lists of people who had not voted. With 15 minutes to spare, the candidate drove to the houses of three Democratic-leaning citizens and convinced them to get into her car and go to the polls so they could vote. All three ended up casting ballots, and Shea won the election by exactly three votes.

As this story demonstrates, campaign GOTV efforts, even on Election Day, can be highly targeted. In the age of microtargeting, campaigns are becoming even more specific in terms of who they target and how they are targeted. For the most part, campaigns will avoid "untargeted" activities like handing out leaflets to random strangers at grocery stores or shopping malls or canvassing precincts with low candidate support (Burton and Shea 2010). Instead, they favor strategies such as phone calls and in-person canvassing if possible, and they are far more likely to concentrate their influence on the citizens they want to mobilize and avoid any unintended consequences of more generalized mobilization efforts that might mobilize an opponent's supporters instead.

Insights from studies conducted over the past decade or so that subject mobilization tactics to rigorous experimental manipulation reveal wide variation in their effectiveness (Gerber and Green 2000; Green and Gerber 2012; Green et al. 2013). Appeals delivered in-person appear to be most effective, while impersonal approaches are less reliable, for example. A recent meta-analysis that examined the findings from hundreds of field experiments found in-person contact via door-to-door canvassing to be most effective in mobilizing voters to the polls, boosting the likelihood of voting by about 2.5 percentage points on average, while phone calls by volunteers raise turnout by about 1.9 percentage points on average and calls by commercial phone banks by about 1.0 percentage points on average (Green et al. 2013). Automated phone messages, like robocalls, are largely ineffective, whereas direct mail exerts a relatively small but statistically significant positive effect on turnout on average (Green et al. 2013). Voters seem to be less responsive to variations in message content, although mobilization appeals that emphasize social voting norms, even subtly (Panagopoulos et al. 2014), reliably elevate turnout, both when delivered by direct mail or even by pre-recorded phone calls (Green et al. 2013). Voting messages delivered via text messages advertisements have also been shown to be effective, while emails routinely fail to boost turnout levels (Green and Gerber 2012).

Field experimental studies have also shed light on other aspects of strategic importance to political campaigns. One strand of experimental research exploring whether there are cumulative or synergistic effects from exposure to multiple mobilization appeals, using either the same or different tactics to deliver these messages, finds little evidence of such effects (Gerber et al. 2013). Other researchers have randomized the timing of mobilization message delivery. While some evidence suggests mobilization appeals delivered closer to Election Day are most effective (Nickerson 2007), other studies find few differences in the potency (or impotency) of mobilization appeals attributable to timing, implying messages delivered earlier can be as effective (or not) in stimulating participation, perhaps because they "plant a seed" with voters or sensitize them to the upcoming election in a way that galvanizes their interest (Panagopoulos 2011). Researchers have also demonstrated that responsiveness to grassroots mobilization tactics can vary depending on individual differences, like baseline propensity to vote, for instance. Arceneaux and Nickerson (2009) argue that mobilization has the strongest effects on voters who are indifferent about participating and that these voters differ across election cycles. Reanalyzing data from 11 face-to-face mobilization experiments, the authors found low-propensity voters to be more responsive to mobilization efforts in high-salience elections (like presidential elections), compared to lower-salience elections, while habitual voters are likely to be most responsive in low-salience elections; the authors also suggest mobilization efforts should target occasional voters in mid-level salience elections, like congressional midterms of mayoral elections (Arceneaux and Nickerson 2009). Enos, Fowler and Vavreck (2014) similarly analyzed experimental data to show that high-propensity voters overall are generally more responsive to voter mobilization, a tendency that widen disparities in participation by mobilizing high-propensity individuals, who tend to be wealthier and better educated, more than under-represented, low-propensity citizens including less affluent voters and minorities.

Campaigns often make a concerted effort to target minority voters in their GOTV efforts. The passage of the Voting Rights Act in 1965 led to the end of disenfranchising election laws aimed at preventing turnout among black voters. Since then, African Americans have been brought into the electoral fold, primarily as the target of mobilization by the Democratic Party (Wielhouwer 2000). The mobilization of black voters has often taken place in the context of black churches because large majorities are affiliated with the black church. It is not unusual for candidates to make appearances at black churches for campaign events and for churches themselves to coordinate with candidates in GOTV drives explicitly encouraging their congregants to take advantage of early voting (Herron and Smith 2012).

Recently, Latino voters have also become a prime target for campaign mobilization efforts. They are a fast-growing segment of the population in the United States that campaigns on both sides of the aisle are courting, although their levels of participation lag behind the general population as well as other racial and ethnic groups (Abrajano and Alvarez 2012). The U.S. Census Bureau estimates Latinos comprised 17.4 percent of the U.S. population in 2014 and projects Latinos to comprise 28.6 percent of the national population by 2060. Over the past two decades, campaigns have begun to increasingly use Spanish-language GOTV messages in efforts to mobilize Latino voters. Spanish-language appeals are particularly effective among Latino voters with a low probability of turning out and, not surprising, among those whose primary language is Spanish (Abrajano and Panagopoulos 2011). Campaigns can also use radio mobilization messages to target Latinos in particular because they tend to listen to radio programming far more often than their non-Hispanic counterparts. Evidence suggests that Spanish-language radio ads are a cost-effective and efficient means of raising Latino turnout in federal elections (Panagopoulos and Green 2011).

ADVANCES IN FIELD EXPERIMENTS

As I discussed above, advances in the social, behavioral and political sciences brought about mainly by randomized field experiments conducted over the past 10-15 years have produced numerous insights about voting behavior and electoral mobilization. Because subjects in field experiments are assigned randomly to treatments, creating groups that are otherwise identical on average, these tests can reliably isolate the effects of these interventions on behaviors like voting. Unlike laboratory experiments that generally occur in more artificial, controlled settings, field experiments are also appealing to campaigns because they are conducted in natural, real-world settings which presumably elicit more realistic reactions from voters (Gerber 2011).

Recent years have witnessed a resurgence in field experimental campaign interventions, often conducted in partisan settings in partnership with political campaigns or advocacy groups, but the method can be traced back to a pioneering study conducted in the 1924 by the political scientist Harold Gosnell (1927). The modern relaunch of field experimental research in campaign settings can be attributed to the political scientists Donald Green and Alan Gerber, whose studies inspired renewed interest in the methodology to study the effectiveness of a wide range of campaign tactics (Gerber and Green 2000; Green and Gerber 2012). The findings uncovered by these studies were enormously relevant for political campaigns which had previously relied on less reliable, observational or anecdotal information to evaluate the effectiveness of campaign tactics. In contemporary elections, campaigns routinely seek input from scholars with experimental expertise to develop sophisticated tests to inform their data-driven and evidence-based campaign operations and decision-making. In 2012, David Nickerson, a political scientist now at Temple University, served as "director of experiments" for President Barack Obama's reelection campaign. Nickerson used his scholarly expertise to execute randomized field experiments that tested campaign messages. This was the first time any presidential campaign had a director of experiments. Nickerson also helped to found the Analyst Institute, a research consortium allied mainly with labor groups that invested heavily in the 2000s in the deployment of field experimental research. One of Nickerson's colleagues referred to the efforts as "drug trials for democracy—testing campaign methods against one another using the electorate as lab rats" (Issenberg 2014).

Some of the more recent advances in field experiments have focused on the individual-level foundations and the psychological underpinnings of voting behavior. This means moving beyond which GOTV method works best to the types of messages that might stimulate greater turnout. Social pressure, for example, can be an effective form of motivation that is essentially "shaming" a voter to turn out. Multiple field experiments have explored the effects of threatening to publicize one's voting record to friends, family, and neighbors and have found that this type of social pressure can indeed promote higher participation (Gerber et al. 2008, 2010). In addition, the shaming effect comes in multiple forms, from messages that include information about subjects' own voting histories to the threat of publicizing voting behavior to neighbors (Gerber et al. 2008). More generally, giving citizens the sense that their behavior is being observed appears to make individuals more likely to perform their civic duty and vote. Even cues as subtle as being exposed to a mobilization message that features a pair of eyes that appear "watchful" can effectively mobilize individuals (Panagopoulos 2014a, c).

Some scholars contend the effects described above arise in part because individuals are psychologically, or even evolutionarily, programmed to be concerned about their reputations and want to be perceived by others as conforming to social norms (like voting) and caring about society. Research by Sinclair (2012) reinforces further the notion that individuals' social networks exert strong influences on participation in general. When members of one's social group engage in behaviors like voting, others in the group tend to notice and to imitate this behavior. The effects are most pronounced when such behaviors are observable. As we will discuss in Chapter 9, the growing visibility of individual behavior on social networks like Facebook and Twitter can potentially accentuate this dynamic in the context of politics.

Recent voting studies also reveal a more nuanced view of how socio-psychological forces may affect voting. Although negative inducements to vote (like shaming), for example, seem to generally exert a positive effect on turnout, the findings are less consistent for positive, pro–social mobilization messages. For example, pride-based motivations to vote, such as publicizing the name of all verified voters in local newspapers, only increase turnout among those already more likely to vote, whereas shame-based motivations have a greater effect, motivating both high- and low-propensity voters to turn out (Panagopoulos 2010a). Other positive forms of motivation also fall short relative to their negative counterparts. When citizens receive messages of "hope" and are then reminded to vote, they are not more likely to turn out and vote (Panagopoulos 2014b). However, social pressure focusing on the rewards of voting (for example, receiving a mailing that lists which of one's neighbors have a "perfect" voting record presented as a "civic honor roll" that encourage "imperfect" voters to join) also seems to mobilize voters. These effects carry across different subgroups of voters, including minorities and women, and high- and low-likelihood voters more generally (Panagopoulos 2013b). Furthermore, positive messages expressing gratitude to citizens for voting in previous elections appears to boost participation in future elections. Such a strategy was used during the 2010 midterm elections by the political consultant Hal Malchow, who was working for the freshman Democratic senator Michael Bennet. In the last days of the race, Democratic constituents in the state of Colorado received a simple message from the senator, which simply thanked the recipient by first name for having voted in 2008 and said that he looked forward to being able to express such gratitude again after the upcoming elections. The strategy appeared to work: Bennett won the race by 15,000 votes (Issenberg 2012d). Experiments that have tested the effects of emphasizing descriptive norms, like the rates at which voters in one's community overall are voting, usually fail to produce large effects (Gerber et al. 2013).

Thanks to these advances and to our understanding of what types of mobilization messages work, campaigns have become more sophisticated in their mobilization efforts. But new information also comes with new challenges. Recent evidence suggests that both personality traits and the context in which individuals are receiving messages can influence the extent to which individuals are mobilized to participate (Mondak et al. 2010). As Funder (2008: 568, 577) writes, "What people do depends both on who they are—their dispositions such as personality traits—and the situation they are in . . . dispositions and situations interact to determine what people do. Which dispositions and *which* aspects of situations (specifically) affect which behaviors? The search for specific answers to this seemingly straightforward question lays out a formidable research agenda."

These discoveries challenge campaigns to dig even deeper to measure the dispositions of voters and mobilize them using messages that are most responsive to their personalities. For example, personality traits have the potential to blunt the effects of some campaign messages more than others. Although extroverts were less responsive to a social pressure treatment, individuals scoring high on the personality trait of openness were more likely to say they would vote (Gerber et al. 2013). In contrast, extroverted individuals exposed to otherwise negative information about candidates running for office are more likely to participate in politics, whereas more agreeable individuals are less likely to do so (Weinschenk and Panagopoulos 2014).

In part because campaigns can now leverage insights gleaned from field experiments to mobilize voters effectively, campaigns may be prioritizing mobilization over persuasion in recent elections (Panagopoulos 2015). In many ways, persuasion is a much more difficult and unpredictable task, so campaigns reason it may be easier and less risky to convince likely supporters to turn out than to persuade voters to support a candidate and then also to vote. As I discussed in Chapter 6, it is plausible that this shift toward an emphasis on mobilization, relative to persuasion, has played a part in increasing polarization in the American public and may itself be driven by the extent to which Americans have become more sorted into their parties and polarized in their preferences. Evidence from the 2008 presidential election further suggests that the impact of this renewed focus on mobilization might be getting stronger over time. It is estimated that the improved and more successful grassroots mobilization efforts by both parties in this election accounted for an estimated increase in the national turnout of 14.5 million votes (Panagopoulos and Francia 2009).

CONSEQUENCES FOR DEMOCRACY

For decades, political scientists and campaigns alike have puzzled over the questions of why citizens vote and what can be done to increase turnout. Almost all empirical studies of voter turnout concern themselves with the normative goal of improving citizen engagement in politics, asking, for example, what explains the persistently low electoral turnout in the United States, what factors increase individuals' likelihood of voting, and what legal-institutional changes might be made to improve voter turnout (Rosenstone and Hansen 1993; Timpone 1998; Lijphart 1997). In contrast, campaigns are not interested in improving overall voter turnout or increasing *everyone's* likelihood of voting. They are above all interested in learning what can be done to increase turnout among their supporters. As such, the goals of political scientists and campaigns can in some respects be at odds with one another.

In the late 1950s, Downs (1957) pioneered the rational choice concept of voting, which was further updated by Riker and Ordeshook (1968). The idea behind this theory is that it is rational for citizens to vote only if the policy benefits they receive outweigh the costs of voting. Of course, if one takes this calculation to its logical extreme, it is a wonder that anyone ever votes. Political scientists have since come to understand that voting is not necessarily based on a clear-cut rational calculation of costs and benefits, but can be influenced by a number of individual factors such as available time, education level, and employment status (Brady et al. 1995; Verba and Nie 1972) as well as considerations of civic duty or other social or material incentives. Using the field experiments highlighted in this chapter, political scientists have developed continually more fine-grained understandings of what can improve the likelihood of individual turnout and overall voter turnout. However, turnout is also contingent on the behavior of politicians. Aldrich (1993) in particular places importance on the role that campaigns play in influencing voter turnout, especially in the context of highly competitive elections.

A deeper, scholarly understanding of the forces that drive voting behavior does not necessarily translate into higher overall participation, however. As I have noted, campaigns are motivated to win, and to do so they must be strategic in who they mobilize and how they allocate resources to achieve victory. As Enos et al. (2014) suggest, grassroots mobilization efforts may have the unintended consequence of exacerbating participation gaps in ways that perpetuate inequality and polarization. Some studies also suggest the Democratic party tends to be systematically more inclusive in its mobilization efforts compared to the GOP (Citrin et al. 2013). These findings may have troubling implications for democracy. Such selective mobilization essentially neglects many voters, creating information imbalances that could keep many would-be voters from the polls on Election Day (Lassen 2005).

Routine patterns of disparities in electoral participation across socio-demographic groups are also a source of alarm for many. Even as scholars acknowledge differences in individuals' motivation, resources and capacity to participate by registering to vote, voting, donating, volunteering or other forms of engagement (Brady et al. 1995; Schlozman et al. 2012), gaps in participation that generally render the electorate more white, wealthy and educated create concerns about representation and responsiveness in American politics (Rosenstone and Hansen 1993; Gilens and Page 2014; Schlozman et al. 2012; Verba et al. 1995). Evidence from the U.S. Census Bureau's Current Population Survey about registration and voting rates in the 2012 general election by several key demographic groups including race, gender, income, age and education displayed in Figures 7.1 through 7.5 reinforce these concerns. As I discussed above, it is possible that voter mobilization efforts may actually be helping to sustain these patterns (Enos et al. 2014). Despite important differences in policy preferences, for example, between wealthy and poor Americans on matters of economic policy (Rigby and Springer 2011; Leighley and Nagler 2013), lawmakers may be more responsive to affluent voters who participate at higher rates (Gilens and Page 2014). Nevertheless, as rigid as these patterns can be, they are not necessarily immutable; for the first time in U.S. history, for instance, black Americans turned out higher rates than their white counterparts in 2012 (Taylor 2012), providing hope that participation disparities among other segments of the electorate can also be abated in the future.

For their part, political campaigns can help or hinder the causes of democratic engagement, information and representation. Often, much of how campaigns unfold hinges on competition, which can potentially spur candidates to be more encompassing in the policy positions, to create more informative environments, and to mobilize more citizens—or not. In an era of microtargeting capabilities, it is unclear whether these approaches remain intact, but it is clear competition matters. As Lipsitz (2011) writes, "Voters learn when elections are competitive, not because they are motivated to seek out more information, but because they cannot help but learn from the rich information environments that competitive elections generate. They are more likely to vote, not because they think their vote is more likely to matter, but because political elites prod them into doing so" (179). In addition, elected officials representing competitive districts seem to be more responsive to their constituents' preferences.

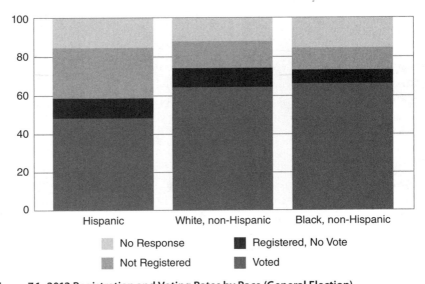

Figure 7.1 2012 Registration and Voting Rates by Race (General Election)
SOURCE: Current Population Survey: Voting and Registration Supplement, U.S. Census Bureau (2012)

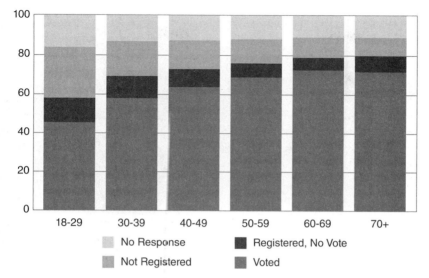

Figure 7.2 Voting and Registration Rates by Age (General Election)
SOURCE: Current Population Survey: Voting and Registration Supplement, U.S. Census Bureau (2012)

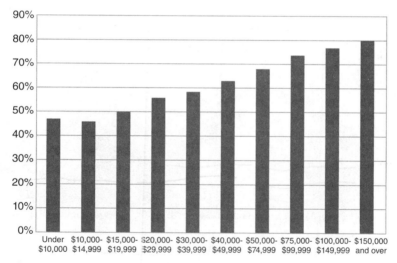

Figure 7.3 Voter Turnout by Income (General Election)
SOURCE: Current Population Survey: Voting and Registration Supplement, U.S. Census Bureau (2012)

Without electoral competition, incentives for campaigns to inform, represent, and mobilize diminish. Over the past 50 years, competition in congressional elections, for example, has steadily declined (Abramowitz et al. 2006; Abramowitz 1991; Jacobson and Carson 2015); as campaigns respond to this changing context, the democratic corollaries that often accompany competition may fade away.

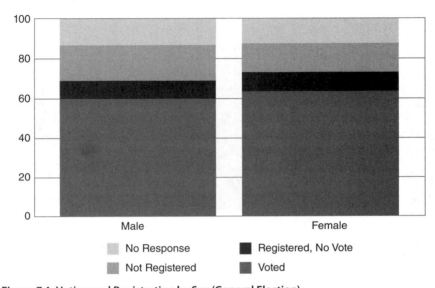

Figure 7.4 Voting and Registration by Sex (General Election)
SOURCE: Current Population Survey: Voting and Registration Supplement, U.S. Census Bureau (2012)

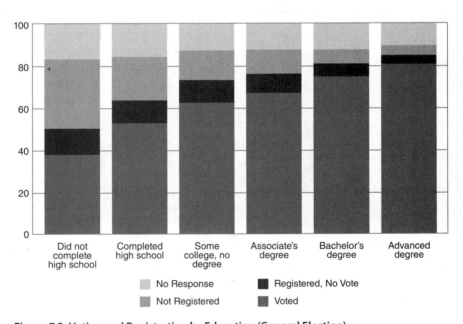

Figure 7.5 Voting and Registration by Education (General Election)
SOURCE: Current Population Survey: Voting and Registration Supplement, U.S. Census Bureau (2012)

On the upside, there are hints that we may have turned the corner in the U.S. on declining participation. Postwar voter turnout rates in federal cycles displayed in Figure 7.6 reveal voting has been on an upward trajectory, at least in presidential cycles since 2000.

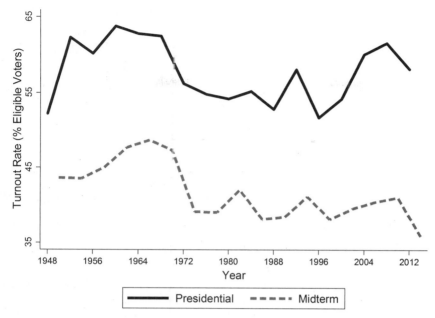

Figure 7.6 Voter Turnout in Presidential and Midterm Elections, 1948–2014
SOURCE: United States Election Project (McDonald 2015)

Before wrapping up our discussion of voter turnout and engagement, it is important to emphasize that enhanced participation can bring unintended consequences. One possibility is that higher turnout could entail a partisan bias. Because the types of voters who tend to abstain are also more likely to identify as Democrats, higher turnout would most likely benefit the Democratic Party and harm the prospects for Republican candidates. So while greater participation may be good for democracy writ large, it may not necessarily be better for both major parties, and (even nonpartisan) efforts to stimulate voting overall may ultimately advantage Democrats. Several studies find that higher turnout would result in a net benefit for Democrats, but it is unlikely that higher turnout would have changed election outcomes by much (Sides, Schickler and Citrin 2003; Citrin, Schickler and Sides 2003; Martinez and Gill 2005). Still, higher (or universal) turnout could have tipped the 2000 and possibly even the 2004 presidential elections in the Democrats' favor (Sides, Schickler and Citrin 2003), and lower turnout could have cost Democrats victories in both 1960 and 1976 (Martinez and Gill 2005). Even so, Martinez and Gill (2005: 1248) observe that the Democratic advantages from higher turnout (and Republican advantages from lower turnout) have steadily ebbed since 1960, corresponding to the erosion of class cleavages in U.S. elections. By contrast, higher turnout can advantage challengers. Studies find incumbents run for reelection and win more frequently in locales with low-turnout institutions in place; these can include no mailings of polling place locations, holding non-concurrent elections and establishing registration deadlines farther from Election Day (Trounstine 2013). Trounstine (2013) also finds these institutions are associated with policy outcomes that favor highly interested subgroups that are likely to vote even when the costs of participating are high. She concludes the higher reelection rates combined with the narrower focus of policy suggests that low-turnout environments may create fewer incentives for elected officials to be responsive to a broad base of constituents (Trounstine 2013). Hansford and Gomez (2010) find similar advantages for incumbent candidates and parties in presidential elections.

CONCLUSION

Widespread participation in the electoral process is a central goal in democratic polities, but it is important to acknowledge that campaigns' main motivation is to win. In contemporary elections, political operatives have growing access to the resources and tools required to expand—or contract—their outreach efforts in pursuit of this goal. The very same tools that can help engage more and more voters can be used to stifle participation by neglecting large swaths of the electorate. Perhaps it is too much to expect that political campaigns will conduct themselves in ways that expand the electorate to incorporate more citizens' voices into the democratic process, but it is conceivable that at least some candidates (or parties) will find electoral advantage in inclusivity; others may follow suit, resulting in greater engagement and participation overall.

KEY TERMS

Calculus of voting
Civic duty
Free-riding
Grassroots mobilization
High-propensity voter

High-salience election
Low-propensity voters
Low-salience election
Randomized
    experiment

Robocall
Voting costs
Voting-age population

SUGGESTED READINGS

Green, D. P., and A. S. Gerber. 2012. *Get out the Vote: How to Increase Voter Turnout*, 3rd ed. Washington, D.C.: Brookings Institution.
Leighley, J. and J. Nagler. 2013. *Who Votes Now? Demographics, Issues, Inequality and Turnout in the United States*. Princeton: Princeton University Press.
Rosenstone, S. J., and J. M. Hanson. 1993. *Mobilization, Participation, and American Democracy*. Reissued as a part of the Longman Classics in Political Science series (2002). New York: Pearson.
Schlozman, K., S. Verba and H. Brady. 2012. *The Unheavenly Chorus: Unequal Political Voice and the Broken Promise of American Democracy*. Princeton: Princeton University Press.
Verba, S., K. Schlozman, and H. Brady. 1995. *Voice and Equality: Civic Voluntarism in American Politics*. Cambridge: Harvard University Press."

CHAPTER 8

Vote Choice

Political scientists are good at predicting presidential election outcomes. In the 2008 race, almost all forecasting models predicted a Democratic victory, and most models were estimated weeks (and even months) before Election Day (Campbell 2008). These models are based on years of research and studies of how voters make decisions and include factors that are largely out of the control of political campaigns, so-called "fundamentals," such as the state of the economy, presidential approval ratings, and even partisan identification. Most famously, Nate Silver, a well-known statistician who launched the fivethirtyeight.com blog, predicted Obama would win 50.8% of the popular vote in the 2012 presidential election. In the end, Obama captured 50.6% of the popular vote, making Silver's estimate shockingly accurate. Silver also correctly predicted how every state would vote in the 2012 presidential election and provided accurate predictions for 49 of the 50 states in the 2008 election. Silver's predictions rely heavily on polling data and are updated throughout the campaign as new polls are conducted and made available (Silver 2012).

The growing predictability of elections, based on what is known about the way citizens make vote choices, ostensibly flies in the face of the way the news media often characterize elections; the endless pursuit of ratings and profit creates incentives to portray races as "horse races"—uncertain and dramatic, with each, new development potentially shaking up a race in significant ways. Of course, such shifts are rare, and elections are predictable in part because voters are predictable. Vote choices at the polls are influenced by short and long-term factors (Campbell et al. 1960). Early studies of voting developed the concept of a "funnel of causality" to describe how these forces operate. Long-term forces include voters' values and sociological situations (the socio-demographic groups they to which belong); these help shape individuals' partisan attachments which exert both direct effects on voting choices but also moderate the impact of more proximate, short term forces that can include media influence, economic conditions, issue opinions, candidate image, and campaign activity

(Campbell et al. 1960). Accordingly, partisan attachments are critical, affecting votes both directly and indirectly. These attachments, and, similarly, political preferences, tend to be stable and resistant to change (Zaller 1992), although they are not completely impervious to political and economic developments (Erikson et al. 2002). These factors typically cause most voters to make up their minds about which candidates they intend to support well before (often months ahead) of Election Day (Panagopoulos and Endres 2015). We may want to believe, as some scholars assert (Downs 1957) that voters are rational, consuming and weighing abundant amounts of information about the available options and then deciding which candidates will best represent their interests. As we will see, the reality of political decision-making is generally quite messier. As a result, convincing voters to support a candidate can be challenging for campaigns, especially when voters' ideological or partisan affinities do not predispose them to do so in the first place; it is also virtually impossible for campaigns to change the basic fundamentals (for example, the national economy) of the political climate in which they are operating. But persuasion is not impossible. Even if campaigns are unable to alter the objective conditions, they *can* shift voters' perceptions of reality by influencing the information environment, shifting levels of issue salience, for instance, or the frames with which voters evaluate issues. Understanding how voters reach decisions about which candidates to support is central to devising effective campaign strategies.

As I contend above, campaigns matter for many reasons. Campaigns can affect election outcomes in combination with national forces such as the state of the economy and incumbent records. Campaign events in particular, such as debates and conventions, play a significant role in shifting public opinion during the course of a campaign (Holbrook 1996). Campaigns also serve as an important link between these campaign events and the formation, crystallization, and revision of citizen preferences; in intensely competitive contests, such as those in battleground states, hard-hitting and frequent campaign advertisements and mobilization efforts augment the effects of campaign events (Panagopoulos 2012). During the 2012 elections, for example, shifts in voter preferences could be explained in part by major events happening over the course of the campaign: the major party conventions, the presidential and vice presidential debates, and late-in-the-game developments like the landfall of Hurricane Sandy, a massive storm that ravaged the East Coast just a week before the general election (Panagopoulos 2013a).

At the individual level, campaigns matter partly because they seem to "enlighten" voters, helping them to sort things out over the course of a campaign in a way that guides their voting decisions to be in line with their underlying predispositions, ultimately pushing them toward candidates they were naturally inclined to support (Gelman and King 1993). The intensity of a campaign also has a distinct effect on the preferences of voters over the course of an election cycle. Preference changes are far more pronounced, for example, in battleground states during presidential elections where campaigns are active, as opposed to safe states where campaigns have little incentive to try to actively persuade and mobilize voters (Panagopoulos 2009a).

In the sections that follow, I summarize some key findings about the factors scholars have determined influence vote choice, in particular, the role of cues (or "heuristics" or cognitive shortcuts) including partisanship and candidate traits and other characteristics. I also bring in emerging findings about how personality traits, genetic predispositions, and other dimensions of voter psychology have challenged campaigns to think of new and creative ways to garner support. Finally, I discuss the role of affect and emotions in vote choice and how campaign strategies can evoke affective reactions on behalf of their candidates or causes. In an era where campaigns are becoming more and more data driven with each election cycle, these findings motivate campaigns to continually refine the ways they can influence voters and data they can use to tap into all of the known dimensions, from personality to affect, which are known to influence vote choice. As with the growing findings regarding the microlevel foundations of voting discussed in Chapter 7, advances in our understanding of vote choice pose unique challenges and opportunities for contemporary campaign strategy.

THE ROLE OF CUES AND CANDIDATE TRAITS

In an ideal democracy, all citizens would be perfectly informed about the policy positions of candidates for elected office. In reality, studies reveal an electorate whose political knowledge is limited and that is generally poorly informed about politics (Delli Carpini and Keeter 1997). Voters are rarely able to recall issue stances taken by U.S. House candidates (Krasno 1994), for instance, and the accuracy with which they describe incumbents' roll call votes is often scarcely better than one might do by chance (Ansolabehere and Jones 2007). Large swaths of the electorate cannot even recognize or recall the names of the candidates running for the U.S. House in their districts (Jacobson and Carson 2015). Almost always, voters are faced with more information than they can possibly handle. Instead, it is understood that citizens use heuristics, that is, cognitive shortcuts, that help them to arrive at their voting decisions. This is also known as "low information rationality." The idea behind this type of rationality is that it is not conceivable or feasible for individuals to learn every detail about candidates and issues. Instead, voters use information they gain in their daily lives about candidates to make their vote choices. Information received from media sources is used in discussions with friends and family to help develop opinions, ultimately helping individuals to align with like-minded candidates when making their vote choices (Popkin 1994).

Individuals rely on a multitude of heuristics to make decisions, such as endorsements of candidates by other politicians and cultural figures, opinion polls, and the opinion of trustworthy elites like journalists and other elected officials. Voters also rely on heuristics not directly related to politics when making vote choices, such as stereotypes about a candidate's race (Mendelberg 2001), gender

(Sanbonmatsu 2002), religion (Layman 1997), or occupation (McDermott 2009). Religion, in particular, has a long history of being associated with vote choice in American elections. In 1928, the Democrat Al Smith lost his presidential election bid in large part, it is suspected, because he was a Catholic running at a time when there was deep suspicion of Catholicism in a largely Protestant United States (Burner 2008). John F. Kennedy made history by becoming the first Catholic to be elected president in 1960. In the 2008 election, Barack Obama came under attack from his opponents when allegations surfaced he was Muslim because he had been enrolled as a Muslim in a Catholic school in Indonesia between the first and third grades (Dobbs 2008), a belief that seemed to persist for some even after the news media made efforts to debunk the claim (Hollander 2010).

Voters tend to stereotype based on gender as well, inferring that female candidates will favor more liberal policy positions (Koch 2000) or perceiving women to be more competent than men at handling issues like child care, poverty, health care, education, the environment, and women's issues, but not others, such as economic development, defense, trade, taxes, and agriculture (Dolan 2010; Huddy and Terkildsen 1993). As a result, conservatives are less likely to vote for female candidates, whereas liberals tend to favor them (McDermott 1997). Voters will also believe that specific groups, parties in particular, "own" certain issues and assume a candidate belonging to a party associated with those issues will be more competent than his or her opponent once in office. Some of these divisions can be seen when breaking down how different groups of voters voted in a given election. For example, as illustrated in Table 8.1, black voters have long gravitated toward the Democratic Party as being best at addressing their concerns (Dawson 1994). The 2012 presidential election followed this pattern, with 93% of black voters supporting Obama compared to a majority of white voters (59%) supporting Romney. Table 8.1 breaks down the vote choices of different groups for president during the 2012 presidential election. Obama won the support of the majority of women, young people, and minorities, whereas Romney fared better with men, older people, and white voters. Obama also won the support of 90% of voters who rated the national economy as excellent or good; Romney won the support of 60% of voters who thought the economy was poor or not doing so well. As expected, Obama won the support of most voters who approved of the job he was doing as president, whereas most of the voters who disapproved voted for Mitt Romney.

Despite citizens' regular use of such cues in making vote choices, campaigns can do little to change voter's basic inclinations, such as their partisan identifications. On rare occasions, they may be able to induce voters to shift their opinions on one or two issues that are crucial to an election. But for the most part, candidates must work around basic voter inclinations, prompting voters to instead answer the question, "What is this election about?" in a way that persuades them to support their candidacy and not their opponent's. In other words, campaigns try to lead a voter toward the candidate he or she is likely to support anyway, whether or not the voter is aware of this inclination (Lodge and Taber 2013). Candidates must work to increase the salience of issues that puts them at an

Table 8.1 Vote Share by Demographic Group in the 2012 Election

		OBAMA (%)	ROMNEY (%)
Gender	Female	55	44
	Male	45	52
Race and ethnicity	Asian	73	26
	Black	93	6
	Latino	71	27
	White	39	59
Age	18–29	60	37
	30–44	52	45
	45–64	47	51
	65+	44	56
Education	No college degree	51	47
	Some college	49	48
	College	47	51
	Postgrad	55	42
Income	Under $30,000	63	35
	$30,000–$49,999	57	42
	$50,000 or more	45	53
	$100,000 or more	44	54
Evaluation of the economy	Excellent or good	90	9
	Not so good or poor	38	60
Obama job approval	Approve	89	9
	Disapprove	3	94

SOURCE: Adapted from 2012 National Election Pool, a consortium of ABC News, Associated Press, CBS News, CNN, Fox News, and NBC News.

advantage and their opponent at a disadvantage. Political scientists have observed that each of the major parties is perceived to be more competent in handling certain issues. The Democratic Party is advantaged when it comes to civil rights, labor, and social welfare issues, for example, whereas Republicans are considered more competent on law and order, defense, taxes, and family values (Petrocik 1996; Petrocik et al. 2003). Performance issues, such as the economy and the United States' standing in the world, are not automatically owned by either party but can, depending on the circumstances, advantage either side. Studies find candidates are more successful when they emphasize issues their party owns compared to those on which the opposing party is advantaged (Petrocik 1996; Petrocik et al. 2003). Further, candidates receive more favorable news coverage when the media focuses on issues their party owns (Hayes 2008).

Campaigns, then, try to control which heuristics are most salient in a given election in a way that best advantages their candidate (Druckman 2004). Campaigns will raise the prominence of a number of other factors for voters to consider, such as the state of the economy (Vavreck 2009), ideological and issue-based considerations (Bartels 2006; Hillygus and Shields 2008), and past candidate behavior and image, all of which can bear on voters' choices.

Perhaps the most important heuristic on which voters rely routinely in elections is the partisan affiliation of the candidates. Party labels signal policy positions, allowing voters to make inferences about candidates and their likely positions on issues, without engaging in extensive and time-consuming information gathering. Most of the time, although clearly not always, these judgments will be accurate, so it can be efficient for voters to simply match candidates' party labels to their partisan inclinations and to vote accordingly. The concept of partisan identification in the electorate has been debated extensively by scholars, with some viewing it as a psychological attachment (Campbell et al. 1960), while others see it more like a social identity (Green, Palmquist and Schickler, 2002), but there is a general consensus that it is formed early in life; that, for the most part, it tends to be stable and resistant to change; and that it shapes our political attitudes and preferences. Voters who identify with a political party generally vote for that party's candidates for elective office. Table 8.2 shows the percentage of partisans voting for their party's presidential candidate between 1956 and 2012. Since 2000, both Democrats and Republicans have voted for their respective candidates at rates between 92% and 94%. Historically, voters have aligned with political parties not only because of their stances on various policies, but also because a particular party reflected a class, ethnic, or religious background they too shared (Berelson et al. 1954). In addition to priming partisanship,

Table 8.2 Party-Line Voting Rates, 1956–2012

YEAR	DEMOCRATS	REPUBLICANS
1956	0.75	0.96
1960	0.81	0.93
1964	0.89	0.73
1968	0.80	0.93
1972	0.58	0.94
1976	0.82	0.86
1980	0.77	0.95
1984	0.78	0.96
1988	0.84	0.92
1992	0.91	0.89
1996	0.95	0.87
2000	0.92	0.92
2004	0.92	0.94
2008	0.92	0.93
2012	0.94	0.92

SOURCE: American National Election Studies (Cumulative File).

campaigns also must consider the social identities of the voters they are trying to court. African Americans have overwhelmingly supported the Democratic Party since the passage of the Voting Rights Act in 1965, whereas evangelical Christians have been more inclined to support Republican candidates because they endorse more conservative social policies on matters such as abortion and gay rights. In these kinds of ways, campaigns try to connect voters to social identities that may be important to them.

As I discuss above, researchers consistently find partisan identification exerts outsized influence on voting decisions. As Figure 8.1 shows, the vast majority of Americans since 1952 have identified with (or at least leaned toward) one of the two major parties (Flanigan et al. 2015); in fact, the distribution of partisan identification in the electorate has not fluctuated dramatically over the past six decades. Even as some scholars have suggested Americans have become increasingly independent or detached from the political parties, others find these claims to be a myth, arguing instead that most of these citizens are "closet partisans" (Keith et al. 1992). As Figure 8.1 reveals, the number of "pure independents" in the electorate, in other words, those with no major-party attachments or who do not even lean toward one of the two major parties, is relatively small, representing only about one in ten Americans in recent cycles (see also Flanigan et al. 2015). Evidence suggests that partisanship shapes policy and candidate preferences (Campbell et al. 1960), and to an increasing degree, over the course of elections (Erikson et al. 2010; Erikson and Wlezien 2012). Early studies found issue voting *per se* was rare (Campbell et al. 1960; Lazarsfeld et al. 1944), perhaps because voters did not hold coherent policy positions or to link these to candidates (Converse 1964), but evidence of issue consistency and issue voting increased since the 1970s (Nie, Verba and Petrocik 1976).

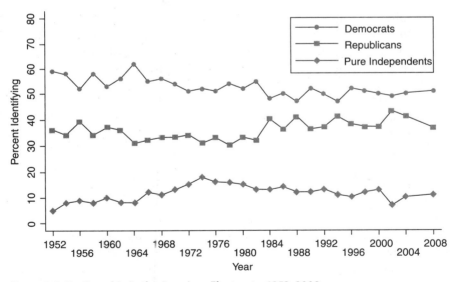

Figure 8.1 Partisanship in the American Electorate, 1952–2008

SOURCE: American National Election Studies (Panagopoulos and Weinschenk 2016: 109)

Some view partisanship as a rational, running tally of political assessments that are continually updated and changed as citizens receive more information about a party (Gerber and Green 1998). Fiorina (1981) suggests that partisanship involves retrospective evaluation of prior candidate performance. Others suggest it is a more pervasive, internal force that shapes and potentially biases citizens' perceptions of campaigns, as argued by Bartels (2002), Green et al. (2002), and Cohen (2003).

Sides et al. (2014) highlight three reasons why partisan identification is relevant for both elections scholars and campaigns alike. First, party identification is an extremely reliable predictor of how citizens will ultimately vote. As I discuss above, about 90% of both Republicans and Democrats in recent presidential elections voted for their party's nominee, and party loyalty has been increasing since the 1950s (Bartels 2000). If all else fails, this makes partisanship a dependable heuristic on which campaigns can rely to lead voters to choices that favor their candidates.

Second, parties serve as a perceptual screen through which information about candidates must pass; information that aligns positively with one's party identification will be accepted, whereas information that reflects poorly on that party might be rejected, even if it is both factual and from a reliable source. This process is known as motivated reasoning, whereby citizens, especially strong partisans, are motivated to believe information that positively reflects on their identities (partisan or otherwise) and reject information that does not (Kunda 1990). Kim et al. (2010) define motivated reasoning as "the discounting of information that challenges priors [attitudes] along with uncritical acceptance of attitude consistent information" (1).

The literature on motivated reasoning in political science boasts some striking examples of the concept in action. For example, in one study, different groups of partisans were asked to estimate the number of deaths that had occurred during the Iraq war in the mid-2000s, when the war was popular with Republicans and increasingly unpopular with Democrats. Republicans underestimated the number of American deaths, whereas Democrats overestimated the number. When provided with the correct information, strong partisans updated their factual beliefs, but this did not lead them to update their opinions on the policies for the war. In other words, although they received more accurate information, the two groups of partisans maintained their polarized policy positions (Gaines et al. 2007).

This tendency explains why campaigns are able to lead voters to certain choices based on incomplete or misleading information. Although candidates cannot typically get away with outright lying, they can spin the information they present and frame it in such a way that cues certain voters to support them. Even if such information is debunked as untruthful or inaccurate by the news media or the opposing campaign, this does not mean strong partisans will update their opinions or change their vote intentions. Contemporary campaigns must grapple with engaging an electorate that is increasingly polarized and resistant to updating its views and evaluations of candidates and parties (Kim et al. 2015).

Finally, party identification matters because it motivates people to vote. The stronger one's partisanship, the more likely individuals are to participate in politics. The effect of strong partisanship can be seen in European parliamentary-style democracies, where the existence of multiple parties often induces a stronger identification with parties and, ultimately, higher turnout, a factor I will discuss in greater detail in Chapter 11 (Powell 1986).

The effects of partisanship on vote choice, although fairly consistent, are not absolute. As always, there are exceptions to the rule. There are circumstances which cause reliable partisans to defect to the opposing party. Sometimes, these reflect short-term influences related to issues, candidates or the campaign environment (Campbell et al. 1960; Hillygus and Shields 2008). Even if the number of partisans who defect is not enormous, in certain cases it can be enough to tip the race in the opposing party's favor, in both direct and indirect ways. In his race against the Democratic Illinois governor Pat Quinn, the Republican Bruce Rauner actively courted African Americans in Chicago, a group that overwhelmingly supports Democratic candidates. Although he did not end up with droves of African American supporters, his efforts did convince some white swing voters with conservative tendencies who nevertheless shy away from any candidate who appears to be racially discriminatory (Bevan 2014).

Frequently, candidates "trespass" on traits or issues owned by their opponents' party in an effort to woo supporters from the other side. Sometimes they succeed, but the strategy is risky and requires candidates to overcome deeply rooted perceptions within the electorate. Furthermore, campaigns identify and exploit persuadable voters by highlighting issues that serve as "wedges," that is, issues that pit the preferences of certain individuals on one policy against their partisan identification. These individuals are also known as "cross-pressured" voters, that is, voters whose partisan identification is at odds with their preferences on certain issues. Most partisans are cross-pressured to some degree. Approximately two-thirds of partisans agree with the opposing party on one or more issues that they consider personally important (Hillygus and Shields 2008). Cross-pressured voters will sometimes cross over and vote for the other party if the issue on which they disagree with their party is made salient over the course of a campaign. For example, socially conservative, anti-abortion Democrat may be inclined to support a pro-life Republican candidate even if they disagree with the candidate's other policy stances. Detailed information about voters' positions and priorities, or projections supplied by predictive analytics, enable campaigns to emphasize wedge issues in their appeals to select audiences. Thus, instead of avoiding controversial or divisive issues, campaigns can use them to target narrow sections of the electorate they deem potentially persuadable based on their position as cross-pressured voters (Hillygus and Shields 2008).

Beyond partisanship and issue positions, candidate traits also play a role in vote choice. Not surprisingly, candidates perceived to embody attractive character traits, such as honesty, empathy, and strong leadership, are more likely to receive votes than candidates identified with less desirable traits (Lawson et al. 2010; Kinder et al. 1980).

Campaigns routinely attempt to manipulate how voters perceive candidates, but these perceptions are not usually entirely within their control. Candidates must contend with how portrayals by the media and their opponents shape perceptions. In 2012, the Republican presidential nominee Mitt Romney faced what the *Wall Street Journal* called an "image" problem. To many, Romney appeared cold and disconnected from the average American worker and voter, an image that was intensified by his massive wealth and elitist persona from his years of working at Bain Capital (Henninger 2012).

There is also evidence that candidate experience affects perceptions. Consider the case of military experience, widely considered to be a plus for candidates seeking elective office. The empirical evidence suggests the effects of highlighting military service in campaigns may not be so clear cut. A recent study finds the impact of military service on voter support likely depends on voters' own positions on military issues, as well as partisan ownership of these issues. It may be advantageous, for example, for Democrats who are veterans to emphasize their military service in campaigns, whereas Republican veterans may be better off focusing on other aspects of their background (McDermott and Panagopoulos 2015).

Hayes (2005) has extended the logic behind issue ownership to candidate traits and argues that Americans view Republicans as stronger or more moral, whereas Democrats are perceived as more compassionate and empathetic. Studies reveal that assessments of candidates' character and personal traits can be reduced to four basic dimensions (leadership, integrity, competence, and empathy) (Kinder 1986) and that these influence voting decisions significantly (Holian and Prysby 2014).

As important as heuristics are in shaping voter preferences and choices, it is important to recall the cues are often subtle, generally operating below the level of conscious awareness. For example, someone watching the speech of a presidential candidate might be inspired to vote for that candidate because he or she sees the candidate as being patriotic, but might not realize that the reason the candidate is seen that way is because he or she wore an American flag pin or because there was an American flag waving in the background. This example highlights what until recently has been a problematic assumption of a great deal of political science research on opinion formation and vote choice: many researchers assume that people are actually able to access their true beliefs and understand why they hold them. Instead, Lodge and Taber (2013) suggest, "unconsciously processed cues operating in the political realm can impact the evaluations of known candidates and their electoral success" (6). In other words, citizens may not be aware or mindful of the cues that are actually affecting their evaluations.

Lodge and Taber argue that people regularly rely on subconsciously and in-stinctively generated thoughts and feelings when explaining their political preferences.

Because people are for the most part vaguely aware of the reasons that certain thoughts or considerations come to mind, such preferences may be difficult to change even when someone is encouraged to think about why they hold them. Lodge and Taber's findings are consistent with other theories that suggest that for most citizens, there is not a need to resolve or recognize reactions to events that may be contradictory to prior responses they have given. As Zaller and Feldman (1992) write, "for most people, most of the time, there is no need to reconcile or even to recognize their contradictory reactions to events and issues. Each represents a gen-uine feeling, capable of coexisting with opposite feelings and, depending on its sa-lience in the person's mind, controlling responses to survey questions" (609).

Lodge and Taber (2013) suggest there can be some merit to these "top of the head" responses in helping citizens to rationalize and make accurate political assessments. A prominent example comes from the 1960 Nixon–Kennedy presi-dential election debate, the first presidential debate aired on television. Nixon refused makeup for the occasion and had also recently been hospitalized, whereas Kennedy was tan after a recent campaign trip to California. Television viewers overwhelmingly thought Kennedy had won the debate, whereas radio listeners thought Nixon was the obvious winner. Television viewers apparently saw Nixon, looking wan and unshaven, as untrustworthy and disconnected, whereas radio viewers, having nothing to go on but the debate itself, were not affected by Nixon's appearance. In their discussion of this incident, Lodge and Taber (2013) suggest that there is something positive that resulted from trusting one's subconscious instincts. They note, "Nixon did indeed turn out to be shifty and untrustworthy. Viewers' implicit, affective responses to the candidates' appearances proved to be more accurate than judgments based presumably on a less biased, more careful consideration of positions and politics" (6).

As this example illustrates, there may be more normative merit to these types of preference formations. What this means for campaigns, however, is that there is far more to influencing vote choice than simply reaching voters with their messages. Thanks to new findings on the role of personality traits, emotions, and even genetic predispositions, campaigns are challenged to create strategies that evoke reactions on behalf of their candidates and tap into dimensions of voter predispositions that cannot be accessed by simply surveying voters regarding their preferences.

THE ROLE OF PERSONALITY TRAITS, GENETIC PREDISPOSITIONS, AND VOTER PSYCHOLOGY

Advances in personality psychology have enabled political scientists to explore more in depth the relationships between personality traits and political pref-erences. The first and most influential book on the matter was *The Authoritarian*

Personality (Adorno et al. 1950), inspired by a drive to understand the individual-level experiences and characteristics that led to the authoritarian behavior and fascist traits that ran rampant during the war. Following this line of research, Herbert McClosky (1958) developed research on the types of personalities that led to a more conservative outlook. He did not define "liberal or conservative" in the sense that they were inventions of political elites, but suggested there was a relationship among conservatism, liberalism, and one's personality. He concluded that conservatives tended to score high on the "undesirable" and poorly adapted side of personality variables, arguing that extreme conservatives were more likely to be hostile and suspicious, rigid and compulsive, and quicker to condemn others for their imperfections and weaknesses, as well as more intolerant and unyielding in their perceptions and judgments. McClosky's work suggested that there is a personality-driven relationship between one's needs and impulses and one's perceptions of the world.

McClosky's work formed the foundation for that of later scholars who would explore more in depth the relationship between different personality traits and political preferences. Personality psychologists developed a conception of personality traits that can be collapsed into five key traits (known as the Big Five model): agreeableness, openness (to experience), emotional stability (or its inverse, neuroticism), conscientiousness, and extroversion. Political scientists have explored whether (and how) these personality traits form the basis of political preferences or shape behavior (Mondak 2010) as well as whether they condition responsiveness to political messages (Gerber at al. 2010). Gerber (2010) and his colleagues suggest that personality traits shape responses to different stimuli (campaign messages, for example), which lead to the formation of attitudes that are contingent on personality. Conscientiousness, for example, is associated with holding more conservative opinions on both economic and social policies, whereas openness is more associated with liberal preferences. However, the relationship between these traits and the opinions developed is affected by contextual differences that change the meaning of the political stimuli. The upshot is that how elites frame their messages and the context of a given election can have important implications for individual-level preferences.

Digging deeper into the microfoundations of preference formation and voting, political scientists have teamed up with geneticists to better understand the biological foundation of political preferences. Whereas the development and transmission of political attitudes was previously thought to be largely sociological and cultural, scientists are now uncovering evidence that there are actually genetic differences that help explain the tendency toward a number of different sociopolitical attitudes. In other words, reasoned and careful considerations of the facts, even the use of cues, do not always explain individual political preferences. Rather, just as biological differences influence a number of other tendencies in humans, they also affect individual orientations to politics. Pathways from DNA to social behavior are complicated by a number of external factors, involving not only networks of different genes, but also one's growth and development, as well as environmental contingencies. Nonetheless, there is a growing consensus that political orientations may arise from the same biological sources as other individual predispositions and psychological traits, both of which have been increasingly associated with individual-level biological differences (Hatemi et al. 2011; Hibbing et al. 2014).

THE ROLE OF AFFECT AND EMOTIONS

Once considered irrelevant in rational conceptualizations of preference formation and voting, renewed scholarly interest in affect, or emotions, has demonstrated strong connections between emotions and political attitudes and behavior (Brader 2006; Marcus et al. 2000). Heightened anxiety, for example, causes people to rely less on their political habits and to consider (and potentially update) their preferences more carefully (Redlawsk et al. 2010; Marcus et al. 2000). High anxiety has also been shown to be related positively to risk aversion; Americans who experienced high levels of anxiety were less supportive of military action by President Bush and favored an increase in American isolationism (Huddy et al. 2005). Similarly, and harkening back to our discussion above about the connections between personality, emotions and political views, Glenn Wilson (1973) suggests that conservative attitudes arise as an ego-defensive function in response to feelings of insecurity, inferiority, and a generalized fear of uncertainty. Wilson suggests these attitudes are inherent, but they are reinforced by culture and social structure.

Campaign advertisements in particular make intentional efforts to appeal to voters by activating emotional responses. As Brader (2006: 13) demonstrates, they use "symbolic images and evocative music to trigger emotional responses from viewers." Brader's evidence suggests that these tactics work. Certain emotional appeals can be particularly effective at mobilizing and persuading voters. Enthusiasm, for example, activates existing partisan loyalties, reminds voters of prior beliefs, and encourages participation. Fear, in contrast, provokes voters to be more vigilant and to seek more information about candidates and can be effective at persuading viewers to change their preferences (Brader 2006).

For decades, political scientists underplayed the role of affect in the formation of political attitudes and behaviors; much greater emphasis was placed on rationality. In recent years, however, researchers have demonstrated that affect and emotions likely play a much more influential role in political decision making. Lodge and Taber (2013: 1) argue that individual variation in beliefs and behavior is rooted in powerful affective and cognitive forces that operate outside of conscious awareness and that "all thinking is suffused with feelings . . . that arise automatically within a few milliseconds of exposure to a sociopolitical object or event" (19). In fact studies have shown that feelings enter the decision stream *before* any cognitive considerations come consciously to mind, suggesting the temporal primacy of affect over cognition (Lodge and Taber 2013, 48). In other words, we feel before we think about political stimuli. Moreover, the "hot cognition" hypothesis posits that all political stimuli individuals have thought about in the past are tagged to positive and/or negative feelings; tallies of these emotional connections stored in our minds are conjured up each time we encounter these stimuli, and these bias our attention and the ways in which we react to stimuli (Lodge and Taber 2013).

The theory of affective intelligence, developed by Marcus, Neuman, and MacKuen (2000), also ascribes considerable importance to the role of affect and emotions in political judgment. The authors leverage insights from neuroscience to show that people generally rely on learned routines, or habits, to manage the many realities of political choice until the "surveillance system" operating in our subconscious minds alerts us to the possibilities of threat or danger by activating specific emotions (for instance, anxiety). The surveillance system is an emotional system that is constantly scanning our surroundings for signals of threat or uncertainty; when it detects these, it interrupts ongoing activity to shift attention to potential pitfalls and focuses our attention on new situations (Marcus et al. 2000). Without this mental jolt, we would continue to behave in routine ways; but when our emotions have prompted us to reconsider our political judgments and behaviors, we may (or not) (re)act differently. Affective intelligence may help explain why citizens are often responsive to negative political messages or situations (for example, a bad economy). More generally, these insights favor an emerging consensus that affect and emotions play a crucial role in influencing political attitudes and behavior, and research is increasingly revealing nuances in the ways it is doing so.

IMPLICATIONS OF PERSONALITY, GENETICS, AND EMOTION: FINDINGS FOR CAMPAIGN CONDUCT

Advances in the microlevel understanding of citizen preference formation and vote choice provide challenges and new opportunities for campaigns. As we will see in the next chapter, these findings have the potential to place a premium on finding and storing more and more detailed information about voters in voter files so as to be as precise as possible in predicting which messages will be the most effective for which types of voters. For example, if stimulating anxiety provokes voters to reconsider their opinions and update their preferences based on new information, it may be more advantageous to release campaign messages that invoke anxiety. The implications of the findings regarding personality and genetics may prove to be more of a challenge for campaigns to incorporate into their strategies. Information on individual personality throughout the electorate is not widely available, and such information may only be attained through in-depth surveys of voters, which can be costly and not ultimately necessary for candidates to win an election.

Genetic information on voters is likely even more difficult to come by. To that end, even political scientists are unclear as to what the importance of a genetic understanding of politics will be, both for the discipline and for campaigns writ large. In an introduction to genopolitics written by the journalist

Thomas Edsall, the political scientist Gary Jacobson is quoted as asking *the* question that puzzles campaigns and political scientists alike: "What I do with this knowledge is another matter. How do I look at public opinion differently knowing that some of what I measure has a genetic basis? I'm not sure what the answer is" (Edsall 2013). In other words, it is likely that there are links between genetic traits and political preferences, but what does this actually mean? Edsall suggests that "with so much riding on political outcomes—from default on the national debt to an attack on Syria to attitudes toward climate change—understanding key factors contributing to the thinking of elected officials and voters becomes crucial" (Edsall 2013). But for others, the implications of genetics for politics are far less clear. Bartels (2013) writes, "If we could identify the genetic factors that make some people more likely than others to support abortion rights while opposing the death penalty, we could indeed 'explain' why some people are more likely than others to support abortion rights while opposing the death penalty. But would doing so help us understand why that particular combination of views is more prevalent now than it was a generation ago? Or why support for the death penalty has declined substantially over the past 20 years? Or why abortion has become a more salient partisan issue in recent campaigns? I don't see how." Although biological information may never be incorporated into voter files, researchers who do study the link between biology and politics argue that "another of the real contributions of the growing empirical evidence on the relevance of biology—and even genetics—to politics is the realization that politics runs very deep" (Hibbing 2013). This realization is not so different from the motivation behind the use of microtargeting in politics; characteristics of voters that seemingly have nothing to do with politics have the potential to provide insight into their political attitudes and preferences.

CONSEQUENCES FOR DEMOCRACY

Voters are commonly viewed as "cognitive misers" (Stroh 1995: 207), navigating conflicting goals of *accuracy* (choices that reflect their substantive values) and *efficiency* (expending minimal cognitive effort) to reach political judgments (Basinger and Lavine 2005) by relying extensively, but not exclusively, on information shortcuts. Even so, citizens seem to vote "correctly," in line with their preferences, more often than not (Lau and Redlawsk 1997). Voters are less likely to support candidates and to use issue-based information when they are uncertain about a candidate's positions (Alvarez 1997). But reliance on heuristics can be rational given the costs of information acquisition, helping to align candidates' positions with voters' interests (Lupia 1994; Lau and Redlawsk 2006; Kahneman et al. 1982). Campaign intensity, however, along with individual characteristics like partisan ambivalence and political knowledge, can moderate the degree to which voters rely on heuristics to make electoral choices (Basinger and Lavine 2005). As Kahn and Kenney (1999) argue, individuals adjust their decision rules depending on the closeness of contests, relying more heavily on sophisticated criteria, like ideology and issues, rather than cognitive shortcuts in more com-petitive, high-intensity campaigns. The effectiveness of heuristic decision-making can also depend on issues framing (Tversky and Kahneman 1981).

Knowledge about voters' reliance on heuristics and persistent stereotypes can also tempt campaigns to follow sinister paths. Tali Mendelberg has shown that campaigns exploit entrenched, racial stereotypes, for example, to appeal to white voters by using subtle terms like "welfare" or "crime" to prime racial biases against blacks (Mendelberg 2001). Fortunately, she finds that such im-plicitly racial messages lose their appeal, even among their target audiences, when their content and sinister motives are exposed (Mendelberg 2001)," but these tactics are not uncommon. Allegations of racial and even sexist under-tones in statements made by Donald Trump during the 2016 presidential cam-paign have renewed concerns about the corrosive effects of such campaign discourse.

From a normative perspective, concerns about manipulation become more acute if we believe campaigns have a responsibility to present accurate and com-plete information to voters. Oftentimes, the line between different interpreta-tions and deliberately misleading is thin. In recent years, the emergence of fact-checking organizations to scrutinize and evaluate the veracity of candidates' claims offers some hope of setting the records straight. Nevertheless, as Kuklinski et al. (2000) and Nyhan (2010) argue, misinformation is difficult to correct, even with new facts; partisans generally have a tendency to reject inconvenient truths (Mattes and Redlawsk 2014), although some studies find citizens do update their political judgments when exposed to new facts (Gilens 2001).

Although the study of the relationship between genetics and political pref-erences leaves unanswered integral questions of why preferences change and develop over time, there is a normative upshot to this new evidence as it relates to how political opponents, both candidates and average citizens, relate to one another. Proponents of the use of genetic research in politics suggest it might improve relationships between political opponents. John R. Alford and his co-authors suggest that the key to getting along in politics is not the ability of one side to suddenly see the problem in its thinking, but the ability of both sides to see the other as inherently different not only in a political sense, but also in a physical and biological sense. "Political disputes," notes the cover of the authors' seminal book on the topic (Hibbing et al. 2014), "typically spring from the as-sumption that those who do not agree with us are shallow, misguided, unin-formed, and ignorant." This becomes more difficult to justify if the bases of political preferences have immutable biological origins. New research on the biology of political preferences contends that political opponents are hard-wired to experience and process the world in different ways, suggesting that although opposing candidates may not necessarily be able to convert one another or their supporters to their way of thinking, they may be able to adopt a greater willing-ness to compromise in light of the biological factors that separate their opinions (Hibbing et al. 2014).

CONCLUSION

Elections are the primary means by which citizens in a democracy can express their preferences to elected officials. Hillygus and Shields (2008) argue that "information about the voters shapes campaign messages and candidate strategies, and information from the campaign influences voter decision making" (193). In other words, "vote choice" is a reciprocal process whereby campaign strategy simultaneously seeks to influence and is also influenced by the characteristics and preferences of voters. This dynamic leads candidates to emphasize some issues over others and, just as important, make highly specific decisions about how to frame and present these issues so as to evoke reactions from citizens that ultimately lead to votes on Election Day. Ideally, the news media's coverage of campaigns also serves to "enlighten" voters, that is, to give them enough information so they can make up their minds by Election Day (Gelman and King 1993). And campaigns do enlighten voters, particularly low-information voters who become both more informed and certain of candidate positions throughout the course of a campaign (Alvarez 1997).

KEY TERMS

Affective intelligence theory	Issue trespassing	Rational choice
"Big Five" personality traits	issue voting	Retrospective voting
	Hot cognition	Stereotypes
Cross-pressured voter	Motivated reasoning	Wedge issue
Funnel of causality	Partisan identification	
Heuristics	Low-information rationality	
Issue salience	Predispositions	

SUGGESTED READINGS

Brader, T. 2006. *Campaigning for Hearts and Minds: How Emotional Appeals in Political Ads Work.* Chicago, IL: University of Chicago Press.

Campbell, A., P. E. Converse, W. E. Miller, and D. E. Stokes. 1960. *The American Voter.* Chicago, IL: University of Chicago Press.

Hibbing, J. R., K. B. Smith, and J. R. Alford. 2014. *Predisposed: Liberals, Conservatives, and the Biology of Political Differences.* New York: Routledge.

Lodge, M., and C. S. Taber. 2013. *The Rationalizing Voter.* New York: Cambridge University Press.

Marcus, G. E., R. Neuman, and M. MacKuen. 2000. *Affective Intelligence and Political Judgment.* Chicago, IL: University of Chicago Press.

Mondak, J. 2010. *Personality and the Foundations of Political Behavior.* New York: Cambridge University Press

Popkin, S. L. 1994. *The Reasoning Voter. Communication and Persuasion in Presidential Campaigns*, 2nd ed. Chicago, IL: University of Chicago Press.

CHAPTER 9

Technology and Contemporary Campaigns

Although Howard Dean lost the 2004 Democratic presidential nomination to John Kerry, his campaign marked a watershed moment for campaign strategy in American elections. As Steven Friess (2012), a reporter for the online news organization *Politico* notes, "Almost every innovation now commonplace in politics—search ads, social networking, online video hubs, do-it-yourself grassroots tools—has traceable roots to a ragtag bunch of techies whose dream candidate was a loser." The Dean campaign's innovative use of technology served as a signal for candidates and campaign managers across the country of what the future of American elections would look like, propelling campaign tactics into an era of seemingly constant technological innovation and development.

Dean's campaign used the then-fairly nascent power of the Internet mainly to raise money and engagement with the campaign. However, the burgeoning power of the Internet was not completely positive for Dean. His infamous scream at a campaign rally after his loss in Iowa turned out to be one of the earliest "viral" political moments and was the beginning of the end of Dean's campaign (Roberts 2004). Nevertheless, the Dean campaign inspired a group of new technological innovators who, after his political demise, branched out, started their own companies, and formed the foundation of what is now a well-established cornerstone of political campaigning. For Dean, the same Internet that helped send him to front-runner status for the Democratic presidential ticket also became the source of his downfall. The Internet and its various trappings have changed the rules of the political game, and campaigns must find a way to efficiently incorporate it into their campaign strategies or be left out in the cold.

If 2004 was a turning point for the development and use of technology in political campaigns, the 2008 presidential race brought it front and center, creating buzz in all circles about the effects of the online political revolution. From the onset of the election, campaigns were posting clips of their speeches to YouTube, using Facebook to create different groups and events to consolidate supporters, advertising on social media, and making important announcements via online videos (Panagopoulos 2009b). The Internet has dramatically changed campaigns and will continue to do so. The first candidate websites appeared in 1996 and the first e-mail blasts from candidates in 1998. By 2000, the McCain campaign began to take advantage of online fundraising. The Dean campaign of 2004 put online fundraising to further use and propelled the role of the Internet in political campaigns forward. By 2006, candidates were regularly using social networking sites like YouTube and MySpace (Cornfield and Rainie 2006). In 2012, President Barack Obama's reelection bid became well known for its innovative use of data to track and mobilize supporters (Issenberg 2012a; 2012d).

Advances in technology have changed almost every facet of contemporary campaigns, from GOTV efforts to messaging, fundraising, soliciting of volunteers, and handling of media. Developing technologies have arguably influenced every aspect of contemporary campaigns that have been covered in this volume thus far. It is now almost unheard of, at least at the level of higher-profile campaigns, for strategists to not rely on massive databases of voter information and web-based tools to identify, keep track of, and communicate with voters.

The Internet has become vital for almost every aspect of campaign strategies and has changed the way campaign analysts think about and implement strategy. Gone are the days of mass marketing, when campaign messages were designed to appeal to broader swaths of the public. Now, thanks to developments in technology and the data that come from the increasing usage of the Internet by Americans, contemporary campaigns have entered an era of mass customization and individualized persuasion, in which campaigns are able to narrowly target the voters they want to communicate with across a multitude of different platforms, both online and offline. As I will show, the mass customization made possible by changes in technology and increasing amounts of available data can influence not only campaign persuasion and mobilization efforts, but also volunteer recruitment and fundraising.

In this chapter, I discuss how political campaigns are being revolutionized by changing technology and the growth of new and social media. I discuss the role of campaign software and data availability for a variety of campaign activities and consider how a candidate's online presence and social media platforms like Facebook and Twitter have affected campaign conduct. I conclude with a discussion of the normative implications of these technological developments.

CAMPAIGN SOFTWARE AND DATA AVAILABILITY

In contemporary elections in the United States, most campaigns use some form of computer-generated database for voter contact and tracking. Although campaigns still employ traditional methods of voter contact, such as phone calls, in-person canvassing, direct mail, and, more recently, e-mail, massive voter databases help ensure that these efforts are reaching the right people. Campaigns generally use these databases to produce three types of estimates: behavior, support, and responsiveness. Behavior estimates gauge which individuals are likely to turn out to vote, contribute money, or volunteer. Support estimates are used to predict preferences for particular candidates and issue positions. And responsiveness estimates are designed to predict how an individual would respond if contacted by the campaign (Nickerson and Rogers 2014). Responsiveness estimates are the most difficult to generate. Behavior estimates are the most reliable since they are heavily dependent on an individual's past behaviors.

The content of the databases is generally considered proprietary information, but the content of voter files that they are built from is publicly available. At the most basic level, voter files are lists of all registered voters in an area. The files include all of the information that is collected when an individual registers to vote (address, date of birth, gender, and history of turnout in primaries and general elections). A handful of states collect race and/or ethnicity when individuals register and this information is also included in the files. States with party registration (see Chapter 5) make this information available as well.

The existence and widespread use of voter files was facilitated by the passage of the 2002 Help America Vote Act. In the wake of the controversial 2000 presidential elections in Florida and the recount that ensued, the act resulted in a greater standardization of election procedures across the country for federal elections and mandated that states create and maintain an electronic list of individuals registered to vote by 2006 (Hersh 2015). Whereas previous campaigns had to acquire their own data county by county, statewide databases became available through secretaries of state after passage of the act (Blaemire 2012). Almost overnight, the once arduous task of developing voter files became far easier and today the use of computer databases of voter files is ubiquitous in contemporary campaigns.

Entrepreneurial companies have been established that merge state voter information with commercially obtained data to provide candidates with a more complete picture of voters. Voter files are now massive databases that contain highly detailed information about voters that goes far beyond their registration status. Prior to the development and widespread use of the Internet, an entry for an individual might contain information about his or her partisan identification (if known), vote history, and some basic demographic characteristics. Now, voter files are available to campaigns (at a cost) that have this information *plus* a host of other variables including hobbies, occupation, homeownership status, income, and magazine subscription status. That said, consumer information such as magazine subscriptions and past purchases are considerably more expensive for campaigns to purchase and are less useful to campaigns than the information provided by the states since consumer information is only available for a relatively small subset of registered voters (Nickerson and Rogers 2014). Other information can be acquired inexpensively from federal and state governments through requests made under the Freedom of Information Act, such as which registered voters have a hunting license. The primary goal is still to identify supporters and persuadable voters, so the most valuable information included in the files is that regarding party identification (Hersh 2015). For states without consistent records of the partisanship of registered voters, however, the newly available consumer information enhances the campaign's ability to identify supporters and the issues that they may consider important.

Of course, such substantial change typically begets more change. With the increasing adoption of the Internet, online tools were developed that allow individual campaigns to do what previously specialized consultants had been doing for them. This type of competition led to the development of online voter files that candidates could access and use on their own, for a price. One of the first online voter file systems, called the Voter Activation Network, is still in use today, marketing itself as a company that helps Democrats and other progressive campaigns. In its wake followed a number of companies such as Leverage, Catalist, and rVotes, all designed to help candidates access voter information. Some of these companies, like Voter Activation Network and rVotes, market their services to one side of the partisan/ideological spectrum or the other—in this case, Democrats and Republicans, respectively. On its homepage, the nonpartisan company Aristotle boasts that its "national voter file contains over 190 million voter records, including voting histories, demographics, hobbies, income, donor histories and over 500 data fields. These records are constantly updated and vetted, providing you with the most up-to-date information from more than 4,000 election boards, county clerks, and voter registrars." Aristotle further elaborates, stating it delivers "valuable (and detailed!) data to candidates about potential supporters. In fact, don't be surprised if the candidates know more about you than you do about them."

Because the use of detailed voter files is now commonplace in contemporary campaigns, companies like Aristotle must compete for candidates as clients. Robert Blaemire (2012), the founder of Leverage, notes, "The existence of a voter file is almost an assumption in modern campaigns, and the competition among vendors isn't between those who have them and those who don't but the amount of data appended and the flexibility that will be made available for accessing that data. It is far more an assessment of quality over quantity" (107). It is no longer a matter of *whether* a campaign is going to use voter files; it is a matter of which service will provide them with the most detailed and accessible files for their purposes.

One of the recent changes in companies that provide access to voter files is that clients no longer pay them to build files on a case-by-case basis. Instead, organizations and campaigns can pay flat-rate subscriber fees in exchange for access to and use of as much data as needed. With the increasing centralization of massive amounts of voter data, companies like Catalist are now able to process huge amounts of information to model and predict voter behavior. Using large amounts of data made available through central databases operated by the Democratic and Republican national committees, for example, these companies can help candidates target voters by partisanship in states where citizens do not register by party and predict whether someone will vote even if they have a poor voting history (Blaemire 2012). With the massive amounts of voter information now available to candidates that can help them fine-tune their *messages* for specific people, future uses of voter databases might involve determining the most effective *method* for contacting a given voter.

The development of voter databases has enormous implications for campaign strategy. As Sasha Issenberg (2012a), an election journalist writes, voters are "no longer trapped in old political geographies or tethered to traditional demographic categories such as age or gender, depending on which attributes pollsters asked about or how consumer marketers classified them for commercial purposes. Instead, the electorate could be seen as a collection of individual citizens who could each be measured and assessed on their own terms. Now it was up to a candidate who wanted to lead those people to build a campaign that would interact with them the same way."

With the ever-increasing amounts of data available to campaigns comes the need to develop software to manage it as well as the many other digital activities that campaigns undertake. Now, many companies offer web-based software as a service application for campaigns. Some help campaigns manage the financial side of campaigning, whereas others help manage voter contact and volunteer management, giving candidates the ability to leverage voter information and technology as efficiently as possible. Their applications include enormous amounts of data that can be used simultaneously by thousands of different campaigns, including but not limited to voter files. They help build political websites that send data in real time to their applications, provide contact management and e-mail services, and help process online contributions.

The sophisticated services and applications available to candidates today were not developed overnight. Nathaniel Pearlman (2012), the founder of NGP Software, now NGP VAN, Inc., had strong skills as a computer programmer and was interested in U.S. elections and politics when he started the then-named NGP Software, Inc., in the late 1990s. In early company statements, Pearlman said, "Democratic candidates and fundraisers are poorly served in the current political software market. Most current products are over-priced, aging, incomplete, or poorly supported" (190). Pearlman's goal was to develop affordable software that would be easy to use and efficient for clients. NGP's fundraising compliance and contribution processing software were particularly popular with Democratic presidential bids during the 2004 elections. NGP ultimately merged with Voter Activation Network (VAN). At the time of the merger, VAN was considered a leading provider of database software enabling voter contact, volunteer management, and organizing tools to Democratic campaigns, labor unions, and non-profit organizations," while NGP was a top provider of fundraising and compliance and new media software to Democrats and their allies. They joined forces to provide both financial and voter data services to Democratic candidates and their organizational allies.

Another technological development shaping the way campaigns operate is the availability of databases of campaign media ads. Kantar Media has a highly sophisticated tracking system that uses satellite technology originally developed for the U.S. military to track and store advertisements as they are aired. The

Campaign Media Analysis Group (CMAG) is a subsidiary of Kantar Media, focusing specifically on creating advertising databases that allow political campaigns to monitor their own and opponents' ads in near real time to get a sense of who is being targeted and what content is being used. CMAG uses custom tracking systems to capture and record all occurrences of an ad and then provides its clients, which include thousands of local, state, and national political and issue advocacy campaigns across the United States, detailed information on the occurrence of relevant ads and ad buy data. As a part of these services, campaigns get electronic copies of ads, full-color storyboards and audio transcripts, digital video files of television ads, tracking reports, and access to historical research. CMAG helps candidates ensure their advertising spots are reaching the right audiences and notifies them of what their competition is buying, how much they are paying, and what they are saying in new spots. They can also notify campaigns of their competition's target demographic and who is sponsoring their ads, a tool that has become increasingly relevant with the rising prevalence of outside groups that air advertisements in favor of and against specific candidates These services are relatively affordable; a competitive U.S. House campaign, for example, can procure weekly reports on placement messaging, and estimated spending for all broadcast television ad activity in the district, including details about the sponsor or sponsor type, party, the issue(s) covered in ad, the market, station, program, airdate and time, and tone of every individual airing, along with links to view the ad itself, for the duration of the campaign at a cost of about $5,000.[1]

ONLINE PRESENCE AND SOCIAL MEDIA PLATFORMS

Every year, more Americans turn to the Internet to get campaign information. Figure 9.1 illustrates this trend over time in comparison to other sources of campaign information (Caumont 2013). Online sources include not only major news websites, but also new forms of news aggregators and explainers like Vox Media and The Skimm that collect and explain news from other sources, featuring user-friendly graphics and quick, pithy explanations of current events and campaign developments. The Skimm, for example, is a news aggregator aimed at women that is delivered via e-mail. It is designed to allow readers to "skim" the daily news headlines without having to take the time to read in-depth articles. Many of these news aggregators come in the form of apps that allow people to get news on their cell phones; as of 2014, a quarter of registered voters got political news on their cell phones (Smith 2014). More and more Americans are also getting campaign information from social media, filtered not through major news outlets or even new forms of news gathering, but through their friends, family, and others in their social networks, as well as updates from candidate pages

---

[1]Personal e-mail communication with Elizabeth Wilner (Kanthar Media/CMAG). June 15, 2015.

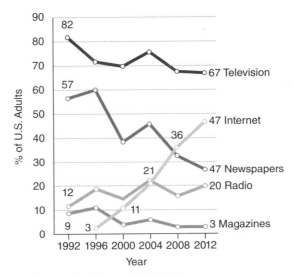

Figure 9.1 Sources of Campaign News, 1992–2012
SOURCE: Caumont (2012)

themselves. As illustrated in Figure 9.2, during the 2014 midterm elections, more than twice as many Americans reported following candidates on social media than during the 2010 midterm elections, with notable increases among older age groups (Smith 2014).

Because of the increasing use of the Internet and social media by millions of Americans as sources of campaign information, more than ever, candidates must develop a consistent online presence and maintain vigilant watch over potentially damaging developments across a wide variety of information sources. Whereas in the late 1990s candidate websites were more or less a novelty, today it is essentially required for a candidate to have not only a website, but also a presence on social media platforms like Facebook and Twitter. Indeed, candidates now routinely announce their candidacies and other developments via social media platforms, as did Republican candidate for president, Tim Pawlenty, in 2012 (Finn and Ruffini 2012). In the 2016 presidential race, GOP contender Donald Trump tweeted over 4,000 times to his 5.9 million followers, between June 2015, when he announced his candidacy, and January 2016 (Lee and Quealy 2016). Although online campaigning is to some extent contingent on strategic and structural factors such as the competiveness of a given election or the number of people who live in a candidate's district, a purely "offline" campaign has more or less become a relic of the past (Herrnson et al. 2007). A candidate's web presence has become integral to his or her success in fundraising and developing electoral support and is especially useful for gathering small-donor contributions, raising fast money after primary victories, and consolidating support

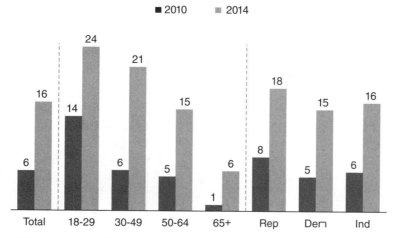

Figure 9.2 Americans Following Candidates on Social Media by Age Group

NOTE: Percent (%) of registered voters who follow candidates for office, political parties or elected officials on social networking sites like Facebook or Twitter. Survey conducted Oct. 15–20, 2014. Based on registered voters.

SOURCE: Pew Research Center (as cited in Smith 2014)

early on (Christenson et al. 2014). Such factors are especially important considering the prominence of the "invisible" primary discussed in previous chapters, in which large war chests can signal viability to prospective donors and supporters, and even opponents.

Indeed, fundraising was one of the first areas of campaign strategy to be substantially affected by the rise in the Internet. In contemporary campaigns, candidates now solicit donations through websites, e-mail blasts, and social media, which are far cheaper than direct mail, phone calls, or in-person appeals for money. Because of the advances in social media, campaigns are also able to send out requests for money that incorporate a whole gamut of technological advances, including the use of online videos and personal messages. Many of these approaches are designed to give a candidate a more personal and approachable feel because they often include ostensibly unedited videos that give supporters a look at a candidate's life outside of politics (Panagopoulos 2009b). Now, strategists considering their online fundraising options must ask themselves a multitude of questions when crafting solicitations for money. Do certain subject lines and senders lead to greater responses? Are there some incentives (such as a sticker, t-shirt, or coffee mug) that are more attractive than others? Today, online fundraising is not just a matter of having a link on one's website where supporters can enter credit card information. It is a complex operation that has become as important as phone calls, canvassing, and direct mail were in decades past (Mele 2012).

The impact of a candidate's online presence is not limited to the capacity of the Internet for fundraising, however. More than ever, candidate messages and information are disseminated to a diverse array of online outlets, from social media websites to the blogosphere. The increasing proliferation of social media and the ease with which information is now spread provides both opportunities and challenges for candidates (Gueorguieva 2009).

On the one hand, it is a cost-effective way for candidates to gain exposure at little to no cost and solve one of the key problems of digital campaigns, "that you only ever preach to the choir" (Finn and Ruffini 2012: 26). Because of this change in technology, campaigns can become more efficient in their targeting, more often reaching voters who have the highest probability of supporting them on Election Day. Social media also allows candidates to develop more personal connections with voters, encouraging voters to access aspects of their identities that may closely align with a candidate's own identity and issue positions. The photograph-based social media platform Instagram, for example, gives users a peak into the personal lives of candidates, and politicians such as Barack Obama, Joe Biden, and Paul Ryan host their own accounts or have their organizing committees host one for them. Figure 9.3 shows examples of the types of posts candidates share to give an inside look at their personal lives beyond their roles as elected officials. Vice President Joe Biden posted a photo of himself and his wife promoting reading awareness as well as a candid photo of himself and the president high-fiving, for example. President Barack Obama gave his wife a birthday

Figure 9.3 Politician Instagram Accounts

Figure 9.3 (*Continued*)

shout out on Instagram and also shared a picture of the two from their wedding day on their anniversary. The former GOP vice presidential candidate and speaker of the House, Paul Ryan, shared a photo of himself and his family at a Green Bay Packers football game as well as multiple pictures of his family hunting and on skiing trips.

On the other hand, although social media allows candidates to give the public an inside look at their lives off the political stage, the proliferation of social media also means that campaigns have less control over the portrayal of a candidate's image, which is central to election success. Social media is novel and challenging because it is free and user driven; users contribute and disseminate as much as they consume (Boutin 2006). Citizens are no longer passive receptors of campaign advertisements on television, endorsements in newspapers, or candidate speeches and debates. They can now contribute to and shape candidates' images in potentially significant ways. Because of this, campaigns now must hire Internet strategists to maintain online communications operations, monitor social networking sites to deal with "rogue" users posting negative messages about candidates, and help spread the content that campaigns want others to see (Greenfield 2007). Furthermore, to successfully leverage the power of the Internet and social media platforms, campaigns must do more than set up a Facebook page, YouTube account, or Twitter feed. They must make use of these resources in ways that seem authentic, credible, and personal while maintaining an integrated message, although social media allows them to reach a far broader swath of the electorate than ever before (Slotnick 2009).

Different formats of social media serve different purposes depending on the type of content they host. Whereas Instagram allows citizens to peer into the lives of candidates through photos, YouTube serves as a venue for candidates to share videos of their lives, make important announcements, share speeches, and disseminate campaign ads without having to pay for television ad time. The impact of online videos for campaigns is enormous and provides just as many challenges as it does opportunities. Clips that are posted can be viewed multiple times and spread around on almost every conceivable online platform.

When done creatively, online campaign videos can be a big hit. When Hillary Clinton was running for the 2008 Democratic nomination, she released a video that made fun of her talents as a singer and asked voters for her help in picking a campaign song. After a few weeks, she released another video that incorporated some of the negative feedback she had received from YouTube members, finally announcing the song in a video featuring herself and Bill Clinton spoofing the series finale of the *Sopranos* to reveal the winning song (Panagopoulos 2009b). Although it is a campaign's dream to have a video that reflects positively on the candidate "go viral," it can also be their nightmare if a video goes viral for the wrong reason. In 2010, after securing the Republican Party's nomination for the Delaware Senate seat formerly held by Vice President Joe Biden, Christine O'Donnell had to deal with the fallout from the comedian Bill Maher's airing of a 1999 clip in which she admitted to dabbling in witchcraft and told a story about having a "midnight picnic on a satanic alter." O'Donnell's response was to air a 30-second ad in which she stated, "I'm not a witch, I'm nothing you've heard, I'm you." Her ad backfired, ultimately having a more negative impact on her campaign than Maher's original clip (Konstantinides 2013).

Social media sites like Facebook and Twitter serve as interactive and dynamic rallying points for candidates and their supporters to "gather" and for candidates to disseminate their messages. These sites can host not only written content in the form of status updates, but also photos, videos, and links to campaign websites and fundraising efforts. Because they are largely made up of communities of like-minded followers and supporters of candidates, they are somewhat akin to a virtual campaign rally where candidates can digitally reach large numbers of supporters with the click of a button. Political information about candidates that social media users encounter can be a catalyst for greater political involvement. Individuals perusing Facebook for nonpolitical reasons may suddenly find themselves on the page of a previously unknown candidate for elected office and be motivated to get further engaged by donating, volunteering, or sharing that candidate's information with their friends if they like what they see.

For contemporary campaigns, social media platforms have the potential to create a virtual cascade effect of candidate awareness and campaign involvement; each retweet increases the probability of more retweets, and each "like" on a candidate's status update increases the number of people who will see that status update. Hashtags have become a key tool in viral political networking because campaigns seek to proliferate the use of hashtags among users that will get spread widely enough to be considered "trending" on these sites. Twitter in particular has brought about a new kind of ad war for political campaigns to engage in. For the first time, during the 2012 elections, the presidential candidates Barack Obama and Mitt Romney purchased "Promoted Trends" on Twitter, which are ad units that create more prominence for a Twitter hashtag by putting it at the top of the Trends lists on Twitter pages. Obama, for example, ran the hashtag #Forward2012, encouraging supporters to add the tag to their tweets. Romney's campaign, for its part, purchased the hashtag trend #RomneyRyan2012 for the nominee's acceptance speech and added #AreYouBetterOff shortly thereafter. The estimated cost of a one-day buy of a promoted trend on Twitter is about $120,000 (Mazmanian 2012). If they have the cash, campaigns no longer have to hope to go viral; they can literally buy it.

In addition to serving as rallying points for supporters and additional venues for candidates to share their campaign messages, social media also creates new data for candidates to collect on potential voters. Because social media creates a sort of online public square where people are exposed to and can discuss politics with friends and family, each comment, like, and click has the potential to become a data point that is then captured and analyzed by political campaigns (Finn and Ruffini 2012: 26). In addition, these interactions are linking users with trusted sources of information, their friends, which can further enhance the effect of candidate messages (Sinclair 2012).

Related to this point, some evidence suggests that through the use of social media to encourage their followers to vote, campaigns have the potential to improve voter turnout. Bond et al. (2012) experimentally tested the power of social media to increase turnout. Facebook users encountered messages encouraging them to vote, information about where to vote, a digital "I voted" button they could share, and a counter telling them how many other Facebook users had reported voting and pictures of their Facebook friends who had already reported voting. Others were given the same treatment without seeing their friends' faces, and a third group received no message. Individuals exposed to messages with their friends photos turned out at a rate that was about 0.4 percentage points higher than the other groups on average. Although this study was nonpartisan in nature, it is conceivable that partisan efforts along these lines delivered via social media can have the capacity to nudge turnout in ways that could be consequential in competitive elections (Lipsitz 2011).

CONSEQUENCES FOR DEMOCRACY

Many observers see the technological developments of the past decade as influencing campaign conduct in a way that is positive for the democratic ideals of engagement, information, and representation. Technology has the power to help bring more people into the political process and to mobilize people around a common candidate or cause in ways that just a few decades ago were unimaginable.

Advances in software and data availability have arguably allowed campaigns to deliver messages effectively, no longer relying on an individual's voting history alone to determine whether a voter should be targeted. Even people with spotty voting histories can be targeted by campaigns based on other characteristics that indicate they will turn out and vote for a given candidate when supplied with an effective motivating message. In this way, advances in the ability of campaigns to store and analyze large amounts of data may help engage more citizens in the electoral process and encourage them to participate in ways that were unimaginable in previous decades. On the downside, as I discussed in Chapter 5, if this detailed information is used to manipulate voters, there is a risk voters will eventually become disillusioned over time as their preferences are ignored, potentially withdrawing from the political process.

Also troubling is new software that allows incumbent candidates in state legislatures to pinpoint the partisan composition of geographic areas to redistrict them in ways that are electorally advantageous for one party or another. Redistricting happens in state legislatures every 10 years after the gathering of census data and often goes under the radar of many ordinary citizens. Redistricting can lead to contentious battles between parties, especially if one party holds the state House of Representatives and the other holds the Senate. In 2001, when Illinois Democrats won control of the Illinois House and Republicans retained the Senate, Barack Obama worked with a Democratic consultant, John Corrigan, to draw himself a new district that would be more electorally advantageous. In 2002, Obama won a seat as an Illinois state senator, and the Illinois Democrats took control of the Senate (Sides et al. 2014; Lizza 2008). The increasing ability of incumbent state legislators to draw districts that favor their parties with such precision naturally has implications for the extent to which elections are actually competitive and, in turn, engaging and informative for citizens. On the flip side, however, citizens can also access new redistricting software and use it to create and present alternatives to their legislature. In certain states, citizens can monitor the process of redistricting as it occurs and get more directly involved. In 2008, California voters passed the Voters First Act via referendum, which reallocated the responsibility for drawing district boundaries for the state Senate from the state legislature to the newly created Citizens Redistricting Commission. In 2010, voters passed a similar act adding congressional districts to the commission's responsibilities. New redistricting requirements established a 14-member, bipartisan commission to draw state political boundaries and set explicitly nonpartisan criteria for the redrawing of districts to allow for the fair representation of Californians. Some of these criteria include the requirement that population equality should be achieved to the furthest extent possible and that districts should be geographically contiguous (League of Women Voters n.d.).

For campaigns, the Internet has the potential to help lower the entry costs for newcomers to the political arena and equalize the playing field with respect to institutional realities like the primary calendar that generally favor front runners. As I discussed in previous chapters, candidates must compete early to gather funds and gain enough recognition to be seen as viable to future donors and supporters. The Internet appears to be combating this inequity as it provides fundraising and organizational opportunities to dark-horse candidates at relatively low costs, relieves the burden of fundraising necessities that seems to have plagued so many campaigns, and places far greater control of the nomination process in the hands of broader swaths of grassroots activists and small-dollar donors (Christenson et al. 2014). A more equalized playing field in terms of candidate entry into political races means that citizens can potentially have a more diverse and representative array of options to choose from when determining which candidates to support. Candidates with strong ideas may no longer be left out of the political fray because of a lack of startup money and support at the onset of a campaign season.

The Internet, too, has compounded the ability of campaigns to disseminate information. Information about policy positions and opponent stances can be shared with supporters with the click of a button. In addition, it appears that candidates are being held to a higher standard of honesty and integrity because armies of fact-checkers can spend time scouring the Internet for information that contradicts a candidate statement or otherwise undermines his or her credibility. Websites like the *Tampa Bay Times*'s Politifact and Factcheck.org post regular updates and analysis of statements made by candidates and elected officials.

Advances in social media also have implications for citizen engagement. Preliminary findings discussed in this chapter suggest that encouraging people to vote on Facebook can have an impact on turnout. But beyond turnout, social media encourages discussion and engagement among citizens about politics and organizes members by different geographic and organizational networks, which makes the possibility of in-person meetings and organizing more likely. Indeed, Facebook "events" have become a staple for local candidate organizers to rally supporters for different campaign events, such as debate viewings or candidate appearances. Broadly, then, social media has the potential to generate a new "online" form of civic engagement where candidates and elected officials can mobilize citizens to all kinds of political action (Williams and Gulati 2009).

There are also normatively troubling developments that come with the increasing role of technology in political campaigns. Druckman et al. (2009) demonstrate that resources are still a critical component that determines campaign strategy; candidates who raise more money and who have larger staffs are better able to utilize technology and present campaign information in a way that is potentially more persuasive. Furthermore, campaigns appear to be able to use their web presence as a means to control their message, at least as it pertains to their websites. The extent to which candidates allow interaction with and among supporters on their websites depends on the competiveness of a given race. Candidates who have large leads or deficits tend to have websites that have more communication features and potential for user interaction. As Druckman et al. (2009) note, "candidates who feel they have little to lose often seem to embrace the idea of online deliberation and discussion as a part of a healthy campaign" (41).

The same is not true when the race tightens. When races are close, the public's interest in a candidate increases, journalists are more interested in covering a particular race, and support tends to increase. Unfortunately, as Druckman and his co-authors note, this is exactly when candidates try to assert the most control over their message and allow for less user interactivity with their websites. Although campaigns have less control over user interactions on their social media websites (for instance, candidates cannot turn off comments on Instagram), it seems logical that they would try to exercise similar discretion over these platforms in highly competitive contexts. These findings raise questions over the extent to which competition actually helps promote democratic accountability and representation, although many see it as a key mechanism for ensuring these norms (Schattschneider 1960). It was hoped that the Internet would give citizens a voice and allow them to easily hold politicians accountable, but this is potentially difficult to achieve if campaigns still largely seek to control their agenda in competitive elections.

Finally, the increasing amount of voter data available to campaigns also has implications for democratic norms. On the one hand, highly specialized voter file data may help candidates to inform, engage, and mobilize citizens who would normally be unreachable. On the other hand, armed with data and models that allow candidates to provide voters with the messages the voter *wants* to hear can potentially cause mischief and result in manipulation.

Privacy concerns are also on the rise given the sheer volume of detailed information about Americans available to campaigns and the potential for mischief and violations. Legal experts argue laws regulating the collection and use of this data are virtually nonexistent (Rubinstein 2014). In fact, Rubinstein suggests (2014: 861) the political dossiers campaigns exploit to deploy big data strategies, "may be the largest unregulated assemblage of personal data in contemporary American life." In the 2012 election cycle, for example, political data vendor Aristotle partnered with Intermarkets, a digital ad firm, and Lotame, a data management and analytics firm, to track Americans' online activity and match voter files with online, cookie-based profiles, in order to target digital ads to potential voters (Rubinstein 2014). Sometimes, this information can end up in the wrong hands, as it did in the 2016 presidential election cycle when the Democratic National Committee temporarily suspended the Sanders' campaign access to its databases after it was discovered that a software vendor glitch enabled a Sanders staffer to access the Clinton campaign's private database (Sherfinski 2015).

Although it seems clear that the technological advances of the past few decades have had a lasting effect on the conduct of campaigns, it remains to be seen whether this conduct will, over time, help or hinder the advancement of democratic norms. Our understanding is likely to be further complicated as more technological advances make their way into the arena of political campaigning, with new updates and assessments coming to light every election cycle.

KEY TERMS

Behavior estimates	Online fundraising	Social media
CMAG database	Predictive analytics	Support estimates
Help America Vote Act	Promoted trends	Voter file
Mass customization	Responsiveness	
News aggregators	estimates	

SUGGESTED READINGS

Hersh, E. D. 2015. *Hacking the Electorate: How Campaigns Perceive Voters*. New York: Cambridge University Press.

Hillygus, D. S., and T. G. Shields. 2008. *The Persuadable Voter: Wedge Issues in Presidential Campaigns*. Princeton, NJ: Princeton University Press.

Issenberg, S. 2012. *Victory Lab: The Secret Science of Winning Campaigns*. New York: Crown.

Nickerson, D. W., and T. Rogers. 2014. "Political Campaigns and Big Data." *The Journal of Economic Perspectives* 28, no 2: 51–74.

CHAPTER 10

Contemporary Campaigns
and the Evolving Electoral Process

In 2003, Gavin Newsom was elected mayor of San Francisco, a city where mayoral elections are often competitive and hard fought. In May 2003, Newsom's campaign began its voter identification program, pinpointing voters who were likely to support or oppose Newsom's candidacy or who were on the fence. Volunteers were sent out asking voters to "endorse" Newsom for mayor. The campaign was not looking for just anyone to sign a petition; they wanted to specifically identify Newsom supporters. After six weeks, the campaign had identified 24,000 supporters, who were then entered into a database and matched against voter files. Those supporters who were not registered to vote had an application sent to them by Newsom volunteers, and the campaign ultimately registered 5,000 new voters.

After this initial push, the Newsom campaign called every registered voter who had not yet expressed support for Newsom, which produced another 25,000 likely Newsom supporters, many of whom lived in neighborhoods that the campaign would not otherwise have considered supportive of Newsom. By September, the campaign had almost 50,000 identified supporters, and nearly half were voters who would not normally vote in an off-year election. All supporters were "aggressively encouraged" to apply to vote by mail; the campaign mailed applications to each voter and called them with requests to return the application (Ross 2004). Each received an application and a call, up to three times, until he or she was registered to vote by mail. Furthermore, Newsom volunteers walked through every precinct in the city and knocked on the doors of identified supporters, urging them to vote by mail, which created 10,000 further applications from Newsom supporters, more than half of which were not for regular voters. By Election Day, the campaign had turned out more than 8,000 voters using its vote-by-mail strategy, and 90% of those voters who applied to vote by mail returned their ballots.

The campaign went into a runoff, after which the Newsom campaign continued its voter identification process. To overcome the massive support his opponent had from a group of united progressive voters in San Francisco, Newsom had to turn out his supporters at "unprecedented" rates (Ross 2004). The campaign used paid phone banks to identify an additional 30,000 Newsom supporters. They matched these supporters with those who had failed to vote in the November campaign, finding 10,000 new potential voters. By the deadline for voting by mail, the campaign had created 9,000 applications to vote by mail.

Newsom won the election partly because he received 20,000 more votes by mail than his opponent, Matt Gonzalez. He won the election with a 5 percentage point margin, 14,000 votes, well within the range of absentee votes he had generated.

This story illustrates many of the campaign tactics I have discussed throughout this volume, including the importance that voter targeting and persistent mobilization play in campaign success. But it also demonstrates how the changing contexts in which campaigns operate and the availability of new methods of voting can both cause campaign headaches and provide campaigns with new opportunities for victory. Beyond the changing mechanisms of electioneering itself, the context of the evolving electoral process creates special challenges and opportunities for political campaigns. The dramatic rise in convenience voting as well as the introduction of same-day registration, and potentially online or Internet-based voting, has forced campaigns to capitalize on these developments to their advantage. Indeed, changes to election laws and reforms that have been passed across many American states since the 1970s form much of the changing context with which campaigns must contend, so our focus will be on these.

In this chapter, I discuss the effects and implications of changing electoral contexts and describe how contemporary campaigns are adapting to these new environments. I briefly touch on the major electoral reforms that have taken place in the United States since the 1960s at the federal level and then focus more in depth on changes taking place at the levels of states and municipalities. Finally, in my discussion of the normative implications of these changes to the American electoral system, I discuss empirical evidence on the effects of these reforms and consider the role that campaigns have played in either enhancing or diminishing their effects.

ELECTORAL REFORMS: VOTER REGISTRATION AND VOTING PROCEDURES

The electoral process in the United States differs from that of many other democracies. To vote, citizens must go through a two-step process, that is, first register and then cast a vote (Timpone 1998). The legal-institutional characteristics of electoral systems have important effects on voting behavior (Lijphart 1997). In the United States, there is enormous variation in the extent to which election laws increase the costs of voting for citizens. These differences result from the federal nature of American governance, which I touched on in Chapter 2, and have their origins in the U.S. Constitution. Keyssar (2009) notes that the Constitution "left the federal government without clear power or mechanisms, other than through constitutional amendment, to institute a national conception of voting rights, to express a national vision of democracy. Although the Constitution was promulgated in the name of 'We, the people of the United States,' individual states have, for the most part, held the power to define voter eligibility and requirements" (20).

As a result, campaigns must contend with differences in election laws across American states, laws that seem to be undergoing almost continuous revision. This variation poses unique challenges for campaigns depending on the context of the election they are operating; campaign strategies should theoretically be quite different in states that permit early voting compared with states that do not, for example. These challenges are especially significant for campaigns operating in multiple jurisdictions, particularly presidential campaigns, which must contend with electoral-legal variation across the different states where their campaigns are active.

The 1965 Voting Rights Act marked a distinct departure in American election law; for the first time, states were expressly prohibited from passing laws aimed, whether implicitly or explicitly, at disenfranchising their citizens. Prior to the Voting Rights Act, several states, primarily in the South, used different forms of registration and voting restrictions like literacy tests and poll taxes to prevent mainly African Americans from voting. With the passage of the act, African American participation in the electorate increased dramatically. For political campaigns, this meant having to account for this new wave of participation by counting African American votes among the supporters they needed to mobilize.

In the wake of the Voting Rights Act, a few states began to experiment with even more expansive changes to their voting laws. In the late 1970s, California and Washington became the first states to allow for early voting in the form of no-excuse absentee voting. Previously, absentee voters had to provide a legitimate excuse and were generally drawn from the elderly, the military, and those who planned to be out of town on Election Day. In the late 1980s, Texas became the first state to allow in-person early voting, setting up different polling sites where citizens could cast their vote in person in the weeks leading up to Election Day. Table 10.1 presents the year of the first election in which no-excuse absentee voting and early voting were enacted in each state. Table 10.1 also includes similar information for universal mail-in registration and Election Day registration.

During this time, other states began to experiment with easing the costs of voter registration. As I highlighted in Chapter 7, voter registration has been identified time and again as one of the more significant barriers to voting (Gosnell 1927; Rosenstone and Wolfinger 1978). In the late 1970s, Minnesota, Wisconsin, and Maine adopted same-day registration (also known as Election Day registration) in an attempt to make the two-step voting process easier on their citizens. In these states, citizens could now register to vote and cast their ballot in the same place on the same day, instead of having to take the additional step of registering prior to an election. This was a significant change because other states have stricter voter registration deadlines, requiring citizens to register to vote as much as 30 or more days before an election.

In 1993, Congress enacted the National Voter Registration Act, the provisions of which were enforced across all states. According to the U.S. Department of Justice, it was designed to "enhance the voting opportunities for every American" by

Table 10.1 Voter Registration Laws and Voting Procedures

STATE	REGISTRATION		VOTING	
	UNIVERSAL MAIL-IN	ELECTION DAY	IN-PERSON EARLY	UNIVERSAL ABSENTEE
AL	1994	—	—	—
AK	1976	—	1996	1996
AZ	1992	—	1994	1992
AR	1996	—	1996	—
CA	1976	—	1998	1978
CO	1996	—	1992	1992
CT	1988	—	—	—
DE	1982	—	—	—
FL	1996	—	—	—
GA	1996	—	—	—
HI	1988	—	1994	1994
ID	1996	1994	1994	1994
IL	1996	—	—	—
IN	1996	—	—	—
IA	1976	—	—	—
KS	1972	—	1996	1996
KY	1924	—	—	—
LA	1996	—	—	—
ME	1984	1974	2000	2000
MD	1974	—	—	—
MA	1994	—	—	—
MI	1996	—	—	—
MN	1974	1974	—	—
MS	1992	—	—	—
MO	1996	—	—	—
MT	1972	—	2000	2000
NE	1986	—	2000	2000
NV	1992	—	1994	1992
NH	—	1994	—	—
NJ	1974	—	—	—
NM	1994	—	2000	1990
NY	1976	—	—	—
NC	1996	—	2000	2000
ND	*	*	—	1998
OH	1978	—	—	—
OK	1996	—	1992	1992
OR	1976	1920, 26; 76–84	—	1980
PA	1976	—	—	—
RI	1996	—	—	—
SC	1986	—	—	—
SD	1996	—	—	—
TN	1972	—	1994	—
TX	1966	—	1988	—
UT	1976	—	—	—
VT	1998	—	—	—
VA	1996	—	—	—
WA	1994	—	1998	1974
WV	1984	—	—	—
WI	1976	1976	2000	2000
WY	—	1994	—	1992

NOTES: Cells indicate the first election year after adoption. ND eliminated its voter registration requirement in 1951.

SOURCE: Adapted from Tables 4.2 and 4.3 in Springer (2014).

making it easier for Americans to register and vote (U.S. Department of Justice 2015). Following the passage of the act, individuals were offered the opportunity to register to vote at the same time they applied for a driver license, at all offices that provide public assistance or state-funded programs involved in providing services to those with disabilities, and were also able to register to vote by mail.

Around the time of the adoption of the National Voter Registration Act and in the years that followed, the United States saw an explosion in the adoption of convenience voting reforms like early voting, with a few more states also making the move to adopt same-day registration. To date, 13 states have adopted Election Day registration, and 33 states allow any qualified voter to cast a ballot in person or by absentee before Election Day with no excuse or justification required (see Table 10.1). Three states—Colorado, Oregon, and Washington—have adopted reforms that require votes to be cast entirely by mail (National Conference of State Legislatures 2015a, b). Oregon made the move to all-mail voting after a series of successful trial runs in local elections. More recently, Colorado and Washington passed laws instituting universal vote-by-mail programs. As of 2016, four states (Oregon, California, West Virginia, and Vermont) have also adopted automatic voter registration.

Some states have arguably moved in the other direction by instituting reforms that require voters to show identification when they register and/or vote. Proponents of voter identification laws argue that they reduce fraud and ensure that eligible voters decide elections. Opponents argue that they place an undue burden on subsets of eligible voters who have a greater difficulty obtaining the proper identification. To date, 36 states have passed laws requiring voters to show some form of identification. However, these laws are often subject to legal challenges and some of the passed laws have yet to be fully enacted (National Conference of State Legislatures 2015c). The most controversial identification laws require voters to show a form of state-issued photo identification. Figure 10.1 shows the current identification requirements for each state. "Strict identification" laws require individuals to show the proper identification to vote, and if he or she does not present a valid ID, the individual has the option to cast a provisional ballot that will only be counted if he or she takes additional steps to confirm his or her identity. "Nonstrict" laws allow individuals without the proper identification to vote. These states will verify the identity of voters through another mechanism—such as verifying his or her signature—and count the votes once eligibility is established (National Conference of State Legislatures 2015c).

CHALLENGES FOR CAMPAIGNS

Although same-day registration has undoubtedly influenced the calculus of contemporary campaigns in some respects, it is the increasingly widespread adoption and use of early voting that poses the greater challenge for political campaigns. Early voting, which influences both when and how citizens cast their ballots, changes the timing considerations of campaigns. This change seems to have affected how campaigns allocate their resources. For example, campaigns

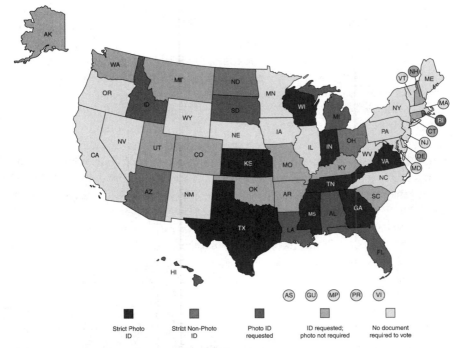

Figure 10.1 Voter Identification Laws in Effect during 2015

SOURCE: National Conference of State Legislatures

run significantly more ads in states with early voting than in those without it (Dunaway and Stein 2012). In addition, early voting also affects the timing and content of news coverage; there are substantially more campaign news stories per day in states with early voting and these stories are far more oriented toward horse-race type coverage emphasizing the competiveness between two candidates than in states without early voting (Dunaway and Stein 2013). As more and more citizens vote early, campaigns can no longer target their spending on advertising and other mobilization strategies as close to Election Day as possible. Instead, in states with early voting, Election Day has been turned into election weeks because citizens have a broader window during which to cast their votes. These challenges are even more pronounced in states that have adopted all-mail voting. The dynamics of early voting increase levels of uncertainty for campaigns, in terms of both dealing with a potentially expanded electorate and navigating a lengthier mobilization period.

Although there is not a great deal of empirical evidence to date, campaign managers across the political spectrum acknowledge that the increasing number of early voters has changed the dynamics of campaigns, making them more unpredictable and costly. Cathy Allen, a campaign consultant from Seattle, Washington, who worked with the Democrats in the mid-1990s, notes, "It means I have two elections. The first one comes when the absentee ballots go out, and the next one on Election Day" (as cited in Conklin 1996). After the state of Washington allowed citizens to be permanently listed as absentee voters, this changed the calculus of political campaigns even more. "In the old days . . . you didn't go on the air until after Labor Day when the campaign really began," notes the Republican consultant Bill Brader. "Now you might go on as much as a month before. . . . All of this has made campaigns more costly, probably 25 percent more costly—and much more complicated" (Conklin 1996). Candidates now must get on air earlier, mobilize sooner, and dig into the psyche of absentee voters, who, in some ways, seem to be different from the average Election Day voter (Stein 1998). For example, early voters tend to be older, better educated, and more interested in campaigns and politics more generally (Gronke and Toffey 2008). In 2008, Evan Tracey, then-president of a company that monitors political advertising, Campaign Media Analysis Group, noted large amounts of spending in Colorado, Iowa, Nevada, and New Mexico, all states that have early voting and were competitive in the 2008 presidential election (Nagourney 2008).

Early voting poses particular challenges for campaigns because it requires a massive up-front investment to secure the votes of citizens who cast their ballot well before Election Day. During the 2012 Republican presidential nomination race, Mitt Romney mastered early voting in part because his campaign had the funding, infrastructure, and sophistication to do so. This meant, for example, running a campaign at full throttle in Florida for six weeks before the primary Election Day. As soon as the absentee-ballot period opened in late December, Romney's team downloaded daily lists made by Florida election officials and compared the names of those who had requested ballots with the campaign's highly specific microtargeted lists of likely supporters. Anyone matched up on the list was aggressively pursued with GOTV pressure that usually does not occur until the last weekend before Election Day (Issenberg 2012d).

In recent years, early voting mobilization strategies have become part and parcel of top ticket campaigns. Consultants for recent presidential contenders note the strategic changes and challenges the law has brought about. Jon Carson, the field director of the 2008 Obama presidential campaign, said that early voting "was our strategy. I sat down and said, 'where early voting is no excuse, and convenient, I will begin the day that early voting starts.'" Michael Duhamel, the political director of the 2008 McCain Presidential Campaigns stated, "Election Day can be spread out over weeks. That means your get out the vote costs are more than ever" (as cited in Nagourney 2008: A20).

Early voting is now commonplace in several American states, and campaigns in early adopting states were quick to try to adapt to the challenges posed by the law. But these adaptations were not only occurring at the level of higher-ballot races. Local campaigns were making note of the strategic changes they could make to benefit from the new laws. In the election for county executive in King County in the state of Washington in 1995, the campaign of Republican Tim Hill made especially effective use of the state's no-excuse absentee voting. Hill's campaign analyzed dozens of reliably Republican precincts, making note of those that gave Ronald

Reagan at least 65% of their vote in the 1984 presidential election and also elected two other Republicans. In those precincts, tens of thousands of registered voters were sent absentee-ballot applications along with materials from the Hill campaign. It was estimated that more than one-third of the absentee ballots issued in King County that year had been generated by the Hill campaign alone (Larsen 1985).

Even more than having the option to vote absentee or early in person, vote-by-mail programs are challenging political campaigns to come up with creative ways to keep voter interest over a longer election period, to navigate far more uncertainty in terms of when people vote, and to gain access to the resources needed for longer and more expensive election cycles. Ballots are in the hands of every registered citizen for sometimes three weeks prior to the end of an election period, not just those citizens who have opted to vote absentee or early in person. Voters can mail them in at any time, meaning candidates must campaign at full force for about a month to make sure they do not miss out on the opportunity to mobilize any potential supporters (Cain 2000).

Evidence from the state of Oregon, the first state to conduct all-mail elections, suggests that this electoral reform substantially improves turnout in special elections, like school bond elections and elections for local offices, but has far smaller effects on turnout in primary and general elections (Southwell 2009). The impact of these effects can be seen, for example, in school levy proposals. For example, West Valley school officials in the state of Washington faced the implications of higher turnout during a levy election held in May 2000. The increased number of citizens voting by mail meant that more people were voting in an election where school officials were used to only having to target school supporters who were, more often than not, the only ones who voted in this type of election, resulting in successful passage of previous measures. With more and more citizens being mailed ballots, interest and concern over the school levy election increased. In light of higher participation, school district officials needed to do more to convince citizens of why the school needed more tax dollars. To address the increase in participation, the school district engaged in mailing campaigns and phone calls that were far more aggressive than in previous election years (Pohlig 2000). Although high-profile, big-ticket campaigns seem the most likely to have the resources to adapt to early voting reforms, even races as far down the ballot as school levy elections are not immune from the effects of these changes to how citizens vote and are forced to adapt as well.

Nevertheless, all-mail elections may pose less of a challenge to higher-ticket campaigns than elections that feature both early voting and Election Day voting. Without the specter of a final Election Day push, campaigns can more efficiently allocate their resources throughout a vote-by-mail period, although they still must contend with the uncertainty that stems from not knowing when citizens are actually casting their ballots. This uncertainty seems to be mitigated in some states by additional election law caveats. In Oregon, for example, campaigns can find out precisely who has voted and who has not during the vote-by-mail period. In 2000, then–secretary of state Bill Bradbury noted that campaigns and interest groups can "orchestrate a really effective get-out-the-vote campaign that is actually targeted at the people who haven't voted yet." In Oregon, this tactic has been used by supporters of schools and community college districts that file for levies to get the required 50% of registered voters to cast ballots in the areas where the levies have been requested (Young 2000).

Little evidence suggests that registration-based reforms, like same-day registration, pose the same magnitude of challenges to political campaigns that early voting does. In fact, in addition to improving overall voter turnout, same-day registration has the potential to work to a campaign's advantage. Campaigns may need to grapple with greater participations, but they can tie more traditionally timed campaign mobilization activities in with this reform. Same-day registration occurs on Election Day itself and is more aligned with the traditional rhythms of an election cycle in which the intensity of mobilization efforts reach a peak closer to Election Day. Campaign efforts often increase citizen interest in elections close to Election Day, but in states where registration deadlines have already passed, this interest cannot translate into voting. Same-day registration allows late-in-the-game campaign efforts to lead to higher turnout among supporters if these efforts are strategically targeted (Francia and Herrnson 2004).

FUTURE REFORMS?

One oft-proposed reform that has yet to take hold for the vast majority of American elections is Internet voting. On March 10, 2000, Arizona became the first state to hold a binding Internet vote, as Democrats voted in their party's presidential primary. The event was not without its problems. Voters had to call in because of technical misunderstandings, site failures, and lost voter identification numbers (Raney 2000). Fifteen years later, the United States is not much closer to adopting widespread Internet voting, although some states, like Alaska, allow any absentee voters to vote online, and many service members in the military are also able to take advantage of this form of voting. However, service members who are allowed to vote via the Internet must sign a form saying they understand that, given the system, their ballot might not be secret. Voters in Alaska are notified they are voluntarily waiving their rights to a secret ballot and taking on the risk that mistakes may be made in the transmission of their vote (Urbina 2000; State of Alaska Division of Elections n.d.).

Opponents of Internet voting have concerns about the potential for hacking and voter fraud, and some speculate that Internet voting may exacerbate the socioeconomic divide between voters and nonvoters (Alvarez and Nagler 2000). The latter concern, however, may be waning because more and more Americans have regular access to the Internet over time. Nevertheless, security and reliability concerns remain. Dan Wallach, an expert on electronic voting systems and professor of computer science, contends that no Internet voting system will be perfectly secure. He points to corporations like JP Morgan, Target, and Home Depot, all of which have had web-based security breaches and all of which have more money and expertise available to them than local election officials (Weise 2014). One compelling tale of such a threat came in 2010, when Washington, D.C., developed an Internet voting project and invited hackers to try to break into the system during a mock election period. Three computer scientists from the University of Michigan were able to gain access to the system, change every vote, and reveal almost every secret ballot. Their efforts were not detected by elections officials in Washington, D.C., for almost two business days (Wolchok et al. 2012).

The widespread adoption of Internet voting would likely exacerbate some of the challenges campaigns face with higher levels of early voting and an increasing number of all-mail elections. However, it might also provide new platforms for candidates to mobilize their supporters. Instead of encouraging voters to go to their polling place, apply for absentee ballots, or vote early in person, campaigns would be able to direct individuals to a website where they could vote from the comfort of their own homes, offices, or even smartphones without having to go to the mailbox, post office, or polling place.

Other, institutional reforms adopted in some states may also be on the horizon. In June 2010, California voters approved Proposition 14, a constitutional amendment to adopt a "top-two" primaries system. (Also called a nonpartisan blanket primary, jungle primary or qualifying primary, similar systems are in place in several other places, including Louisiana where runoffs between the top two candidates regardless of party face off in general elections if no one receives a majority of the vote in the primary.) The reform consolidates all primary elections for a particular office and places all candidates on a single, primary ballot that is identical for all voters. The two candidates with the most votes move on to compete in the general election. In June 2016, California's top-two primary system resulted in pitting, for the first time since U.S. Senators have been directly elected in California's history, two Democrats (Attorney General Kamala Harris and 10-term Congresswoman Loretta Sanchez) against each other in the U.S. Senate general election contest to succeed retiring, Democratic Senator Barbara Boxer. This example illustrates how institutional arrangements, like the type of primary systems jurisdictions adopt, can affect context and campaign strategy in response.

CONSEQUENCES FOR DEMOCRACY

Reforms like early voting and same-day registration are often touted as simple "convenience" voting reforms designed to make voting easier and improve turnout. In theory, they represent a move toward the democratic norm of greater engagement in politics by the American public. In practice, however, the results of their implementation on overall voter turnout and individuals' likelihood of voting have been mixed.

Of the electoral institutional changes discussed in this chapter, same-day registration is one of the few reforms that seems to have had a significant effect on turnout over time. This reform makes it all but certain that a voter who takes advantage of the law will vote because it effectively eliminates the two-step process of registration and voting that increases the costs of doing so for many Americans. Studies suggest that same-day registration can increase overall turnout along the lines of 3% to 5% (Brians and Grofman 2001; Fitzgerald 2005; Hanmer 2009), but it seems to have less substantive effects on resource-disadvantaged individuals, especially poorer citizens. Those with lower levels of education, young adults, and recent movers have improved their representation in the electorate in modest ways in places where this reform is in place, but it has not had a major impact on turnout among individuals with lower incomes (Hanmer 2007, 2009; Knack and White 2000).

Some findings suggest that campaigns can play a positive role in enhancing the extent to which same-day registration improves political engagement in the American public. Francia and Herrnson (2004) demonstrate that the interactive combination of campaign spending and party GOTV efforts can have a synergistic effect on turnout in states that have Election Day registration. As the authors note, "Campaign efforts excite and motivate citizens, especially as Election Day nears. But without Election Day registration, those who have not registered to vote, but become interested later in the campaign, cannot vote" (Francia and Herrnson 2004: 85). Election Day registration allows campaigns to capitalize on such late-in-the-game interest and improves the prospects for engagement for individuals who would otherwise be unable to vote in elections.

The normative implications of the adoption of early voting and vote-by-mail reforms are less clear-cut. First, early voting, especially in-person early voting, appears to simply make it easier for those already likely to turn out and vote (Berinsky 2005; Giammo and Brox 2010). There is empirical evidence demonstrating that early voting actually exacerbates the gap in turnout between economically advantaged and disadvantaged citizens (Rigby and Springer 2011). These effects seem to be the most pronounced for in-person early voting. But perhaps more concerning for our purposes is the role that campaigns potentially play in producing these effects. Because longer voting periods necessitate campaigns to more efficiently allocate their resources and stretch their most intense spending periods over a number of weeks, there is a diminished intensity as Election Day nears in states with early voting in comparison to other states. This diminished intensity can mean fewer mobilization efforts close to Election Day, leaving citizens who would normally be mobilized closer to Election Day out. In fact, some evidence suggests that early voting can actually lead to lower turnout if not accompanied by same-day registration (Burden et al. 2014). In states with highly competitive elections, such as presidential battleground states, early voting also seems to exacerbate gaps in turnout between the wealthy and the poor, an effect that is not apparent in states that are noncompetitive. This suggests that high-intensity campaign efforts in these places may play a role in creating this normatively undesirable gap between advantaged and disadvantaged voters precisely in the places where high turnout and a more representative electorate are needed most (Suttmann-Lea 2014).

The dynamics of the relationship between campaigns and early voting suggest other normative implications beyond political engagement. As mentioned previously, early voting has effects both on the quantity and on the timing of news coverage dedicated to political campaigns as well as the content of that coverage; horse-race or "game" coverage is far more likely in the context of elections that feature early voting (Dunaway and Stein 2013). In addition, early voting appears to affect the number and distribution of campaign advertisements (Dunaway and Stein 2012). These findings have implications for the information citizens receive from political campaigns and the news media. Although citizens seem to receive more news coverage of campaign happenings in states with early voting, if this news coverage focuses more on the competition between two candidates instead of substantive policy issues, this can have negative implications for the quality of information received. An increase in the number of negative political advertisements in particular and the time in which they are aired may also be crucial for the relationship between campaign conduct and citizen engagement and interest in politics and the information they receive. As we learned in Chapter 6, negative advertisements can be more informative than other ads, but they do little to improve political interest, can lower feelings of political efficacy and trust in government, and are potentially detrimental to citizen turnout depending on who the advertisements are reaching (Lau et al. 2007).

All-mail elections have forced local election officials and administrators like school board representatives to reach out to an electorate beyond narrow constituent bases, potentially improving representation of citizens to avoid undesirable special election outcomes. All-mail elections seem to have a modest impact on overall participation, although again, like other forms of early voting, they increase the likelihood of *retaining* voters, that is, encouraging regular voters to continue to vote and turning semihabitual voters into regular voters, as opposed to bringing new voters into the electorate (Monroe and Sylvester 2011; Southwell and Burchett 2000). In other words, all-mail elections seem to increase turnout, but do not necessarily make the electorate more representative of the voting-age population in terms of descriptive representation (Berinsky et al. 2001; Karp and Banducci 2000).

There are concerns that if citizens vote early (whether by mail or in person), they may be doing so before they have gotten all of the arguments from campaigns and information they need to make an informed decision. This potentially leaves voters armed with incomplete amounts of information. Reformers must assess whether the risks of poor information outweigh the participatory benefits of early voting. In the contentious 2014 Oregon Republican U.S. Senate primary race that pitted Monica Wehby against Tea Party candidate Jason Conger, allegations surfaced that Wehby had a history of harassment, with multiple partners coming forward with accusations in the final week of the election, when many voters had already cast their ballots (Bresnahan 2014). Similarly, in 2000, only five days before the presidential election, the Republican nominee George W. Bush was forced to acknowledge that he was arrested for drunk driving in 1976. Exit polling indicated this admission cost him some votes. In

Tennessee, however, where Bush barely won, more than one-third of the votes were cast before Election Day. This means that some voters did not have the information about his drunk-driving arrest when they cast their ballots (Becker 2004). This dynamic is troubling because there was an asymmetry in the information environment when voters cast their ballots. In close races, these late-breaking developments can affect election outcomes, but this is much harder when sizable segments of the electorate have already voted. Returning to the case of the 2000 presidential election, absentee ballots cast before Bush's drunk-driving incident broke could have tipped the scale in favor of the Democrat Al Gore in Florida, which ultimately decided the fate of the election by a mere 537 votes. A reversal in Tennessee, Gore's home state, would have also been sufficient to propel the Democrat to victory.

Although entertaining such what-if scenarios can be intriguing, empirical evidence suggests the impact of late-breaking developments on early voting results is likely limited. Early voters tend to be stronger partisans and generally committed to candidates (Stein 1998; Gronke 2008; Gronke and Toffey 2008), implying vote choices may be impervious to news about a scandal or an unsavory policy allegation (Niquette 2006). This is consistent with the earlier discussion about motivated reasoning that suggests strong partisans are less likely to update their preferences upon receiving new information about a candidate if that information contradicts strongly held beliefs about their party and a given candidate (Kunda 1990; Kim et al. 2010; Gaines et al. 2007). Nevertheless, concerns that early voting could prevent voters from taking all of the available information into account before casting a vote are palpable.

The changing electoral process in the United States puts constraints on political campaigns, but it does not leave them unable to adapt. Rather, as with other developments in technology and new media, campaigns adjust to remain competitive and relevant in the electoral process. With some changes, as with the adoption of same-day registration, these adaptations appear to lead to normatively desirable outcomes. With others, as with the adoption of early voting and all-mail elections, the relationship among these changes, campaign conduct, and consequences for democratic norms is murkier. It is not uncommon for reformers to grapple with trade-offs that often pin one democratic ideal (e.g., engagement) against another (e.g., information). The empirical evidence covered in this chapter suggests that campaigns may adapt to changes in voting laws that alter when and how citizens vote in ways that are actually maladaptive to the advancement of democratic norms. More broadly, it is apparent that political scientists and advocates of reforms designed to increase citizen engagement in the electoral process must also consider the extent to which these reforms incentivize campaigns to adapt their strategies in ways that are actually harmful for democracy.

KEY TERMS

Absentee ballot

All-mail election

Convenience voting

In-person early
  voting

Internet voting

National Voter
  Registration Act

No-excuse absentee
  voting

Same-day registration

Top-two primary

Two-step voting process

Vote-by-mail

Voter identification
  laws

Voting Rights Act of
  1965

SUGGESTED READINGS

Erikson, R. S., G. C. Wright, and J. P. McIver. 1993. *Statehouse Democracy: Public Opinion and Policy in the American States.* New York: Cambridge University Press.

Springer, M. J. 2014. *How the States Shaped the Nation: American Electoral Institutions and Voter Turnout, 1920–2000.* Chicago, IL: University of Chicago Press.

CHAPTER 11

Political Campaigns
in International Context

A merican campaigns have evolved to adapt to changing contexts and circumstances ushered in mainly by developments in the sociopolitical and technological landscapes, changes that extend well beyond national boundaries. This chapter offers a glimpse into how political campaigns operate in democracies abroad, highlighting similarities and differences between countries and how variations in key institutional features affect campaign conduct across the range of democratic polities. In some respects, elections in other democracies have changed in ways that run parallel to shifting campaign contexts in the United States. Elections abroad, like those in the United States, used to be highly labor intensive, with candidates, members of parties, and loyal volunteers doing most of the heavy lifting. Campaigns relied on direct interactions among candidates, their staffs, and volunteers and the voters. Now, just as they have in the United States, campaigns in many other democracies have shifted to become far more capital intensive. Campaign professionals are often at the helm, especially in national elections, and the extent to which candidates have direct contact with voters is often mediated.

In this chapter, I first provide an introduction to changing trends in campaigns run in democracies around the world, emphasizing the debate over the extent to which campaigns abroad have become more or less "Americanized." I discuss the empirical evidence to date of this phenomenon, providing an overview of the different structural and regulatory components that can play a role in the extent to which parties and candidates can, for lack of a better term, import American-style campaigns. With this framework in mind, I consider differences in the media and communications infrastructure as well as how campaign finance regulations vary from country to country. As in previous chapters, I conclude with a discussion of how the relationship among campaign contexts, conduct, and norms varies between the United States and democracies across the world.

It is nearly impossible to discuss electoral contexts and campaign conduct in other democracies without recognizing the pervasive influence of developments in American electioneering. Although campaigns in other countries retain, in part, strategies that are idiosyncratic to their particular context, there is no doubt that there is an increasing move toward American-style campaign professionalization in many countries (Plasser and Plasser 2002). Most agree that these patterns have been fueled, in part, by the increasing activity of American campaign consultants abroad. Well-known American political consultants have worked abroad since the 1970s, bringing their expertise to Latin America and Western Europe in the 1980s and to the countries of the former Soviet Union after 1989 (Plasser 2000). Indeed, it is not uncommon to have U.S. consultants competing against one another in election campaigns abroad. For example, during the 1998 Honduras presidential campaign, the well-known Democratic consultant James Carville worked for Carlos Flores, whereas Dick Morris worked for Flores's opponent, Nora de Melgar. Both Carville and Morris have worked for campaigns in a number of different countries. Carville, for example, has served as a consultant in both Argentinian and Israeli elections.

There are differing views on the extent to which campaigns in other countries increasingly resemble American campaigns in terms of their strategic decisions, communication styles, and media approaches. There is debate over whether campaign strategies have *diffused* from the United States to other democracies around the world in a one-way direction or whether the adoption of campaign strategies that are more Americanized is part of a broader process of *modernization* and change in politics and media systems across democracies (Gurevitch 1999). According to the former explanation, campaign strategists in other democracies adopt strategies that are similar to those used in American elections independent of the institutional and cultural factors present in a given country. This has also been described as an *adoption model* of campaign adaptation, in which foreign campaign managers adopt the methods used by American consultants and campaign experts with little regard for the electoral structures that are unique to a given country.

In the latter explanation, the increasing presence of Americanized campaign components, such as personalization, management of candidate perception in the mass media, and increased negativity, might be borrowed from American practices, but country-specific institutions, norms, and regulations still influence strategic decisions. This has also been described as the *shopping model*, whereby campaign strategies from the United States are considered and in some cases implemented, but while still taking into account the political context of the country in which a given campaign is operating with an eye toward retaining country-specific campaign styles (Farrell 2002).

In reality, there is no single path of diffusion by which changes have occurred to campaigning in democracies around the world. Contrary to what many observers see as a one-way exporting of American style campaign strategies, Plasser (2000) uncovers multiple ways in which campaign expertise is disseminated. First and most influential is the proliferation of techniques developed in the context of U.S. campaigns. However, there are also distinct patterns of "West

Europeanization" emerging in East Central and Eastern Europe, as well as a Third World style of campaigning originating in Latin America that incorporates some components of U.S. campaigns but maintains a stronger emphasis on more traditional, party-centered modes of mobilization. Other countries have adopted a *hybrid* form of campaigning, combining elements of the U.S. approach such as television campaigns with constituency campaigning at the grassroots level that is more characteristic of the United Kingdom and Third World strategies of mass rallies and parades to promote mass interest in elections.

Although the United States model seems to be the most influential, it is not the only approach in the development of campaign strategies around the world. Instead, as Plasser (2000) notes, there are "highly complex patterns of interactions and connections with the ongoing process of a worldwide proliferation of U.S. campaign practice and expertise" (50). There is a clear desire for market- and money-driven campaign techniques, such as those featured in the United States, as evidenced by the networks of cooperation between American consultants and foreign campaign managers. But there are naturally differences in the degree of Americanization from country to country contingent on factors particular to these other countries (Plasser 2000). Table 11.1, from Plasser and Plasser (2002, 19), highlights the different models by which campaigns around the world choose to incorporate American campaign strategies.

There are some stark exceptions to the rule that campaigns around the world have adopted increased modernization and professionalization in the Americanized sense of terms, although this trend seems to predominate in Western European countries (Farrell et al. 2001). In Latin America, in contrast, Boas (2010) contends that the development of presidential election campaign strategies in three nascent democracies, Chile, Brazil, and Peru, explicitly contradicts the cross-national convergence thesis that campaigns are moving inexorably toward greater professionalization and Americanization. In Chile, for example, candidates across the ideological spectrum value maintaining direct ties with voters, avoid negative campaigning and

Table 11.1 Two Models of the Global Diffusion of American Campaign and Marketing Techniques

SHOPPING MODEL	ADOPTION MODEL
Implementation of select U.S.-campaign techniques and practices	Adoption of U.S. strategems of successful campaigning
Professionalization of political campaigns outside the United States	Transformation of political campaigns outside the United States
Hybridization	**Standardization**
Country-specific supplementation of traditional campaign practices with select features of the American style of campaigning	Gradual phase-out of country-specific traditional campaign styles and their substitution by capital-intensive media- and consultant-driven practice

SOURCE: Plasser and Plasser (2002).

divisive appeals, and focus on empathy-based strategies with popular concerns as opposed to campaigning on detailed policy proposals to solve them. Brazilian candidates also emphasize direct ties with voters and try to avoid divisive campaigning, but instead focus far more on outlining policy proposals. In Peru, candidates do not seem to have converged on a common strategy at all; some focus on policy, some try to leverage societal divisions, and some try to retain direct contact with voters. Instead of relying solely on bringing in outside expertise and strategists, campaigns have learned from each other's mistakes, which has led, in the case of Chile and Brazil, to a within-country convergence of campaign strategy and, in the case of Peru, greater diversity in strategies after no clear "best practices" have emerged (Boas 2010: 637).

More broadly, the extent to which campaign practices around the world converge around American-style campaigning is dependent on contextual factors within a given country such as the electoral system and level of competition, the regulation and structure of elections, the media, and the presence of campaign finance regulations. Differences in national political cultures, such as whether a country has a history of high or low voter turnout and whether voting is compulsory, also play a role. For example, campaigns in countries where turnout is consistently high face a greater risk of neglecting broad swaths of the electorate if they craft their messages to cater to the preferences of narrow groups of base or swing voters. This is especially true in countries where voting is compulsory and turnout rates generally exceed 80–90 percent of the eligible electorate.

Well-meaning institutional arrangements and changes in a given country can also have unintentionally led to the proliferation of Americanized campaign techniques. In the United Kingdom, for example, a 2011 electoral reform limited the power of the British prime minister and his or her party to call for elections at moments that were favorable to their political fortunes. Although almost certainly an unintended consequence of this shift, the British parliament now faces reelection on a set date, as in the United States, instead of navigating relatively short election campaign seasons set on the fly as in years past. This has led to longer campaigns and increased adoption of American styles of political campaigning. In the past, of course, American consultants have worked on British campaigns; president Bill Clinton's pollster, Stanley Greenberg, also worked to help elect the British prime minister Tony Blair. But since the change in British election law, longer election cycles in which campaigns can prepare far in advance have made way for the most up-to-date advances in American electioneering, specifically data mining and microtargeting. Jim Messina, who headed Barack Obama's 2012 reelection campaign, was hired by the Tory party in August 2015 to provide advice similar to what he gave the Obama campaign: how to craft the right messages to share with voters who are most likely to respond to it (Allison 2015).

Thus, there are a number of factors that mitigate the complete adoption of American methods in campaigns abroad (Farrell 1996; Swanson and Mancini 1996). In this way, just as the contexts in which American campaigns operate and strategize have changed, so too have campaigns in democracies around the world, but in ways that are unique to the region or country under consideration.

One of the primary differences between the United States and many democracies around the world is that the United States has a two-party system and holds majoritarian elections; candidates need only one more vote than their closest rival to win. The electoral system in the United States rewards the two major parties, Republicans and Democrats, and provides few incentives for alternative third parties to step forward. Theoretically, this is because two-party, majoritarian systems value effective working governments to the exclusion of third-party and other minority voices (Duverger 1972). However, the extent to which the United States' form of government can continue to function effectively has been called into question given the polarization and legislative gridlock that has plagued the U.S. Congress in recent years. Other democracies that use similar systems include the United Kingdom, Canada, and India.

In contrast, many democracies are situated in multiparty systems that generally award seats in legislatures by proportional representation based on the number of seats in chambers of government based on the number of votes each party receives in an election (although there is typically a minimum number of votes required for a party to obtain seats). Table 11.2 showcases the diversity of electoral systems in place in select democracies across the world.

The nature of a country's party system can determine, in part, the extent to which campaigns are more candidate centered or party based. Campaign practices in candidate-based electoral systems, such as the United States, lead to more individualized, personalized, and decentralized campaigns that focus on the district level and on a candidate's particular constituency. Even presidential elections in the United States feature candidates traveling from battleground state to battleground state, vying for votes by making state-specific appeals. In a campaign stop on October 20, 2008, in Florida, then–presidential candidate Barack Obama highlighted the economic woes that Floridians in particular were dealing with during the economic meltdown that was occurring under the Bush administration. In his speech, he said, "115,000 workers lost their jobs in Florida this year, more than any other state in the country. Wages are lower than they've been in a decade, at a time when the cost of health care and college has never been higher" (Obama 2008).

Proportional representation systems with multiple parties, in contrast, do not feature decisive "battleground" districts or states. Rather, candidate and party strategies must often coincide to maximize their nationwide share of the vote. National parties in these systems generally allocate their resources to a few highly competitive campaigns in two-party, majoritarian systems, whereas campaigns operating in party-based systems must more broadly distribute their resources and address their electorates at a national level. In party-centered systems, it can be more difficult, although by no means impossible, to import the decentralized and candidate-focused campaign tactics found in U.S. elections. There are also mixed electoral systems that feature some combination of proportional

Table 11.2 Electoral Systems of Selected Democracies

COUNTRY	SYSTEMS OF REPRESENTATION
Australia	Single-member districts with preferential voting, but uses proportional representation for senate elections
Austria	Proportional representation
Belgium	Proportional representation
Canada	Single-member districts
Czech Republic	Proportional representation
France	Single-member districts with a runoff if no one gets at least 50% in the first round
Germany	Combination of single-member districts and proportional representation
Greece	Proportional representation
Ireland	Proportional representation
Italy	Combination of single-member districts and proportional representation
Japan	Combination of single-member districts and proportional representation
Republic of Korea	Combination of single-member districts and proportional representation
Mexico	Combination of single-member districts and proportional representation
Netherlands	Proportional representation
Romania	Proportional representation
South Africa	Proportional representation
Spain	Proportional representation
Sweden	Proportional representation
United Kingdom	Single-member districts
United States	Single-member districts

SOURCE: Center for Voting and Democracy (adapted from Wayne 2014).

party-based and majoritarian-based politics, such as in Italy, Mexico, and Russia. These electoral systems seem to provide campaigns with greater opportunities to run individualized, candidate-centered campaigns that are more in line with the likes of what might be seen in the United States.

DIFFERENCES IN REGISTRATION AND TURNOUT

Electoral participation in the United States consistently lags behind many other nations (Norris 2004). Figure 11.1, which compares voting rates in the 2012 elections in the United States with voting in recent elections in 16 other democracies, confirms the U.S. is near the bottom of the list (although the U.S. fares better when comparing turnout amongst registered voters). In part, these patterns

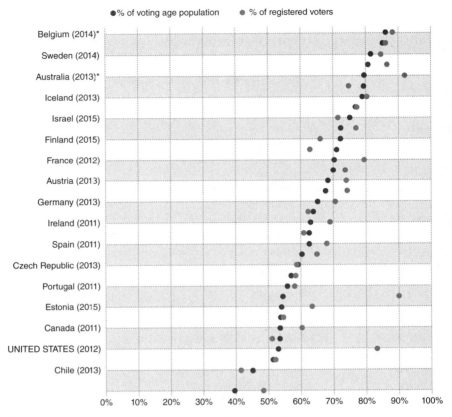

Figure 11.1 Comparison of Voter Turnout in Recent Elections

NOTES: (1) Pew Research Center calculations, based on data from International Institute for Democracy and Electoral Assistance, European Election Database, United States Election Project, House Clerk's office, and various national election authorities. (2) In some countries, the estimated voting age population is smaller than the estimated number of registered voters. (3) * denotes countries with national laws making voting compulsory. In addition, one Swiss canton has compulsory voting.
SOURCE: Pew Research Center

persist because electoral institutions in many other countries impose fewer barriers on registration and voting (Powell 1986; Norris 2004). Twenty-three countries, including established democracies like Australia, Belgium, and Luxembourg, actually compel citizens to vote by making voting mandatory (Norris 2004), while others automatically register voters, or schedule elections less frequently or on weekends (LeDuc, Niemi, and Norris 2002). Majorities of voters in some U.S. states support transitioning to automatic voter registration, a reform that, as we discussed in Chapter 10, has already been adopted in 4 states, but support nationally is weaker (Alvarez et al. 2011). As we also discussed, there are differences in the overall structure of their political systems, including whether the systems are proportional or majoritarian (or some combination), presidential or parliamentary, or whether the party systems are two-party or multiparty, that can affect the rate at which citizens vote (Norris 2004). Researchers have exploited this variation to show that electoral arrangements matter for participation: proportional representation with small electoral districts, regular but infrequent elections, competitive party systems, presidential systems, and institutions that reduce the costs of voting, like automatic registration, postal and weekend voting, and especially mandatory voting all seem to maximize participation (Norris 2004; LeDuc et al. 2002). Individual-level factors, like socioeconomic status and partisan loyalties, also help to explain turnout rates in countries across the globe, as they do in the U.S., but these analyses confirm the electoral arrangements also matter in terms of voting (Norris 2004; LeDuc et al 2002).

DIFFERENCES IN MEDIA AND POLITICAL COMMUNICATION

Crossnational media and communications infrastructures and landscapes vary greatly across the globe, and especially compared to the U.S. Most other democratic countries place restrictions on campaign communications in the media, and on television advertising in particular (Plasser and Plasser 2002). In decades past, free airtime was given to parties and candidates in a few countries, but by the end of the 20th century, this was the case in almost all democracies, the United States being the notable exception. However, by the 1970s, paid television advertising had made inroads not only in the United States, but also in countries like Australia, Canada, and Japan. This trend expanded to other countries late in the 20th century and in the 21st century, although there are still a number of countries, particularly in Western Europe and Africa, that do not allow paid political advertising. Furthermore, even in countries where paid advertising is permitted, there are often regulations on how much can be spent and when ads can be aired. Table 11.3, adapted from Plasser and Lengauer (2009: 262), highlights the democracies around the world that allow paid political television advertising.

In Belgium, France, Great Britain, and Spain, candidates and parties are not allowed to buy airtime on commercial or public television. Instead, these countries provide free airtime on either commercial or public television networks, although there are restrictions on when and how this advertising can be aired. Whereas in the United States the major distinction in the use of media involves *paid* versus *free* or *earned* media, which I discussed in Chapters 3 and 6, in other countries one must distinguish between those that provide free air time and those that allow more traditional advertising paid for by candidates or political parties. In some countries, particularly those in Eastern and Western Europe, parties and candidates spend more effort trying to garner earned media by organizing press conferences, orchestrating messages that cycle through the news, creating camera-ready events, and having representatives participate on political talk shows and in debates (Plasser and Lengauer 2009). Switzerland, for example, prohibits advertising on television and radio during election and referendum campaigns based on the

Table 11.3 Access to Paid Political Television Advertising Worldwide

ANGLO-AMERICA	LATIN AMERICA	WESTERN EUROPE	EASTERN EUROPE/CIS	ASIA-PACIFIC AND CARIBBEAN	AFRICA
Canada	Argentina	Austria[a]	Albania	Aruba	Botswana
United States	Columbia	Denmark[a]	Armenia	Australia[a]	Gambia
	Costa Rica[b]	Finland[a]	Azerbijian	Bahamas	Ghana
	Dominican Republic	Germany[a]	Bulgaria	Barbados	Lesotho
	Ecuador	Greece[a]	Estonia[a]	Indonesia[b]	Malawi
	El Salvador	Italy[b]	Georgia	Japan[c]	Mozambique
	Guatemala	Malta	Hungary	Mauritius	Namibia
	Honduras	The Netherlands[a]	Latvia	New Zealand	Uganda
	Mexico[a]		Lithuania	The Philippines	
	Nicaragua		Macedonia	Samoa	
	Panama		Mongolia	South Korea	
	Paraguay		Montenegro	Taiwan	
	Peru		Poland	Vanuatu	
	Uruguay		Romania		
	Venezuela		Russia		
			Serbia		
			Ukraine		

NOTES: [a]In private television stations only. [b]Out of the official election campaign period only. [c]For political parties only.

SOURCE: Plasser and Lengauer (2009).

assumption that parties would not have the means to pay for the ads or airtime, as well as to protect the print media, which plays a major role in Swiss elections (Holtz-Bacha and Kaid 2006).

In many countries, as in the U.S., campaign advertisements and news coverage are increasingly personalized. *Personalization* places an emphasis on candidate traits and characteristics rather than their (or their party's) policy positions. Even in electoral systems that have more party-centered campaigns, like Austria and Italy, there appears to be a move toward personalization in television advertisements and coverage of elections. This pattern is consistent across a number of different types of campaigns, from presidential to parliamentary races, and occurs in different types of electoral systems, including majoritarian and proportional representation systems (Plasser and Lengauer 2009).

In some countries, hard-hitting, 30-second negative campaign ads that are characteristic of American elections are also becoming more prominent. Israel provides an excellent example of the influence that American consultants can have on a country's media and advertising focus during political campaigns and in bringing about these kinds of changes. Prior to 1996, Israeli campaigns aired television ads during prime time during the last three weeks of a campaign. The ads featured dynamic debates between parties and candidates concerning issues (Caspi 1996). When American consultants took over in 1996, the format of political advertising shifted to increasingly negative 30-second advertising spots lambasting opponents rather than the engaging back and forth between candidates that previously had been the norm (Nagourney 1999).

Campaign communications internationally can also be affected by whether the national press is free or state controlled. In the United States, free speech is constitutionally safeguarded, but this is not necessarily the case in all places that hold elections. In Russia, for example, where the press is state controlled, incumbents are typically presented in overtly positive ways by the state-controlled media and the opposition is portrayed unfavorably in order to preserve the status quo. It can be difficult for opposition candidates to leverage earned media to criticize ruling parties or incumbents in such systems (Plasser and Lengauer 2009), although social media can potentially help overcome these constraints.

DIFFERENCES IN CAMPAIGN FINANCE

As is the case in the United States, the ways in which campaigns are funded and the regulations in place on donations have an impact on the strategic decisions made by campaigns abroad (Administration and Cost of Elections Project 2012). Limitations on campaign spending, private contributions, and strict disclosure laws are far more likely to be in place in countries that provide public campaign funds, reimbursements to campaigns that disclose their expenditures, or tax incentives for citizens who donate to political campaigns (Alexander 2000; Alexander and Shiratori 1994). Table 11.4 illustrates the different limits on campaign expenditures around the world. The contribution of public campaign funds to political parties in particular can enhance the extent to which campaign strategies are party centered as opposed to candidate centered (P. Mair 2000). In contrast, as is seen in the United States and other countries where private funding of campaigns is more prominent candidate-centered campaigns feature heavily (Pinto-Duschinsky 2001). In these elections, money plays a large role, incumbents typically have larger war chests than challengers, and the influence of national party organizations is diminished. Table 11.5 documents the level of public funding from select democracies.

DEVELOPMENTS IN NEW TECHNOLOGIES

The technological developments I discussed in Chapter 9 are by no means limited to the United States. In most countries around the world, citizens receive information from a number of different sources, including multiple television

Table 11.4 Limits on Expenditures in Europe and Other Established Democracies

COUNTRY	CEILING ON PARTY ELECTION EXPENDITURE	WHAT IS THE CEILING?
Belgium	Yes, per election cycle	1 million EUR
Bulgaria	Yes, per election cycle	More than 1.5 million EUR
Canada	Yes	Registered political parties and candidates must not exceed the election expense limits calculated by the chief electoral officer under the formulas provide in the Canada Elections Act.
France	Yes	In presidential elections, a party and its candidates may spend more than 16 million EUR in the first round and more than 20 million EUR in the second round. For parliamentary election, both parties and candidates have a ceiling of 40,000 EUR plus more than 0.20 EUR per inhabitant.
Hungary	Yes	The ceiling is per candidate and per election.
Ireland	Yes	The ceiling is per candidate and per election.
Italy	Yes	The ceiling is per candidate and per election. There are additional limits for parties that present candidates in all constituencies.
Latvia	Yes	For parliamentary elections: 0.20 Centas per voter.
Lithuania	Yes	1,000 times the average minimum wage for a list of candidates in a multicandidate electoral area.
Poland	Yes	More than 3,500,000 EUR (presidential elections).
Portugal	Yes	3,008,600 EUR
Spain	Yes	Per election cycle. Established for each electoral cycle by the general accounting court.
United Kingdom	Yes	18,840,000 GBP (this figure is for political parties only and excludes candidate spending).
United States	No/yes	Generally no limits but there are limits for certain local elections and voluntary limits for the presidential election.

SOURCE: International Foundation for Electoral Systems (as reported in Ohman et al., p. 52).

Table 11.5 Level of Public Funding in Different Countries

No public funding	Afghanistan, Bahamas, Ghana, New Zealand
Private funding dominates	United Kingdom, United States, Italy, Australia, Egypt
Private and public funding at par	Denmark, France, Japan
Public funding dominates	Austria, Sweden, Hungary, Mexico, Portugal
Only public funding	Uzbekistan

SOURCE: International Foundation for Electoral Systems (as reported in Ohman et al., p. 70).

channels, newspapers, websites, and social media networks. As in the United States, some campaigns are increasingly able to reach wider swaths of citizens and target them in highly efficient ways. These changes, however, have not occurred at the same levels in all countries. The extent to which postmodern strategies of campaigning such as microtargeting have been adopted in other countries depends on the media environment in which a campaign is acting, the extent to which advertising is regulated, and how much money campaigns have on hand (Wlezien 2014).

In many countries, citizens access to technology is not as widespread as it is in the United States. Access to technology, the Internet, and even television, as well as levels of computer literacy, also vary widely. Even in more advanced regions like Europe, the use of tools like social media in campaigns is not ubiquitous. In a study of candidates running for the European parliament, for example, Vergeer et al. (2011) found that, even as of 2009, most candidates were reluctant to use social media platforms like Twitter.

Advertising regulations and restrictions also affect how political campaigns develop and deploy their communications plans. Parties and candidates in countries that provide free advertising are generally prohibited from procuring other, paid advertisements. Even in countries that permit paid advertising, there are typically limited spots made available. Where paid advertising is prohibited, including in several Western European nations, campaigns have been turning increasingly to the Internet and to social media to promote their candidates. In countries with high Internet penetration and usage levels, Internet-based campaigning seems to be taking off in ways similar to that seen in the United States (Ward et al. 2008; Stromer-Galley and Sheinheit 2012).

Finally, access to financial resources also affects campaigns' ability to develop and disseminate personalized messages for highly targeted groups of voters via a variety of media platforms. Although in most countries there are few limits on how much candidates can spend, differences in fundraising across countries reflect, in large part, different funding regulations. Many countries provide limited public funding for elections. In addition, the type of funding differs from country to country. Funding can be either tax incentive based (citizens get a tax break for campaign contributions) or come directly from the tax revenues of a given country. Limited access to financial resources can determine whether campaigns can afford to pay for high-level political consultants and advanced means of voter contact and communication.

In general, the use of and access to different media, restrictions on advertising, and availability of campaign funding in large part determine the intensity of contemporary international campaigns, their use of technology, and the extent to which they are the highly professionalized, targeted affairs that exist in the United States (Wlezien 2014). Even in terms of microtargeting, sophisticated voter databases are unavailable in many countries, whereas other countries (Scandanavia, for instance) provide access to databases that are often more comprehensive, detailed, accurate, and up to date than those in the United States.

CONSEQUENCES FOR DEMOCRACY

The normative tenets against which we have measured American campaigns throughout this volume are by no means of unique importance in the context of the United States. Campaigns around the world, too, can be evaluated based on the extent to which they help or hinder the advancement of the norms we have focused on: representation, information, and engagement. In his analysis of campaign strategy in Latin American democracy, Boas (2010) notes,

> The types of appeals candidates present to voters and the means by which they mobilize support carry great import for the quality of new democracies around the world. Electoral strategies matter for whether citizens exercise real influence over the political agenda. . . . Campaign styles affect whether people participate enthusiastically in democratic politics or whether apathy and abstention remain high. Approaches to campaigning help determine whether elected officials can be held accountable for their promises or whether instead they claim a right to govern at will based on a vague mandate for change (636).

Here, I briefly assess how different electoral structures and regulatory regimes in democracies around the world help advance representation and engagement of citizens and the quality of information they receive during elections. The diffusion of Americanized electoral practices has no doubt influenced the extent to which democracies around the world have campaigns that help or hinder the advancement of these norms. In some ways, the normative concerns we have highlighted in previous chapters apply when considering campaigns in other countries. However, in many cases, a country's electoral structure and system of regulations mitigates the extent to which campaign practices bring about normatively undesirable consequences.

There has been extensive debate among political scientists over which type of democratic electoral system—two party or multiparty—is more effective at ensuring citizens are informed, represented, and engaged in politics. Advocates of systems of proportional representation, for example, suggest such an institutional design is superior in terms of advancing democratic ideals. They suggest that systems of proportional representation increase representation by providing a legitimate space for minority voices to be heard; coalitional government building is all but essential for effective governance in multiparty systems. Greater representation, in turn, leads to more citizen participation in politics. Empirical evidence suggests some validity to these claims; voters tend to have stronger partisan preferences in proportional representation systems, which in turn enhances political efficacy and increases participation in politics (Karp and Banducci 2008).

In terms of advances in political communication and media in democracies around the world, the increasing influence of television, in particular, has led to broader normative concerns about the pervasive role this medium plays in helping to promote democratic ideals. Television advertising has become a near-universal tool of political campaigns. In nearly all countries where data are available, television is widely perceived to be the central provider of political information (Plasser and Plasser 2002). Campaign strategists, candidates, and political parties alike recognize the importance of having a well-crafted television advertising strategy wherever it is allowed. In Latin America, for example, the shift of campaign activities from rallies, parades, and intensive, dynamic discussions in public squares to more scripted events on television has been referred to by some as an "impoverishment of the public space," a development that means less engagement and lower-quality information for citizens (Plasser and Plasser 2002). In other countries, such as Russia, strong interference by the ruling party in government leads to even more explicit normative concerns about the extent to which citizens are properly informed about their political options; candidates not affiliated with the government in power typically have difficulties controlling the content of television coming from state- and Kremlin-affiliated television stations in Russia, for example (Plasser and Lengauer 2009).

Do stricter campaign finance regulations, restrictions on political advertising, or the provision of free advertising improve campaign conduct in ways that produce more normatively desirable outcomes in countries around the world? In many ways, it is conceivable that such electoral and regulatory systems have the capacity to advance democratic priorities. But arguments to the contrary can also be made; critics may claim that such restrictions ultimately limit the amount of information campaigns can convey, depriving the public of useful details that could help them make informed decisions. Others, however, might argue that regulations that place restrictions on negative and attack advertising force candidates to be more positive and potentially more straightforward about their policy positions. There have also been concerns over whether campaign finance restrictions, in particular publicly financed campaigns, might adversely affect challengers given that spending matters more for challenger success than for incumbent success (Katz and Mair 1995; Jacobson 2004). In contrast, there is evidence suggesting that public funding evens the playing field and helps nascent parties in their election bids; public funding given to new parties in their early years seems to increase their likelihood of success in subsequent elections (Ikstens et al. 2002). In reality, the correct answer to the central question posed above is likely somewhere in the middle: some things probably do a better job at promoting democratic norms, while others fall short. Panaceas, when it comes to perfectly democratic goals, are elusive.

Many critics decry the adoption of American-style campaign tactics in democracies around the world. Primary concerns revolve around the contention that American-style campaigning could be at least partly responsible for eroding public confidence in government and interest in politics and drawing the public's attention away from the serious consideration of public policies, all of which proponents of party-centered politics argue are critical features of such systems (Gurevitch 1999). As we assess the consequences of political campaign approaches for democracy, these concerns are legitimate, not only for citizens of other countries, but for Americans as well.

KEY TERMS

Adoption model
Compulsory voting
Electoral institutions
Free press
Multiparty system

Party-based election
Professionalization
Proportional
   representation
Shopping model

Single-member district
State-controlled press
Two-party system

SUGGESTED READINGS

LeDuc, L., R. G. Niemi, and P. Norris. 2014. *Comparing Democracies 4: Elections and Voting in a Changing World*. London: Sage.

Norris, P. 2004. *Electoral Engineering: Voting Rules and Political Behavior*. Cambridge, UK: Cambridge University Press.

Plasser, F., and G. Plasser. 2002. *Global Political Campaigning: A Worldwide Analysis of Campaign Professionals and Their Practices*. Westport, CT: Praeger.

Powell, G. B., Jr. 1986. "American Voter Turnout in Comparative Perspective." *The American Political Science Review* 80, no. 1: 17–43.

CHAPTER 12

Assessments and Reflections
on the Future of Political Campaigns

On October 5, 2008, about a month before the historic 2008 election, I participated in a forum titled "The Media and the Presidency—Playing Politics" hosted by the Howard & Virginia Bennett Forum on the Presidency at the Truman Library in Kansas City, Missouri. One of the other panelists was Ted Sorensen, the famed advisor and speechwriter to President Kennedy. Backstage, I reflected on the sea change that political campaigns have undergone over the past five decades. I remember Sorensen telling me he believed that "few things had changed as much as campaigns" since the 1960s.

Two years later, when I was editor in chief of *Campaigns & Elections*, I asked Mr. Sorensen to pen some reflections on campaigns to commemorate the 50th anniversary of the 1960 presidential race. Many of the insights he offered were particularly relevant in light of the election of the first black president, Barack Obama, in 2008. Of Kennedy's election, Sorensen wrote, "Even a young United States senator, inexperienced in executive administration and a member of an oft-disparaged demographic minority group, can, through hard work, defeat a hard-nosed, hard-eyed, hardhearted WASP who scowls more than he smiles, even though a single speech cannot overcome decades of disparagement for his demographic group." He also offered insights that, despite the vast changes that have occurred in American elections since the 1960s, still ring true for political campaigns today. He reminded us that for politicians and political operatives, making friends with journalists, whether they are in print, on broadcast, or blogging online, is imperative for success and that the way to do so is through candidate engagements, honesty, accessibility, and humor. "Do not talk down to the American people with pompous attitudes, piety, and party slogans," he further noted. "Talk about the presidency, patriotism, and the perils facing the country. Avoid factions and quarreling within your team" (Sorensen 2010).

A central premise in this volume is that electoral context influences the ways campaigns are conducted and the strategic choices they make. I have also argued that contexts are fluid, but, as Sorensen reminds us, some lessons carry over from decade to decade. Throughout the book, I have sought to highlight continuity—the more or less stable features of political campaigns—alongside the powerful effects of the changing contexts in which they operate. Another key goal has been to demonstrate that campaigns matter, in many ways.

First, campaigns matter because they can have an impact on citizen preferences. Through their relationship with the media and political parties, they help to enlighten voters and, ideally, lead them to make vote choices that align with their preferences (Gelman and King 1993). Campaign events foster voter preferences to form and crystallize over the course of a campaign season. In a study examining how the structure of vote choice changes during an election season, Erikson et al. (2010) demonstrate that partisanship becomes an increasingly important predictor of voting preferences over the course of an election cycle. Since partisan identity is generally stable, we can interpret this finding to support the notion that campaigns likely help voters to sort out their views about the candidates and to ultimately reconcile these with their votes. Voters' actual choices may not change much, but the determinants or structure of such choices seem to evolve over the course of a campaign season. The impact of campaigns is especially notable in the context of battleground states and other competitive environments, where intense and active campaigns serve to amplify and reinforce the impact of events, news, and other developments. These active campaigns encourage citizens to update or solidify their preferences for candidates, effects that are less potent in noncompetitive elections, such as those in nonbattleground states, where campaigns are more or less dormant (Panagopoulos 2012).

Campaigns also matter because they engage some, if not all, citizens as activists, voters, volunteers, and donors, all of which helps enlist them directly in the political process. Again, this is evident especially in highly competitive elections in which campaigns are most active. Intense, lively campaigns engage and excite the electorate, sparking its interest in learning more about campaigns and increasing the likelihood of participation. Voter turnout is almost always higher in competitive elections, holding all else equal (Cox and Munger 1989). Campaigns in competitive contexts may have greater incentives to provide voters with adequate amounts of information. This means, at least in competitive contexts, that voters learn more and receive a greater range of information that they can bring with them to the ballot box when they make their voting decisions (Lipsitz 2011). Of course, the downside of this is that not all elections in the United States *are* competitive. In fact, in House elections, competiveness has been on the decline and incumbency advantage on the rise over time (Abramowitz 2006).

Political campaigns perform another useful function: they help to vet candidates for public office, requiring them to make difficult choices, to interact with ordinary citizens, to defend their views and to compromise, at least sometimes, and to explain complex public policies to voters. They also compel candidates to develop clear platforms and to adopt positions that can in turn be used by voters in subsequent elections to hold elected officials accountable for differences between their campaign promises and policy actions. This is a critical dimension of democracy, and campaigns serve to reinforce this dimension by forcing candidates to make promises on issues and policies that best serve their constituents and, once they are in office, to follow up on those promises. Finally, even if campaigns are simply a form of political theater or ritual, they nonetheless reinforce the practice of democracy in America. Campaigns serve as reminders that even if the consequences of campaign conduct do not always live up to ideal democratic norms, Americans have the right to debate, be informed, and ultimately decide who governs their democracy. If nothing else, there is value in that dynamic.

In each chapter of this volume, I have evaluated in detail the contexts and ways in which campaign conduct matters: for election outcomes, the information that citizens have, their engagement in politics, and, ultimately, their representation in government. In this chapter, I highlight the current state of campaigns, summarizing how the changing contexts highlighted throughout this volume contribute to the changing nature of campaigns in the United States. I then summarize and reflect on how well the campaign activities I have discussed help achieve the goals of democratic representation, information, and engagement. Although there are countless normative dimensions against which to benchmark campaign performance in terms of democratic theory, I focus on these three tenets because they are the ones most directly related to campaign strategy and execution.

In Chapter 3, I discussed how external actors like parties, interest groups, and the media affect campaign decisions. Over the past several decades, the role of political parties in American politics has changed dramatically, with significant consequences for campaigns. We have observed a shift from party-centered campaigns to candidate-centered campaigns, but we are currently seeing a resurgence in the role that party labels and endorsements play in campaign strategy. To put it simply, although the relationship between parties and campaigns has shifted over the years, any candidate trying to run a successful campaign in American politics will have a difficult time without attachment to a major party. Interest groups, too, have risen to even greater prominence, in large part because of the deregulation of campaign finance. They now not only contribute to campaigns, but also head up their own PACs and run separate campaigns that more often than not lambast candidates who do not align with their interests. Furthermore, an increasingly fragmented, diverse, and 24-hour news cycle means campaigns must stay on top of stories that may potentially harm their campaign more than ever; each day offers new opportunities for positive coverage as well as the risk of negative coverage that can affect a campaign's success.

Chapter 4 highlighted some of the more substantial changes to campaign finance that have affected the way campaigns operate. Individuals can now donate unlimited amounts of money overall to candidates, parties, and PACs during an election cycle, although limits still remain on the amount one can contribute to individual candidates. In the wake of the *Citizens United v. Federal Election Commission* Supreme Court ruling, super PACs can now collect contributions of any size. These changes, as well as others, require candidates to raise more money than ever, not only to avoid being outspent by their opponents, but also to counter the increasing number of negative attacks from well-funded independent expenditure groups.

These changes have had a substantial impact on the campaign strategies, communications efforts, and GOTV efforts I discussed in Chapters 5 through 7. The job of campaign communications professionals has grown much more complicated, often necessitating the hiring of an array of different media consultants to deal with different social media platforms and website development and to manage a campaign's conventional media presence. Although the opportunity for "free media" is certainly more abundant given the growing number of news outlets, this does not mean candidates have to compete any less for attention. In addition, they must worry more about negative news stories that may break on smaller outlets and then be picked up by larger sources. Whereas in eras past campaigns had to concern themselves only with coverage by nightly news broadcasts and daily newspapers, developing a campaign strategy that communicates a clear-cut message has grown more difficult in light of the multiple voices in the arena of contemporary elections. Related to these challenges, of course, is the fact that campaigns must compete for voters' attention amid an entertainment world that seems to offer an infinite array of options to take their attention away from elections and campaign activities.

Not all of these developments have created challenges for campaigns, however. Advances in data collection and big data analytics have allowed strategists to target voters and with greater precision, exposing them to messages to which they are likely to be responsive. As I discussed in Chapter 9, centralized voter lists are now available to most campaigns, along with more efficient ways of storing, managing, and modeling data. New technologies and advances in social media make it easier than ever for candidates to reach a number of citizens in efforts to persuade them and solicit donations. More and more, campaigns are relying on the expertise of political scientists engaged in field experiments to determine which types of messaging and methods of contact are more effective in getting out the vote, as I discussed in Chapter 7.

In Chapter 10, I highlighted how recent institutional changes in the electoral process in the United States have changed the structural constraints under which campaigns operate, posing new challenges in targeting and mobilizing voters, but not across all states. The adoption of practices like early voting and all-mail elections increase uncertainty for campaigns as more and more citizens cast their ballots before Election Day and threaten to add to the already high costs of running a campaign. Same-day registration can also add more voters to the registration rolls, prodding campaigns to reach out to previously unregistered and nonhabitual voters, and aligns well with the traditional rhythms of election cycles. These changes are especially consequential for campaigns that must simultaneously operate in different jurisdictions, in particular presidential campaigns, which must navigate a variety of different legal-institutional environments in crafting their campaign strategies. But they can also matter in statewide elections when counties and municipalities have different election laws, as in Washington State. In the past, Washington has implemented all-mail elections in some counties but not others, posing challenges for statewide campaigns and congressional campaigns that straddle multiple jurisdictions.

Many of the changing contexts and strategies observed in American campaigns are now also found in democracies around the world. Although campaigns in other countries often retain unique characteristics dictated by their own electoral systems and political cultures and must operate within the constraints of their country's election laws, more and more campaigns abroad are becoming professionalized, personalized, and, some say, Americanized as expertise from American consultants makes its way abroad. This means the normative implications I have considered throughout this volume in relationship to American contexts and campaign conduct will likely have increasing relevance for other democracies.

Of course, there is no guarantee that changes and advances in campaign strategies will carry over from election to election. For example, lessons and best practices learned by the Obama campaign, which according to many observers and social scientists was groundbreaking in its use of data and development of extensive volunteer networks, may not necessarily be available to other campaigns and remain instead proprietary to Obama's organizing committee, Obama for America. Although companies like Aristotle and Catalist, which I discussed in Chapter 9, have made it easier for campaigns across the political spectrum to get more detailed voter files and manage such data, there is wide variation in how much information is shared between campaigns. Campaigns are, by their nature, competitive. Not only are they competing with their opponents and opposing parties, but also candidates of the same party are in competition for attention from national, state, and local party organizations, interest groups, and potential donors, all of whom have a finite amount of resources to share. In many cases, campaign organizations are left to reinvent the wheel. There is little institutional memory because most campaign staffs dissipate after the election is over. The continuity that was once provided to campaigns by parties running the show is now less prevalent as well. Today, much of the institutional memory for campaign operations is provided by consultants, whose approaches can vary widely.

Throughout this volume, I have discussed how the evolution of campaign conduct in response to differences and changes in contexts, in different places and over time, has had consequences for three central tenets of democratic theory: representation, information, and engagement. Representation refers to how well campaign practices help elect accountable representatives who reflect the preferences of their constituents. For my purposes, representation refers primarily to substantive representation, in the sense that elected officials adopt policy positions and support laws that align with their constituency's preferences. But political scientists also often refer to descriptive representation in the sense that elected officials, in some respect, reflect the different backgrounds and life experiences of their constituents. Many observers bemoan the fact that Congress, for example, remains on the whole populated by wealthy white males who do not reflect the diversity of their constituents. Accurate and reliable information that guides citizens' vote choices and enables them to make informed decisions is also indispensable in democratic politics. Finally, democratic societies depend on broad citizen participation and engagement, not only in terms of voting but also in terms of other political activities such as volunteering, donating, and contacting representatives about policy concerns.

To what extent have campaigns lived up to these ideals? My evaluations of campaigns by these standards of representation reveal a murky, although not entirely bleak, picture of the extent to which campaign conduct in contemporary elections helps uphold these norms.

Campaigns must operate and make strategic decisions under the constraints that are imposed on them. The goals of campaigns are not primarily to promote broad democratic ideals, but to engage in strategies and make decisions that help candidates win elections. From a rational perspective, campaigns have few incentives to inform, engage, and represent all citizens, or even all citizens within their districts. In some cases, their decisions can nevertheless help promote these democratic norms. In others, they may exacerbate problems such as biases in representation, misinformation of citizens, and citizen participation rates between the wealthy and the poor. Thinking about the consequences of campaign conduct is important for society. Returning to the analogy of campaigns as military expeditions in the preface, it is crucial that, as campaigns seek victories in electoral battles, society does not end up losing the war in terms of the quality and integrity of our democratic process.

Nevertheless, elections do seem to perform an important function for citizen representation: they may increase the incentives for legislators to be representative of their constituents as elections approach. Legislators appear to be more moderate in their positions and responsive as elections approach. Evidence from California suggests that representation of constituent preferences increases substantially during an election year and that they are especially likely to increase if the likelihood of reelection may be adversely affected by being tied to the party of an unpopular president. The same evidence also suggests that members of the California state house stay consistently in line with the preferences of their constituencies throughout their two-year terms (Kuklinski 1978). Presidents, too, tend to be more responsive to the public during their first term, when their popularity is middling and prospect for reelection is up in the air (Canes-Wrone 2006). More broadly, there is evidence that legislators generally adopt the policies that citizens support and that changes in policy are fairly responsive to macro changes in public opinion (Erikson, MacKuen and Stimson 2002; Stimson 2015).

In Chapter 1, I introduced the concept of polarization and speculated on the extent to which it has influenced campaign conduct. Most scholars agree that polarization is increasing among political elites, that is, that the ideological centers of the two major American parties are moving farther apart. However, there is a contentious debate over whether polarization has occurred in the American public as well or if voters are simply becoming better sorted into their parties, that is, with less ideological overlap between parties but not necessarily farther apart. Abramowitz and Saunders (2008) suggest that ideological polarization has indeed increased among the public, especially among those segments of it that care about and are engaged in politics. Others resist these claims, arguing that the results are simply a methodological byproduct. When the same data were reexamined with different coding and aggregation procedures, the evidence seemed to disappear (Fiorina et al. 2008). A review of existing evidence, taking into account the difficulties with developing accurate indicators of polarization, suggests that the American public may not be more polarized than it was in previous decades, whether one looks at voters' positions on a general liberal to conservative ideological scale or considers their preferences on specific positions. Sorting, in contrast, has occurred, most clearly between members of the Democratic and Republican parties, but this does not mean that Americans are farther apart in their median positions, ideological or otherwise (Fiorina and Abrams 2008).

Both elite-level polarization and sorting among the American public nevertheless force candidates to adapt their issue positions, who they cater to during campaigns, and the legislation they support once in office. Elite polarization can lead to ugly campaign discourse as candidates speak past one another instead of to one another and can cause gridlock in the legislative process (Jones 2001; Binder 2003). Indeed, opposing legislation that one's party base opposes has come at the expense of not only passing legislation, but also keeping the government running. In 2013, a small group of Republicans in Congress refused to fund the government without the passage of a resolution that defunded Obamacare, the highly polarizing piece of health care legislation opposed by many hardline Republicans, both in the public and among the elites (Narula et al. 2013). Presumably, this strategy, like House votes to repeal the act, was designed in part to give Republican representatives with a hardline party base the opportunity to advertise their position to their supporters come reelection time.

Polarization may have some normatively desirable consequences, however. When campaigns cater more strongly to strong partisan identities, participation and interest in politics and the extent to which citizens are informed can be increased (Abramowitz and Saunders 2008). Individuals who strongly identify with a party are more likely to participate in the political process, and campaign responses to polarization may aid this tendency. Indeed, explanations for high turnout and activism in the 2004 presidential election include heightened degrees of partisan polarization as well as meaningful differences in issue positions that accentuated the policy differential between the major-party candidates. It is perhaps no coincidence that that election also featured a renewed effort at personal contact and grassroots mobilization by both political parties (Abramowitz and Stone 2006; Bergan et al. 2005).

In our discussion of the increasing need for campaigns to raise more and more money with every successive election cycle, I highlighted the implications of campaigns' inclinations to focus on donors who can provide them with the largest amounts of money. Simply put, raising large sums of money from a few wealthy donors involves far less time than attempting to reach a wide variety of small-dollar contributors. This leads to concerns over the extent to which candidates will take policy positions that are more representative of wealthy donors and interest groups than the preferences of the average citizen (Gilens and Page 2014). However, as we saw in Chapter 9, advances in fundraising through a range of online platforms, both website and social media based, have allowed candidates to reach out to broader donor bases, increasing the number of small-dollar donations campaigns have seen in recent years. In the 2008 and 2012 presidential elections, for example, candidates like Barack Obama actually touted their success in raising small-dollar contributions, raising the profile of this normatively desirable campaign conduct and ideally pushing other candidates to reach out to small donors as well. A greater reliance on small-dollar donors means candidates, once in office, may be able to pay more attention to the preferences of their constituents rather than worrying about retaining large-dollar contributions for their next reelection bids.

In our discussion of campaign communications, advertising, and the relationship between campaigns and the news media, I assessed how well contemporary campaigns contribute to this goal through their strategic decisions. The behavior of the news media, too, helps determine the extent to which citizens are informed about candidates' substantive policy positions. Unfortunately, evidence suggests that the news media may be more focused on the horse-race or nonsubstantive aspects of political campaigns rather than the merits of candidate's policy positions, particularly when races are more competitive (Hayes 2010). Candidates, too, have an incentive to focus on communicating messages to voters that emphasize personal characteristics more than substantive policy concerns and are putting forth increasingly negative advertisements with each new election cycle. But empirical evidence suggests that negative advertisements might not be all bad for democratic norms; they can lead to a more informed and engaged citizenry by increasing the likelihood that individuals will choose one candidate over the other (Krupnikiov 2012).

Additionally, the increased use of highly sophisticated microtargeting techniques has both positive and negative implications for democratic norms. Some have concerns that microtargeting might create greater opportunities for campaigns to misinform citizens while avoiding scrutiny by the news media (Jamieson 2013). Furthermore, as I highlighted in Chapter 7, it is often inefficient for campaigns to aim their GOTV efforts at broad, nonspecific groups of voters. Advances in voter data and microtargeting techniques have only improved campaigns' ability to engage in highly efficient and precise GOTV efforts, isolating likely supporters and leaving those less likely to vote out in the cold. In this way, campaigns are increasingly able to lead the right people—for their purposes—to the polls on Election Day and to rely less on persuading those on the fence, turning out new voters, and improving citizen engagement.

On the upside, contemporary campaigns can rely on tools like data analytics to maximize the effectiveness of their mobilization and persuasion tactics. Microtargeting can now be used to ensure voters receive absentee ballot applications, to know where their polling locations are, and to be aware of voter registration deadlines. In addition, the advances in the details provided on voter lists I discussed in Chapter 9 mean candidates can now rely on more than an individual's voter history to predict whether he or she will actually turn out and vote. Even those with a spotty history of turnout may be mobilized based on other known factors that, with the right message, will lead them to cast a ballot. Furthermore, it is possible that campaign messages tailored to specific groups and individuals will cause voters to pay greater attention to the information they receive.

As I have emphasized throughout this volume, contemporary campaigns in the United States are by no means perfect, but they are also not entirely antithetical to the advancement of democratic ideals. Campaigns engage and inform at least some citizens, at least some of the time. There seems to be greater concern over the extent to which the nature of contemporary campaigns can promote greater representation by elected officials once they are in office. In light of these findings, political scientists and reformers have proposed a series of improvements meant to progress the conduct of American campaigns and democracy writ large. It may be feasible to implement some of these reforms in the near future, but others face steep uphill battles in the face of questions about their constitutionality and degree of public support.

One of the most prominent areas where advocates for reform have proposed change is in the domain of campaign finance. Especially in light of recent Supreme Court decisions, there are concerns among pundits and the public alike over the rising role that money plays in American elections. Indeed, as I highlighted in previous chapters, there is empirical evidence to substantiate these concerns because elected officials seem to be more responsive to the preferences of wealthy Americans and interest groups than to those of the average citizen (Gilens and Page 2014). Limitations to campaign spending are frequently debated, but the U.S. Supreme Court has made clear that such restrictions would violate free speech protections.

Some suggest that requiring full disclosure of major political spending would better inform the public and deter secretive donations in exchange for political favors. Although direct contributions of $200 or more to candidates for federal office are required to be reported to the FEC, super PACs are able to conceal the identity of their donors if they choose because donations are only required to be disclosed if the donors themselves designate their contribution as political spending. Reforms would require the full disclosure of all political contributions, from private citizens as well as lobbyists, corporations, and other organizations, such as unions.

Public funding of elections has also been floated as a means to weaken the influence of money in American elections. As I highlighted in previous chapters, public funding lessens the extent to which candidates *must* rely on big donors, potentially making them more responsive to their broader constituencies. Some evidence suggests that certain forms of public funding, such as multiple matching systems where small contributions from individual donors are matched by public funds, can increase voter participation, campaign contributions from those with lower incomes, and competition (Center for Governmental Studies 2003; Levin 2006; Migally and Liss 2010), but other studies call these effects into question (Panagopoulos 2011). The American public, however, seems ambivalent about this reform. Opinions seem to depend on the extent to which campaign finance is in the national spotlight; in the wake of the Watergate scandal, a majority of Americans supported providing public money to candidates for contributions to Congress as well as for the presidency, as long as all private contributions were limited. This support has dwindled in recent years, with only about a fifth of the public supporting public financing in 1997 and 2000 (Panagopoulos 2004).

Another common area where reformers advocate for change is in the area of the laws that structure voting and registration. As discussed in Chapter 10, the system of elections in the United States is unique in the sense that it requires citizens to engage in a two-step process to cast a vote. As a result, the United States has low turnout compared to many other democratic countries (Powell 1986) and participation is skewed toward the resource advantaged in American society such as wealthier and more educated individuals (Schlozman et al. 2012). Reforms like early voting and same-day registration have already been put in place in a number of states, but most scholars conclude that of these two reforms, same-day registration stands to be the most effective at improving voter turnout and decreasing biases in voting between the resource advantaged and the resource disadvantaged (e.g., Burden et al. 2014; Springer 2014; Rigby and Springer 2011). As promising as these reforms are, it is unclear, perhaps even doubtful, that they have the capacity to improve citizen engagement.

Other proposed reforms have yet to take off across most American states. Some states feature online voter registration, allowing citizens to register to vote from the convenience of their homes, or automatic registration. Online voter registration has had a positive influence on turnout in places like California, especially among young voters who are otherwise less likely to participate in elections (Cha and Kennedy 2014). Other reform advocates have proposed more dramatic changes to the U.S. system of voter registration such as implementation of universal voter registration. This would put the government in charge of registering people to vote as opposed to placing the onus on citizens themselves. This reform does not appear to be one that candidates and campaigns across the partisan and ideological spectrum would necessarily oppose, but some have argued that "certain people just shouldn't be voting." Such opponents express concerns that many Americans do not know enough about politics to vote correctly (Malkin 2008). It is also suggested that those who oppose this type of reform do so to protect their own electoral prospects, namely Republican candidates, who would be disadvantaged as the result of an expanded electorate; some empirical evidence suggests there is legitimacy to this argument (Bentele and O'Brien 2013).

More drastic reforms that would improve citizen access to the ballot and engagement in politics, such as compulsory voting, are unlikely to be adopted in the near future. Although the idea of compulsory voting has been floated, that is, requiring all citizens to vote or pay a penalty, proponents would face an uphill battle given that states generally control the structure and administration of their elections. Americans have consistently disapproved of the idea of compulsory voting at levels of approximately 70% (Panagopoulos 2004). In 2015, however, President Barack Obama did make a public speech indicating that the United States should consider the adoption of compulsory voting. But neither he nor any of his counterparts in Washington seems likely to take legislative action toward this reform forward any time soon (Somin 2015).

Many reforms that might theoretically improve the normative conduct of political campaigns and American democracy lack public support. Alternatively, the public may express support for changes that could have potentially detrimental, even if unintended, consequences for American democracy. For example, many Americans support voter identification laws to prevent election fraud. The most stringent form of these laws requires citizens to show a form of photo identification and verify their signature when voting, which opponents argue unfairly targets minority, less educated, and low-income voters who are less likely to have the means to obtain such identification. African Americans in particular are less likely to have the types of identification typically required—a driver license or state-issued identification card—and are thus more likely to be disenfranchised by such laws (Wilson 2014). Early examinations suggest voter identification laws may not necessarily reduce participation overall, but more stringent policies seem to depress turnout among registered voters with lower levels of education, potentially widening inequalities or disparities in participation (Alvarez et al. 2007). However, the most stringent laws can negatively impact some individuals' likelihood of voting relative to the least stringent laws and can decrease the likelihood that registered voters with lower levels of education will vote, many of whom may also be a part of disadvantaged minority populations (Alvarez et al. 2007). Opponents of voter ID laws have called into question advocates' motivations, positing the reform is often supported by politicians who would likely benefit from lower participation by members of these groups (Haygood 2011). Empirical evidence suggests there may be some merit to these arguments because these reforms are most often adopted in states where Republicans control state legislatures and that are generally competitive in presidential elections (Bentele and O'Brien 2013). In opinion polls, majorities of the American public seem to favor voter identification laws, although there is little evidence to suggest that voter fraud is a significant problem in American elections (Minnite 2010). On the whole, however, Americans seem to be ambivalent about reforms that could potentially raise turnout considerably, such as same-day registration and automatic registration. (Alvarez et al. 2011).

In the absence of major reforms, American campaigns seem to be on a trajectory toward increasingly expensive, data-driven, and technologically advanced campaigns. These changes bear on the extent to which the "permanent" campaign will become even more prominent in American politics. Coined by Sidney Blumenthal in his 1980 book (Blumenthal 1980), the concept of a "permanent campaign" posits that shifts in American politics from strong party-based elections and organizations to more candidate-centered, technologically advanced elections have led to an era in which governing itself has become a form of campaigning. In particular, Blumenthal noted how political consultants and pollsters were increasingly being consulted on important matters of policy to ensure that candidates' or elected officials' issue positions were palatable to the constituents needed to win election or reelection.

The permanent campaign has given way to roll call votes taking place in Congress that are meant to serve as talking points and provide fodder for campaign commercials. In this volume, I highlighted House Republicans' use of this strategy in their repeated votes to repeal President Obama's health care law. Such votes were explicitly symbolic and designed to allow freshmen congressmen to be able to "advertise" their roll call votes to their constituents back home. This example highlights the extent to which almost every move that elected officials make is in service to their image as a candidate running for office, to the increasing detriment of their position as policy makers representing their constituencies.

More broadly, a system of permanent campaigning tends to reward candidates who are talented campaigners, not necessarily politicians who have the best policy solutions. From a cynical perspective, American campaigns have become more about who can present their policy ideas in the most fashionable and palatable way than about which candidates have policy positions and ideas that are the most effective and representative of constituent preferences.

ELECTION ADMINISTRATION AND DEMOCRACY

This book has focused primarily on political campaigns' strategies and efforts to persuade voters to support specific candidates and then to get them to the polls on Election Day, or to the mailboxes, voting centers or administrative offices, to register these preferences. For the most part, a campaign's job is done once voters get to the vote sites to cast their ballots. But what happens at voting locations— election administration—can also have important consequences for democracy. As we discussed, elections in the United States have historically been managed at the state and local levels. Counties and municipalities generally finance elections, which can be quite costly. A report issued by the CalTech/MIT Voting Technology Project in 2001 found that the cost of administering the 2000 presidential election was about $1 billion nationally, or about $10 per vote cast. On a per-voter basis, counties and local governments spend approximately $3.50 per voter on voter registration, $1.50 per voter to acquire and maintain voting equipment and about $1.50 per voter to run the election on Election Day; another $3.50 per voter is spent on administrative overhead (Voting Technology Project 2001). Despite the enormous expense, it is estimated that between 4 and 6 million votes were lost in that election cycle (Voting Technology Project 2001). Moreover, election costs appear to be on the rise; despite potential cost savings promised by reforms like vote-by-mail, voting centers and new technology, election administration expenditures are only escalating. Consider the case of Weld County, Colorado: With 121,116 registered voters, the county paid $594,723 to conduct the November 2004 election, including $88,280 just to print ballots; by November 2008, overall costs had risen 63%, to $970,476, even though the number of registrants had only grown 15%, to 138,873 voters (Montjoy 2010).

The federal government has gradually become more involved in overseeing election administration, especially since the 2000 presidential election debacle, through several changes in election law, most notably, the passage of the Help America Vote Act (HAVA) in 2002. Authorizing federal funds for election administration improvements for the first time—over $3 billion—HAVA mandated that all states and localities adopt new technological innovations (by upgrading voting equipment, for example) and procedures, including poll worker training and improvements in registration processes, in order to enhance the efficiency and efficacy of election operations (Alvarez and Hall 2005). Nevertheless, there is considerable variation in jurisdictions across the country in the quality of election administration and in the effectiveness of the implementation of voting procedures.

The nature and quality of election administration can affect citizens and campaigns in important ways. Selections about voting technology and variations in how election machinery performs (Alvarez, Ansolabehere, and Stewart 2005; Ansolabehere and Stewart 2005), poll worker effectiveness (Alvarez and Hall 2005; Atkeson and Saunders 2007; Hall, Monson and Patterson 2007), and related reforms (Berinsky 2005) can be consequential. Poll workers and election administrators, for example, perform key functions that include configuring polling places, posting voting information, verifying voter identification and eligibility, counting votes, and most importantly, interacting with voters (Alvarez and Hall 2005; Hall, Monson, and Patterson 2007). These individuals' performance and effectiveness can significantly impact the quality of voters' experiences at the polls (Alvarez and Hall 2005; Claassen, Magleby, Monson and Patterson 2008; Hall, Monson and Patterson 2007). Incidences of extending voting hours at poll sites due to poor management, poll workers' absenteeism or failure to operate voting machines properly are commonplace, as are long lines at polling places and instances of discrimination, factors which may ultimately lower voter turnout and decrease voter confidence in the voting process (Atkeson and Saunders 2007; Claassen et al. 2008). Atkeson, Bryant, Hall, Saunders, and Alvarez (2010) have also shown that poll workers have applied voter identification laws differentially, asking minority voters for identification more often than white voters. Such biases, whether intentional or not, can potentially have far-reaching social and political consequences (Alvarez and Hall 2005). Moreover, conflicts can potentially arise because election administrators are often partisans (Kimball, Kropf, and Battles 2006), or improper training and monitoring mechanisms can impair performance (Alvarez and Hall 2005). Poll worker errors can even directly endanger election outcomes. In the 2004 primary election in California, for example, poll workers who were unfamiliar with the new electronic voting system incorrectly distributed ballots to over 7,000 Orange County voters. In the 21 precincts where the problem was most apparent, there were more ballots cast than registered voters (Herndon and Pfeifer 2004). Evidence that perceptions about poll worker performance affects voter confidence in the electoral process is abundant (Hall and Moore 2011). Hall, Monson and Patterson (2010) found that voters who were satisfied with their poll workers were more likely to think that their votes would be counted accurately and tended to hold stronger views on the fairness of the outcome of the election. Alvarez, Hall, Levin and Stewart (2011) analyzed data from the 2008 Survey of the Performance of American Elections, a nationwide survey on the voters' election experiences, to show that voters were very sensitive to problems that occurred during voting and held their poll workers responsible and accountable for such problems; as a result, voters who encountered difficulties expressed lower levels of confidence that their votes were accurately counted. Although generally beyond the purview of campaigns' control, fair, effective and efficient election administration is an important part of the electoral process and can affect campaigns indirectly by influencing individuals' attitudes about the system or behavior and even election outcomes directly. Reforms in recent years have improved many, but certainly not all, aspects of how U.S. elections are administered.

CONCLUDING REMARKS

I conclude on an optimistic note. As I reflect on the nature of campaigns over the past quarter-century since I was a candidate for the Massachusetts state legislature in 1992, I observe both continuity and change. Some of the changes advance democratic ideals and the quality of our electoral system, whereas others present challenges. All things considered, however, my view is that both the machinery of electioneering and the character of democracy in America have improved over the past few decades. Campaigns and voters both seem to have become more savvy in how they interact with each other in the political sphere. Citizens are not at the mercy of ruthless political operatives who relentlessly manipulate and misguide them for political gain. Although many critics decry the escalating costs of campaigns, the sinister motivations of special interests, the intensification of partisan polarization and gridlock, and the inability of voters to have a say, we must balance those concerns against evidence of enhanced voter participation and engagement in recent election cycles and a willingness—and ability—to hold elected officials accountable when responsiveness dwindles and to defend democratic principles when they are threatened. As political entities, campaigns may have evolved to adapt to contextual changes in the political environment but so, too, have voters, who, in the end, remain the sole audience of any successful campaign. Admittedly, campaigns are imperfect and increasingly complex, and they do not always advance the democratic principles citizens espouse. It is our duty as citizens to remain attentive to these shortcomings and to pursue reform. When all is said and done, one must wonder whether democracy in America would be better off without political campaigns. Inevitably, I conclude it would not be. An electoral process that involves candidates hashing out ideas in public forums and interacting directly with voters to attract broad citizen support is, in my view, warts and all, superior to a system in which political elites call the shots in the proverbial smoke-filled rooms that were a feature of American elections for much of the nation's history. To paraphrase the inimitable E. E. Schattschneider (1942), democracy in America is essentially unworkable save in terms of political campaigns.

References

Abrajano, M., and R. M. Alvarez. 2012. *New Faces, New Voices: The Hispanic Electorate in America*, 2nd edition. Princeton, NJ: Princeton University Press.

Abrajano, M., and C. Panagopoulos. 2011. "Does Language Matter? The Impact of Spanish versus English-Language GOTV Efforts on Latino Turnout." *American Politics Research* 39(4): 643–663.

Abramowitz, A. I. 1991. "Incumbency, Campaign Spending, and the Decline of Competition in U.S. House Elections." *Journal of Politics* 53(1): 34–56.

Abramowitz, A. I., B. Alexander, and M. Gunning. 2006. "Incumbency, Redistricting, and the Decline of Competition in U.S. House Elections." *Journal of Politics* 68(1): 75–88.

Abramowitz, A. I., and K. L. Saunders. 2008. "Is Polarization a Myth?" *The Journal of Politics* 70(2): 542–555.

Abramowitz, A. I., and J. A. Segal 1986. "The Determinants of Outcomes in U.S. Senate Elections." *Journal of Politics* 48(2): 433–439.

Abramowitz, A. I., and W. J. Stone. 2006. "The Bush Effect: Polarization, Turnout, and Activism in the 2004 Presidential Election." *Presidential Studies Quarterly* 36(2): 141–154.

Abramowitz, M. 2006. "GOP Candidates Claim Degrees of Separation from President." *The Washington Post*. Retrieved March 2, 2015, http://www.washingtonpost.com/wp-dyn/content/article/2006/08/04/AR2006080401807.html/.

Administration and Cost of Elections Project. 2012. "Parties and Candidates: Campaigning." Retrieved May 15, 2015, https://aceproject.org/ace-en/topics/pc/pcc/pcc08/.

Adorno, T. W., E. Frenkel-Brunswick, D. Levinson, and N. Sanford. 1950. *The Authoritarian Personality*. New York: Harper & Brothers.

Aguiar-Conraria, L., Magalhães, P. C. and Soares, M. J. 2013. "The Nationalization of Electoral Cycles in the United States: a Wavelet Analysis." *Public Choice*, 156(3–4): 387–408.

Aldrich, J. H. 1993. "Rational Choice and Turnout." *American Journal of Political Science* 37(1): 246–278.

Aldrich, J. H. 2011. *Why Parties? A Second Look*. Chicago: University of Chicago Press.

Aldrich, J. H., B. H. Bishop, R. S. Hatch, D. S. Hillygus, and D. W. Rohde. 2014. "Blame, Responsibility, and the Tea Party in the 2010 Midterm Elections." *Political Behavior* 36(3): 471–491.

Alexander, H. E. 2000. "Election Finances." In *The International Encyclopedia of Elections*, edited by R. Rose, 77–82. Washington, DC: Congressional Quarterly Press.

Alexander, H. E. and R. Shiratori. 1994. *Comparative Political Finance among the Democracies.* Boulder, CO; Westview.

Allen, C. 1990. "GOTV." *Campaigns & Elections* October.

Allison, B. 2015. "Micro-targeting Is America's Latest Political Export." *Sunlight Foundation.* Retrieved May 26, 2015, https://sunlightfoundation.com/blog/2015/05/07/micro-targeting-is-americas-latest-political-export/.

Almond, G. A., and S. Verba. 1963. *The Civic Culture.* Princeton, NJ: Princeton University Press.

Althaus, S. L. 1998. "Information Effects in Collective Preferences." *American Political Science Review* 92(3): 545–558.

Alvarez, R. M. 1997. *Issues and Information in Presidential Elections.* Ann Arbor, MI: University of Michigan Press.

Alvarez, R. M. 1999. *Information and Elections.* Ann Arbor: University of Michigan Press.

Alvarez, R. M., S. Ansolabehere and C. Stewart. 2005. "Studying Elections: Data Quality and Pitfalls in Measuring of Effects of Voting Technologies." *Policy Studies Journal* 33: 15–24.

Alvarez, R. M., D. Bailey, and J. Katz. 2007. "The Effect of Voter Identification Laws on Turnout." *Caltech/MIT Voting Technology Project*, VTP Working Paper 57, Version 2.

Alvarez, R. M. and T. E. Hall. 2005. "Rational and Pluralistic Approaches to HAVA Implementation: The Cases of Georgia and California." *Publius: The Journal of Federalism* 35(4): 559–577.

Alvarez, R. M., T. E. Hall, I. Levin, and C. Stewart III. 2011. "Voter Opinions about Election Reform: Do They Support Making Voting More Convenient?" *Election Law Journal* 10(2): 73–87.

Alvarez, R. M., and J. Nagler. 2000. "Likely Consequences of Internet Voting for Political Representation." *Loyola of Los Angeles Law Review* 34: 1115–1154.

American Political Science Association. 1950. "Toward a More Responsible Two-Party System: A Report of the Committee on Political Parties." *American Political Science Review* 44(3): 1–99.

Ansolabehere, S. and C. Stewart. 2005. "Residual Votes Attributable to Technology." *Journal of Politics* 70: 754–766.

Ansolabehere, S., J, M. de Figueiredo, and J. M. Snyder Jr. 2003. "Why Is There so Little Money in U.S. Politics?" *The Journal of Economic Perspectives* 17(1): 105–130.

Ansolabehere, S., and S. Iyengar. 1994. "Of Horseshoes and Horse Races: Experimental Studies of the Impact of Poll Results on Electoral Behavior." *Political Communication* 11: 413–430.

Ansolabehere, S. and S. Iyengar. 1995. *Going negative: How campaign advertising shrinks and polarizes the electorate.* New York: The Free Press.

Ansolabehere, S., S. Iyengar, A. Simon, and N. Valentino. 1994. "Does Attack Advertisement Demobilize the Electorate?" *American Political Science Review* 88(4): 829–838.

Ansolabehere, S., and P. Jones. 2007. "Constituents' Policy Perceptions and Approval of Their Members of Congress." Unpublished manuscript. MIT. Retrieved March 20,

2015, http://projects.iq.harvard.edu/cces/publications/constituents-policy-perceptions-and-approval-members-congress/.

Arbitron. 2001. *Arbitron Outdoor Study: Outdoor Media Consumer and Their Crucial Role in the Media Mix. 2001.* New York: Arbitron.

Arceneaux, K., and Nickerson, D. W. 2009. "Who Is Mobilized to Vote? A Re-Analysis of 11 Field Experiments." *American Journal of Political Science* 53: 1–16.

Arceneaux, K., and Nickerson, D. W. 2010. "Comparing Negative and Positive Campaign Messages: Evidence from Two Field Experiments." *American Politics Research* 38(1): 54–83.

Augenblick, N., and S. Nicholson. 2016. "Ballot Position, Choice Fatigue, and Voter Behaviour." *Review of Economic Studies* 83: 460–480

Atkeson, L. R. and K. Saunders. 2007. "The Effect of Election Administration on Voter Confidence: A Local Matter?" *PS: Political Science & Politics* 40: 655–660.

Atkeson, L. R., L. Bryant, T. E. Hall, K. Saunders and R. M. Alvarez. 2010. "New Barriers to Voter Participation: An Examination of New Mexico's Voter Identification Law." *Electoral Studies* 29(1): 66–73.

AZPM Staff. 2014. "McSally Wins Congressional Seat, Ousting Barber." *Arizona Public Media*. Retrieved March 3, 2014, https://www.azpm.org/s/26810-will-it-be-congresswoman-elect-mcsally-or-2nd-term-for-barber/.

Babad, E. 1999. "Preferential Treatment in Television Interviewing: Evidence from Nonverbal Behavior." *Political Communication* 16(3): 337–358.

Babad, E. 2005. "The Psychological Price of Mass Media Bias." *Journal of Experimental Psychology: Applied* 11(4): 245–255.

Babb, D. 2014. "LBJ's 1964 Attack Ad 'Daisy' Leaves a Legacy for Modern Campaigns." *The Washington Post*. Retrieved April 6, 2015, http://www.washingtonpost.com/opinions/lbjs-1964-attack-ad-daisy-leaves-a-legacy-for-modern-campaigns/2014/09/05/d00e66b0-33b4-11e4-9e92-0899b306bbea_story.html/.

Bachrach, P., and M. S. Baratz. 1962. "Two Faces of Power." *American Political Science Review* 56(4): 947–952.

Bafumi, J., R. Erikson, and C. Wlezien. 2010. "Balancing, Generic Polls and Midterm Congressional Elections." *Journal of Politics* 72(3): 705–719.

Ballotpedia. 2014. "Incumbents with No Primary or General Election Challenger in 2014 State Legislative Elections." *Ballotpedia: An Interaction Almanac of U.S. Politics*. Retrieved February 17, 2015, http://ballotpedia.org/Candidates_with_no_primary_or_general_election_challengers_in_the_2014_state_legislative_elections/.

Ballotpedia. 2015. "States with Initiative or Referendum." *Ballotpedia: An Interaction Almanac of U.S. Politics*. Retrieved May 28, 2015, http://ballotpedia.org/States_with_initiative_or_referendum/.

Barbaro, M., and D. W. Chen. 2009. "Bloomberg Sets Record for His Own Spending on Elections." *The New York Times*. Retrieved March 2, 2014, http://www.nytimes.com/2009/10/24/nyregion/24mayor.html?_r=0/.

Bartels, L. 1988. *Presidential Primaries and the Dynamics of Public Choice*. Princeton, NJ: Princeton University Press.

Bartels, L. M. 1985. "Resource Allocation in a Presidential Campaign." *Journal of Politics* 47(3): 928–936.

Bartels, L. 2000. "Partisanship and Voting Behavior, 1952–1996." *American Journal of Political Science* 44(1): 35–50.

Bartels, L. M. 2002. "Beyond the running tally: Partisan bias in political perceptions." *Political Behavior* 24(2): 117–150.

Bartels, L. 2006. "Priming and Persuasion in Presidential Campaigns." In *Capturing Campaign Effects*, edited by H. Brady and R. Johnston, 78–112. Ann Arbor, MI: University of Michigan Press.

Bartels, L. M. 2008. *Unequal Democracy: The Political Economy of the New Gilded Age.* Princeton, NJ: Princeton University Press.

Bartels, L. 2013. "Your Genes Influence Your Political Views. So What?" *The Washington Post: Monkey Cage.* Retrieved May 1, 2015, http://www.washingtonpost.com/blogs/monkey-cage/wp/2013/11/12/your-genes-influence-your-political-views-so-what/.

Basinger, S. and H. Lavine. 2005. "Ambivalence, Information and Electoral Choice." *American Political Science Review* 99(2): 169–184.

Bawn, K., Cohen, M., Karol, D., Masket, S., Noel, H. and Zaller, J. 2012. "A Theory of Political Parties: Groups, Policy Demands and Nominations in American Politics." *Perspectives on Politics* 10(03), pp. 571–597.

Beard, C., and B. Shultz. 1912. *Documents on the Statewide Initiative, Referendum, and Recall.* New York: Macmillan.

Beaudry, A., and B. Schaeffer. 1986. *Winning local and state elections.* New York, NY: Free Press.

Beckel, M. 2013. "In Montana, Dark Money Brings Down a Judicial Candidate." *Salon.* Retrieved March 2, 2015, http://www.salon.com/2013/05/16/in_montana_dark_money_brings_down_a_judicial_candidate_partner/.

Becker, J. 2004. "Many Voters Will Make Their Choice before Election Day." *South Bend Tribune.* August 29: B6.

Bentele, K. G., and E. E. O'Brien. 2013. "Jim Crow 2.0? Why States Consider and Adopt Restrictive Voter Access Policies." *Perspectives on Politics* 11(4): 1088–1116.

Berelson, R. B., P. N. Lazarsfeld, and W. M. McPhee. 1954. *Voting: A Study of Opinion Formation in a Presidential Campaign.* Chicago, IL: University of Chicago Press.

Bergan, D. E., A. S. Gerber, D. P. Green, and C. Panagopoulos. 2005. "Grassroots Mobilization and Voter Turnout in 2004." *Public Opinion Quarterly* 69(5): 760–777.

Berinsky, A. J. 2005. "The Perverse Consequences of Electoral Reform in the United States." *American Politics Research* 33(4): 471–491.

Berinsky, A. J., N. Burns, and M. W. Traugott. 2011. "Who Votes by Mail? A Dynamic Model of the Individual-Level Consequences of Voting-by-Mail Systems." *Public Opinion Quarterly* 65(2): 178–197.

Berkovitz, T. 1996. "Political Media Buying: A Brief Guide." *The Case Program, Kennedy School of Government, Harvard University.* Retrieved May 22, 2015, http://www.hks.harvard.edu/case/3pt/berkovitz.html/.

Berman, R. 2015. "Why Republicans Are Voting to Repeal Obamacare—Again." *The Atlantic.* Retrieved March 9, 2015, http://www.theatlantic.com/politics/archive/2015/02/why-republicans-are-voting-to-repeal-obamacare-again/385105/.

Berry, W. D., M. B. Berkman, and S. Schneiderman. 2000. "Legislative Professionalism and Incumbent Reelection: The Development of Institutional Boundaries." *American Political Science Review* 94(4): 859–874.

Besley, T., and S. Coate. 2008. "Issue Unbundling via Citizens' Initiatives." *Quarterly Journal of Political Science* 3(4): 379–397.

Bevan, T. 2014. "What Bruce Rauner Can Teach His Fellow Republicans." *Real Clear Politics.* Retrieved April 28, 2015, http://www.realclearpolitics.com/articles/2014/11/07/what_bruce_rauner_can_teach_his_fellow_republicans_124590.html/.

Binder, S. A. 2003. *Stalemate: Causes and Consequences of Legislative Gridlock.* Washington, D.C.: Brookings Institute.

Bingham, A. 2012. "Top 13 Quotes in Mitt Romney's Leaked Fundraiser Video." *ABC News.* Retrieved March 9, 2015, http://abcnews.go.com/Politics/OTUS/top-13-quotes-mitt-romneys-leaked-fundraiser-video/story?id=17264969#4/.

Blaemire, R. 2012. "An Explosion of Innovation: The Voter-Data Revolution." In *Margin of Victory: How Technologists Help Politicians Win Elections,* edited by N. G. Pearlman, 79–92. Santa Barbara, CA: Praeger.

Blais, A. 2000. *To Vote or Not to Vote?* Pittsburgh, PA: University of Pittsburgh Press.

Blake, A. 2012. "Michigan Democratic Party Encourages Crossover Voting in GOP Presidential Primary." *The Washington Post.* Retrieved April 24, 2015, http://www.washingtonpost.com/blogs/the-fix/post/michigan-democratic-party-encourages-crossover-voting-in-gop-presidential-primary/2012/02/22/gIQA1qjoTR_blog.html/.

Blumenthal, S. 1980. *The Permanent Campaign.* New York: Simon & Schuster.

Blumenthal, P. 2016. "Trump Has Spent Less Than Any Other Primary Front-Runner." *The Huffington Post.* Retrieved April 10, 2016. http://www.huffingtonpost.com/entry/donald-trump-campaign-spending_us_56f172e6e4b03a640a6bcda2.

Blumenthal, P., and A. Bycoffe. 2014. "Here Are the Top Super PAC Mega-Donors in 2014 Elections." *The Huffington Post.* Retrieved May 20, 2015, http://www.huffingtonpost.com/2014/10/31/super-pac-donors-2014_n_6084988.html/.

Boas, T. C. 2010. "Varieties of Electioneering: Success Contagion and Presidential Campaigns in Latin America." *World Politics* 62(4): 636–675.

Bonanos, C. 2016. "Read the Actual Reynolds Pamphlet from *Hamilton*, Page by Original Page." *Vulture.* Retrieved May 26, 2016, http://www.vulture.com/2016/01/read-the-actual-reynolds-pamphlet-from-hamilton.html.

Bond, R. M., C. J. Fariss, J. J. Jones, A. D. I. Kramer, C. Marlow, J. E. Settle, and J. H. Fowler. 2012. "A 61-Million Person Experiment in Social Influence and Political Mobilization." *Nature* 489(7415): 295–298.

Bonneau, C. W. 2004. "Patterns of Campaign Spending and Electoral Competition in State Supreme Court Elections." *The Justice System Journal* 25(1): 21–38.

Bor, S. 2014. "Using Social Network Sites to Improve Communication between Political Campaigns and Citizens in the 2012 Election." *American Behavioral Scientist* 58(9): 1195–1213.

Bovee, J. 1998. "How to Do Opposition Research on the Internet." *Campaigns & Elections* September.

Boutin, P. 2006. "A Grand Unified Theory of YouTube and MySpace: Point-and-Click Sites That Don't Tell You What to Do." *Slate.* Retrieved May 1, 2015, http://www.slate.com/articles/technology/technology/2006/04/a_grand_unified_theory_of_youtube_and_myspace.html.

Bowler, S. and T. A. Donovan. 2000. *Demanding Choices: Opinion, Voting, and Direct Democracy.* Ann Arbor, MI: University of Michigan Press.

Box-Steffensmeier, J. and S. De Boef. 2001. "Macropartisanship and Macroideology in the Sophisticated Electorate." *Journal of Politics* 63(1): 232–248.

Brader, T. 2005. "Striking a Responsive Chord: How Political Ads Motivate and Persuade Voters by Appealing to Emotions." *American Journal of Political Science* 49(2): 388–405.

Brader, T. 2006. *Campaigning for Hearts and Minds: How Emotional Appeals in Political Ads Work.* Chicago, IL: University of Chicago Press.

Brady, H. E., S. Verba, and K. L. Schlozman. 1995. "Beyond SES: A Resource Model of Political Participation." *The American Political Science Review* 89(2): 271–294.

Brennan Center for Justice. 2015. "Money in Politics." Brennan Center for Justice at New York University School of Law. Retrieved May 21, 2015, http://www.brennancenter .org/issues/money-politics/.

Bresnahan, J. 2014. "Second Harassment Accusation vs. Monica Wehby." *Politico*. Retrieved May 27, 2015, http://www.politico.com/story/2014/05/monica-wehby-harassment-106854.html/.

Brians, C. L., and Grofman, B., 2001. Election day registration's effect on US voter turnout. *Social Science Quarterly, 82*(1):170–183.

Bridges, A. 1997. *Morning Glories: Municipal Reform in the Southwest.* Princeton, NJ. Princeton University Press.

Broockman, D. 2009. "Do Congressional Candidates Have Reverse Coattails? Evidence from a Regression Discontinuity Design." *Political Analysis* 17(4): 418–434.

Broockman, D. E., and D. P. Green. 2013. "Do Online Advertisements Increase Political Candidates' Name Recognition or Favorability? Evidence from Randomized Field Experiments." *Political Behavior* 36(2): 263–289.

Brooks, D. J., and M. Muroy. 2012. "Assessing Accountability in a Post–*Citizens United* Era: The Effect of Attack Ad Sponsorship by Unknown Independent Groups." *American Politics Research* 40(3): 383–418.

Brown, C. 2015. "7 Reasons Your Campaign Should Never Stop Polling." *Campaigns & Elections.* Retrieved March 31, 2015, http://www.campaignsandelections.com/campaign-insider/2413/7-reasons-your-campaign-should-never-stop-polling/.

Bucy, E. P., and Grabe, M. E. 2007. "Taking Television Seriously: A Sound and Image Bite Analysis of Presidential Campaign Coverage, 1992–2004." *Journal of Communication,* 57: 652–675.

Burden, B. C., D. T. Canon, K. R. Mayer, and D. P. Moynihan. 2014. "Election Laws, Mobilization, and Turnout: The Unanticipated Consequences of Election Reform." *American Journal of Political Science* 58(1): 95–109.

Burner, D. 2008. "Alfred E. Smith." *American National Biography Online.* Retrieved May 25, 2015, http://www.anb.org/articles/06/06-00608.html?a=1&n=al%20smith&d=10&ss= 1&q=2/.

Burton, M. J., and D. M. Shea. 2010. *Campaign Craft: The Strategies, Tactics, and Art of Political Campaign Management.* Santa Barbara, CA: Praeger.

Cain, B. 2000. "Oregon Voters Going Postal in Election First." *The Seattle Times,* May 7: B1.

Cain, B., J. Ferejohn, and M. Fiorina. 1987. *The Personal Vote: Constituency Service and Electoral Independence.* Cambridge, MA: Harvard University Press.

Cain, S. A. 2011. "An Elite Theory of Political Consulting and Its Implications for U.S. House Election Competition." *Political Behavior* 33: 375–405.

Campaign Finance Institute. 2008. "Outside Soft Money Groups in 2008 Election." Retrieved April 5, 2016. http://www.cfinst.org/press/Preleases/08-10-31/Outside_ Soft_Money_Groups_in_2008_Elections.aspx.

Campaign Finance Institute. 2010. "New Figures Show That Obama Raised About One-Third of His General Election Funds from Donors Who Gave $200 Or Less." Retrieved April 5, 2016, http://www.cfinst.org/Press/PReleases/10-01-08/Revised_ and_Updated_2008_Presidential_Statistics.aspx.

Campaign Finance Institute. 2013. "Money vs. Money-Plus: Post-Election Reports Reveal Two Different Campaign Strategies." Retrieved March 16, 2015, http://www.cfinst

.org/Press/PReleases/13-01-11/Money_vs_Money-Plus_Post-Election_Reports_
Reveal_Two_Different_Campaign_Strategies.aspx/.

Campaign Finance Institute. 2014. "Senate Campaign Expenditures: Incumbents and Challengers, Major Party General Election Candidates by Election Outcome, 1980–2012 (full cycle, mean net dollars)." Retrieved March 16, 2015, http://www.cfinst.org/pdf/vital/VitalStats_t6.pdf/.

Campbell, A., P. Converse, W. Miller, and D. Stokes. 1960. *The American Voter.* New York: John Wiley and Sons.

Campbell, J. E. 1986. "Presidential Coattails and Midterm Losses in State Legislative Elections." *American Political Science Review* 80(1): 45–63.

Campbell, J. E. 2008. *The American Campaign: U.S. Presidential Campaigns and the National Vote.* College Station, TX: Texas A&M University Press.

Campbell, J. E. 2008b. "Editor's Introduction: Forecasting the 2008 National Elections." *PS: Political Science & Politics* 4: 679–682. doi:10.1017/S1049096508081006.

Campbell, J. E., and J. A. Sumners. 1990. "Presidential Coattails in Senate Elections." *American Political Science Review* 84: 513–24.

Canes-Wrone, B. 2006. *Who Leads Whom? Presidents, Policy, and the Public.* Chicago, IL: University of Chicago Press.

Cann, D. M., and J. B. Cole. 2011. "Strategic Campaigning, Closeness, and Voter Mobilization in U.S. Presidential Elections." *Electoral Studies* 30(2): 344–352.

Carey, J. M., R. G. Niemi, and L. W. Powell. 1998. "The Effects of Term Limits on State Legislatures." *Legislative Studies Quarterly* 23(2): 271–300.

Carey, J. M., R. G. Niemi, and L. W. Powell. 2000. "Incumbency and the Probability of Reelection in State Legislative Elections." *Journal of Politics* 66(3): 671–700.

Carney, D. 2015. "How We Won Texas." *Politico.* Retrieved April 1, 2015, http://www.politico.com/magazine/story/2015/02/greg-abbott-texas-114972.html#.VRxQfWYoMmQ/.

Carsey, T. M., and G. C. Wright. 1993. "State and National Factors in Gubernatorial and Senatorial Elections." *American Journal of Political Science* 42(3): 994–1002.

Caspi, D. 1996. "American-Style Electioneering in Israel: Americanization versus Modernization." In *Politics, Media, and Modern Democracy: An International Study of Innovations in Electoral Campaigning and their Consequences*, edited by D. L. Swanson and P. Mancini, 173–182. Westport, CT: Praeger.

Caumont, A. 2013. "12 Trends Shaping Digital News." *Pew Research Center: Fact Tank, News in the Numbers.* Retrieved May 26, 2015, http://www.pewresearch.org/fact-tank/2013/10/16/12-trends-shaping-digital-news/.

Center for Governmental Studies. 2003. "Investing in Democracy: Creating Public Financing of Elections in Your Community." Retrieved June 13, 2014, http://policyarchive.org/collections/cgs/index?section=5&id=231/.

Cha, J. M., and L. Kennedy. 2014. "Millions to the Polls: Practical Policies to Fulfill the Freedom to Vote for All Americans." *Demos.* Retrieved June 2, 2014, http://www.demos.org/millions-polls/.

Chaptman, D. 2008. "Negative Campaign Ads Contribute to a Healthy Democracy, Political Scientists Argues." *University of Wisconsin–Madison News.* Retrieved May 25, 2015, http://www.news.wisc.edu/14606/.

Christenson, D., C. D. Smidt, and C. Panagopoulos. 2014. "Deus ex Machina: Candidate Web Presence and the Presidential Nomination Campaign." *Political Research Quarterly* 67(1): 108–122.

Christenson, K. S. 2009. "Building a Database for Fundraising." *Campaigns & Elections.* Retrieved March 12, 2015, http://www.campaignsandelections.com/magazine/2083/building-a-database-for-fundraising/.

Christie, B., K. Kruesi, and A. DeMillo. 2015. "In Age of Campaign Mega-Groups, Solo Spenders Still Compete." *The Daily Mail.* Retrieved February 9, 2015, http://www.dailymail.co.uk/wires/ap/article-2945456/In-age-campaign-mega-groups-solo-spenders-compete.html.

Cilliza, C. 2007. "Romney"s Data Cruncher." *The Washington Post.* Retrieved April 6, 2015, http://www.washingtonpost.com/wp-dyn/content/article/2007/07/04/AR2007070401423.html/.

Cilizza, C., and A. Blake. 2012. "What Mitt Romney Did Right." *The Washington Post.* Retrieved May 26, 2015, http://www.washingtonpost.com/blogs/the-fix/wp/2012/11/29/what-mitt-romney-did-right/.

Citrin, J., E. Schickler, and J. Sides. 2003. "What If Everyone Voted? Simulating the Impact of Increased Turnout in Senate Elections." *American Journal of Political Science* 47(1): 75–90.

Claassen, R. L., D. B. Magleby, J. B. Monson and K. D. Patterson. 2008. "At Your Service: Voter Evaluations of Poll Worker Performance." *American Politics Research* 36: 612–634.

Clinton, W., and A. Clinton. 1999. "Telephone and Direct Mail." In D. Perlmutter, ed. *The Manship School Guide to Political Communication.* Baton Rouge, LA: LSU Press.

CMAG.n.d. "Methodology." *Tns Media Intelligence/CMAG.* Retrieved May 26, 2015, http://mycmag.kantarmediana.com/methodology.asp/.

Cohen, G. L. 2003. "Party over Policy: The Dominating Impact of Group Influence on Political Beliefs." *Journal of Personality and Social Psychology* 85(4): 808–822.

Cohen, M., D. Karol, H. Noel, and J. Zaller. 2008. *The Party Decides: Presidential Nominations before and after Reform.* Chicago, IL: University of Chicago Press.

Coleman, K. J. 2012. "The Presidential Nominating Process and the National Party Conventions, 2012: Frequently Asked Questions." *Congressional Research Service.* Retrieved May 27, 2015, https://www.fas.org/sgp/crs/misc/R42533.pdf/.

Confessore, N., and S. Cohen. 2016. "How Jeb Bush Spent $130 Million Running for President With Nothing to Show for It." *The New York Times.* Retrieved April 10, 2016. http://www.nytimes.com/2016/02/23/us/politics/jeb-bush-campaign.html.

Converse, P. E. 1964. "The Nature of Belief Systems in Mass Publics." in David E. Apter, (ed.), *Ideology and Discontent.* New York: Free Press.

Cornfield, M., and L. Rainie. 2006. "The Internet and Politics: No Revolution, Yet." *Pew Research Center, Pew Internet & American Life Project.* Retrieved May 1, 2015, http://www.pewresearch.org/2006/11/06/the-internet-and-politics-no-revolution-yet/ on May 1, 2015.

Costa, R. 2015. "Jeb Bush and His Allies Form Leadership PAC and Super PAC, Both Dubbed Right to Rise." *The Washington Post.* http://www.washingtonpost.com/blogs/post-politics/wp/2015/01/06/jeb-bush-forms-new-pac-right-to-rise/.

Cox, G. W., and J. N. Katz. 1996. "Why Did the Incumbency Advantage in U.S. House Elections Grow?" *American Journal of Political Science* 40(2): 478–497.

Cox, G. W., and J. N. Katz. 2002. *Elbridge Gerry's Salamander: The Electoral Consequences of the Reapportionment Revolution.* New York: Cambridge University Press.

Cox, G. W., and M. C. Munger. 1989. "Closeness, Expenditures, and Turnout in the 1982 U.S. House Elections." *The American Political Science Review* 83(1): 217–231.

Cruikshank, B. 2015. "Disclosure and Reporting Requirements." *National Conference of State Legislatures.* Retrieved May 26, 2016, http://www.ncsl.org/research/elections-and-campaigns/public-financing-of-campaigns-overview.aspx.

Crupi, A. 2011. "In Their Prime Broadcast Spot Costs Soar: Gap between Network and Cable CPMs Remains Vast " *Adweek*. Retrieved May 22, 2015, http://www.adweek .com/news/television/their-prime-broadcast-spot-costs-soar-132805/.

Cunningham, Anne, and Renita Coleman. 2003. "Outdoor Recall: An Examination of Outdoor Advertising Recall Effectiveness." Retrieved March 9, 2015, http:// halloutdooradvertising.com/benefits/Outdoor_Recall_Study.pdf.

Dahl, R. A. 1961. *Who Governs? Democracy and Power in an American City*. New Haven, CT: Yale University Press.

Dahl, R. A. 1971. *Polyarchy: Participation & Opposition*. New Haven, CT: Yale University Press.

Davey, M. 2010. "Under Fire for Abortion Deal, Stupak to Retire." *The New York Times*. Retrieved March 8, 2015, http://www.nytimes.com/2010/04/10/us/politics/10stupak .html?_r=0/.

Dawson, M. C. 1994. *Behind the Mule: Race and Class in African American Politics*. Princeton, NJ: Princeton University Press.

Delli Carpini, M. 1984. "Scooping the Voters? The Consequences of the Networks' Early Call of the1980 Presidential Race." *Journal of Politics* 46(3): 866–885.

Delli Carpini, M. X., and S. Keeter. 1997. *What Americans Know about Politics and Why It Matters*. New Haven, CT: Yale University Press.

Dickerson, J. 2011. "Obama's Victory Plan" *Slate*. Retrieved April 1, 2015, http://www.slate .com/articles/news_and_politics/politics/2011/12/president_obama_s_campaign_ advisers_reveal_the_outlines_of_his_re_election_strategy_it_s_not_pretty_.html/.

Dickerson, J. 2012. "Why Romney Never Saw It Coming." *Slate*. Retrieved February 10, 2015, http://www.slate.com/articles/news_and_politics/politics/2012/11/why_romney_was_ surprised_to_lose_his_campaign_had_the_wrong_numbers_bad.html/.

Dinkin, R. J. 1989. *Campaigning in America: A History of Election Practices*. Westport, CT: Greenwood Press.

Dobbs, M. 2008. "Was Obama Ever a Muslim?" *The Washington Post, the Fact Checker*. Retrieved May 25, 2015, http://voices.washingtonpost.com/fact-checker/2008/06/ was_obama_a_muslim.html/.

Doherty, B. J. 2007. "The Politics of the Permanent Campaign: Presidential Travel and the Electoral College." *Presidential Studies Quarterly* 37(4): 749–773.

Doherty, J. W. 2006. "The Hidden Network: Political Consultants Form Party Infrastructure." *Campaigns & Elections* 27(7): 39–42.

Dolan, Kathleen. 2010. "The Impact of Gender Stereotyped Evaluations on Support for Women Candidates." *Political Behavior* 32: 69–88.

Dowling, C. M., R. D. Enos, A. Fowler, and C. Panagopoulos. 2012. "Does Public Financing Chill Political Speech? Exploiting a Court Injunction as a Natural Experiment." *Election Law Journal: Rules, Politics, and Policy* 11(3): 302–315.

Downs. A. 1957. *An Economic Theory of Democracy*. Boston, MA: Addison–Wesley.

Druckman, J. N. 2004. "Priming the Vote: Campaign Effects in a U.S. Senate Election." *Political Psychology* 25(4): 577–594.

Druckman, J. N., and A. Lupia. 2000. "Preference Formation." *Annual Review of Political Science* 3: 1–24.

Druckman J. N., M. J. Kifer, and M. Parkin. 2009. "The Technological Development of Candidate Websites: How and Why Candidates Use Web Innovations." In *Politicking Online: The Transformation of Election Campaign Communications*, edited by Costas Panagopoulos, 249–271. New Brunswick, NJ: Rutgers University Press.

Dulio, D. A. 2004. *For Better or Worse?: How Political Consultants Are Changing Elections in the United States.* New York: State University of New York Press.

Dunaway, J., and R. M. Stein. 2012. "The Effects of Early Voting on Campaign Advertising." Presented at the State Politics and Public Policy Conference, Rice University, Houston, Texas.

Dunaway, J., and R. M. Stein. 2013. "Early Voting and Campaign News Coverage." *Political Communication* 30(2): 278–296.

Duverger, M. 1972. *Party Politics and Pressure Groups: A Comparative Introduction.* New York, NY: Thomas Y. Crowell.

Easley, J. 2014. "Five Reasons Mary Landrieu Lost." *The Hill.* Retrieved April 1, 2015, http://thehill.com/blogs/ballot-box/226238-five-reasons-mary-landrieu-lost/.

Edsall, T. B. 2013. "Political Beliefs Encoded in Our DNA?" *The New York Times: Opinionator.* Retrieved May 1, 2015, http://opinionator.blogs.nytimes.com/2013/10/01/are-our-political-beliefs-encoded-in-our-dna/?_r=1/.

Eggers, A. C., A. Fowler, J. Hainmueller, A. B. Hall, and J. M. Snyder Jr. 2015. "On the Validity of the Regression Discontinuity Design for Estimating Electoral Effects: New Evidence from over 40,000 Close Races." *American Journal of Political Science* 59(1): 259–274.

Elving, R. 2012. "Santorum & Co. Left to Mourn What Might Have Been in Michigan." *NPR.* Retrieved April 6, 2015, http://www.npr.org/blogs/itsallpolitics/2012/02/29/147615426/santorum-co-left-to-mourn-what-might-have-been-in-michigan/.

Endres, K. 2016. "The Accuracy of Micro-targeted Policy Positions." *PS: Political Science and Politics* (forthcoming).

Enns, P. K. and C. Wlezien. 2011. "Group Opinion and the Study of Representation." In *Who Gets Represented?*, P. K. Enns and C. Wlezien, eds. New York: Russell Sage Foundation.

Enos, R., A. Fowler and L. Vavreck. 2014. "Increasing Inequality: The Effect of GOTV Mobilization on the Composition of the Electorate." *Journal of Politics* 76(1): 273–288.

Enten, H. 2014. "Eric Cantor Upset: What Happened?" *Five Thirty Eight*: http://fivethirtyeight.com/datalab/the-eric-cantor-upset-what-happened/.

Erie, S. 1988. *Rainbow's End: Irish Americans and the Dilemmas of Urban Machine Politics.* Berkeley, CA: University of California Press.

Erikson, R. S., M. B. MacKuen, and J. A. Stimson. 2002. *The Macro Polity.* New York: Cambridge University Press.

Erikson, R., and T. Palfrey. 2000. "Equilibria in Campaign Spending Games: Theory and Data." *American Political Science Review* 94(3): 595–609.

Erikson, R. S., C. Panagopoulos, and C. Wlezien. 2010. "The Crystallization of Voter Preferences during the 2008 Presidential Campaign." *Presidential Studies Quarterly* 40(3): 482–496.

Erikson, R. S., Panagopoulos, C. and Wlezien, C. 2004. "Likely (and unlikely) voters and the assessment of campaign dynamics." *Public Opinion Quarterly*, 68(4): 588–601.

Erikson, R. S., and C. Wlezien. 2012. *The Timeline of Presidential Elections: How Campaigns Do (and Do Not) Matter.* Chicago, IL: University of Chicago Press.

Fahri, P. 2015. "2016 Campaigns Are Beefing Up Staffs. So Are the Media Who Will Cover Them." *The Washington Post.* Retrieved April 6, 2015, http://www.washingtonpost.com/lifestyle/style/2016-campaigns-are-beefing-up-staffs-so-are-the-media-who-will-cover-them/2015/02/23/9f1d2152-a66b-11e4-a7c2-03d37af98440_story.html/.

Farrell, D. 1996. "Campaign Strategies and Tactics." In *Comparing Democracies: Elections and Voting in Global Perspective*, edited by L. LeDuc et al. pp. 160–183. Thousand Oaks, CA: Sage.

Farrell, D. M. 2002. "Shopping in the U.S. Political Market: Campaign Modernization and the West European Party." In: Luther, R., Mueller-Rommel, F (eds). Political Parties in the New Europe. Oxford: Oxford University Press.

Farrell, D. M., R. Kolodny, and S. Medvic. 2001. "Parties and Campaign Professionals in a Digital Age." The Harvard International Journal of Press/Politics 6: 11–30.

Faucheux, R. 2002. Running for Office: The Strategies, Techniques and Messages Modern Political Candidates Need to Win Elections. New York: M. Evans and Company.

Federal Communications Commission (FCC). 2012. "Evolution of Cable Television." Federal Communications Commission. Retrieved April 6, 2015, http://www.fcc.gov/encyclopedia/evolution-cable-television/.

Federal Election Commission. (FEC). 2014. "Alison Grimes Lundergan and Mitch McConnell." Federal Election Commission. Retrieved March 3, 2014, http://www.fec.gov/data/CandidateSummary.do/.

Federal Election Commission (FEC). 2015. "Contribution Limits 2013–2014." Retrieved March 11, 2015, http://www.fec.gov/pages/brochures/contriblimits.shtml/.

Fineman, H., and P. Blumenthal. 2012. "Political Consultants Rake It In, $466 Million and Counting in 2012 Cycle." The Huffington Post. Retrieved February 10, 2015, http://www.huffingtonpost.com/2012/06/05/political-consultants-2012-campaign-big-money_n_1570157.html/.

Finn, M., and P. Ruffini. 2012. "The Quest for Victory: Campaigning Online for President." In Margin of Victory: How Technologists Help Politicians Win Elections, edited by N. G. Pearlman, 15–28. Santa Barbara, CA: Praeger.

Fiorina, M. P. 1981. Retrospective Voting in American National Elections. New Haven, CT: Yale University Press.

Fiorina, M. P., and S. J. Abrams. 2008. "Political Polarization in the American Public." Annual Review of Political Science 11: 563–588.

Fiorina, M. P., and S. J. Abrams. 2014. "Americans Aren't Polarized, Just Better Sorted." The Washington Post. Retrieved May 18, 2015, http://www.washingtonpost.com/blogs/monkey-cage/wp/2014/01/21/americans-arent-polarized-just-better-sorted/.

Fiorina, M. P., S. J. Abrams, and J. C. Pope. 2008. "Polarization in the American Public: Misconceptions and Misreadings." Journal of Politics 70(2): 556–560.

Fiorina, M. P., S. J. Abrams, and J. C. Pope. 2010. Culture War? The Myth of a Polarized America. London: Longman.

Fishkin, J. S. 2006. "Beyond Polling Alone: The Quest for an Informed Public." Critical Review 18: 157–165.

Fitzgerald, M. 2005. "Greater Convenience but Not Greater Turnout: The Impact of Alternative Voting Methods on Participation in the United States." American Politics Research 33(6): 842–867.

Fitzpatrick, A. 2012. "Obama, Romney Take over the Web with Advertisements." Mashable. Retrieved May 22, 2015, http://mashable.com/2012/09/11/obama-romney-web-ads/.

Flanigan, W., N. Zingale, E. Theiss-Morse, M. Wagner. 2015. Political Behavior of the American Electorate. 13th edition. Thousand Oaks, CA: CQ Press.

Fowler, L. 1993. Candidates, Congress and the American Democracy. Ann Arbor, MI: University of Michigan Press.

Fowler, E. F., and T. N. Ridout. 2010. "Advertising Trends in 2010." The Forum 8(4): 1–16.

Fowler, E. F., and T. N. Ridout. 2013. "Negative, Angry, and Ubiquitous: Political Advertising in 2012." *The Forum* 10(4): 51–61.

Fowler, E. F., Michael M. Franz and T. N. Ridout. 2016. *Political Advertising in the United States*. Boulder, CO: Westview Press.

Francia, P., J. Green, P. Herrnson, L. Powell, and C. Wilcox. 2003. *The Financiers of Congressional Elections: Investors, Ideologues and Intimates*. New York: Columbia University Press.

Francia, P. L., and P. S. Herrnson. 2003. "The Impact of Public Finance Laws on Fundraising in State Legislative Elections." *American Politics Research* 31(5): 520–539.

Francia, P. L., and P. S. Herrnson. 2004. "The Synergistic Effect of Campaign Effort and Election Reform on Voter Turnout in State Legislative Elections." *State Politics & Policy Quarterly* 4(1): 74–93.

Franz, M. M. 2013. "Interest Groups in Electoral Politics: 2012 in Context." *The Forum* 10(4):62–79.

Franz, M. M. and Ridout, T. N. 2007. "Does political advertising persuade?" *Political Behavior* 29(4), 465–491.

Franz, M. M. and T. N. Ridout. 2010. "Political Advertising and Persuasion in the 2004 and 2008 Presidential Elections." *American Politics Research* 38(2): 303–329.

Franz, M. M., P. R. Freedman, K. M. Goldstein, and T. M. Ridout. 2007. *Campaign Advertising and American Democracy*. Philadelphia, PA: Temple University Press.

Friedenberg, R., and J. Trent. 2011. *Political Campaign Communication: Principles and Practices*, 7th ed. Lanham, MD: Rowman & Littlefield.

Friess, S. 2012. "How Howard Dean's Bid Gave Birth to Web Campaigning." *Politico*. Retrieved April 30, 2014, http://www.politico.com/news/stories/0912/81834.html/.

Fuller, J. 2014. "Obamacare Will Likely Help Republicans in 2014. But, 2016 Is a Different Deal." *The Washington Post*. Retrieved May 26, 2015, http://www.washingtonpost.com/blogs/the-fix/wp/2014/04/28/do-republicans-benefit-from-obamacare-in-2014-maybe-but-it-isnt-likely-to-help-them-in-2016/.

Fuller, J. 2014. "From George Washington to Shaun McCutcheon: A brief-ish history of campaign finance reform." *The Washington Post*. Retrieved May 26, 2016, https://www.washingtonpost.com/news/the-fix/wp/2014/04/03/a-history-of-campaign-finance-reform-from-george-washington-to-shaun-mccutcheon/.

Gaebler. 2015a. "WBBM Radio Advertising Costs." *Gaebler.com: Resources for Entrepreneurs*. Retrieved May 22, 2015, http://www.gaebler.com/WBBM-FM-IL-Radio-Advertising-Costs++19026/.

Gaebler. 2015b. "WAAG Radio Advertising Costs." *Gaebler.com: Resources for Entrepreneurs*. Retrieved May 22, 2015, http://www.gaebler.com/WAAG-FM-IL-Radio-Advertising-Costs++18658/.

Gaines, B. J., J. H. Kuklinski, P. J. Quirk, B. Payton, and J. Verkuilen. 2007. "Same Facts, Different Interpretations: Partisan Motivation and Opinion on Iraq." *Journal of Politics* 69(4): 957–974.

Garthwaite, C., and T. J. Moore. 2012. "Can Celebrity Endorsements Affect Political Outcomes? Evidence from the 2008 U.S. Democratic Presidential Primary." *The Journal of Law, Economics, & Organization* 29(2): 355–383.

Gearan, A., and M. Gold. 2014. "Hillary Clinton Begins Weighting Details of a 2016 Bid, with a Spring Announcement Likely." *The Washington Post*. Retrieved March 6, 2015, http://www.washingtonpost.com/politics/hillary-clinton-begins-weighing-details-of-a-2016-bid-with-a-spring-announcement-likely/2014/12/11/088bccac-80a5-11e4-9f38-95a187e4c1f7_story.html/.

Geer, J. 2006. *In Defense of Negativity: Attack Ads in Presidential Campaigns*. Chicago, IL: University of Chicago Press.

Gelman, A., and G. King. 1990. "Estimating Incumbency Advantage without Bias." *American Journal of Political Science* 34(4): 1143–1164.

Gelman, A., and G. King. 1993. "Why Are American Presidential Election Campaign Polls So Variable When Votes Are So Predictable?" *British Journal of Political Science* 23(4): 409–451.

Gerber, A. S. 2011. "Field Experiments in Political Science." In *The Handbook of Experimental Political Science*, edited by J. N. Druckman et al., 115–138. New York: Cambridge University Press.

Gerber, A. S., J. G. Gimpel, D. P. Green, and D. R. Shaw. 2011. "How Large and Long-Lasting Are the Persuasive Effects of Television Campaign Ads? Results from a Randomized Field Experiment." *American Political Science Review* 105(1): 135–150.

Gerber, A., and Green, D. P. 1998. Rational learning and partisan attitudes. *American journal of political science* 42(3):794–818.

Gerber, A. S., and D. P. Green. 2000. "The Effect of Canvassing, Telephone Calls, and Direct Mail on Voter Turnout: A Field Experiment." *The American Political Science Review* 94(3): 653–663.

Gerber, A. S., D. P. Green, and C. W. Larimer. 2008. "Social Pressure and Voter Turnout: Evidence from a Large-Scale Field Experiment." *American Political Science Review* 102(1): 33–48.

Gerber, A. S., D. P. Green, and C. W. Larimer. 2010. "An Experiment Testing the Relative Effectiveness of Encouraging Voter Participation by Including Feelings of Pride or Shame." *Political Behavior* 32(3): 409–422.

Gerber, A. S., G. A. Huber, D. Doherty, C. M. Dowling, and S. E. Ha. 2010. "Personality and Political Attitudes: Relationships across Issue Domains and Political Contexts." *American Political Science Review* 104(1): 111–133.

Gerber, A. S., G. A. Huber, D. D. Doherty, C. M. Dowling, and C. Panagopoulos. 2013. "Big Five Personality Traits and Responses to Persuasive Appeals: Results from Voter Turnout Experiments." *Political Behavior* 35(4): 687–728.

Gerber, A. S., D. Karlan, and D. Bergan. 2009. "Does the Media Matter? A Field Experiment Measuring the Effect of Newspapers on Voting Behavior and Political Opinions." *American Economic Journal: Applied Economics* 1(2): 35–52.

Gerber, E. R., and R. B. Morton. 1998. "Primary Election Systems and Representation." *Journal of Law, Economics, & Organization* 14(2): 304–324.

Giammo, J. D., and B. J. Brox. 2010. "Reducing the Costs of Participation: Are States Getting a Return on Early Voting?" *Political Research Quarterly* 63(2): 295–303.

Gilens, M. 2001. "Political Ignorance and Collective Policy Preferences." *American Political Science Review* 95(2): 379–396.

Gilens, M. 2012. *Affluence and Influence: Economic Inequality and Political Power in America*. Princeton, NJ: Princeton University Press.

Gilens, M., and B. I. Page. 2014. "Testing Theories of American Politics: Elites, Interest Groups, and Average Citizens." *Perspectives on Politics* 12(3): 564–581.

Gimpel, J. G., K. M. Kaufmann, and S. Pearson-Merkowitz. 2007. "Battleground States versus Blackout State: The Behavioral Implications of Modern Presidential Campaigns." *Journal of Politics* 69(3): 786–797.

Girzynski, A., and D. Breaux. 1991. "Money and Votes in State Legislative Elections" *Legislative Studies Quarterly* 16(2): 203–217.

Goldstein, K., and P. Freedman. 2002 "Campaign Advertising and Voter Turnout: New Evidence for a Stimulation Effect." *Journal of Politics* 64(3): 721–740.

Goldstein, K., and T. N. Ridout. 2004. "Measuring the Effects of Televised Political Advertising in the United States." *Annual Review of Political Science* 7(1): 205–226.

Gosnell, H. 1927. *Getting Out the Vote: An Experiment in the Stimulation of Voting.* Chicago, IL: University of Chicago Press.

Gowrisankaran, G., M. F. Mitchell, and A. Moro. 2004. "Why Do Incumbent Senators Win? Evidence from a Dynamic Selection Model." (No. W10748). *National Bureau of Economic Research Working Paper Series.*

Graber, D. 2000. *Processing Politics: Learning from Television in the Internet Age.* Chicago, IL: University of Chicago Press.

Grading State Disclosure Laws. 2008. *Grading State Disclosure: Evaluating States' Efforts to Bring Sunlight to Political Money.* Retrieved March 3, 2015, http://campaigndisclosure.org/gradingstate/.

Green, D. and A. Gerber. 2012. *Get Out the Vote! 3rd edition.* Washington, DC: Brookings Institution Press.

Green, D., B. Palmquist, and E. Schickler. 2002. *Partisan Hearts and Minds.* New Haven, CT: Yale University Press.

Green, D. P., and J. S. Krasno. 1988. "Salvation for the Spendthrift Incumbent: Re-estimating the Effects of Campaign Spending in House Elections." *American Journal of Political Science* 32(November): 884–907.

Green, D. P., J. S. Krasno, A. Coppock, B. D. Farrer, B. Lenoir, J. N. Zingher. 2016. "The Effects of Lawn Signs on Vote Outcomes: Results from Four Randomized Field Experiments." *Electoral Studies* 41: 143–150.

Green, D. P., M. C. McGrath, and P. M. Aronow. 2013. "Field Experiments and the Study of Voter Turnout." *Journal of Elections, Public Opinion & Parties* 23(1): 27–48.

Green, D. P., and J. K. Smith. 2003. "Professionalization of Campaigns and the Secret History of Collective Action Problems." *Journal of Theoretical Politics* 15(3): 312–339.

Greenfield, H. 2007. "YouTube Boon May Mean New Jobs on Campaigns." *National Journal* January. http://nationaljournal.com/about/technologydaily/

Grim, R., and S. Siddiqui. 2013. "Call Time For Congress Shows How Fundraising Dominates Bleak Work Life." *The Huffington Post.* Retrieved March 12, 2015, http://www.huffingtonpost.com/2013/01/08/call-time-congressional-fundraising_n_2427291.html/.

Gronke, Paul. 2008. "Early Voting Reforms and American Elections." *William and Mary Bill of Rights Journal* 17: 423–451.

Gronke, P., and D. K. Toffey. 2008. "The Psychological and Institutional Determinants of Early Voting." *Journal of Social Issues* 64(3): 503–524.

Grossman, M. 2012. *The Not-So-Special Interests: Interest Groups, Public Representation, and American Governance.* Stanford, CA: Stanford University Press.

Grossman, M., and C. B. K. Dominguez. 2009. "Party Coalitions and Interest Group Networks." *American Politics Research* 37(5): 767–800.

Gueorguieva, V. 2009. "Voters, MySpace, and YouTube." In *Politicking Online: The Transformation of Election Campaign Communications*, edited by Costas Panagopoulos, 233–248. New Brunswick, NJ: Rutgers University Press.

Gurevitch, M. 1999. "Wither the Future? Some Afterthoughts." *Political Communication* 16(3): 281–284.

Gurian, P. H. 1993. "Primaries versus Caucuses: Strategic Considerations of Presidential Candidates." *Social Science Quarterly* 74(2): 310–321.

Hajnal, Z. L. 2009. *America's Uneven Democracy: Race, Turnout, and Representation in City Politics.* New York: Cambridge University Press.

Hall, R. L., and F. W. Wayman. 1990. "Buying Time: Moneyed Interests and the Mobilization of Bias in Congressional Committees." *American Political Science Review* 84(30): 797–820.

Hall, T. E. and M. K. Moore. 2011. "Election Administration." In S. K. Medvic, ed. *New Directions in Campaigns and Elections* (pp. 1–16). New York: Routledge.

Hall, T. J., Q. Monson and K. D. Patterson. 2007. "Poll Workers and the Vitality of Democracy: An Early Assessment." *PS: Political Science & Politics* 40: 647–654.

Hallin, D. C. 1992. "Sound Bite News: Television Coverage of Elections, 1968–1988." *Journal of Communication* 42: 5–24.

Hanmer, M. 2007. "An Alternative Approach to Estimating Who Is Most Likely to Respond to Changes in Registration Laws." *Political Behavior* 29(1): 1–30.

Hanmer, M. 2009. *Discount Voting: Registration Reforms and Their Effects.* New York: Cambridge University Press.

Hansford, T. G., and B. T. Gomez. 2010. "Estimating the Electoral Effects of Voter Turnout." *American Political Science Review* 104(2): 268–288.

Harbridge, L. 2015. *Is Bipartisanship Dead? Policy Agreement and Agenda-Setting in the House of Representatives.* New York: Cambridge University Press.

Harwood, D. 2004. "Election System a Failure." *The Denver Post*, October 31, 2004.

Hatemi, P. K., N. A. Gillespie, L. J. Eaves, B. S. Maher, B. T. Webb, A. C. Heath, S. E. Medland, D. C. Smyth, H. N. Beeby, S. D. Gordon, G. W. Montgmery, G. Zhu, E. M. Byrn, and N. G. Martin. 2011. "A Genome-Wide Analysis of Liberal and Conservative Political Attitudes." *Journal of Politics* 73(1): 271–385.

Hayes, D. 2005. "Candidate Qualities through a Partisan Lens: A Theory of Trait Ownership." *American Journal of Political Science* 49(4): 908–923.

Hayes, D. 2008. "Party Reputations, Journalistic Expectations: How Issue Ownership Influences Election News." *Political Communication* 25(4): 377–400.

Hayes, D. 2010. "The Dynamics of Agenda Convergence and the Paradox of Competiveness in Presidential Elections." *Political Research Quarterly* 63(3): 594–611.

Haygood, R. P. 2011. "The Past a Prologue: Defending Democracy against Voter Suppression Tactics on the Eve of the 2012 Elections." *Rutgers Law Review* 64: 1019–1064.

Hedlin, S. 2015. "Do Long Ballots Offer Too Much Democracy?" The Atlantic. November 3. Accessed online on May 20, 2016 at: http://www.theatlantic.com/politics/archive/2015/11/long-ballots-democracy/413701/.

Heerwig, J. A., and B. J. McCabe. 2009. "Education and Social Desirability Bias: The Case of a Black President." *Social Science Quarterly* 90(3): 674–686.

Heerwig, J. A., and K. Shaw. 2014. "Through a Glass, Darkly: The Rhetoric and Reality of Campaign Finance Disclosure." *The Georgetown Law Journal* 102: 1443–1500.

Helliker, K. 2007. "Political Ads Stage a Comeback in Newspapers." *The Wall Street Journal*. Retrieved April 5, 2016. http://www.wsj.com/articles/SB118541344062578440.

Hendricks, M. 2012. "Newspaper Readers Vote, and Voters Read Newspapers: Key Election Study Underscores American Voters' Media Use." *Newspaper Association of America.* Retrieved May 27, 2015, http://www.naa.org/News-and-Media/Press-Center/Archives/2012/Newspaper-Readers-Vote-and-Voters-Read-Newspapers.aspx/.

Helling, D. 2014. "Outsiders Spending Millions in Kansas Governor's Race." *The Kansas City Star*. Retrieved March 2, 2015, http://www.kansascity.com/news/government-politics/article1601763.html/.

Henninger, D. 2012. "Romney's Image Problem." *The Wall Street Journal*. Retrieved May 1, 2015, http://www.wsj.com/articles/SB10000872396390444914904577617570848363612/.

Herndon, R. F. and S. Pfeifer. 2004. "7,000 Orange County Voters Were Given Bad Ballots." *Los Angeles Times*. Retrieved May 26, 2016, http://articles.latimes.com/2004/mar/09/local/me-machines9.

Herrnson, P. 2000. *Congressional Elections: Campaigns at Home and in Washington*, 3rd ed. Washington, D.C.: CQ Press.

Herrnson, P. S., A. K. Stokes-Brown, and M. Hindman. 2007. "Campaign Politics and the Digital Divide: Constituency Characteristic, Strategic Considerations, and Candidate Internet Use in State Legislative Elections." *Political Research Quarterly* 60(1): 31–42.

Herron, M. C. and Smith, D. A. 2012. Souls to the polls: Early voting in Florida in the shadow of House Bill 1355. *Election Law Journal*, 11(3): 331–347.

Hersh, E. D. 2015. *Hacking the Electorate: How Campaigns Perceive Voters*. New York: Cambridge University Press.

Hersh, E. D., and B. F. Schaffner. 2013. "Targeted Campaign Appeals and the Value of Ambiguity." *Journal of Politics* 75(2): 520–534.

Hibbing, J. 2013. "Why Biology Belongs in the Study of Politics." *The Washington Post: Monkey Cage*. Retrieved October 30, 2015, https://www.washingtonpost.com/news/monkey-cage/wp/2013/11/27/why-biology-belongs-in-the-study-of-politics/.

Hibbing, J. R., K. B. Smith, and J. R. Alford. 2014. *Predisposed: Liberals, Conservatives, and the Biology of Political Differences*. New York: Routledge.

Hill, S. J., J. Lo, L. Vavreck, and J. Zaller. 2013. "How Quickly We Forget: The Duration of Advertising Effects from Mass Communication." *Political Communication*. 30(4): 521–547.

Hillygus, D. S., and T. G. Shields. 2008. *The Persuadable Voter: Wedge Issues in Presidential Campaigns*. Princeton, NJ: Princeton University Press.

Hogan, R. E. 2004. "Challenger Emergence, Incumbent Success, and Electoral Accountability in State Legislative Elections." *Journal of Politics* 66(4): 1283–1303.

Hogan, R. E. 2005. "State Campaign Finance Laws and Interest Group Electioneering Activities." *Journal of Politics* 67(3): 887–906.

Holbrook, A., and J. Krosnick. 2010. "Social Desirability Bias in Voter Turnout Reports: Tests Using the Item Count Technique." *Public Opinion Quarterly* 74(1): 37–67.

Holbrook, T. M. 1994. "Campaigns, National Conditions, and U.S. Presidential Elections." *American Journal of Political Science* 38: 973–998.

Holbrook, T. M. 1996. *Do Campaigns Matter?* Thousand Oaks, CA: Sage.

Holian, D., and C. Prysby. 2014. "Candidate Character Traits in the 2012 Presidential Election." *Presidential Studies Quarterly* 44(3): 484–505.

Hollander, B. A. 2010. "Persistence in the Perception of Barack Obama as a Muslim in the 2008 Presidential Campaign." *Journal of Media and Religion* 9(2): 55–66.

Holtz-Bacha, C., and L. L. Kaid. 2006. "Political Advertising in International Comparison." In *The Sage Handbook of Political Advertising*, edited by C. Holtz-Bacha and L. L. Kaid, 3–13. Thousand Oaks, CA: Sage.

Hopkins, D. 2014. "All Politics Is Presidential." *Five Thirty Eight*. Retrieved March 2, 2015, http://fivethirtyeight.com/features/all-politics-is-presidential/.

Huber, G. A., and K. Arceneaux. 2007. "Identifying the Persuasive Effects of Presidential Advertising." *American Journal of Political Science* 51(4): 957–977.

Huddy, L., S. Feldman, C. Taber, and G. Lahav. 2005. "Threat, Anxiety, and Support of Anti-Terrorism Policies." *American Journal of Political Science* 49(3): 493–608.

Huddy, L., and N. Terkildsen. 1993. "Gender Stereotypes and the Perception of Male and Female Candidates." *American Journal of Political Science* 37: 119–147.

Ikstens, J., Smilov, D. and Walecki, M. 2002. "Campaign finance in Central and Eastern Europe: Lessons learned and challenges ahead." *IFES Report,* Washington DC.

Issenberg, S. 2012a. "A More Perfect Union: How President Obama's Campaign Used Big Data to Rally Individual Voters." *Technology Review.* Retrieved May 18, 2015, http://www.technologyreview.com/featuredstory/508836/how-obama-used-big-data-to-rally-voters-part-1/.

Issenberg, S. 2012b. "Can You Win a Campaign without Conducting Polls?" *Slate.* Retrieved April 1, 2015, http://www.slate.com/articles/news_and_politics/victory_lab/2012/03/rick_santorum_can_the_former_pennsylvania_senator_win_a_campaign_without_conducting_a_single_poll_.2.html/.

Issenberg, S. 2012c. "Early Bird Gets the Delegates." *Slate.* Retrieved May 26, 2015, http://www.slate.com/articles/news_and_politics/victory_lab/2012/03/mitt_romney_s_early_voting_mastery_his_rivals_never_stood_a_chance_.html/.

Issenberg, S. 2012d. *Victory Lab: The Secret Science of Winning Campaigns.* New York: Crown.

Issenberg, S. 2012e. "Why Obama Is Better at Getting Out the Vote: Lots of Door-Knocking—and Years of Statistical Analysis." *Slate.* http://www.slate.com/articles/news_and_politics/victory_lab/2012/11/obama_s_get_out_the_vote_effort_why_it_s_better_than_romney_s.html/.

Issenberg, S. 2014. "Dept. of Experiments: Obama's Campaign Turned Politics into a Science. But What If There Are Still Some Things in Politics That Money Can't Buy?" *Politico.* Retrieved April 27, 2015, http://www.politico.com/magazine/story/2014/02/campaign-science-dept-of-experiments-103671.html#.VT5l1GYoMnQ/.

Iyengar, S. 2002. "The Effects of Media-Based Campaigns on Candidate and Voter Behavior: Implications for Judicial Elections." *Indiana Law Review* 35: 691–700.

Iyengar, S., and D. R. Kinder. 1987. *News That Matters.* Chicago, IL: University of Chicago Press.

Jacobs, A. 2006. "Evicted, Newark's Mayor Finds Another Blighted Street." *The New York Times.* Retrieved May 26, 2015, http://www.nytimes.com/2006/11/20/nyregion/20newark.html?fta=y.

Jacobson, G. C. 1978. "The Effects of Campaign Spending in Congressional Elections." *American Political Science Review,* 72(June): 469–491.

Jacobson, G. C. 1980. *Money in Congressional Elections.* New Haven, CT: Yale University Press.

Jacobson, G. C. 1990. "The Effects of Campaign Spending in House Elections: New Evidence for Old Arguments." *American Journal of Political Science* 34(2): 334–362.

Jacobson, G. C. 2004. *The Politics of Congressional Elections. 6th ed.* New York: Harper Collins.

Jacobson, G. C. 2006. "Measuring Campaign Spending Effects in U.S. House Elections." In *Capturing Campaign Effects,* edited by Henry E. Brady and Richard Johnston, 199–220. Ann Arbor, MI: University of Michigan Press.

Jacobson, G. C. 2009. "The 2008 Presidential and Congressional Elections: Anti-Bush Referendum and Prospects for the Democratic Majority." *Political Science Quarterly* 124(1): 1–30.

Jacobson, G. C. 2014. "Barack Obama and the Nationalization of Electoral Politics." *Electoral Studies* 40: 471–481.

Jacobson, G. C. 2015. "How Do Campaigns Matter?" *Annual Review of Political Science* 18(1): 1–17.

Jacobson, G. C., and J. Carson. 2015. *The Politics of Congressional Elections*, 9th ed. Lanham, MD: Rowman & Littlefield.

Jacobson, G. C., and S. Kernell. 1981. *Strategy and Choice in Congressional Elections*. New Haven: Yale University Press.

Jamieson, K. H. 2013. "Messages, Micro-Targeting, and New Media Technologies." *The Forum* 11(3): 429–435.

Jan, T. 2013. "For Freshman in Congress, Focus Is On Raising Money." *The Boston Globe.* Retrieved May 20, 2015, http://www.bostonglobe.com/news/politics/2013/05/11/freshman-lawmakers-are-introduced-permanent-hunt-for-campaign-money/YQMMMoqCNxGKh2h0tOIF9H/story.html/.

Jester, D., and K. Roberts. 2013. "The Next Evolution in Media Buying." *Campaigns & Elections.* Retrieved May 21, 2015, http://www.campaignsandelections.com/magazine/1758/the-next-evolution-in-media-buying/.

Johnson, D. W. 2000. "The Business of Political Consulting." In *Campaign Warriors: Political Consultants in Elections*, edited by James A. Thurber and Candice J. Nelson, 37–52. Washington, D.C.: Brookings Institution.

Johnston, R., M. G. Hagen, and K. H. Jamieson. 2004. *The 2000 Presidential Election and the Foundations of Party Politics*. Cambridge, UK: Cambridge University Press.

Jones, A. 2012. "Political Newcomers Face High Costs and Difficult Odds" *CNN*, January 22. Retrieved February 9, 2015, http://www.cnn.com/2012/01/22/politics/newcomers-campaign-costs/.

Jones, D. R. 2001. "Party Polarization and Legislative Gridlock." *Political Research Quarterly* 54(1): 124–141.

Judd, D. R., and T. Swanstrom. 2008. *City Politics: The Political Economy of Urban America, 6th edition*. London, UK: Longman.

Kahn, K. F., and P. Kenney. 2004. *No Holds Barred: Negativity in U.S. Senate Campaigns.* Upper Saddle River, NJ: Pearson Prentice Hall.

Kahn, Kim Fridkin, and Patrick J. Kenney. 1999. *The Spectacle of U.S. Senate Campaigns.* Princeton, NJ: Princeton University Press.

Kahneman, D., P. Slovic, and A. Tversky. 1982. *Judgment under Uncertainty: Heuristics and Biases.* New York: Cambridge University Press.

Kalla, J. L., and Broockman, D. E. 2015. "Campaign Contributions Facilitate Access to Congressional Officials: A Randomized Field Experiment." *American Journal of Political Science.* doi:10.1111/ajps.12180.

Kardish, C. 2014. "Outsiders Add Money and Negativity to State and Local Elections." *Governing: The States and Localities.* Retrieved March 2, 2015, http://www.governing.com/topics/elections/gov-outside-spending-state-local-elections.html/.

Karp, J. A., and S. A. Banducci. 2000. "Going Postal: How All-Mail Elections Influence Turnout." *Political Behavior* 22(3): 223–239.

Karp, J. A., and S. A. Banducci. 2008. "Political Efficacy and Participation in Twenty-Seven Democracies: How Electoral Systems Shape Political Behavior." *British Journal of Political Science* 38(2): 311–334.

Katz, C. 2009. "Mayor Bloomberg Spent $102M on Campaign to Win Third Term—or $175 per Vote." *NY Daily News.* Retrieved March 2, 2015, http://www.nydailynews.com/new-york/mayor-bloomberg-spent-102m-campaign-win-term-175-vote-article-1.414005/.

Katz, R. S. and Mair, P. 1995. "Changing Models of Party Organization and Party Democracy the Emergence of the Cartel Party. *Party politics* 1(1): 5–28.

Kazee, T., and M. Thornberry. 1990. "Where's the Party? Congressional Candidate Recruitment and American Party Organizations." *The Western Political Quarterly*, 43(1), 61–80.

Kazin, M., R. Edwards, and A. Rothman. 2011. *The Concise Princeton Encyclopedia of American Political History*. Princeton, NJ: Princeton University Press.

Keith, B. E., D. B. Magelby, C. J. Nelson, E. Orr, M. C. Westlye, and R. E. Wolfinger. 1992. *The Myth of the Independent Voter*. Berkeley, CA: University of California Press.

Kenski, K., B. W. Hardy, and K. H. Jamieson 2010. *The Obama Victory: How Media, Money, and Message Shaped the 2008 Election*. New York: Oxford University Press.

Key, V. O. 1942. *Politics, Parties, and Pressure Groups*. New York: Crowell.

Key, V. O. 1949. *Southern Politics in State and Nation*. Knoxville, TN: University of Tennessee Press.

Key, V. O. 1966. *The Responsible Electorate*. New York: Vintage Books.

Keyssar, A. 2009. *The Right to Vote: The Contested History of Democracy in the United States*. New York: Basic Books.

Kim, S., C. S. Taber, and M. Lodge. 2010. "A Computational Model of the Citizen as Motivated Reasoner: Modeling the Dynamics of the 2000 Presidential Elections." *Political Behavior* 32(1): 1–28.

Kimball, D. C., M. Kropf and L. Battles. 2006. "Helping America Vote? Election Administration, Partisanship and Provisional Votes in the 2004 Presidential Election." *Election Law Journal* 5: 447–461.

Kinder, D. R., M. D. Peters, R. P. Abelson, and S. T. Fiske. 1980. "Presidential Prototypes." *Political Behavior* 2(4): 315–337.

Kinder, Donald R. 1986. "Presidential Character Revisited." In *Political Cognition*, edited by Richard R. Lau and David O. Sears. Hillsdale, NJ: Erlbaum.

King, G., and A. Gelman. 1991. "Systematic Consequences of Incumbency Advantage in U.S. House Elections." *American Journal of Political Science* 35(1): 110–138.

Klapper, J. T. 1960. *The Effects of Mass Communication*. New York, NY: Free Press.

Klar, S. 2013. "The Influence of Competing Identity Primes on Political Preferences." *Journal of Politics* 75(4): 1108–1124.

Klein, J. 2007. *Politics Lost: How Politicians Have Become Less Courageous and More Interested in Keeping Power Than in Doing What's Right for America* reprint ed. New York: Broadway Books.

Knack, S., and J. White. 2000. "Election Day Registration and Turnout Inequality." *Political Behavior* 22(1): 29–44.

Koch, J. W. 2000. "Do Citizens Apply Gender Stereotypes to Infer Candidates' Ideological Orientations?" *Journal of Politics* 62(2): 414–429.

Kolodny, R. and M. Hagen. (2009). "What Drives the Cost of Political Advertising?" In *Routledge Handbook of Political Management*, D. Johnson, ed. New York: Routledge. pp. 194–207.

Konstantinides, A. 2013. "Viral Videos That Derailed Political Careers." *ABC News*. Retrieved May 1, 2015, http://abcnews.go.com/Politics/viral-videos-derailed-political-careers/story?id=21182969/.

Krasno, J. 1994. *Challengers, Competition and Reelection: Comparing Senate and House Elections*. New Haven, CT: Yale University Press.

Kraus, J. 2011. "Campaign Finance Reform Reconsidered: New York City's Public Finance Program at Twenty." In *Public Financing in American Elections*, edited by C. Panagopoulos. Philadelphia PA: Temple University Press.

Krebs, T. B. 1998. "The Determinants of Candidates' Vote Share and the Advantages of Incumbency in City Council Elections." *American Journal of Political Science* 42(3): 921–935.

Krupnikov, Y. 2012. "Negative Advertising and Voter Choice: The Role of Ads in Candidate Selection." *Political Communication* 29(4): 387–413.

Kuklinski, J. H. 1978. "Representativeness and Elections: A Policy Analysis." *American Political Science Review* 72(1): 165–177.

Kuklinski, J. H., P. Quirk, J. Jerit, D. Schneider, and R. F. Rich. 2000. "Misinformation and the Currency of Democratic Citizenship." *Journal of Politics* 62(3): 790–816.

Kunda, Z. 1990. "The Case for Motivated Reasoning." *Psychological Bulletin* 108(3): 489–498.

Lachman, S. 2014. "NRA Takes on the Tea Party in Competitive GOP Primary." *The Huffington Post.* Retrieved March 8, 2015, http://www.huffingtonpost.com/2014/03/17/nra-mike-simpson-_n_4978722.html/.

Lane, C. 2006. "Justices Reject Vermont's Campaign Finance Law." *The Washington Post.* Retrieved March 16, 2015, http://www.washingtonpost.com/wp-dyn/content/article/2006/06/26/AR2006062600407.html/.

Larsen, R. W. 1985. "Hill Campaign Well-Targeted." *The Seattle Times*, November 6: A16.

Lassen, D. D. 2005. "The Effect of Information on Voter Turnout: Evidence from a Natural Experiment." *American Journal of Political Science* 49(1): 103–118.

Lau, R. and D. Redlawsk. 1997. "Voting Correctly." *American Political Science Review* 91(3): 585–598.

Lau, R., and D. Redlawsk. 2006. *How Voters Decide.* New York: Cambridge University Press.

Lau, R. R., S. Sigelman, and I. B. Rovner. 2007. "The Effects of Negative Political Campaigns: A Meta-Analytic Reassessment." *Journal of Politics* 69(4): 1776–1209.

Lawless, Jennifer. 2012. *Becoming a Candidate: Political Ambition and the Decision to Run for Office.* New York: Cambridge University Press.

Lawson, C., G. S. Lenz, A. Baker, and M. Meyers. 2010, "Looking Like a Winner: Candidate Appearance and Electoral Success in New Democracies." *World Politics* 62(4): 561–593.

Layman, G. C. 1997. "Religion and Political Behavior in the United States: The Impact of Beliefs, Affiliations, and Commitment from 1980 to 1993." *Public Opinion Quarterly* 61(2): 288–316.

Layman, G. C., and T. M. Carsey. 2002. "Party Polarization and 'Conflict Extension' in the American Electorate." *American Journal of Political Science* 46(4): 786–802.

Layman, G. C., T. M. Carsey, and J. M. Horowitz. 2006. "Party Polarization in American Politics: Characteristics, Causes, and Consequences." *Annual Review of Political Science* 9: 83–110.

Lazarsfeld, P. F., B. Berelson, and H. Gaudet. 1944. *The People's Choice: How the Voter Makes up His Mind in a Presidential Campaign.* New York: Duell, Sloan, & Pearce.

League of Women Voters. n.d. "Redistricting California: Voters Choose a Citizens Commission Instead of the Legislature." *League of Women Voters of California: Education Fund.* Retrieved May 26, 2015, https://cavotes.org/issues/redistricting-implementation/citizens%20redistricting%20commission/.

Leahy, M. P. 2013. "'Inside the Cave.' Documents Obama Campaign Tech Superiority over GOP." *Breibart News.* Retrieved May 18, 2015, http://www.breitbart.com/big-government/2013/01/07/inside-the-cave-documents-obama-campaign-tech-superiority-over-gop/.

LeDuc, L., R. Niemi, and P. Norris. 2002. *Comparing Democracies 2: New Challenges in the Study of Elections and Voting.* Thousand Oaks, CA: Sage.

Lee, J. and K. Quealy. 2016. "Introducing the Upshot's Encyclopedia of Donald Trump's Twitter Insults." January 28. Retrieved April 10, 2016, http://www.nytimes.com/2016/01/29/upshot/introducing-the-upshots-encyclopedia-of-donald-trumps-twitter-insults.html.

Leff, Lisa. 2008. "Calif. Gay Marriage Ban Backers Target Businesses." *USA Today*, October 24. http://usatoday30.usatoday.com/news/politics/2008-10-24-668737864_x.htm

Leff, Lisa. 2009. "Donors Pumped $83M to Calif. Gay Marriage Campaign." *The Christian Post.*,February2.http://www.christianpost.com/news/donors-pumped-83m-to-calif-gay-marriage-campaign-36755/

Leighley, J. E., and J. Nagler. 2013. *Who Votes Now? Demographics, Issues, Inequality, and Turnout in the United States.* Princeton, NJ: Princeton University Press.

Leonard, J. 2014. "A $250,000 Election? This Year's City Council Race Is Shaping Up as the Most Expensive in History." *Ann Arbor Observer*. http://annarborobserver.com/articles/a__250_000_election__full_article.html/.

Levin, S. M. 2006. "Keeping It Clean: Public Financing and American Elections." *Center for Governmental Studies*. Retrieved March 2, 2015, http://users.polisci.wisc.edu/kmayer/466/Keeping_It_Clean.pdf/.

Levine, B. J., and M. Johnston. 2014. "Campaign Contributions Should Be Anonymous." *The Washington Post*. Retrieved May 21, 2015, http://www.washingtonpost.com/opinions/making-campaign-contributions-anonymous/2014/09/04/65f2b8d8-2e39-11e4-9b98-848790384093_story.html/.

Levinthal, D. 2012. "The Fight for the 5$ Donation." *Politico*. Retrieved May 21, 2015, http://www.politico.com/news/stories/1012/81888.html/.

Lewis-Beck, M. S., and M. Stegmaier. 2000. "Economic Determinants of Electoral Outcomes." *Annual Review of Political Science* 3: 183–219.

Lieberman, David. 2007. "Presidential Coffers Set to Boost Ad Spending." *USA Today*. December 5.

Lijphart, A. 1997. "Unequal Participation: Democracy's Unresolved Dilemma." *American Political Science Review* 91(1): 1–14.

Lioz, A., and B. Bowie. 2013. "McCutcheon Money: The Projected Impact of Striking Aggregation Contribution Limits." *Demos: An Equal Say and an Equal Change for All* and *U.S. PIRG: Federation of State PIRGs*.

Lipsitz, K. 2009. "The Consequences of Battleground and "Spectator" State Residency for Political Participation." *Political Behavior*, 31(2): 187–209.

Lipsitz, K. 2011. *Competitive Elections and the American Voter*. Philadelphia, PA: University of Pennsylvania Press.

Lipsitz, K., and C. Panagopoulos. 2009. "Filled Coffers: Campaign Contributions and Contributors in the 2008 Elections." *Journal of Political Marketing* 10(1–2): 43–57.

Lizza, R. 2008. "Making It: How Chicago Shaped Obama." *The New Yorker*. Retrieved April 10, 2016. http://www.newyorker.com/magazine/2008/07/21/making-it

Lodge, M., and C. S. Taber. 2013. *The Rationalizing Voter*. New York: Cambridge University Press.

Lowi, T. 1979. *The End of Liberalism*. New York: Norton.

Lueders, B. 2011. "Campaign Financing Dead in Wisconsin." *WisconsinWatch.org*. Retrieved March 12, 2015, http://wisconsinwatch.org/2011/06/campaign-financing-dead-in-wisconsin/.

Lundry, A. 2012. "Making It Personal: The Rise of Micro-targeting." In *Margin of Victory: How Technologists Help Politicians Win Elections*, edited by Nathaniel G. Pearlman, 161–174. Santa Barbara, CA: Praeger.

Lupia, A. 1994. "Shortcuts versus Encyclopedias: Information and Voting Behavior in California Insurance Reform Elections." *American Political Science Review* 88(1): 63–76.

Madison, J. 1961 [1787–1788]. *The Federalist Papers*, edited by Clinton Rossiter. New York: New American Library.

Mair, L. 2012. "Ignore at Your Peril: Campaigns and the Blogosphere." In *Margin of Victory: How Technologists Help Politicians Win Elections*, edited by N. G. Pearlman, 41–52. Santa Barbara, CA: Praeger.

Mair, P. 2000. "Public Aid to Parties and Candidates." In *The International Encyclopedia of Elections*, edited by R. Rose, 241–243. Washington, D.C.: Congressional Quarterly Press.

Malbin, M. 2012. "48% of President Obama's 2011 Money Came from Small Donors— Better Than Doubling 2007. Romney's Small Donors: 9%." *The Campaign Finance Institute*. Retrieved March 12, 2015, http://cfinst.org/Press/PReleases/12-02-08/Small_Donors_in_2011_Obama_s_Were_Big_Romney_s_Not.aspx/.

Malbin, M. 2006. *The Election after Reform: Money, Politics, and the Bipartisan Campaign Reform Act*. Oxford: Rowman & Littlefield.

Malhotra, N. 2008. "The Impact of Public Financing on Electoral Competition: Evidence from Arizona and Maine." *State Politics & Policy Quarterly* 8(3): 263–281.

Malkin, M. 2008. "Universal Voter Registration?" Retrieved June 4, 2014, http://michellemalkin.com/2008/11/10/universal-voter-registration/#comments/.

Marcus, G. E., R. Neuman, and M. MacKuen. 2000. *Affective Intelligence and Political Judgment*. Chicago, IL: University of Chicago Press.

Marquardt, A. 2008. "Obama says Palin's family off limits." CNN. Retrieved May 26, 2016, http://www.cnn.com/2008/POLITICS/09/01/obama.palin/.

Marshall, J. 2013. "What Online Ads Really Cost." Retrieved March 9, 2015, http://digiday.com/publishers/what-online-ads-really-cost/.

Martinez, M., and J. Gill. 2005. "The Effects of Turnout on Partisan Outcomes in U.S. Presidential Elections 1960-2000." *Journal of Politics* 67(4): 1248–1274.

Masket, S. E., and J. B. Lewis. 2007. "A Return to Normalcy? Revisiting the Effects of Term Limits on Competiveness and Spending in California Assembly Elections." *State Politics and Policy Quarterly* 7(1): 20–38.

Matsusaka, J. G. 2005. "The Eclipse of Legislatures: Direct Democracy in the 21st Century." *Public Choice* 124(1–2): 157–177.

Matsusaka, J. G. 2006. "Direct Democracy and Electoral Reforms." In *The Marketplace of Democracy: Electoral Competition and American Politics*, edited by Michael P. McDonald and John Samples, 151–170. Baltimore: Brookings Institution Press.

Mattes, K., and D. Redlawsk. 2014. *The Positive Case for Negative Campaigning*. Chicago, IL: University of Chicago Press.

Mayer, K. R., T. Werner, and A. Williams. 2006. "Public Funding Programs and Competition." In *The Marketplace of Democracy: Electoral Competition and American Politics*, edited by Michael P. McDonald and John Samples, 245–267. Baltimore: Brookings Institution Press.

Mayhew, D. R. 1974. *Congress: The Electoral Connection*. New Haven, CT: Yale University Press.

Mazmanian, A. 2012. "Obama, Romney in Hashtag Battle on Twitter." *Yahoo! News*. Retrieved May 1, 2015, https.//www.yahoo.com/news/obama-romney-hashtag-battle-twitter-143001590--politics.html.

McCain, J., and R. Feingold. 2004. "A Campaign Finance Law That Works." *The Washington Post*, October 23: A22 Retrieved May 21, 2015, http://www.washingtonpost.com/wp-dyn/articles/A55769-2004Oct22.html.

McClosky, H. 1958. "Conservatism and Personality." *American Political Science Review* 52(1): 27–45.

McCormick, R. L. 1979. "The Party Period and Public Policy: An Exploratory Hypothesis." *Journal of American History* 66(2): 279–298.

McCoy, T. 2012. "The Creepiness Factor: How Obama and Romney Are Getting to Know You." *The Atlantic*. Retrieved May 21, 2015, http://www.theatlantic.com/politics/archive/2012/04/the-creepiness-factor-how-obama-and-romney-are-getting-to-know-you/255499/.

McDermott, M. L. 1997. "Voting Cues in Low-Information Elections: Candidate Gender as a Social Information Variable in Contemporary United States Elections." *American Journal of Political Science* 41(1): 270–283.

McDermott, M. L. 2009. "Religious Stereotyping and Voter Support for Evangelical Candidates." *Political Research Quarterly* 62: 340–354.

McDermott, M. L., and C. Panagopoulos. 2015. "Be All That You Can Be: The Electoral Impact of Military Service as an Information Cue." *Political Research Quarterly* 68(2): 293–305.

McDonald, M. P. 2015. "National General Election VEP Turnout Rates, 1789–Present." *United States Elections Project*. Retrieved May 25, 2015, http://www.electproject.org/national-1789-present/.

McKenna, E., and H. Han. 2014. *Groundbreakers: How Obama's 2.2 Million Volunteers Transformed Campaigning in America*. New York: Oxford University Press.

McKinley, Jesse, and Johnson, Kirk. 2008. "Mormons Tipped Scale in Ban on Gay Marriage." *New York Times*, November 15. http://www.nytimes.com/2008/11/15/us/politics/15marriage.html?_r=4&hp=&oref=slogin&pagewanted=print/.

Medvic, S. K. 2001. *Political Consultants in U.S. Congressional Elections*. Columbus, OH: Ohio State University Press.

Medvic, S. K. 2014. *Campaigns & Elections: Players and Processes*, 2nd ed. New York: Routledge.

Mele, N. 2012. "Skyrocketing Numbers: Online Fundraising for Political Campaigns." In *Margin of Victory: How Technologists Help Politicians Win Elections*, edited by N. G. Pearlman, 15–28. Santa Barbara CA: Praeger.

Mendelberg, T. 2001. *The Race Card: Campaign Strategy, Implicit Messages and the Norm of Equality*. Princeton, NJ: Princeton University Press.

Migally, A., and S. Liss. 2010. "Small Donor Matching Funds: the NYC Election Experience." *Brennan Center for Justice*. Retrieved March 2, 2015, http://www.brennancenter.org/page/-/Small%20Donor%20Matching%20Funds-The%20NYC%20Election%20Experience.pdf/.

Miller, W. 1955. "Presidential Coattails: A Study in Political Myth and Methodology." *The Public Opinion Quarterly* 19(4): 353–368.

Milyo, J., D. Primo, and M. Jacobsmeier. 2011. "Does Public Financing of State Election Campaigns Increase Voter Turnout?" In *Public Financing in American Elections*, edited by C. Panagopoulos. Philadelphia, PA: Temple University Press.

Minnite, L. 2010. *The Myth of Voter Fraud*. Ithaca, NY: Cornell University Press.

Moe, A. 2015. "Congress Sends Obamacare Repeal to President for First Time." *NBC News*. Retrieved May 25, 2016, http://www.nbcnews.com/news/us-news/congress-send-obamacare-repeal-president-n491316.

Mondak, J. 1990. "Determinants of Coattail Voting." *Political Behavior* 12(3): 265–288.

Mondak, J. 2010. *Personality and the Foundations of Political Behavior*. New York: Cambridge University Press.

Mondak, J. J., M. V. Hibbing, D. Canache, M. A. Seligson, and M. R. Anderson. 2010. "Personality and Civic Engagement: An Integrative Framework for the Study of Trait Effects on Political Behavior." *American Political Science Review* 104(1): 85–110.

Monroe, N. W., and D. E. Sylvester. 2011. "Who Converts to Vote-By-Mail? Evidence from a Field Experiment." *Election Law Journal*. 10(1): 15–35.

Montjoy, R. 2010. "The Changing Nature . . . and Costs . . . of Election Administration." *Public Administration Review* 70(6): 867–875.

Morain, Dan, and Garrison, Jessica. 2008. "Prop. 8 Foes, Fans Amass $60 Million." *Los Angeles Times*, October 25. http://articles.latimes.com/2008/oct/25/local/me-marriagemoney25/.

Morris, D. 2008. "Money Is Losing Its Mojo." *Campaigns & Elections* 29(2): 50.

Morris, J. S. 2005. "The Fox News Factor." *The International Journal of Press/Politics* 10(3): 56–79.

Morris, J. S. 2007. "Slanted Objectivity? Perceived Media Bias, Cable News Exposure, and Political Attitudes." *Social Science Quarterly*. 88(3): 707–728.

Mutz, D. 1995. "Effects of Horse-Race Coverage on Campaign Coffers: Strategic Contributing in Presidential Primaries." *Journal of Politics* 57(4): 1015–1042.

Nadeau, R., and M. S. Lewis-Beck. 2001. "National Economic Voting in U.S. Presidential Elections." *Journal of Politics* 63(1): 159–181.

Nagler, J., and Jan Leighley. 1992. "Presidential Campaign Expenditures: Evidence on Allocations and Effects." *Public Choice* 73(3): 319–333.

Nagourney, A. 1998. "New D'Amato Ad Attacks Missed Votes by Schumer." *The New York Times*. Retrieved April 6, 2015, http://www.nytimes.com/1998/10/02/nyregion/new-d-amato-ad-attacks-missed-votes-by-schumer.html/.

Nagourney, A. 1999. "Sound Bites over Jerusalem." *The New York Times Magazine*, April 25, 41–70. Retrieved May 15, 2015, http://www.nytimes.com/1999/04/25/magazine/sound-bites-over-jerusalem.html/.

Nagourney, A. 2008. "Campaigns Adjust Their Pace to Meet Short Season." *The New York Times*. Retrieved May 11, 2015, http://www.nytimes.com/2008/09/10/us/politics/10schedule.html?pagewanted=print&_r=0/.

Nagourney, A., and J. Zeleny. 2008. "Obama Forgoes Public Funds in First for Major Candidate." *The New York Times*. Retrieved March 12, 2015, http://www.nytimes.com/2008/06/20/us/politics/20obamacnd.html?_r=0.

National Conference of State Legislatures. 2011. "Contribution Limits: An Overview." Retrieved May 20, 2015, http://www.ncsl.org/research/elections-and-campaigns/campaign-contribution-limits-overview.aspx/.

National Conference of State Legislatures. 2013. "Public Financing of Campaigns: An Overview." http://www.ncsl.org/research/elections-and-campaigns/public-financing-of-campaigns-overview.aspx/.

National Conference of State Legislatures. 2015a. "Absentee and Early Voting." Retrieved May 11, 2015, http://www.ncsl.org/research/elections-and-campaigns/absentee-and-early-voting.aspx/.

National Conference of State Legislatures. 2015b. "Same Day Voter Registration." Retrieved May 11, 2015, http://www.ncsl.org/research/elections-and-campaigns/same-day-registration.aspx/.

National Conference of State Legislatures. 2015c. "Voter Identification Requirements/Voter ID Laws." Retrieved November 3, 2015, http://www.ncsl.org/research/elections-and-campaigns/voter-id.aspx/.

Narula, S. K., R. Jacobs, and J. Dhikuare. 2013. "32 Republicans Who Caused the Government Shutdown: Meet the House Conservative Hardliners." *The Atlantic.* Retrieved May 28, 2015, http://www.theatlantic.com/politics/archive/2013/10/32-republicans-who-caused-the-government-shutdown/280236/.

New York Times. 1988. "George Bush and Willie Horton." November 4. Retrieved April 6, 2015, http://www.nytimes.com/1988/11/04/opinion/george-bush-and-willie-horton.html/.

NGP VAN n.d. "Voter Activation Network and NGP Software to Merge." Retrieved April 30, 2015, https://www.ngpvan.com/voter-activation-network-and-ngp-software-merge/.

Nickerson, D. W. 2007. "Quality Is Job One: Professional and Volunteer Voter Mobilization Calls." *American Journal of Political Science* 51: 269–282.

Nickerson, D. W., and T. Rogers. 2014. "Political Campaigns and Big Data." *The Journal of Economic Perspectives* 28(2): 51–73.

Nie, N., S. Verba, and J. Petrocik. 1979. *The Changing American Voter.* Cambridge: Harvard University Press.

Nielsen, R. K. 2012. *Ground Wars: Personalized Communication in Political Campaigns.* Princeton, NJ: Princeton University Press.

Niquette, M. 2005. "Opponents Make Case to Kick Amendments off Ballot: Blackwell Mistakenly Allowed Out-Of-State Petition Circulators, Ohio First Argues." *The Columbus Dispatch.* September, 9: 03B.

Niquette, M. 2006. "Primary Voting Begins Tuesday—Relaxed Absentee Ballot Rules Will Be Put to Test." *The Columbus Dispatch*, March 27: 01C.

Nordheimer, J. 1992. "Cable Becomes New Player in Political Ad Game." *The New York Times.* Retrieved April 6, 2015, http://www.nytimes.com/1992/11/03/nyregion/cable-becomes-new-player-in-political-ad-game.html/.

Norris, P. 2004. *Electoral Engineering: Voting Rules and Political Behavior.* New York: Cambridge University Press.

Nyczepir, D. 2012. "A Rapid Response Battle on Twitter." *Campaigns & Elections.* Retrieved May 21, 2015, http://www.campaignsandelections.com/campaign-insider/467/a-rapid-response-battle-on-twitter/.

Nyhan, B. 2010. "Why the 'Death Panel' Myth Wouldn't Die: Misinformation in the Health Care Reform Debate." *The Forum* 8(1): 1–24 (Article 5).

Obama, B. 2008. "Campaign Stop in Florida." *Presidentialrhetoric.com.* Retrieved May 15, 2015, http://www.presidentialrhetoric.com/campaign2008/obama/10.20.08.html/.

Ohman, M., H. Zainulbhai, J. Santucci, and M. Walecki. N.d. "Political Finance Regulation: The Global Experience." *The International Foundation for Electoral Systems.* Retrieved May 27, 2015, http //www.eods.eu/library/IFES.Political_Finance_Regulation_The_Global_Experience.pdf

Oliver, J. E., and S. E. Ha. 2007. "Vote Choice in Suburban Elections." *American Political Science Review* 101(3): 393–408.

OpenSecrets.org. 2015a. "Election Stats." *Center for Responsive Politics.* Retrieved March 11, 2015, https://www.opensecrets.org/bigpicture/elec_stats.php?cycle=2012/.

OpenSecrets.org. 2015b. "Expenditures." *Center for Responsive Politics.* Retrieved May 21, 2015, https://www.opensecrets.org/expends/.

OpenSecrets.org. 2015c. "Super PACs." *Center for Responsive Politics*. Retrieved March 16, 2015, https://www.opensecrets.org/pacs/superpacs.php/.

OpenSecrets.org. 2015d. "Top 50 Federally Focused Organizations." *Center for Responsive Politics*. Retrieved March 16, 2015, http://www.opensecrets.org/527s/527cmtes.php?level=C&cycle=2014/.

OpenSecrets.org. 2015f. "Outside Spending." *Center for Responsive Politics*. Retrieved March 16, 2015, https://www.opensecrets.org/outsidespending/.

Orr, J. 2012. "Barack Obama's 'Horses and Bayonets' Comment Becomes Internet Hit." *The Telegraph*. Retrieved April 6, 2015, http://www.telegraph.co.uk/news/worldnews/us-election/9628566/Barack-Obamas-horses-and-bayonets-comment-becomes-internet-hit.html/.

Panagopoulos, C. 2004. "The Polls—Trends: Electoral Reform." *Public Opinion Quarterly* 68(4): 623–640.

Panagopoulos, C. 2006. "Vested Interests: Interest Group Resource Allocation in Presidential Campaigns." *Journal of Political Marketing* 5(1/2): 59–78. Reprinted in *Campaigns and Political Marketing*, edited by W. Steger et al. Binghamton, NY: Hayworth Press, 2006.

Panagopoulos, C. 2009a. "Campaign Dynamics in Battleground and Non-Battleground States." *Public Opinion Quarterly* 73(10): 119–129.

Panagopoulos, C. 2009b. *Politicking Online: The Transformation of Election Campaign Communications*. New Brunswick, NJ: Rutgers University Press.

Panagopoulos, C. 2009c. "Street Fight: The Impact of a Street Sign Campaign on Voter Turnout." *Electoral Studies* 28(2): 309–313.

Panagopoulos, C. 2010a. "Affect, Social Pressure and Prosocial Motivation: Field Experimental Evidence of the Mobilizing Efforts of Pride, Shame, and Publicizing Voting Behavior." *Political Behavior* 32(3): 369–386.

Panagopoulos, C. 2010b. "Are Caucuses Bad for Democracy?" *Political Science Quarterly* 125(3): 425–442.

Panagopoulos, C. 2011. "Voter Turnout in the 2010 Congressional Midterm Elections." *PS: Political Science & Politics* 44(2): 317–319.

Panagopoulos, C. 2012. "Campaign Context and Preference Dynamics in U.S. Presidential Elections." *Journal of Elections, Public Opinion & Parties* 22(2): 123–137.

Panagopoulos, C. 2013a. "Campaign Effects and Dynamics in the 2012 Election." *The Forum* 10(4): 36–39.

Panagopoulos, C. 2013b. "Positive Social Pressure and Prosocial Motivation: Evidence from a Large-Scale Field Experiment on Voter Mobilization." *Political Psychology* 34(2): 265–275.

Panagopoulos, C. 2013c. "Who Participates in Exit Polls?" *Journal of Elections, Public Opinion and Parties* 23(4): 444–455.

Panagopoulos, C. 2014a. "I've Got My Eyes On You: Implicit Social Pressure and Prosocial Behavior." *Political Psychology* 35: 23–33.

Panagopoulos, C. 2014b. "Raising Hope: Hope Inducement and Voter Turnout." *Basic and Applied Social Psychology* 36(6): 493–501.

Panagopoulos, C. 2014c. "Watchful Eyes: Implicit Observability Cues and Voting." *Evolution and Human Behavior* 35: 279–284.

Panagopoulos, C. 2015. "Bases Loaded: Changing Campaign Strategies in U.S. Presidential Elections." *Party Politics*. 22(2): 179–190.

Panagopoulos, C., and D. Bergan. 2004. "Contributions and Contributors in the 2004 Presidential Election Cycle." *Presidential Studies Quarterly* 36(2): 155–171.

Panagopoulos, C., and J. Bowers. 2012. "Do Newspaper Ads Raise Voter Turnout? Evidence from a Randomized Field Experiment." *Working Paper.*

Panagopoulos, C., and K. Endres. 2015. "The Enduring Relevance of National Presidential Nominating Conventions." *Forum* 13(4): 559–576.

Panagopoulos, C., and B. Farrer. 2014. "Polls and Elections Preelection Poll Accuracy and Bias in the 2012 General Elections." *Presidential Studies Quarterly* 44(2): 352–363.

Panagopoulos, C., and P. L. Francia. 2009. "Grassroots Mobilization in the 2008 Presidential Election." *Journal of Political Marketing* 8(4): 315–333.

Panagopoulos, C., and D. P. Green. 2008. "Field Experiments Testing the Impact of Radio Advertisements on Electoral Competition." *American Journal of Political Science* 52(1): 156–168.

Panagopoulos, C., and D. P. Green. 2011. "Spanish-Language Radio Advertisements and Latino Voter Turnout in the 2006 Congressional Elections: Field Experimental Evidence." *Political Research Quarterly* 64(30): 588–599.

Panagopoulos, C., C. W. Larimer, and M. Condon. 2014. "Social Pressure, Descriptive Norms, and Voter Mobilization." *Political Behavior* 36(2): 451–469.

Panagopoulos, C., and J. Thurber. 2003. "Do Image-Makers Need a Makeover? (Or, Why Do Americans Hate Political Consultants?) Assessing Public Perceptions about Political Consultants." *Campaigns & Elections* October/November.

Panagopoulos, C., and P. W. Wielhouwer. 2008. "The Ground War 2000–2004: Strategic Targeting in Grassroots Campaigns." *Presidential Studies Quarterly* 38(2): 347–362.

Panagopoulos, C., and A. Weinschenk. 2016. *A Citizen's Guide to U.S. Elections: Empowering Democracy in America.* New York: Routledge.

Parti, T. 2011. "Will 2012 Be the End of the Presidential Public Financing System?" *OpenSecrets.org: Center for Responsive Politics.* Retrieved May 21, 2015, http://www.opensecrets.org/news/2011/08/the-end-of-presidential-public-financing/.

Pearlman, N. G. 2012. "Bootstrapping an Enterprise: NGP and the Evolution of Campaign Software." In *Margin of Victory: How Technologists Help Politicians Win Elections,* edited by N. G. Pearlman, 79–92. Santa Barbara, CA: Praeger.

Pearson, R., B. Secter, and J. Chase. 2014. "Quinn, Rauner in Final Frenzy to Get Out the Vote." *The Chicago Tribune.* Retrieved April 28, 2015, http://www.chicagotribune.com/news/ct-quinn-rauner-get-out-vote-met-1102-20141101-story.html#page=1/.

Pelissero, J. P. 2003. "The Political Environment of Cities in the Twenty-First Century." In *Cities, Politics, and Policy: A Comparative Analysis,* edited by. John P. Pelissero, 10. Washington, D.C.: CQ Press.

Penhale, E. 1997. "Paul Allen Stars in TV Ad to Sway Stadium Voters." *Seattle Post-Intelligencer.* June 3: B1.

Petrocik, J. R. 1996. "Issue Ownership in Presidential Elections, with a 1980 Case Study." *American Journal of Political Science* 40(3): 825–850.

Petrocik, J. R., W. L. Benoit, and G. J. Hansen. 2003. "Issue Ownership and Presidential Campaigning, 1952–2000." *Political Science Quarterly* 118(4): 599–626.

Pew Research Center. 2014. "Political Polarization in the American Public: How Increasing Uniformity and Partisan Antipathy Affect Politics, Compromise, and Everyday Life." *Pew Research Center: U.S. Politics & Policy.* Retrieved May 18, 2015, http://www.people-press.org/2014/06/12/political-polarization-in-the-american-public/.

Pinto-Duschinsky, M. 2001." Overview." In *Handbook on Funding of Parties and Election Campaigns.* Stockholm: International IDEA.

Plasser, F. 2000. "American Campaign Techniques Worldwide." *The Harvard International Journal of Press/Politics* 5(4): 33–54.

Plasser, F., and G. Lengauer. 2009. "Television Campaigning Worldwide." In *Routledge Handbook of Political Management*, edited by D. W. Johnson, 253–271. New York: Routledge.

Plasser, F., and G. Plasser. 2002. *Global Political Campaigning: A Worldwide Analysis of Campaign Professionals and Their Practices.* Westport, CT: Praeger.

Pohlig, C. 2000. "West Valley Gets out the Vote on School Levy—Interest Running High in Election That Could Bring Big District Cuts if Voters Defeat Levy." *Yakima Herald Republic*, May 12: 1A-6.

Polsby, N. W. 1968. "The Institutionalization of the U.S. House of Representatives." *American Political Science Review* 62(1): 144–168.

Popkin, Samuel L. 1994. *The Reasoning Voter. Communication and Persuasion in Presidential Campaigns*, 2nd ed. Chicago: University of Chicago Press.

Powell, G. B., Jr. 1986. "American Voter Turnout in Comparative Perspective." *The American Political Science Review* 80(1): 17–43.

Powers, S. 2012. "Newt Gingrich Calls on 'Super PAC' to Pull Anti-Romney Ads in S.C." *The Los Angeles Times.* Retrieved March 9, 2015, http://articles.latimes.com/2012/jan/13/news/la-pn-newt-gingrich-pac-bain-ads-20120113/.

PQ Media. 2004. "Political Media Buying 2004." Retrieved March 9, 2015, http://www.pqmedia.com/pmb2004-es.pdf/.

PQ Media. 2010. "Political Campaign Media Spending 2010." Retrieved March 9, 2015, http://www.pqmedia.com/about-press-20101215-pcms2010.html/.

Primo, D. M., J. Milyo, and T. Groseclose. 2006. "State Campaign Finance Reform and Competitiveness." In *The Marketplace of Democracy: Electoral Competition and American Politics*, edited by Michael P. McDonald and John Samples, 268–285. Baltimore, MD: Brookings Institution Press.

Prior, M. 2007. *Post-Broadcast Democracy: How Media Choice Increases Inequality in Political Involvement and Polarizes Elections.* New York: Cambridge University Press.

Randall, K. 2015. "Neuropolitics, Where Campaigns Try to Read Your Mind." *The New York Times.* Retrieved May 26, 2016, http://www.nytimes.com/2015/11/04/world/americas/neuropolitics-where-campaigns-try-to-read-your-mind.html?_r=0.

Raney, R. F. 2000. "From the Keyboard, Arizonans Cast Votes." *The New York Times.* Retrieved May 11, 2015, http://www.nytimes.com/library/tech/00/03/cyber/articles/10vote.html/.

Rappeport, A. 2015. "'Humble Upbringing' Emerges as an Early G.O.P Campaign Theme." *The New York Times.* Retrieved April 1, 2015, http://www.nytimes.com/politics/first-draft/2015/02/24/walker-and-rubio-take-jabs-at-jebs-wealth/.

Rauf, D. S. 2014. "Ethics Commission Approves Dark Money Regulation." *San Antonio Express News.* Retrieved March 2, 2015,http://www.mysanantonio.com/news/local/article/Ethics-commission-approves-dark-money-regulation-5856198.php.

Redlawsk, D. P., A. J. W. Civettini, and K. M. Emmerson. 2010. "The Affective Tipping Point: Do Motivated Reasoners Ever 'Get It?'" *Political Psychology* 31(4): 563–593.

Reinhard, B. 2015. "Iowa Draws GOPs 2016 Hopefuls to Agriculture Summit." *The Wall Street Journal.* Retrieved March 6, 2015, http://blogs.wsj.com/washwire/2015/03/06/iowa-draws-gops-2016-hopefuls-to-agriculture-summit/.

Ridder, R. 2014. "Politics Is Customizable: The Pitfalls of Micro-Targeting." *Real Clear Politics.* Retrieved May 21, 2015, http://www.realclearpolitics.com/articles/2014/12/08/all_politics_is_customizable_the_pitfalls_of_micro-targeting_124856.html/.

Ridout, T. N. 2009. "Campaign Micro-targeting and the Relevance of the Televised Political Ad." *The Forum* 7(2) Article 5.

Rigby, E., and M. J. Springer. 2011. "Does Electoral Reform Increase (or Decrease) Political Equality?" *Political Research Quarterly* 64(2): 420–434.

Riker, W. H., and P. C. Ordeshook. 1968. "A Theory of the Calculus of Voting." *The American Political Science Review* 62(1): 25–42.

Roberts, J. 2004. "The Rise and Fall of Howard Dean." *CBS News.* Retrieved May 26, 2016, http://www.cbsnews.com/news/the-rise-and-fall-of-howard-dean-18-02-2004/.

Robinson, E. 2012. "Breaking Grover Norquist's Anti-Tax Pledge." *The Washington Post.* Retrieved May 18, 2015, http://www.washingtonpost.com/opinions/eugene-robinson-breaking-grover-norquists-anti-tax-pledge/2012/11/26/49cdcd16-37ee-11e2-8a97-363b0f9a0ab3_story.html/.

Rosenstone, S. J., and J. M. Hansen. 1993. *Mobilization, Participation, and American Democracy.* Reissued as part of the Longman Classics in Political Science series (2002). New York: Pearson.

Rosenstone, S. J., and R. E. Wolfinger. 1978. "The Effect of Registration Laws on Voter Turnout." *American Political Science Review,* 72(01): 22–45.

Ross, J. 2004. "Tilting the Playing Field: Voter ID & Turnout." CompleteCampaigns.com. Retrieved April 20, 2015, http://www.completecampaigns.com/article.asp?articleid=27/.

Rubin, J. 2012. "Romney Slams Obama on Foreign Policy." *The Washington Post.* http://www.washingtonpost.com/blogs/right-turn/post/romney-slams-obama-on-foreign-policy/2012/09/24/1eed3bf2-067c-11e2-afff-d6c7f20a83bf_blog.html/.

Rubinstein, I. 2014. "Voter Privacy in the Age of Big Data." *Wisconsin Law Review* 5: 861–936.

Sabato, L. J. 1989. "How Direct Mail Works." In *Campaigns and Elections: A Reader in Modern American Politics,* edited by Larry J. Sabato, 89–99. Glenview, IL: Scott, Foresman.

Sanbonmatsu, K. 2002. "Gender Stereotypes and Vote Choice." *American Journal of Political Science* 46(1): 20–34.

Schaffner, B. F., M. Streb, and G. Wright. 2001. "Teams without Uniforms: The Nonpartisan Ballot in State and Local Elections." *Political Research Quarterly* 54(1): 7–30.

Schaffner, B. F., M. W. Wagner, and J. Winburn. 2004. Incumbents out, Party in? Term Limits and Partisan Redistricting in State Legislatures. *State Politics & Policy Quarterly* 4(4): 396–414.

Schattschneider, E. E. 1942. *Party Government.* New York: Rinehart.

Schattschneider, E. E. 1960. *The Semisovereign People: A Realist's View of Democracy in America.* New York: Holt, Rinehart, & Winston.

Scherer, M. 2012. "Inside the Secret World of the Data Crunchers Who Helped Obama Win." *Time Magazine.* Retrieved February 10, 2015, http://swampland.time.com/2012/11/07/inside-the-secret-world-of-quants-and-data-crunchers-who-helped-obama-win/.

Schlesinger, J. A. 1991. *Political Parties and the Winning of Office.* Ann Arbor: University of Michigan Press.

Schlozman, K. L., S. Verba, and H. E. Brady. 2012. *The Unheavenly Chorus: Unequal Political Voice and the Broken Promise of American Democracy.* Princeton, NJ: Princeton University Press.

Schouten, F. 2014. "Federal Super PACs Spent Big on Local Elections." *USA Today.* Retrieved March 2, 2014, http://www.usatoday.com/story/news/politics/2014/02/25/super-pacs-spending-local-races/5617121/.

Schumpeter, J. 1942. *Capitalism, Socialism and Democracy*. New York: Harper & Brothers.

Shaw, D. R. 1999. "The effect of TV ads and candidate appearances on statewide presidential votes, 1988–96." *American Political Science Review* 93(2): 345–361.

Shaw, C. 2004. *The Campaign Manager: Running and Winning Local Elections*. Boulder, CO: Westview Press.

Shaw, D. R. 2006. *The Race to 270: The Electoral College and the Campaign Strategies of 2000 and 2004*. Chicago, IL: University of Chicago Press.

Sherfinski, D. 2015. "Bernie Sanders' Camp Suspended from DNC Voter Database After Viewing Hillary Clinton's Data." December 18. Retrieved March 30, 2016, http://www.washingtontimes.com/news/2015/dec/18/bernie-sanders-camp-suspended-dnc-voter-database-a/

Sherman, G. 2012. "How Karl Rove Fought with Fox News over the Ohio Call." *New York Magazine*. Retrieved February 10, 2015, http://nymag.com/daily/intelligencer/2012/11/how-rove-fought-with-fox-over-ohio.html/.

Schreckinger, B. and K. Vogel. 2016. "Donald Trump, 2016's First Loser." Politco.com. February 2. Retrieved April 6, 2016. http://www.politico.com/story/2016/02/donald-trump-iowa-caucus-loser-218604.

Sides, J. 2006. "The Origins of Campaign Agendas." *British Journal of Political Science* 36(3): 407–436.

Sides, J. 2011. "The Moneyball of Campaign Advertising (Part 1). *The New York Times*. Retrieved April 5, 2016. http://fivethirtyeight.blogs.nytimes.com/2011/10/05/the-moneyball-of-campaign-advertising-part-1/?_r=0

Sides, J., E. Schickler and J. Citrin. 2008. "If Everyone Had Voted, Would Bubba and Dubya Have Won?" *Presidential Studies Quarterly* 38(3): 521–539.

Sides, J., and L. Vavreck. 2013. *The Gamble: Choice and Chance in the 2012 Presidential Election*. Princeton, NJ: Princeton University Press.

Sides, J., D. Shaw, M. Grossman, and K. Lipsitz. 2014. *Campaigns & Elections Rules, Reality, Strategy, Choice*. New York: Norton.

Simon, D. M., C. W. Ostrom, Jr. and R. F. Marra. 1991. "The President, Referendum Voting, and Subnational Elections in the United States." *American Political Science Review*, 85, 1177–1192.

Silver, N. 2012. "FiveThirtyEight Forecast." *The New York Times Blogs*. Retrieved May 26, 2016 http://fivethirtyeight.blogs.nytimes.com/fivethirtyeights-2012-forecast/.

Simon, D. M. 1989. "Presidents, Governors, and Electoral Accountability." *Journal of Politics* 51(2): 286–304.

Sinclair, B. 2012. *The Social Citizen: Peer Networks and Political Behavior*. Chicago, IL: University of Chicago Press.

Sizemore, J. M. 2008. "How Obama Did It: Big States, Small States, Caucuses, and Campaign Strategy." *University of Virginia Center for Politics: Sabato's Crystal Ball*. Retrieved May 28, 2015, http://www.centerforpolitics.org/crystalball/articles/jms2008060501/.

Slotnick, A. 2009. "'Friend' the President: Facebook and the 2008 Presidential Election." In *Politicking Online: The Transformation of Election Campaign Communications*, edited by Costas Panagopoulos, 249–271. New Brunswick, NJ: Rutgers University Press.

Smith, A. 2014. "Cell Phones, Social Media, and Campaign 2014." *Pew Research Center: Internet, Science & Tech*. Retrieved May 26, 2015, http://www.pewinternet.org/2014/11/03/cell-phones-social-media-and-campaign-2014/.

Smith, D. 1995. "Campaign Finance Regulation: Faulty Assumptions and Undemocratic Consequences." *The Cato Institute, Policy Analysis, No 238*. Retrieved May 21, 2015, http://www.cato.org/publications/policy-analysis/campaign-finance-regulation-faulty-assumptions-undemocratic-consequences/.

Smith, D. A. 2001. "Homeward Bound?: Micro-Level Legislative Responsiveness to Ballot Initiatives." *State Politics and Policy Quarterly* 1(1): 50–601.

Somers, Terri. 2008. "Calif. Could Lose Lead to Gay-friendly Mass." *San Diego Union-Tribune*. http://legacy.signonsandiego.com/news/business/20081029-9999-1b29prop8.html/.

Sorensen, T. 2010. "13 Lessons from the 1960 Presidential Campaign." *Campaigns & Elections*. Retrieved May 27, 2015, http://www.campaignsandelections.com/magazine/1944/13-lessons-from-the-1960-presidential-campaign/.

Southwell, P. 2009. "Analysis of the Turnout Effects of Vote by Mail Elections, 1980–2007." *The Social Science Journal* 45: 211–217.

Southwell, P., and J. Burchett. 2000. "Does Changing the Rules Change the Players? The Effect of All-Mail Elections on the Composition of the Electorate." *Social Science Quarterly* 81(3): 837–845.

Spiegel, A. 2012. "Can Science Plant Brain Seeds That Make You Vote?" *NPR: All Things Considered*. Retrieved April 27, 2015, http://www.npr.org/2012/07/16/156571493/can-science-plant-brain-seeds-that-make-you-vote/.

Springer, M. J. 2014. *How States Shaped the Nation: American Electoral Institutions and Voter Turnout, 1920–2000*. Chicago, IL: University of Chicago Press.

Squire, P. 1992. "Legislative Professionalism and Membership Diversity in State Legislatures." *Legislative Studies Quarterly* 17(1): 69–79.

Squire, P. 2007. "Measuring State Legislative Professionalism: The Squire Index Revisited." *State Politics & Policy Quarterly* 7(2): 211–227.

Sreenivasan, H. 2012. "How Campaigns Amass Your Personal Information to Deliver Tailored Political Ads." *PBS News Hour*. Retrieved May 22, 2015, http://www.pbs.org/newshour/bb/politics-july-dec12-frontline_10-29/.

Stanley, A. 2008. "Question Reprised, but the Words Come None Too Easy for Palin." *The New York Times*. Retrieved April 6, 2015, http://www.nytimes.com/2008/09/26/us/politics/26watch.html/.

State of Alaska Division of Elections. N.d. "Absentee Voting by Electronic Transmission." Retrieved May 11, 2015, http://www.elections.alaska.gov/vi_bb_by_fax.php/.

Steger, W. P. 2000. "Do Primary Voters Draw from a Stacked Deck? Presidential Nominations in an Era of Candidate-Centered Campaigns." *Presidential Studies Quarterly* 30(4): 727–753.

Steger, W. P. 2007. "Who Wins Nominations and Why?: An Updated Forecast of the Presidential Primary Vote." *Political Research Quarterly* 60(1): 91–97.

Stein, R. M. 1998. "Introduction: Early Voting." *The Public Opinion Quarterly* 62(1): 57–69.

Stimson, J. 2015. *Tides of Consent: How Public Opinion Shapes American Politics. 2nd edition*. New York: Cambridge University Press.

Storey, T. 2014. "State Vote 2014: Election Results." *National Conference of State Legislatures*. Retrieved March 2, 2014, http://www.ncsl.org/research/elections-and-campaigns/statevote-2014-post-election-analysis635508614.aspx/.

Strachan, C. J. 2003. *High-Tech Grass Roots: The Professionalization of Local Elections*. Lanham, MD: Rowman & Littlefield.

Stratmann, T., and F. J. Aparicio-Castillo. 2006. "Competition Policy for Elections: Do Campaign Contribution Limits Matter?" *Public Choice* 127: 177–206.

Strauss, S. 2003. "TV as a Great Way to Get the Word Out—And Empty Your Wallet, Too." *USA Today*. Retrieved May 25, 2015, www.usatoday.com/money/smallbusiness/columnist/strauss/2003-08-25-tv_x.htm/.

Streb, M. J., Burrell, B., Frederick, B. and Genovese, M. A. 2008. "Social desirability effects and support for a female American president." *Public Opinion Quarterly*, 72(1): 76–89.

Stroh, P. 2005. "Voters as Pragmatic, Cognitive Misers: The Accuracy-Effort Trade-off in the Candidate Evaluation Process." In *Political Judgment: Structure and Process*, M. Lodge and K. McGraw, eds. Ann Arbor: University of Michigan Press.

Stromer-Galley, J., and I. Sheinheit. 2012. "Online Campaigning." *Oxford Bibliographies Online*. Retrieved May 15, 2015, http://www.oxfordbibliographies.com/view/document/obo-9780199756841/obo-9780199756841-0059.xml/.

Sullivan, S. 2012. "How The Presidential Campaigns Are Spending Money, in One Chart." *The Washington Post*. Retrieved May 21, 2015, http://www.washingtonpost.com/blogs/the-fix/wp/2012/09/26/how-the-presidential-campaigns-are-spending-money-in-one-chart/.

Sullivan, S. 2014. "Meet Larry Pressler, the One-Man Band Shaking Up the Battle for the Senate Majority." *The Washington Post*. Retrieved February 9, 2015, http://www.washingtonpost.com/blogs/post-politics/wp/2014/10/10/meet-larry-pressler-the-one-man-band-shaking-up-the-battle-for-the-senate-majority/.

Suttmann-Lea, M. 2014. "Election Laws, Campaign Strategy, and Competitive Elections: The Impact of Electoral Reforms on Participatory Equality in American Politics." Presented at the Midwest Political Science Association's Annual Conference, Chicago, IL.

Swanson, D. L., and P. Mancini. 1996. *Politics, Media, and Modern Democracy: An International Study of Innovations in Electoral Campaigning and Their Consequences*. Greenwood Publishing Group.

Taber, C. S., and Lodge, M. 2006. "Motivated Skepticism in the Evaluation of Political Beliefs." *American Journal of Political Science* 50(3): 755–769.

Taylor, P. 2012. "The Growing Electoral Clout of Blacks Is Driven by Turnout, Not Demographics." *Pew Research Center: Social and Demographic Trends*. Retrieved May 25, 2015, http://www.pewsocialtrends.org/2012/12/26/the-growing-electoral-clout-of-blacks-is-driven-by-turnout-not-demographics/.

Timpone, R. J. 1998. "Structure, Behavior, and Voter Turnout in the United States." *American Political Science Review* 91(1): 145–158.

Trounstine, J. 2011. "Evidence of a Local Incumbency Advantage." *Legislative Studies Quarterly* 36(2): 255–280.

Trounstine, J. 2013. "Turnout and Incumbency in Local Elections." *Urban Affairs Review* 49(2): 167–189.

Truman, D. B. 1951 [1981]. *The Governmental Process*, 2nd ed. New York: Knopf.

Turow, J., M. X. Delli Carpini, N. Draper, and R. Howard-Williams. 2012. "Americans Roundly Reject Tailored Political Advertising at a Time When Political Campaigns Are Embracing It." Annenberg School for Communication at the University of Pennsylvania. Retrieved May 21, 2015, http://web.asc.upenn.edu/news/Turow_Tailored_Political_Advertising.pdf/.

Tversky, A., and D. Kahneman. 1981. "The Framing of Decisions and Psychology of Choices." *Science, New Series* 211(4481): 453–458.

Urbina, I. 2000. "States Move to Allow Overseas and Military to Cast Ballots by Internet." *The New York Times.* http://www.nytimes.com/2010/05/09/us/politics/09voting .html/.

U.S. Department of Justice. "About the National Voter Registration Act." Retrieved May 11, 2015, http://www.justice.gov/crt/about/vot/nvra/activ_nvra.php/.

Valentino, N., V. L. Hutchings, and D. Williams. 2004. "The Impact of Political Advertising on Knowledge, Internet Information Seeking, and Candidate Preference." *Journal of Communication* 54(2): 337–354.

Vavreck, J. 2009. *The Message Matters: The Economy and Presidential Campaigns.* Princeton, NJ: Princeton University Press.

Verba, S., and Norman H. Nie. 1972. *Participation in America: Political Democracy and Social Equality.* New York: Harper & Row.

Vergeer, M., J. Hermans, and S. Sams. 2011. "Online Social Networks and Micro-Blogging in Political Campaigning: The Exploration of a New Campaign Tool and New Campaign Style." *Party Politics* 19(3): 477–501.

Villanova, P. 2015. "9 Jersey City Municipal Elections among N.J's Most Expensive: Election Report." Retrieved February 19, 2015, http://www.nj.com/hudson/index .ssf/2015/01/9_jersey_city_municipal_elections_among_njs_costli.html/.

Voting Technology Project. 2001. "Voting: What It Is, What It Could Be." Accessed May 26, 2016, http://vote.caltech.edu/content/voting-what-what-could-be. Report issued by the CalTech/MIT Voting Technology Project.

Wagner, D. 2015. "How Did Big Data Help Obama Campaign?" *Bloomberg Business.* Retrieved May 18, 2015, http://www.bloomberg.com/news/videos/b/78661fa3-93fc-41dd-a1a0-28dc7ac685e5/.

Ward, S., D. Owen, R. Davis, and D. Tars, eds. 2008. *Making a Difference: A Comparative View of the Role of the Internet in Election Politics.* Lanham, MD: Lexington Books.

Washington Post. "Soft Money—A Look at the Loopholes." Retrieved March 11, 2015, http://www.washingtonpost.com/wp-srv/politics/special/campfin/intro4.htm/.

Wattenberg, M. P. 1990. *The Decline of American Political Parties 1952–1988.* Cambridge, MA: Harvard University Press.

Wayne. S. 2014. *Is This Any Way to Run a Democratic Election? 5th edition.* Thousand Oaks, CA: CQ Press.

Weber, D. 2011. "Unlimited Presidential Fundraising: The Curse of Steve Forbes." *OpenSecrets.org.* Retrieved May 28, 2015, http://www.opensecrets.org/news/2011/12/ unlimited-presidential-fundraising/.

Weigel, D. 2013. "Iowa Caucuses 2016: Hillary Clinton's 59-Point Lead, and Other Poll Potpourri." *Slate.* Retrieved May 19, 2015, http://www.slate.com/blogs/weigel/2013/ 07/11/iowa_caucus_2016_hillary_clinton_s_59_point_lead_and_other_poll_ portpourri.html/.

Weinschenk, A., and C. Panagopoulos. 2014. "Personality, Negativity, and Political Participation." *Journal of Social and Political Psychology* 2(1): 164–182.

Weise, E. 2014. "Internet Voting 'Not Ready' For Prime Time." *USA Today.* Retrieved May 11, 2015, http://www.usatoday.com/story/tech/2014/11/02/internet-voting-not-secure/18269285/.

Wesleyan Media Project. 2012. "Presidential Ad War Tops 1M Airings." *Wesleyan Media Project Advertising Analysis.* Retrieved October 29, 2015, http://mediaproject.wesleyan .edu/releases/presidential-ad-war-tops-1m-airings/.

West, D. M. 2010. *Air Wars: Television Advertising in Election Campaigns, 1952–2008*, 5th ed. Washington, D.C.: CQ Press.

Wielhouwer, P. W. 2000. "Releasing the Fetters: Parties and the Mobilization of the African-American Electorate." *Journal of Politics* 62(1): 206–222.

Williams, C. B., and G. J. Gulati. 2009. "The Political Impact of Facebook: Evidence from the 2006 Elections and the 2008 Nomination Contest." In *Politicking Online: The Transformation of Election Campaign Communications*, edited by Costas Panagopoulos, 272–291. New Brunswick, NJ: Rutgers University Press.

Williams, C. B., and G. J. Gulati. 2012. "Social Networks in Political Campaigns: Facebook and Congressional Elections of 2006 and 2008." *New Media & Society* 15(1): 52–71.

Willis, D. 2015. "Online Political Ads Have Been Slow to Catch on as TV Reigns." *The New York Times*. Retrieved May 22, 2015, http://www.nytimes.com/2015/01/30/upshot/why-online-political-ads-have-been-slow-to-catch-on.html?_r=0&abt=0002&abg=1/.

Wilson, G. 1973. *The Psychology of Conservatism*. London: Academic Press.

Wilson, R. 2014. "Report: Voter ID Laws Reduce Turnout More Among African American and Younger Voters." *The Washington Post*. Retrieved May 28, 2015, http://www.washingtonpost.com/blogs/govbeat/wp/2014/10/09/report-voter-id-laws-reduce-turnout-more-among-african-american-and-younger-voters/.

Winer, S. L., L. W. Kenney, and B. Grofman. 2014. "Explaining Variation in the Competitiveness of U.S. Senate Elections, 1922–2004." *Public Choice* 161(3–4): 471–497.

Winston, D. 2013. "Creating a Winning Campaign Strategy." In *Campaigns and Elections American Style*, edited by James A. Thurber and Candice J. Nelson, 24–39. Boulder, CO: Westview Press.

Wlezien, C. 2014. "Election Campaigns." In *Comparing Democracies: Elections and Voting in a Changing World*, edited by L. LeDuc, R. G. Niemie, and P. Norris. Thousand Oaks, CA: Sage.

Wolchok, S., E. Wustrow, D. Isabel, and J. Alex Halderman. 2012. "Attacking the Washington D.C Internet Voting System." *Financial Cryptography and Data Security: Lecture Notes in Computer Science* 7392: 114–128.

Yardley, W. 2010. "Murkowski Wins Alaska Senate Race." *New York Times*. Retrieved May 26, 2016, http://www.nytimes.com/2010/11/18/us/politics/18alaska.html?_r=0.

Young, A. 2000. "Mail Ballots Could Boost Oregon Turnout." *The Columbian*, May 16: B2.

Zaller, J. 1992. *The Nature and Origins of Mass Opinion*. New York: Cambridge University Press.

Zaller, J., and S. Feldman. 1992. "A Simple Theory of the Survey Response: Answering Questions versus Revealing Preferences." *American Journal of Political Science* 36(3): 579–616.

INDEX

bias in, 110, 112
biometric technologies in, 112
data on microtargeting, 118
importance of, 112
methods of, 109
National Election Pool on exit, 67
as non-neutral, 66
poll aggregators for, 66–67
private firms for, 109–10
Santorum not using, 113
split-ballot testing in, 110
use of, 109
poll workers, 237–38
positive messaging, 123
PQ Media
outdoor advertising projections by,
129–30
political media spending report by,
124–25
television *vs.* digital advertising report
by, 137
presidential campaign (2000), 236–37
presidential campaign (2004), 180
presidential campaign (2008)
campaign messaging in, 115
caucuses in, 53, 54, 54*f*
economy in, 214–15
individual contributions in, 92
opposition research in, 113
technology in, 180–81
presidential campaign (2012), 100
campaign spending in, 101, 112*f*
data-driven campaign approach in, 2
hashtag use in, 191
Minnesota results for, 130*f*
Obama campaign tactics for, 98–99
record-breaking spending of, 2
voter demographics in, 166, 167*t*
presidential campaign (2016)
earned media statistics for, 8
Republican discourse in, 44
superdelegates in, 15
Trump using Twitter in, 186
Pressler, Larry, 8
primary election
advertising by interest groups in,
59–60
campaign strategy for, 103
closed, 51, 52*f*, 56
elected candidates influenced by, 56

invisible, 51
open, 51, 52*f*
party registration data and, 107*t*
resource allocation for caucus
versus, 53
semiclosed, 51, 52*f*
top-two system for, 51–52
professionalization, 23
Senate and House of Representatives
and, 27
of state and local elections, 27, 34
Project Narwhal, 2
public financing, 234
benefits of, 39
FECA system for, 80
in general election, 80, 81
matching funds and, 38
minority representation and, 39
Obama opting out of, 81
opting out of, 80–81
in primary election, 80, 81, 82
at state and local level, 82

Quinn, Pat, 148–49, 151
Quinn/Rauner race, 148–49, 151

Rauner, Bruce, 148–49, 151
redistricting, 193
Reid, Harry, 121
representation
citizen engagement increased by,
222–23
defining, 4
in democratic theory, 3
descriptive, 230
international campaigns and
proportional, 214–16, 215*t*
in local elections, 32
microtargeting creating false, 118
polarization impacting, 57
political consultants in, 19
political term and, 230
semiclosed primary increasing, 56
substantive, 230
Republican State Leadership
Committee, 39
responsive estimates, 182
retail campaigning, 12
reverse coattails, 40
Rhoades, Matt, 9